The Book of MOM

Motherhood's Operating Manual

created by Leni Engels RN, CHt

written with many, many Moms!

for Carly and Marlo

... here it is - just like I told you!

And for David, the love of my life.

Welcome to the Sisterhood of Motherhood!

We're so glad to have you join us! But consider this: For nine months you've attended regularly scheduled doctor visits to 'meticulously monitor the Mom' and 'fastidiously focus on the fetus.' There's been scrupulous attention paid to ultrasound pictures, diagnostic lab tests, monitoring the fetal heart rate, vitamins, hemoglobin and blood checks, Lamaze classes, pretend pushing-practice and delivery room tours. Then finally, the much anticipated day arrives... you do the requisite pain, puffing, panting, pushing and POOF someone hands you a squirming, crying bundle of flesh and – and – and – "That's all folks, you're on your own now! Good luck!" they say. They're kidding, right? Now what? Why doesn't this baby come with instructions? The seven-ish pounds of wriggling humanity cradled in your arms, makes the word 'responsibility' take on a whole new meaning - response ability! How do they expect you to take this wiggling mass of human genetic material and turn it into a highly intelligent, literate and humorous person without giving you the slightest hint of how to accomplish it!? Hello......!!!

There isn't a Mother around who hasn't thought, "Where is the owner's manual? Even cheap, throwaway watches come with directions! Do I really have to figure out how to get my infant to sleep through the night? Hasn't someone figured this out already? Millions of Moms have dealt with fussy, whiny children screaming their heads off in the middle of a store – surely someone's figured out how to handle it!" Yes we have, and now it's all here in your hands! Finally!

Let me tell you how this book got started. Every once in a while we all get frustrated, or we just don't feel like giving long, in-depth reasons for everything we decide for our children. Right? Of course right! (You'll see.) One day I was tired and one of my girls asked me another "Why do I have to?" question, so instead of saying "Because I told you to!" I said, "Because it's in the 'Mother's Book' on page 47! When you're a Mother you can look it up." It just popped out of my mouth! To my astonishment the kids believed me... they looked at each other, shrugged and went off to do whatever it was they were asked to do. And I thought – "Holy Moly! That worked!" So a few days later, the rule was on page 53... and so was born the legend of 'The Book.' One could say that I just went 'back to the future,' knowing that this instruction manual was going to be written... one day. By referring to this omniscient book, ALWAYS with a straight face, I could defer the negative and defend my Maternal decisions. But, I reserved 'The Book' only for silly things, certainly not for subjects that deserved my attention or an interactive discussion. After a while when the kids demanded to see this famous reference book, I told them as soon as they became Mothers I'd be happy to share it with them. And I invite you to do the same – after all, this is YOUR secret Mommy handbook, not theirs. Refer to this book often, literally and figuratively, but NEVER, NEVER, NEVER let them see it ... the aura of the mysterious 'Book of Mom' holds great power.

As I said, I began writing this book because of our ongoing family tradition, referring to the legendary 'Book.' Let's just say that before this book became a tangible reality, I just took the expression 'fake it till you make it' to the next level - for about twenty years! But as I began to write, I wondered what magic other Moms used to motivate their children. Making reference to 'The Book' worked well for me and I was sure that they too must have secret strategies. So, I enlisted the help of friends and Mothers everywhere, confident that I could tap into our collective Maternal Wisdom. I've approached Moms in the grocery store line, in theaters, in airports and restaurants, in the ladies room and on hiking trails, at outdoor events, music festivals and in parks … wherever I saw a Mom 'doing something right,' I asked for her help and she gladly shared her thoughts. Thanks to the magic of e-mail I've been able to connect with Moms from all over the globe. And what wisdom I found! Talk about Mothers of invention! I was thrilled to discover that we are all quiet geniuses calmly going about the world's most sacred business – readying the next generation to inherit the planet. We welcome you into the fold! This collection of 'Momisms' was written as our gift to you. Our hope is to provide you with some ideas, direction and inspiration to handle whatever comes your way. It is a collection of our truths. Our tender reminiscences of "Been there done that," and "If only I had known then what I know now." This is certainly not a science or recipe book. Nor is this a definitive, complete or perfect formula for Mothering. It is a practical guide of tried and true motivators, suggestions, strategies and tactics, ideas, personal opinions and philosophies, a couple of true confessions, poems, song lyrics, recipes and stories. More than 200 Moms have contributed to this book and only three offered overlapping ideas! You will find their insightful input throughout this book *written in italics*. All the content that I have contributed is printed in plain text. We offer all of these suggestions to you with love and the hope that you will add your own and pass it on to your children.

From that glorious day you deliver to the day your child goes off into the world, you have but one goal – to raise a healthy, compassionate, warm, wise and friendly human being who will be able to go out into the world, contributing to and integrating fully into the human community. Our job, in a sense, is to make ourselves obsolete. You have about 18 years to help your child achieve 'personhood'… so much to teach in so little time.

So much has to happen between Hello and Goodbye.

Greg Greenway

'Success' will be measured in small increments along the way: potty training, school tests, young friendships, mastering arguments, musical instruments and relationships; but successful personhood should not be judged by how others see the individual as much as how one judges oneself. The ability to love, to laugh easily and enjoy life, listen well, relate to others and contribute to society are the most essential elements of successful living.

The door to success is marked "push" and "pull."
Achieving success is knowing when to do what.

Yiddish Folk Saying

Kids - One day they come toddling over to you with outstretched arms waiting to be caught up in yours. The next day they come running, breathless and giggling as they proclaim that your derriere is 'home base' and no one would dare tag them in your protective space! Through toothless smiles and tearful disappointments, you'll hug them 'tight, tight' and while you go about the business of living each day, the days will slip quickly away. And one day will be the last day. They'll be ready to leave the nest and you might wonder - are they ready? Am I ready? Did I teach them everything they need to know? Did I do a good enough job? That is why we pooled our wisdom. Knowledge really is power, so we'll gladly share ours with you.

Because in the end, when all is said and done, you never want to think back and say, "I should have done better." Hindsight is always 20/20, so we offer you the benefit of our accumulated wisdom. As Maya Angelou has said, "When you know better, you do better."

Of course giving birth is only one road to motherhood. No matter how you came to assume this precious mantle: birthing, adopting, step parenting, custody grand-parenting, foster parenting, parenting as a single Mom or double Mom, or as an 'at home Dad' (formerly known as Mr. Mom,) Motherhood is something like a dress label that promises "One Size Fits All." The challenges are pretty much the same for all of us... a rose by any other name would still be a rose.

The first thing to learn is that YOU will be THE most important person in your child's life, so take pride in your work ... become a Master Mom. Because I feel so strongly that we Moms need to think of ourselves with great respect I have capitalized every reference pertaining to 'Mothers' in this book. Never underestimate your worth! People who have attended the world's finest universities and acquired educational degrees of all kinds are never given the same responsibility as that of 'A Mother.' You may have to work hard, but no matter what else you may accomplish in your lifetime, nothing will ever be as important as the work you are about to perform.

'Experts' are people who study other's work, conduct research and write about their findings to benefit others. Most of the contributors in this book don't have advanced degrees in child psych, but rest assured that we Moms are the true kid experts! Of course what works for one may not work for all, but perhaps something you read will spark your imagination and make manifest your own Maternal Magic. So while we can't guarantee a perfect outcome, what we can guarantee is that raising your children will be challenging, volatile, hilarious, infuriating, fun, rewarding and full of surprises. And then, when the day finally comes that they wave a goodbye and move on, you'll never have to think, "I could have done better."

Think of Motherhood the way a master artist regards a canvas. Plan, think and be careful how you apply the colors of life to your little living, breathing masterpiece. But bear in mind that life isn't a 'paint-by-numbers' kit and your child's life may not turn out the way you have envisioned it would.

Some of us had wonderful mothers – real June Cleaver/ Carol Brady types (they were the completely fictional, quintessential, ideal, fantasy Moms in 1950's and 1970's TV sitcoms) but some of us were not so lucky ... so

Be the mother you wish you had.

We're all in this together - by ourselves.   Lily Tomlin

The hand that rocks the cradle is the hand that rules the world.
                                        William Ross Wallace

You are the bows from which your children as living arrows are sent forth.
                                        Kahlil Gibran

Many Moms, Many Thanks

Time was when the women of a village gathered, pooled their resources and stitched a quilt together. Their aim was to create a warm coverlet for someone in need. No doubt, along with their tiny expert stitches, they shared stories, recipes and confidences as they offered their insights, cures and advice to one another. Each one added to the pool of knowledge. This book has been fashioned much the same way - a modern-day quilt. Tiny stitches tapped out on computer keyboards, snatches of conversations and ideas shared. Some of the 'Moms' quoted don't actually have their own children, but I consider them Mothers just the same because they nourish us all with their words, actions and spirits. Isn't that what Moms do? So thank you to all the Wise Men and Wise Women whose insightful thoughts and quotes I've sprinkled throughout this book. And thank you to all the brilliant Moms who added their stories, inspirations, ideas and experience.

> When you learn, teach.
> When you get, give.
>
> Maya Angelou

Ellen Adelman, Maya Angelou, Shirley Apteker, Mary, Joan Baez, Jeanette M. Barceló, Jackie Bardin, Ellen Becker, Laura Berman, Cathy Black, Annie B. Bond, Cindy Bowers, Elaine Boozler, Jennifer Brinkler, Elyse Brunt, Julie Brown, Ellen Bukstel, Sunny Burdman, Alex Burroughs, Sandy Cash, D. Caolo, Kate Carpenter, Lillian Carter, Caryn, Hazel Case, Wendy Chai, Emily Chappell, Julie Schumacher Ciardiello, Amanda Carlos, Hillary Clinton, M. Cohen, Lui Collins, Cary Cooper, Laura Cox, Brittany Craig, Tricia Dalaba, Susan Davis, Doris Davidoff, Barbara Davidson, Charlotte Diamond, Jeanne Djaballah, Elizabeth Edwards, Donna Ellis, Louise Elwood, Nancy Engels, Rita Engels, Linda Eubank, Anne Feeney, Macki Feinstein, Rabbi Tirzah Firestone, Sharon Fitch, Betty Friedrichsen, H. Friedman, Dawn Gacadack, Kim Gandy, Ann Garth, Jennifer Kelly Geddes, Deborah Geigis Berry, Linda Gennari, Heather Gibson, V. Gilbert, Jenny Gitlitz, Mara Giulianti, Nikki Glantz, Cheryl Gleissner, Patti Glick, Melissa Glozman, Laura Gonzalez, Marilyn Green, Riki Lerner Green, Penny Greenberg, Robby Greenberg, JoAnne Greenstone, Andrea Grossman, Kelly Guidry, Tracey Harris, Kateri Hauck, Sharon Heller, Reba Heyman, Juliane Hiam, Sandy Hingston, Betty Holland, Connie Howard, Ina J. Hughs, Pat Humphries, Mala J., Joanna, Karen Jackson, Donna Jacobs, Liz Jacques, Gail Jenkins, Andrea Johnson, Jane E. Johnson, Lady Bird Johnson, Laura Johnson, Catherine Joyce, Judy Kaufman, Wendy Keilin, Lisa Kent, Mira Kirshenbaum, Meredith Knight, Pat Kracht, Mary L., Patti LaBelle, Valerie Landa, Ann Landers, Jeanne Marie Laskas, Christine Lavin, Linda Lentin, Lori Lennox, Lucie Lerner, Marilyn Lerner, Marilyn Levy, Ravit Levi, Jennifer Lewis, Billie Lister, Rosalee (Peppard) Lockyer, Marisa Lopez, Beverly Low, Madonna, Mary McLaughlin, Donna Magadov, Brandy Mahan, Miriam Mandel, Jennifer Marino, Laurie Marson, Mary Martha, Elinder Martin, Sandra May, Susan May, Mireya Mayor, Lisa McElhaney, Karen McElveen, Mary McLaughlin, Margaret Mead, Golda Meir, Laura Morse, Lindy Meshwork, Linda Miller, Demi Moore, Linda Morris, Graciela Moses, Susan Moss, Laurie Murray, Mother Nature, Narrissa Nields, Christiane

Northrup, Dorothy Law Nolte, Michelle Obama, Rosie O'Donnell, Jackie Kennedy Onasis, Sandy Opatow, Laurie Jennings Oudin, Courtney Page, Nancy Pelossi, Erica Percheski, Angela Perzow, Aidan Quinn, Anna Quindlen, Queen Rania, Julie Riley, Lisal Kayati Roberts, Eleanor Roosevelt, Brona Rosen, Debra Russell, Simone Ryals, Jackie Salvaggio, Barbara Schipper, Barbara Schwartz, Cozy Sheridan, Maria Shriver Shwartzenegger, Geri Shaw, Pat Shays, Sheila Sidline, Diane Sidovnikov, Mindy Lou Simmons, Nancy Singer, Anne Hawn Smith, Peggy Solomunsen, Elizabeth Soutter Schwarzer, Gloria Steinem, Susan Strasberg, Robin Vasquez, Tina Sklar, Ana Veciana Suarez, Joan Sheinwald, Diane Sidovnikov, Deborah Silverstein, Christine Stay, Arlene Stoffmaker, Linda Stone, Saralyn Singer, Stacy, Shirley, Martha Stewart, Susan Sweeney, Maia Szalavitz, Anne Marie Tague, Karenia Tarolli, Lynn Tasker, Mother Teresa, Chris Thompson, Lily Tomlin, Joyce Tritt, Ginny Unser, Abigail Van Buren, Lauren Vesely, D. Vinegrad, Sloan Wainwright, Cheryl Ward, Suzanne Walkins, Amy Carol Webb, Tami Weiser, Annie Wenz, Jean Wenz, Susan Werner, Cheryl Wheeler, Gray Whitestone, Judy Smith Williams, Susan Wilson, Adrienne Wiebe, Nancy Williams, Kate Winslet, Oprah Winfrey, Jody Wood, Melissa Woods, Naomi Wolfe, Kathy Zuckerman.

I welcome your comments, questions, suggestions and/or contributions for the sequel to this book. Please contact me at: **thebookofmom.com**

Cover design: Original Art by Leni Engels
Graphics by designworkshopgroupinc.com

What's Inside

Notes On Motherhood

I always wanted to be a Mom. Even now, some 50 odd years later, I can still remember Mothering my first baby, a hard plastic doll. I take the role of Motherhood very seriously. Having and raising children isn't for the faint of heart. I have had a very different experience than most: three children on very different paths along life's journey. Each has taught me more about life than I ever could have imagined they would. Nobody told me how much kids have to teach us. We are all each other's teachers, no matter our age. Take your time. Enjoy every day. Expect to make mistakes, because you will. And don't blink – your kids will be grabbing the car keys and they'll be gone in an instant.

may I suggest

© 2001 susan werner music
Hear her great music at: susanwerner.com

there is a world that's been addressed to you
addressed to you - intended only for your eyes
a secret world, like a treasure chest for you
of private scenes and brilliant dreams that mesmerize
a tender lover's smile, a tiny baby's hands
the million stars that fill the turning sky at night
o i suggest, yes i suggest to you
o i suggest this is the best part of your life.

there is a hope, that's been expressed in you
the hope of seven generations, maybe more
and this is the faith that they invest in you
it's that you'll do one better than was done before
inside you know, inside you understand
inside you know what's yours to finally set right
and i suggest to you, yes i suggest to you
i suggest this is the best part of your life.

Mom = Wow! (just upside down!)

HELP WANTED: Lifelong Volunteer Position. I guess you could call it a Mom-opoly!

POSITION: Mom, Mommy, Mum, Mummy, Mama, Ma

JOB DESCRIPTION: Long-term team players needed for challenging permanent work in an often chaotic environment. Candidates must possess excellent communication and organizational skills and be willing to work variable hours, which will include evenings and weekends and frequent 24 - hour shifts on call. Some overnight travel required, including trips to primitive camping sites on rainy weekends and endless sports tournaments in far away cities! Travel expenses not reimbursed. Extensive courier duties also required.

RESPONSIBILITIES: For the rest of one's life, the candidate should be willing to be hated, at least temporarily, until someone needs $5. Must be willing to bite tongue repeatedly. Also, must possess the physical stamina of a pack mule and be able to go from zero to 60 mph in three seconds flat in case, this time, the screams from the backyard are not someone just crying wolf. Must be willing to face stimulating technical challenges, such as small gadget repair, mysteriously sluggish toilets and stuck zippers. Must screen phone calls, maintain calendars and coordinate production of multiple homework projects. Must have ability to plan and organize social gatherings for clients of all ages and mental outlooks. Must be willing to be indispensable one minute, an embarrassment the next. Must handle assembly and product safety testing of a half million cheap, plastic toys and battery operated devices. Must always hope for the best but be prepared for the worst. Must assume final, complete accountability for the quality of the end product. Responsibilities also include floor maintenance and janitorial work throughout the facility.

POSSIBILITY FOR ADVANCEMENT & PROMOTION: None. Your job is to remain in the same position for years without complaining, constantly retraining and updating your skills so that those in your charge can ultimately surpass you!

PREVIOUS EXPERIENCE: None required unfortunately. (You may need a license to drive, but they let anyone become the custodian of the future.) On-the-job training offered on a continually exhausting basis.

WAGES AND COMPENSATION: Nope, sorry, you get nothing – in fact you have to pay your employers, offering frequent raises and bonuses along the way! And just when you think you're finished opening your wallet – you find that a balloon payment is due because of the assumption that college will help them become financially independent. When you die, you give your employers whatever is left. The oddest thing about this reverse-salary scheme is that you actually enjoy it and wish you could only do more. In 2007, www.salary.com estimated that a stay-at-home Mom's salary, for a 92-hour 'workweek' is worth $138,095 annually. But, alas, the check is not in the mail.

BENEFITS: While no health or dental insurance, no pension, no tuition reimbursement, no paid holidays and no stock options are offered, this job supplies limitless opportunities for personal growth and free hugs for life if you play your cards right.

Author Unknown

Life's A Dance

Parenting closely resembles an old-fashioned sock-hop, a school-wide dance held in the gym. (Footwear was restricted to socks only, so as not to mar the floor ... they were so civil in the olden days!) As you dance your way through the stages of infancy, childhood and adolescence you'll find they are much like different dances. At first you'll be as hesitant as a middle school 'tween taking the floor to try a slow waltz. You'll fumble, stumble, sway back and forth, and if this is your first, you may have a hard time finding the rhythm in your infant's song. During the toddler years, you'll find yourself doing the hokey pokey, the Macarena, a quick polka or a little two - step. Childhood is hectic; a cha-cha, lots of twirling, line dancing and jitterbugging. The tween and teen years will find both you and your child in the wild and crazy, twist and shout stage. And in every dance sequence, even though you may follow the beat of their drummer, take the lead, guide the way and teach them all the different steps of life. Expect that sometimes you will step on each other's toes, get out of sync, and drift apart to march to your own melody.

If you bungle motherhood nothing else matters. It doesn't matter how successful you are, how many books you write, how good you are on TV - nothing. If you don't get that right, nothing else matters.
Jackie Kennedy Onassis

Having children is asking for trouble. So why do we have kids?
Maybe Pete Seeger said it best, "We do it for the high wages...kisses."

Our children are not us. They are their own people. We mother each child differently because we give them what they need as individuals.
Maria Shriver Schwarzenegger

The only time we really seem to have them is when they're in the womb. And then the process, once they're born, is a process of letting go.
Demi Moore

Try Not To Smother When You Mother

Most Moms agree that in retrospect they'd have done things with a more relaxed, less obsessive, less programmed approach to Mothering, with less hyper-parenting and less helicopter-like hovering, but it's so hard to see yourself in the moment. The essence of Motherhood is simply being present in your child's life. Watch, listen, smile, comment occasionally, cheer, hug and just be there.

If all goes well, a Mother's essence will persist like an echo even when the source of her voice is gone. It will linger in her child's soul forever.

Time Out!

First you were somebody's daughter, then you were somebody's wife and now you're somebody's Mother... don't forget to take time just to be you. "Take time for yourself!" You've heard this said a thousand times before, but there's a good reason for that. 1) You deserve it. 2) You need it. 3) You can't give what you don't have. Soooooooo... for just one minute before you get out of bed and one minute before you nod off, make it a practice think good thoughts and count your blessings. Eat well; exercise even if you just walk for 20 minutes a day, take that time to read, listen to a book or music, or meditate. One night a week, put your coat on and take off! Don't wait till your kids are 'sleeping through,' are in school or are out on their own – do it NOW! Consider this Mom 'time out' your personal reset button. Join a book club, see a movie, go bowling, learn something new – drawing, painting – anything, or take an academic course... whatever it is, you'll feel invigorated, rejuvenated and enlightened! Do something for yourself, by yourself. If you don't fill your own soul, you won't have much to give. You'll also be empowering your partner to take charge and engage with the kids, which isn't called babysitting – it's called Parenting or/and Fathering!

I have always tried to put to put my kids first and then myself a really close second, as opposed to fifth or seventh. One thing I've learned from the male role model is that they don't hesitate to invest in themselves.

Michelle Obama

On Alternative Mothering

While we're on the subject of calm mothering, where is it written that certain child rearing activities, giving birth and breastfeeding notwithstanding, are "motherly" as opposed to "fatherly"? Honestly, folks, this is the USA in 2012! Haven't we evolved beyond male/female stereotypes of nurturing? In my house, we have happily reversed the traditional roles. My husband is definitely the calmer of the two of us - I have allergic reactions to whining. He is usually five times more patient with the kids than I am, and as a result, I have happily ceded most traditional "motherly" roles to him: school drop-off and pick-up, schlepping to activities, taking them to the grocery store and clothes shopping, cooking and doing the dishes, supervising teeth brushing, and doing bedtime routine. While this flurry of motherly (!) activity is underway, I am free to work on the computer in an attempt to earn some extra cash, and to tackle jobs that are traditionally thought of as male: seeding the lawn, changing the oil in the lawnmower, pruning bushes, building tables and shelves for the kids, painting stairwells, tearing down walls and sheet-rocking them back up, designing and building porch railings and patios, hauling garbage and recycling to the dump, etc. I check in with the kids for occasional kisses, I read a bedtime book now and then, and I even make dinner once in a while -but when they need a tushie wiped or a boo-boo kissed, "Daddy!" is heard first. Anyone can wear the proverbial apron or tool belt; if Dad is the calmer of the two of you, make him the mother!

Jenny Gitlitz, Pittsfield, MA

For all the Mothers

For all the Mothers who cry the first time they hold their newborn babies,
For the Mothers who gave homes to babies not born their own,
And to those who gifted them to a family.
For the mothers whose babies never got to take their first breath,
For the mothers yet to be.
For the Mothers who instinctively turn their heads when they hear the word "Mom" even
when their children are far away.
For the Mothers who stayed awake all night with a sick child and whispered "It's OK
honey, Mommy's here"
For the mothers who haven't slept a full night's sleep in years, and for those who do.
For all the Mothers who sat outside a kindergarten class room and cried,
and for those who danced all the way home.
For the mothers who run carpool and bake cookies
and for those who don't.
For the mothers who carry a bag the size of a duffle and for those who just carry keys.
For the Moms who show up at work with stains on their dresses, gummy bears in their
hair, and diapers in their purses.
For the Mothers who've read *Good Night Moon*,
or *I Love You as Much*, every night for two years.
For all the young and old Mothers, working and stay-at-home Moms, married Mothers
and single ones too.
We Thank You

Karenia Tarolli, Denten, TX

A Prayer for The Children

We pray for the children who put chocolate fingers on everything, who love to be tickled, who stomp in puddles and ruin their new pants, who eat candy before supper and who can never find their shoes in the morning.
And we also pray for those who stare at photographers from behind barbed wire, who have never bounded down the street in a pair of new shoes, who have never played 'one potato, two potatoes' and who are born in places that we would not be caught dead in and that they will be.

We pray for the children who gave us sticky kisses and fistfuls of dandelions, who sleep with their dog and who bury their goldfish, who hug us so tightly and who forget their lunch money, who squeeze the toothpaste all over the sink, who watch their fathers shave, and who slurp their soup.
And we also pray for those who will never get dessert, who have no favorite blanket to drag around behind them, who watch their fathers suffer, who cannot find bread to steal, who do not have rooms to clean up, whose pictures are on milk cartons instead of on dressers, and whose monsters are real.

We pray for the children who spend all of their allowance by Tuesday, who pick at their food, who love ghost stories, who shove dirty clothes under the bed and who never rinse the bathtub, who love visits from the tooth fairy, even after they find out who it really is, who do not like to be kissed in front of the school bus, and who squirm during services.
And we also pray for those children whose nightmares occur in the daytime, who will eat anything, who have never seen a dentist, who are not spoiled by anyone, who go to bed hungry and wake up hungry, who live and move and have no address. We pray for those children who like to be carried and for those children who have to be carried, for those who give up and for those who never give up, for those who will grab the hand of anyone kind enough to offer it and for those who find no hand to grab.

For all these children, we pray today, for they are all precious.

Ina J. Hughs

In The Beginning... Oh Baby!

Safety First

Of course safety comes first, but what does this actually mean? Baby proof your house. Here is a partial list:

- Get down (literally!) on your hands and knees and crawl through every square inch of your house, before your baby does! Inspect every corner carefully. Be especially vigilant looking under and around desks, office areas and in the bathrooms. You'll be amazed at how many nails, screws, paper clips, staples and pills you find, in spite of your tireless vacuuming. If you discover anything lurking at least it won't go into your baby's mouth!

- Install smoke and carbon monoxide detectors in different areas of your home.

- Wind up all the mini-blind and drape cords and electrical cords. Insure that that the cords are high enough (knotted and out of the way) so little hands can't pull them down. Shorten phone cords to eliminate slack. Cover all the electrical outlets.

- Put safety latches on all kitchen and bathroom cabinets, even above the sink medicine cabinets – toddlers are notorious climbers.

- Empty your cabinets of all hazardous cleaning materials. Store them on very high shelves. Consider switching to 'green, nontoxic' cleaning products. These cost the same as regular household cleaners and work just as well, but they have the added benefit of not being harmful to you or the environment. If we all used these products, I bet we'd enjoy better health and have a much cleaner country in just a few years.

- We pour 3 billion pounds of pesticides into our gardens and around our homes annually, just in the USA! In general, as a rule of thumb: open the bottle and smell it, if the product has a strong odor and/or it catches in your throat, it's toxic. You don't even have to read the label. Let's all start using more eco-friendly products. (See 'Cleaning Up')

- If you haven't already, sign up and take a CPR course. Better to have this knowledge and never use it than need it and not know it.

Iddy Biddy Baby = Big, Big Business!

Put your wallet away and save a bundle! You really don't need a $900 stroller to move your baby from the car into the store. You don't really need a detachable carrier seat to store your infant in a restaurant. You don't need an air purifying, home sanitizing diaper disposal system. You don't need a bathtub water-splashguard. You don't need specially designed baby support pillows. You don't need a $300 audio-visual baby monitoring system. You don't need a 'baby wipe warmer.' You don't need expensive, brand-name baby clothes. You don't need a $350 car seat. You don't even need a changing table. You can put a lovely, fabric-covered foam slab on top of a regular, waist high dresser.

Save your bucks, you're going to need them! The (2008) national-average cost of raising a child from infancy to age 18 was a staggering $291,570! Don't get caught in the Big Buy-Buy Baby merchandising of infancy and childhood.

Safe Sucking

When you choose pacifiers, nipples and teethers, look for silicone nipples instead of rubber, because rubber can leach carcinogenic nitrosamines. You can easily tell them apart because silicone is clear and rubber is yellow. Choose pacifiers and teethers made without PVC; silicone pacifiers are available, and many companies have stopped using PVC for teethers.
(Source: pollutioninpeople.org/safer/products/kids-products)
To check the safety of any other household item or toy check: healthystuff.org

Don't Get Into Hot Water

You can reduce your electricity bill and your chances of accidentally scalding your baby by simply turning down your hot water heater to 110' - 120' F.

Swaddle Your Babe

Wrapping your baby in a soft blanket will make her feel safe and secure, it is also makes it much easier for you to hold her.

Ellen Bukstel, Southwest Ranches FL

To swaddle your baby: Open a baby blanket and place it on a bed like a diamond. Fold down the top corner, and place the baby's head at the top, ears aligned with the fold. Now pull the right corner around her body and tuck it in under her. Fold the bottom corner up towards her chin and finally pull the left corner around her.
Her arms should be close to her body and she should look like a little 'mummy.' Now you can carry her very securely in a football hold and have one hand completely free.

When 1 = 2 (Really!)

Some Moms discovery that they gave birth to one child in the hospital but come home with two kids, because some first-time Dads (not your husband of course) seem to need so much attention, direction, instruction, demonstration and encouragement. It's as if you have another child to attend to. A two-fer, who knew? Most guys just aren't wired the way we are. Forewarned is forearmed.

Feeling Sad? Bad? - You're Not Alone

In a recent study conducted in Manchester, England, it was noted that many normal new mothers experience negative thoughts. But they rarely discuss these thoughts because society expects Moms to feel happy and content after giving birth. It should be reassuring to new mothers to know that it is more common to experience some negative emotions, such as guilt and sadness, than was previously recognized. But if you are feeling uneasy, have continuing sadness or worry that you may be suffering from postpartum depression, don't wait – check it out. There's no reason to suffer whether it's a chemical or hormonal imbalance. Don't wait another moment, call your doctor and get some help!

Baby, Your Hair Must Fall

When the hormones stop flowing
Your hair will be going!
And it sure helps just knowing
That it's normal – so relax, no baldness will be showing!

To Work or Not To Work

That is the question. Some have the luxury of being able to decide, others have no (financial) choice. But whatever your circumstance please respect the decision of other women for theirs. When women entered the work force en masse, they strived to have it all. Having 'it all' meant managing a career, an immaculate and well-organized home, a storybook marriage and perfect children, all accomplished with creativity, excellence, elegance and humor. Super-moms could accomplish 'it all' by doing everything in moderation and not demanding perfection. Today's super achievers are the so-called Alpha Moms. Whether you're an Alpha Mom or (a more relaxed) Beta Mom – Motherhood is NOT a contest. Just be 'The Mom.' Relax - you really don't need to be perfect. If you need to work, remember that it's easy to get so caught up in the demands of the job that you can easily give it undue priority over the needs your family. Balance is the key.

It isn't about women having to do it all. It's about women NOT having to do it all.
Gloria Steinem, founder Ms. Magazine

You can love your job, but it won't love you back.
Cathy Black, former president and chair of Hearst Publications and USA Today

If you do work outside of your home, make it a practice to spend a few minutes transitioning from one hectic place to the next. Spend an extra few minutes in your car listening to relaxing music to clear your head of all workday pressures. Borrow an idea from the Japanese and change your shoes as you enter your home. This practice sets boundaries and should signal your mind and spirit to separate the outside world from the inner sanctuary of your home. Try making it a habit to sit down for a few minutes as soon as you come in, to unwind, to listen to the kids' stories and relax.

Working mothers continue to face many challenges in this country. Sadly, there remains a real disconnect between our government, the justice department and half of America's workforce – women! According to a report from 'A Woman's Nation,' women today now earn 60 percent of the college degrees awarded each year and fully half of the Ph.D.s and other professional degrees. Almost 40 percent of working women hold managerial and professional positions. Women make 80 percent of the buying decisions in American homes. Companies led by women generally are proving to have healthier bottom lines.
(Source: americanprogress.org/issues/2009/10/womans_nation.html) All that said, it is shameful that blatant employment and pay discrimination are still being tolerated. And it is deplorable that in the USA today, we have better care available, and more protections for our pets and cars than we do for our children. We lag way behind other industrialized countries with regard to family leave, flexible work hours, healthcare and child care. We need more 'feminine understanding' in positions of power. We need more 'estrogen enlightenment' to make this truly a kinder, gentler country. So, whether you work outside your home or not, it's time for us to get involved. And let's inspire our daughters too. Encourage them hold a public office and change our Womb-in's Working World. Because every Mom is a working Mom.

Your kids should have lots of heroes and she-roes
and you should be one of them.

You 2 Should Always Be Number 1

I remember the burning need I felt as I yearned to have a baby. And part of that need was to express my love for my husband and project it onto our beloved little human creation. And even though I fell madly in love with our baby girl, I always made sure that my life partner was my first priority. It is not selfish, but rather healthy, to place your relationship first. If you don't, it will be very apparent to everyone especially your husband. No wonder it is so common for new dads to feel left out and/or jealous as they see you falling in love with the new baby. In time he may well feel displaced and his resentment may grow into anger or indifference as your child(ren) begins to feel an unwarranted sense of undue importance. Children need to feel that they are an important part of a whole family, not your primary or only focus.

How do you ensure your relationship remains number one? Within the first two weeks, get a mature, trustworthy sitter, grab your husband and go out on a date together. This will ensure 4 things: It will reassure you that your baby can indeed survive a few hours without you. It will give you and your beloved some precious time alone. It will set the stage for the future. It will get your baby used to having an alternate caregiver, assuming s/he doesn't sleep through the whole experience. It may be more convenient to go out during the day – for a Sunday brunch and a walk in the park for an hour. The main idea is that you need to connect often and early.

As soon as your baby sleeps through the night, take her/him out of your room and put the baby in her/his own space. And even if his snoring drives you crazy, do not to move your husband into another room. Fix the snoring and keep the relationship intact. As soon as you can, go out on a date together.

When your baby is old enough to be without you for a few hours a week on a regular basis, look for a reliable teenage babysitter and arrange a standing one-night-a-week appointment. We used to pay our babysitter even if we went out of town or planned on staying home that night. This way we were always assured that she'd be there for us - we both had a commitment. It was easier for the kids, too – no separation anxiety, 'the mice didn't play when the cats were away' and they looked forward to playing with the babysitter. She was part of our family. Leave your little one and go out with your husband every week. It is so important for all of you!

Postpartum Sex Talk

Here's a little secret. These are sexiest phrases in the English language. Who could resist a partner who sweetly whispers these special words into the ear of a new Mom? "Honey, what would you like me to wash first? The laundry or the floors?" "Where should I start vacuuming, darling?" "Hey beautiful, what would you like me to make/order for dinner?"

I have four children and my advice is to do everything it takes to keep going out with, and have lots of sex with your husband. Babysitting is expensive but forgetting what led to having kids in the first place is even more expensive!

Juliane Hiam, Pittsfield, MA

Babysitter Check List

- If you have an alarm, demonstrate how to use it. Leave written instructions on its use.

- Keep a clearly written list beside the phone, with your address and phone number on it (in order to verify this info to the police or 911 operator.) List all emergency numbers – Police, 911, poison control, and your closest neighbor.

- Show the sitter where the fire extinguisher is and describe how to use it.

- Discuss what to do if the fire alarm goes off.

- Show the sitter where the first aid supplies are kept. If medication needs to be given, prepare the exact amount to be given (place it in the fridge) and write down time it is to be given.

- Write down your location, your cell phone number or alternate contact info.

- Walk through the house and ensure that all windows and doors are locked.

- Turn on outside lights.

The Chinese symbol for 'crisis' is created by portraying 'danger and opportunity.'

Division of Labor

Teach and expect your husband to participate fully in your child's life. Not just lip service – diaper changing, bathing, feeding, reading, talking, playing, disciplining, home-working, bike riding, parent-teacher nighting … the works.

Don't wait: Start this the bonding process immediately. I used to express breast milk and David would use it to bottle feed our daughter at 11pm or when I was going out 'alone.' The first time I gave him the bottle, he looked at it quizzically and said, "Do I start on the right or left?"!

In order to be a good father, dads need to be given the opportunity to get involved. Make time for the two of them to do things alone together, and allow them to develop their own rituals. About once a month my husband and the girls would ceremoniously troop into the kitchen to bake a batch of gourmet (store bought prepared cookie dough!) cookies. That was sacred Daddy time! I claimed 'cookie incompetence' and stayed out of the way. The reward of a strong lifelong father-daughter/son relationship is built on sharing and experiencing together.

Remember – the behavior you accept in the first 6 months of
<u>any</u> relationship will be the behavior that you live with forever.

Remind your husband that he is the role model for all the future loving relationships your children will aspire to. Encourage and expect him to share, participate and be as involved as you are, or he may end up living emotionally outside of the family unit. Don't allow spectator sports to become a focus or priority. Parallel play is not interactive. Watching a ballgame with one's child is not the same as playing a ballgame with one's child.

Men who change diapers change the world!

Documenting A Life

- Buy a divided spiral notebook. Keep an up-to-date record of immunizations and medical records for each member of your family in the separate sections. Keep a dated list of illnesses, medications (note any allergies or side effects), surgeries and dental work. Organization is 'key' to easy Mothering.

- Instant art: Instead of throwing it out all the baby cards you receive, cut out some of the pictures and arrange a collage, surrounding your infant's picture or baby announcement.

- Get a 'Baby Book' and keep it full of funny anecdotes, funny things that the kids said, milestones reached, childhood illnesses, vaccination records, first steps, first boyfriends etc. Include an annual school picture, list the names each year's teachers, best friends and play friends. Years later you'll have the perfect reference book.

- Hang a calendar in each child's room to record funny or special things s/he does. Committing to one little square a day might be easier than keeping up a daily journal. After several months (or once a year) you can transfer the really hysterical stories into the 'baby book.'

- Never stop taking pictures – you can never have too many! Once the opportunity is gone it's lost forever.

- Make hand and/or foot prints (or tracings) at birth, 3 months, 6 months and yearly. Frame them.

- Keep a special 'birthday tape.' Consider getting a video (or audio) tape recorder and record your child's voice from day one – the sounds of sucking, those delicious early cooing sounds and even a little crying. Keep the tape and add on to it as time passes. When she begins to talk, those first words are priceless and you'll treasure them later. Keep the video separate from all other recordings. Do a yearly interview on each birthday, recording the year's events, name all the best friends, discuss plans and aspirations for the future. As time goes on you'll have an oral or video history of his/her life ... the sound of his/her voice (hairstyle and fashions) will change with time and you'll have captured it all! We vow that we'll always remember those sounds and images but our intentions are always stronger than our memories.

Plant A Tree

Consider planting a sapling tree to mark the arrival of your little one. Plant it where you can watch it grow. With the passage of time, it will be fun to see your child and the tree mature together. And as your child begins to understand the world around him/her, you can be sure s/he'll take pride in knowing that this is "my tree." What a nice way to ensure a healthy respect for nature!

Germs

Don't get too rattled about germs. In my opinion, clean is good, sterile is not. There is something to be said for the slow introduction of a moderate amount of normal germs – wash off the pacifier, but don't sterilize everything your baby puts in her mouth. We have to build up our immune systems in order for them to work. I'm not a proponent of alcohol-based, antibacterial hand sanitizers. I predict that it won't be long before normal bacteria mutates into strains much more harmful than what we are trying to clean away now. New super-bugs may be a direct result of our constant use of these products. We've become totally germaphobic! The truth is we NEED some germs in our lives – we would (quite literally) die without them. We have germs which live on our skin, in our noses and our bowels. There are about one trillion bacteria on each of your feet! Each one of us is a walking zoo - and we're meant to be that way! Problems only arise when some of these itty-bitty micro animals land in places they're not supposed to be. If bacteria from your nose are introduced into your urinary tract – you'll be in trouble. If friendly bacteria from your bowel, somehow comes in contact with your eyes – you'll be in trouble. Just use regular soap. A 2007 study, which appeared in 'Clinical Infectious Diseases' found that washing with regular soap and antibacterial soap was essentially the same. Antibacterial soap contains triclosan and may cause bacteria to become resistant to other drugs in that same class. (Source: Advance For Nurses 12/07). Be mindful of what you touch, wash your hands when you should and leave the hand-sanitizing gel in your diaper bag for emergencies. Use it only when soap and water aren't readily available – perhaps at the park or on a picnic in the woods.

Soap and water at regular intervals is a good thing... sterilizing bottles is a waste of time. Dishwashers are wonderful – use the top rack for plastic toys once in a while.

And while we're 'talking dirty' please fast forward to 'Medical Issues' and read the section regarding vaccinations.

Avoiding Allergies

The most common allergies noted in young children today are to peanuts, tree nuts, wheat, dairy products, fish and eggs. You might be surprised to learn that as we become more fastidious keeping our homes clean, allergies are becoming more and more prevalent. Is there a connection? Many scientists are beginning to think so. The theory is called "The Hygiene Hypothesis." A simple explanation: Every baby is born with an immune system that, although immature, is primed and ready to assimilate itself into the world. While the Mom's antibodies, (supplied in breast-milk) are protecting the infant, the newborn's immune system is actually looking for something to be stimulated by, in order to fulfill the function of producing its own antibodies. If we (inadvertently) deny that need by cleaning away all the germs and antigens, then the baby's immune system is forced to challenge whatever else it's introduced to, thereby creating allergies to things that it might not otherwise. Moral of the story: adopt a relaxed attitude about your household germ warfare.

Breathe In!

Have you noticed that in the past decade there has been considerable attention paid to the air we breathe? No, no, industry is not concerned about air purity – they just want to make sure that our dirty air smells good! Air fresheners, toilet bowl cleaners, mothballs and other deodorizing products contain a chemical compound, (volatile organic compound, VOC 1,4 DCB) which has been recently discovered to cause a modest reduction of lung function in adults – so imagine the impact on a newborn's tiny, immature lungs. The smell of your baby is so delicious. Savor it! Avoid using perfumes, spraying scents, burning incense or scented-candles, air wicks, and plug-in room deodorizers. For bathroom use, I recommend organic, non-toxic sprays available in natural food markets.

Update: According to University of Washington researcher, Ann C. Steinemann, PhD, air fresheners and fragranced laundry products often emit literally dozens of chemicals - some of which are considered toxic by federal law. "I didn't find a brand that didn't emit at least one toxic chemical," she reported. However, there are no laws that require disclosure of the chemicals in fragrances. So I recommend that we stop using store-bought air fresheners altogether, and try the real thing instead - cut open a lemon or orange, gather some mint leaves, or just open a box of baking soda. (Source: Daily Dose 12/09)

A Word About Rocking, Bouncing Or Any Type of Repetitive Motion:

DON'T.

Humans are creatures of habit. If you (even unknowingly) create a habit, your baby will crave it and be at a loss when it's withdrawn. Human beings love and crave consistency, so if you begin rocking, perpetual walking, bouncing, patting or constant back rubbing in order to get your baby to calm down or go to sleep, you may find that variations on this theme will be expected forever. I know many people who innocently started a soft motion and ultimately graduated to baby swings and long distance car rides to get their kids to sleep. Make a conscious decision not to start any repetitive soothing motion – sleep should be equated with stillness and self-soothing.

A Word About Breastfeeding

DO.

This is the best thing you can do for yourself and your new baby. Some of the benefits are: Breast milk provides the perfect nutrition, at the perfect temperature; is readily available in adequate quantities; requires no preparation; provides vital antibodies and over 200 infection-fighting agents which protect the infant from numerous diseases, ear infections, diarrhea, eczema, childhood obesity, respiratory infections and allergies. And new scientific research shows evidence that breast milk may actually alter it's composition to accommodate the baby's changing needs. Fascinating! It's as if your baby has a personal chef, nutritionist and pharmacy all rolled into one! Of course breastfeeding saves money, time and is always convenient no matter where you are. Breast milk can be easily stored (up to 4 days in a clean glass container, stored at the back of the fridge at 39 degrees F.) so that dads can give supplemental feedings. In addition, breastfeeding uses lots of calories to speed you back to your normal body weight and shape. (Well, OK, it actually enhances your 'presentation' and your partner loves it, we know.) Nursing your infant creates a wonderful, warm, physically nurturing relationship between you, which simply cannot be duplicated. Medical science has demonstrated that women who breastfeed (for a total of 24 months over their child-bearing years) have a lower incidence of breast cancer and new studies show there is some cardiac protection as well. (Sources: Obstetrics and Gynecology, 1/2010. Journal of Pediatrics, 1/2010) Let's face it; breastfeeding - it's a good thing.

Some Moms have difficulties with nursing, either experiencing painful nipples or getting their babies to 'latch on.' Using silicone nipple shields can easily cure both of these problems.

If you're still in any doubt that 'breast is best' the recent recall of bug infested baby formula should convince you. After all, there's never been a breast milk recall. Perhaps you heard that Abbott Laboratories had to recall 5 million containers of Similac formula when it discovered that large quantities had been contaminated with Trogoderma variabile beetles. The FDA (Food and Drug Administration) however, was quick to say that the beetle itself is harmless while they did admit that beetle parts and/or larvae pieces in the formula could irritate an infant's digestive tract, lead to stomach aches, and even cause a baby to refuse food (which could, of course, lead to dehydration and death)! Which begs the question, who is the FDA charged with protecting?

In addition, scientists are warning parents to avoid some infant formulas that may contain high levels of arsenic, an extremely poisonous metallic element that has been shown to cause cancer. The hazardous baby formulas are sweetened with arsenic-containing organic brown rice syrup, which some manufacturers are starting to use in place of high fructose corn syrup or other sweeteners.

Still don't want to breastfeed? OK, don't. They never thank you for giving birth 'naturally' either!

Another Mom's Take On Breastfeeding

Breastfeed your kid for as long as you can stand it. They adore it, it's free, healthy, portable, and doesn't get dirty like a pacifier. You can quiet them in 2 seconds when you need to in a public place. If well-meaning but ignorant waitresses, maître d's, lifeguards, and museum docents give you a hard time and/or offer to sequester you in the toilet or some other private place "for your comfort," politely decline and continue what you're doing. If they make a real stink, smile and suggest that they call the cops. Hold your ground! Your kid will thank you for it by growing up loving and confident. BUT, if the breastfeeding is driving you absolutely bonkers—it hurts/itches/tickles or is otherwise driving you to distraction, and if you've consulted with midwives, La Leché, etc. to try to solve the problem but still can't, then honey, give it up before you drive yourself and your kid insane. Kids need a calm mother, not someone who is freaked out.

Jenny Gitlitz, Pittsfield MA

Note: Florida law recognizes that breastfeeding "is an important and basic act of nurture which must be encouraged in the interests of maternal and child health and family values." A mother may legally breastfeed her baby anywhere -- public or private. The law gets even more detailed, specifically stating that a mother may breastfeed "irrespective of whether the nipple of the mother's breast is uncovered during or incidental to the breastfeeding." (Wow!)

Your notes...

Infancy info ...

More On Hormones

Your newborn's genitals may be in a massive looking state,
But don't worry - this is not their normal fate.
Because when pregnancy hormones abate,
Those 'private parts' will completely deflate!
And then the baby will have to wait
For adolescent hormones to compensate and reinstate!

Baby Boobs

A baby who's been floating in Mom's hormones for nine months can sometimes emerge with enlarged breasts - yup, even boys. Glands can even secrete a liquid resembling 'milk' (so-called 'witch's milk.') But don't worry, both conditions go away in a few weeks and are of no concern.

Cradle Cap

If you see thick, scaly patches on your baby's tiny, delicate head you are seeing cradle cap. It's a harmless scalp condition.

According to the Mayo Clinic's Web site, cradle cap usually goes away within a few months but can look pretty unsightly in the meantime. Try applying some baby oil to the scalp, allow it soften the patches for a few minutes, then gently backcomb the scaly patches. Wash your baby's hair once a day using a mild baby shampoo and loosen the scales with a small, soft-bristled brush before rinsing the shampoo.

Bowed Legs

Don't worry about your child's chubby bowed legs. Most babies have slightly curved legs as they learn to stand and walk, but this normal curvature straightens out within a year or so.

Is S/He Getting Enough To Eat?

Rule of thumb: In terms of calories, babies generally need their height in inches multiplied by 40. So if your infant is 20 inches, s/he'll need about 800 calories a day. If you're nursing, just go by your infant's comfort zone. If s/he is peeing and sleeping and happy, s/he is getting enough!

Fever!

Fever is a symptom – not an illness. So if your infant is not 'acting sick,' the immune system is functioning well and s/he's better off just getting over whatever was 'bugging' him.

Is That A Third Nipple?

Most parents are shocked if they see their baby has a third nipple. But according to the National Institute of Health they're actually quite common. Small and not well formed, a third (or perhaps more) nipple may be seen below the regular two. The NIH Web site says no treatment is needed, and there's no need to worry - the extra nipples will never develop into real breasts.

Crossed Eyes

For the first six weeks of life many babies have what appears to be crossed eyes. It's normal, but if it goes on past six weeks, bring it to the attention of your pediatrician. (Source: the Children's Medical Center of Dallas, Texas)

White Eye Alert

Make sure that the pediatrician examines your newborn infant's eyes using dilating drops. Subsequent exams (at each and every visit!) should be done in a darkened room. However, if you ever develop photos and see one eye with a white dot (rather than red) reflection, go to an ophthalmologist and have it checked out! Most of the time it's nothing, but sometimes it indicates a very serious problem (specifically retinoblastoma).

Understanding The Secret Language of Babies

An amazing Australian woman thinks she has deciphered exactly what infants are trying to tell us! Her research has identified five sounds which make up a universal infant language. If you listen closely to the 'pre cry' noises infants make prior to actually crying, you can decode what they are communicating. Priscilla Dunstan says that these sounds are infant reflexes, normally found in all babies from birth through 3 months, after which the reflexes change or vanish and, unfortunately, so does this early communication system.

Listen for: "neh" it means "I'm hungry."
　　　　　　 "owh" it means "I'm sleepy."
　　　　　　 "heh" it means "I'm uncomfortable."
　　　　　　 "ehrr" it means "I have lower intestinal gas."
　　　　　　 "eh"   it means "I need to burp."

For more information look for the DVD, "Dunstan Baby Language.

Skinship

'Skinship' is a translation of a Japanese term for the close physical relationship between mother and infant. Skin to skin contact is so important. Studies show that in our culture, infants are currently spending up to 60 waking hours a week in high chairs, walkers, play-pens, portable cribs, bouncy seats and swings. This will not promote independence. In fact, it may actually create unmet physical tactile needs. Dr. Sharon Heller (in her book The Vital Touch) cites caressing, stroking, hugging and squeezing, rocking, swaying and spinning as feeding the infant's need for sensory input, which leads to healthy brain development. Hold your infant in your arms and free him from our current trend to 'containerize the baby.'

Baby Massage

Give your baby massages! It is both calming and health strengthening. It "connects" both baby's sense of her body, and her bond with you. Massage promotes good circulation, relaxes muscles, it stimulates nerve growth and flexibility. S/he'll respond with happy kicks and giggles, or by going soundly to sleep. I narrated my babies' massages, too, naming body parts, such as "here is your sweet baby hand with one finger, two fingers, three fingers, four, and this is your sweet baby thumb," sometimes making up rhymes. Warm baby lotion between your palms and start with a lightly firm touch all over baby's skin at first, then move on to gentle squeezes along arms and legs as well. Be sure to pay attention to each finger and toe, and each ear along the way. Massage is especially important for Cesarean-born babies, as they don't get that first vigorous squeeze through the birth canal. For further instruction and suggestions check out: infantmassage.com

Amy Carol Webb, Miami, FL

What About Colic?

Colic can be exhausting. On top of making you sleep-deprived and frustrated, it's terrible to see your infant hurting. Colic is a particular type of crying (frequent, prolonged outbursts) often caused by abdominal pain. When defining colic, physicians often refer to the classic "rule of 3's:" periods of intense crying lasting for more than 3 hours per day, at least 3 days per week. (Note that the average baby cries 1 ¾ hours per day.) There are 2 reasons why a baby's tummy might hurt that badly, but thankfully both are treatable:

One possible cause is Reflux, also known as gastroesophageal reflux disease (GERD). This occurs when the circular band of muscle where the esophagus joins the stomach hasn't fully matured. This allows stomach acid to flow into the esophagus, irritating the lining and causing heartburn. Baby heartburn! In addition to inconsolable crying, there may be repeated spitting up after feeding, writhing in pain, frequent wet or sour burps or trouble sleeping.

The treatment is simple: continue to breastfeed as long as possible. Since breast milk empties from the stomach much faster than formula, it will be less likely to lead to reflux. If you're bottle-feeding, feed your baby twice as often, giving her half as much. With either feeding method, keep your baby upright for at least half an hour after s/he's finished and elevate the head of the crib between 30 and 45 degrees. If these treatments don't work, your doctor may prescribe medication to reduce stomach acid.

The second most likely reason for colic is allergies. It might surprise you that your baby might have an allergy to a component of formula or something in a breastfeeding mother's diet. The symptoms are the same as reflux, but are often accompanied by diarrhea and a raised rash, found primarily on the face and trunk. If you're bottle-feeding, try a hypoallergenic formula and offer smaller, more frequent feedings. If breastfeeding, eliminate cow's milk* (the most common infant allergen) from your diet for at least a week to see if your baby feels better. (* Do lions suckle pigs? Do giraffes nurse on hippo's milk? Why do humans drink cow's milk and think it's perfectly natural? Something to think about...) Some other typical allergens are soy, wheat, eggs, onions, cruciform vegetables such as cabbage and broccoli, garlic, chocolate and nuts.

"The 5 S's" - Techniques which may help parents with crying infants:

- Swaddling, especially in combination with carrying the baby for a minimum of 3 hours per day;

- Side or prone positioning while the baby is being held;

- Shushing -- using white noise to calm the baby;

- Sucking a pacifier; and

- Swinging -- activating the vestibular system by using a swinging motion may reduce crying. Per Dr. Irons, "Run [the swing] as fast as it'll operate. Wind it up and let 'em go!"

Of course, not all babies will respond to these methods, since many things can cause colic. But whatever the reason for the constant crying, most babies will outgrow it within three to six months. (I heard that sigh...)

When To Call the Doctor

Fever: Babies younger than 3 months, call if a rectal temperature is 100.5'F or higher. Babies 3 – 6 months, call if a rectal temperature is 101'F or higher. Call if the fever lasts 3 days or longer and/or you see any type of rash.

A Cold: Call if your baby is having difficulty breathing or a cold lasts longer than one week.

Vomiting: Call if the baby is younger than 6 months and has been vomiting, intermittently for 6 hours, especially if you see a rash or if the baby has a fever.

Diarrhea: Call if it's persistent, watery, green and/or foul smelling and especially if accompanied by fever.

Rx for all of the above: Regularly offer small amounts of room temperature water to keep your baby hydrated while waiting to see or hear from the doctor.

* NEVER give aspirin to babies or children unless your doctor orders it specifically. In rare cases aspirin can cause Reyes Syndrome, which is a fatal condition.

Don't be alarmed if your doctor opts not to treat a fever. If it's a low- grade fever with a known cause, studies show that children recover faster if the fever is allowed to run its course. Treat the child, not the thermometer.

And while we're on the subject, in lieu of manufactured oral liquid replacements (which are chock full of artificial chemicals, dyes and sugar) ask your doctor about offering room temperature coconut water. Coconut water (not coconut milk) is Mother Nature's all natural electrolyte and dehydration fluid replacement.

Teething

No one likes to see their child in pain, but Mother Nature has seen fit to introduce us to pain early in life. Perhaps we should adopt a more holistic approach and offer soothing, frozen teething rings and resist the temptation to reach for medications at the first signs of discomfort. There is something to be said for allowing a baby to develop ways of coping, self-soothing skills and some pain tolerance early on.

Signing and Language Development

Across the globe, in almost every culture mothers have a tendency to speak to their newborn infants in high-pitched voices. I don't know why we do this but it's universal, so go ahead. But as soon as you start really talking to your baby, speak as you would like her to. Don't repeat or encourage baby talk. And I would encourage you to communicate with simple sign language as well as the spoken word. There are books which teach the essential signs. Studies have shown that infants understand language very early on, but they lack the verbal skills necessary to reply or make their wishes known. However, they are capable of 'showing' you what you they want! Ask a baby to wave 'bye bye' and you'll see an arm or hand wave. Much the same way, you can easily teach your baby a few basic 'sign language' skills to communicate her/his needs and desires, therefore reducing crying time frustrations. Learning just a few signs such as "I'm hungry, I'm thirsty, I'm tired, I need to be changed" will make life so much easier for both of you. And, you'll have the added benefit of seeing that little brain working! (Check out babysigns.com)

On SIDS

Although there is recent evidence that SIDS (Sudden Infant Death Syndrome) may in fact be triggered by a biological brain condition, here are some guidelines to help reduce the risk. (Source: American Academy of Pediatrics)

- Infants should be placed on their back, for every sleep.
- The sleep surface should be firm.
- The infant should sleep separately from the parents, but nearby.
- A pacifier should be used when placing the infant down to sleep and not be reinserted once the infant falls asleep. It should be cleaned often and replaced regularly. For breast-fed infants, pacifier introduction should be delayed until one month of age.
- Avoid overheating the infant. Dress in light clothes.
- Leave a fan on at a low setting.
- Avoid commercial devices claiming to reduce SIDS risk because none has been adequately tested or proven to be of any benefit.

Our Children's Health Is Nothing to Play With

Plastic is ubiquitous in our environment. Did you know that there are toxic chemicals that leach out of most plastic materials? We are just beginning to uncover some of the hazardous effects that these materials are having on our children. Some chemicals (PVC and phallates, as well as polycarbonates containing bisphenol A, commonly known as BPA) have been linked to hormonal disruptions, obesity, hyperactivity, precocious puberty and genetic mutations, just to name a few.

The chemical phallate is used to make plastic soft and pliable. It is in everything from shower curtains to car dashboards, baby bottles, teething rings and your favorite rubber ducky – it's everywhere. The European Union was so concerned about its detrimental effects that it has banned the use of phallates from any and all products sold in Europe. The FDA has finally (and belatedly, in 2012) banned BPA in baby bottles but has opted not to adopt Europe's cautious concern, so all the products that were deemed too unsafe for European children are now be available for ours to play with! (Except in California, where the governor has taken a progressive, proactive stand and prohibited all plastics containing phallates... let's all move there!) But don't breathe easy just yet, because now that most BPA has been removed from baby bottles (and here's a lesson regarding 'be careful what you wish for') it has been replaced with BPS which has been associated with the same harmful endocrine disruptors as BPA! They merely swapped one bad chemical for the other and hoped no one would notice. We noticed. Buy glass bottles.

Play it safe. Avoid all plastic food containers, baby bottles, juice cups, children's (tooth decay) fillings which contain BPA, credit card and all store receipts, canned foods and plastic food wraps. Particularly avoid plastic marked with the #3, #7 or PC recycling codes.

Use only containers marked with #1, 2, or 5 recycling codes and never use those containers to heat or reheat foods.

- Don't allow plastic toys to be put in children's mouths.
- Don't allow milk to remain in plastic bottles for long periods of time.
- Don't use very hot water or strong detergents to wash plastic bottles or toys.
- Throw out plastic bottles that look scratched or hazy.
- Use only glass, ceramic or metal food containers, dishes and eating utensils.
- Choose glass or lightweight stainless steel baby bottles.
- Look for "PVC Free" labels on toys or choose wooden toys. As previously stated, the U.S.A. has no laws prohibiting the use of dangerous plastics in toys. So if it doesn't say "PVC Free" or "BPA Free" you can be sure it is BPA full!
- If you serve food (cheese or meat) that has been wrapped in plastic, shave off the areas that came into contact with the plastic and store the foods in a glass container.
- Do not microwave foods in plastic containers.
- For more info: environmentcalifornia.org/environmental-health/stop-toxic-toys

And one more item … Every American alive today, including newborn babies, has hundreds of chemicals flowing through their blood. Many of these chemicals are linked to prostate and breast cancers, diabetes, heart disease, lowered sperm counts, early puberty and other diseases and disorders. Yet, of the 82,000 chemicals available for use in the U.S., only about 200 have been required to be tested for safety. And the EPA has succeeded in banning only one group of chemicals, PCBs, from the marketplace. Go as green as you can, look for flame retardant free clothes, PJ's, bedding and furniture. A good product safety resource can be found at: cosmeticsdatabase.com (Source: care2.com/greenliving/toxic-beauty.html)

Bottoms Up

To avoid diaper rash: Expose your baby's bum to the sun and air for about 10 minutes a day. Allowing the sun to shine (where it doesn't usually!) even through a closed window will gently and naturally soothe tender skin.

Diaper Rash

The staff at my child's day care center told me that if a child has really bad diaper rash for no obvious reason, it's probably due to teething. The kids swallow extra saliva, which results in extra acid burning their little bums. My pediatrician was impressed and amazed when I told her that!

Soothing Your Sweetie

Having music playing in the baby's room is valuable in many ways. It is extremely soothing, and at the same time it gets the baby accustomed to hearing noise when s/he is going to sleep. Another benefit is that you don't have to be afraid to talk around the baby while s/he is sleeping.

When the baby begins teething, freeze a wet washcloth and let the baby chew on it. It's much safer than using the numbing medications.

When you are driving in the car and the baby begins to cry, open the windows (weather permitting, of course) and the baby usually stops crying. There's no explanation as to why this works, it just works!

Jackie Bardin, Edison, NJ

Sleep Baby Sleep

White Out!

I heard that newborns like to look at white walls, so I draped white towels on the side of the basinet and the crib. It worked like a charm! It calms them down and helps them to fall asleep.

Turn Up the Volume

Do not keep the house quiet. Make noise and get the baby used to sleeping in a busy noisy home. It works!

Love Them and Leave Them

Always put your infant into the crib while s/he's still awake. Let them learn to fall asleep without your help, or you'll need to stand by every time you want him/her to fall asleep for the next 2 years!

Lisa Kent, Toronto, Canada

Banish Bottles in Bed

Putting babies to sleep with a bottle of anything but water is the surest way to tooth decay.

Getting Your Infant To Sleep Through the Night

If your baby was born at full term, is steadily gaining weight and if s/he weighs approximately 40% more than the birth weight at 6 – 8 weeks, then s/he is physically ready to sleep through the night. Really!

"Leni's Tender Sleep Teaching"

1) Feed her at 11pm. If you're nursing give her an extra 2 – 3 oz. of collected breast milk. (Once your baby sleeps through the night, you'll wake up extremely full of milk. Hold a plastic glass beneath your waiting breast during the first morning feeding and you'll be able to collect a few ounces of milk as it pours out! Express a little more after the feeding.) The 11 p.m. feeding is a great opportunity for your husband to feed the baby. If you're bottle-feeding try offering a little more than usual. Lay her down to sleep while she is drowsy but still awake. Remember, you are trying to 'teach' her how to fall asleep on her own.

2) Night one: When she wakes up at 3 – 4am, wait 3-5 minutes to see if she'll settle on her own. If not, offer her 5 - 6 oz. of room temperature plain water. Do not coo, talk or play. Keep the room dark. Don't change her or handle her too much. Feed her, offer her a pacifier or her fist and put her back to sleep as quickly as possible.

3) Night two: same as night one but offer her only 3 – 4 oz. of plain water.

4) Nights three and four: wait 5 minutes, then proceed as before but don't offer any water, just give her the pacifier or help her find her fist. Be matter of fact – no talking, no playing, no changing, and no lights.

5) That's it – all my kids learned quickly and easily to sleep through the night at 6 weeks old. The first morning feeding was usually about 7 am.

6) After a maximum of 7 – 10 nights of sleep teaching, leave the baby to calm him/herself. Learning to self-calm is an essential process, which we will employ throughout life. Adapting to the night and sleeping through the night is the ideal way to begin.

7) If you have followed the above program and s/he's not sleeping through the night on day 10, s/he's simply not ready. Wait two weeks and start again.

8) I have found that often it's the parents who get in their own way – they check on the baby too frequently, they rearrange the blankets and unwittingly disturb the baby. Some parents think that feeding a baby cereal will help their baby sleep through the night, but it doesn't. Don't wait too long to begin sleep teaching – if you wait until s/he's 6 months old you've waited too long and poor sleep patterns have already been established.

Sleeping During the Day

Nap times are wonderful – when s/he sleeps, you sleep.

Keep soft music (try classical) playing during the day; it's soothing and it distinguishes the day from the night. It also gets the baby used to sleeping with distractions.

Keep the blinds open and allow light to fill the baby's room during the day; then keep the room dark at night. Human learning is based on experience, so not only will you be reinforcing natural circadian rhythms but you will be teaching your baby at the same time.

How much sleep does your baby need?

At 2 months old: Average 14.5 hours over a 24 hour period.
9.5 hours at night, 5 hours during naps.

At 6 months old: Average 14.5 hours
                         11 hours at night, 3.5 hours during naps
At 1 year: Average 14 hours
                         11.5 hours at night, 2.5 hours during nap

Have Your Baby Sleep In Her/His Own Room

Unless it's easier for breastfeeding reasons, move the baby to her/his own room as early as possible — and don't wait until s/he's fully asleep to put her/him into the crib. We made that mistake with our five-month-old. When she woke up in the middle of the night, she wanted me to help her fall back to sleep by rocking her or giving her a bottle she didn't really need. It took a week to get her used to drifting off on her own.

And now, more baby info ...

The Circumcision Decision

Ouch... Should you? Some religions mandate this minor surgery. I've seen many of these procedures and I can assure you that it's no big deal. (Literally and figuratively.) It doesn't cause an infant any more than momentary pain. Some argue that "it's not natural" without stopping to think that all surgery is 'unnatural' – but we do it! Cutting our hair, finger and toe nails, plucking eyebrows, waxing or shaving our legs or facial hair is also unnatural but we do it all the time. As for the claim that male circumcision is mutilation, girls get their ears pierced routinely and no one says boo. Nose jobs, breast reductions and augmentations are practically routine in this country. Medically speaking, circumcision is more hygienic and has been shown to prevent some sexually transmitted diseases and infections (STD's and STI's) from spreading to partners. It also eliminates the possibility of one painful disorder that will absolutely, positively require surgical intervention. (Phimosis is a stricture of the foreskin, which squeezes the head of the penis.) And, let's be honest, most women find circumcised males to be more esthetically pleasing. If your husband insists that his little boy needs to look just like his 'natural daddy' ... ask him if that includes the beer belly too. Of course, it's a personal decision but now that you have some facts, you can make a more informed personal decision.

Start That Engine

We all want smart kids. While there's no guarantee that you can create a genius, there's nothing wrong with priming the engine. Starting in the first week of life you can challenge that little brain to get in gear. Hold the baby on your lap so that she's facing you. Look into her eyes and start sticking your tongue out at her in a rhythmic manner. Watch for her to begin to imitate you. Do this every day for a few minutes and slowly begin to vary your facial signs – add a smile or eye blinks, puff out your cheeks or cluck your tongue. We humans learn by imitating; start that brain engine and as time passes, increase the RPMs – keep making different patterns. If she misses a pattern, repeat it until she has mastered it. Encourage her to follow your lead and eventually (by 1 - 1 ½ years old) she will be able to imitate handclapping, drumbeats, vocalization of nonsense words etc. It's fun to get your husband or other children involved and participating in this game, too. Try it as a round! You'll be amazed at how intricate and fun this becomes: and all the while that little brain is wiring up for music, math, science and reading!

Start Thinking About College!

Start a college fund or sign up for a prepaid college plan. No matter what happens you'll end up a winner – when the time comes, either you'll have college completely paid for or you'll have saved a significant amount of money, which will be returned to you if your child doesn't attend a state college or chooses not to go to college.

Keeping Your Keys Handy

I was always digging through my purse to find my keys with one hand, my son in the other hand and the groceries hanging from my third hand... my mouth! Then I bought a carabineer (a sports clip) and put all of my various key chains (home, car, work, etc.) on it. I attached it to the outside of my bag on my purse strap. Now, I just unclip the keys I need when I need them, and they're no longer clumped together in one big bundle - much easier!
Meredith Knight, MA

Please Don't Cook the Baby!

When you're dressing your infant count the layers you are wearing (excluding your bra) and dress your baby the same way. Body temperature falls during sleep so cover your baby with a light blanket in the summer and a medium-weight blanket in the cooler months. I've seen young mothers in halter-tops and shorts while their infants are wearing under-shirts and winter sleepers, smoldering under heavy blankets.

Little Feet Need To Be Free

Hold off on infant shoe wear. According to Dr. Isadore Rosenfeld, going barefoot actually strengthens a baby's foot muscles and helps babies learn to walk. Canada has even banned the sale of infant walkers because they can affect normal muscle control and mental development.

Avoiding the 'Fountain of Youth'

- To avoid getting accidentally sprayed by your baby boy, keep a stack of clean washcloths on the changing table. Cover his penis while you're cleaning him up: if he starts to spray you'll stay dry!

- Keep stack of disposable paper cups stuffed with tissues on the changing table. If he starts to "go" quickly invert the tissue-stuffed cup over the stream, capture the mess and just toss it away.

The Diaper Bag

- *To better organize all the small items you keep in the diaper bag, put them in a clear make-up pouch. You'll easily see what you need and you can move it easily from bag to bag.*

- Keep an extra T-shirt for yourself in the diaper bag. Mom, emergencies do happen; overflowing milk, foul-smelling cheesy spit up, etc.

- Smell like spit-up? Keep some baking soda in a baggie and rub it directly on baby spit-up to nix the smell quickly.

- For one-step mess control keep a Ziploc bag containing a small amount of laundry detergent in your diaper bag. Anytime you have "spills" you can easily isolate the mess and presoak at the same time.

What's On Your Bag?

Handbags are one item that every woman carries with them. While we may know what's inside our handbags, do you have any idea what's on the outside? Shauna Lake put handbags to the test for bacteria - with surprising results. We carry our handbags everywhere, from the office to public toilets to the floor of the car. It turns out handbags are so surprisingly dirty that even the microbiologist who tested them was shocked. Microbiologist Amy Karen of Nelson Labs says nearly all of the handbags tested were not only teeming with regular bacteria, but they also carried large amounts of harmful kinds of bacteria. Pseudomonas (can cause eye infections), staphylococcus aurous (can cause serious skin infections), salmonella and e-coli that were found on the handbags could all make people very sick. In one sampling, four of five handbags tested positive for salmonella, and that's not the worst of it... there was fecal contamination on the handbags! Leather or vinyl handbags tended to be cleaner than cloth handbags. Consider your bag to be just as dirty as your shoes. You may think twice about where you put your handbag after reading this report. Hang them from hooks when you're in a restaurant or restroom, and never put them down near a food preparation area at home. Clean them with disinfectant wipes from time to time and remember - there's probably more on them than in them.

Diaper Disposal

Many newspapers come wrapped in plastic bags. Instead of throwing them away, recycle them. Keep a bunch in the diaper bag. When you change a dirty diaper you'll have the perfect disposal bag – especially if you're at someone else's house!

Sore Tush

Add 3-5 tablespoons of baking soda in the bath water to soothe diaper rash.

Hangin' Out!

Use shower rings to clip toys onto your baby stroller's handle.

Snap It

If you have your little ones in day care, provide them with a disposable camera to capture milestone moments, funny faces and first friends.

Worried About Autism?

Of course you are. And who wouldn't be? In 1996, experts said that 1 in 2,500 children, was diagnosed with autism. Ten years later the figure was drastically different: 1 in 166. In 2010 the incidence was 1 in 150 children. Now (2012) the incidence is 1 in 88 children! Disturbing, disastrous and devastating for families and society alike. This is a public health crisis and yet the media has been hesitant to sound the alarm bells. I wonder if we'd see the same tepid reaction if 1 out of every 88 toddlers was suddenly going blind? Or losing their pudgy, little right arms? We're in the middle of an epidemic, but because this is a hidden biologic (neurological) problem the media and the medical community has been very slow to react. The medical mindset has become, if you don't understand the problem and you can't offer a drug or solution – don't make waves.

It may be difficult to explain autism simply, especially because it's an umbrella term that covers a wide spectrum of physical conditions and neurological disabilities. But the hallmark of autism is difficulty interacting and relating to other people.

No one understands the cause of autism. Some think it's possibly genetic, environmental or may even be due to some type of post traumatic stress disorder. My opinion? I think the autism epidemic is due to all the modern conveniences we are marinating in, which is overwhelming to an immature, underdeveloped, infant/child's immune system. Every day we bombard our personal universe's with a host of man-made modern marvels such as: flame retardant fabrics and foams, chemical additives in our water supply, chemical preservatives in our food, ultra sound waves, microwaves, cell phone frequencies and cell phone towers, pesticides, plastics, nonstick cookware, man-made toxins, GMO (genetically modified organism) food products, cleaning supplies, antibiotics, pharmaceuticals and all the other ubiquitous chemicals we are saturated with, and an explosion in the C-section rate which not only deprives the infant of the physiologic dynamics of birth but also denies the newborn the beneficial and necessary inoculation of vaginal flora, then we top it all off by filling our babies and small children with multiple vaccinations … and we never give a second thought to what unintended consequences we may be (unknowingly) bringing on ourselves. We have created a very artificial world, but we've convinced ourselves it's all perfectly normal and natural. That's my opinion, but I could be wrong. Whatever the cause, the effects are devastating. Bear in mind that doctors are very reluctant to be the messengers of bad news, and as there is no definitive test, they may opt to delay discussing the possibility of this distressing diagnosis. The APA (American Pediatric Association) has recently mandated that toddlers be screened during a normal well visit, twice before their 2nd birthdays. If you suspect that your child might be autistic, early intensive intervention is key: begin therapy as early as 6 months old and definitely before the child is 3 years old. (Resource information can be found at: generationrescue.org)

Very Early Detection: look for signs of attachment difficulty

1. Extreme passivity (lack of crying, lack of movement, lack of interest) No big smiles or other joyful expressions by six months or thereafter.
2. Hyperactivity (continuous crying for no apparent reason or restlessness.)
3. Refusal to eat or lack of interest in the breast /food (repelled by mother's scent, resistant to nursing.)
4. No reaction to parent's voice or presence.
   If you notice that s/he doesn't turn her/his head toward parent, doesn't smile in response to parent or doesn't react to voices; or if s/he shows no back-and-forth sharing of sounds, smiles or other facial expressions by nine months or thereafter; no babbling by 12 months: no back-and-forth gestures, such as pointing, showing, reaching or waving by 12 months; no words by 16 months; no two-word meaningful phrases (without imitating or repeating) by 24 months or any loss of speech or babbling or social skills at any age, bring it to your doctor's attention.
5. Repelled by touch.
6. No eye contact.
7. Delayed motor development (including hypotonia, poor muscle tone)
8. Unusually rapid head (circumference) growth.

Barbara Schipper, Mifne Treatment Center, Israel, Mary Ellen Egan, Autism Speaks. For more information go to: AutismWeb.com, autism.com, talkaboutcuringautism.org, generationrescue.org, recoveryvideos.com

Getting Rid of the Pacifier

The Disappearing Act!

I suggest you take the pacifier away when the child is 6 months old - they have no way to get it back and they aren't able to whine about it.

Nip It In the Bud

Cut off the very tip of the pacifier. It doesn't even need to be noticeable but it just won't "feel" right, so the comforting sensation will be lost. If you do this before your child turns 1, you won't have pacifier issues when they are 4.

Sour Grapes

Try dipping your toddler's pacifiers in a weakened solution of grapefruit or lemon juice, to sour the taste and make the pacifier less comforting. When s/he complains about the taste, act surprised and explain that this just happens when their time is up.

So near and yet so far...

To help a child give up a pacifier, either purchase a new stuffed animal or pick one of his/her favorites. Make a slit in one of the side seams. Have him/her kiss the pacifier goodbye and then insert it deep into the stuffing of the toy and sew up the seam. Now s/he can sleep with the pacifier still nearby but safely tucked away inside her toy.

Feeding Solid Foods

Whether you are bottle feeding or nursing, I would suggest that you feed on demand for the first month. By then you should be able to move to a more organized and predictable schedule. If you continue to nurse, delay solid food until the baby is 6 months old.

I found it was best to follow Mother Nature's lead and introduce fruits first, beginning with very ripe bananas. They taste remarkably similar to breast milk and are very easy to digest. Offer all the fruits first – slowly introducing one new taste at a time, about one a week… there's no hurry. Fruits are the easiest food to digest and they're so simple to cook and puree. Next offer vegetables - all of them – asparagus, broccoli and squash were my kid's favorites. Sweet potatoes are fine, but wait till later to introduce starchy white potatoes.

Here's a simple, easy way to be sure your baby is getting the purest food in this age of preservatives, additives and hidden ingredients - and contribute to a sustainable environment at the same time! Prepare your favorite vegetables and fruits yourself; simply puree fruits or vegetables in a food processor, spoon into clean ice trays and freeze. Each "food cube" is a perfect portion for a young baby, and can be carried in a reusable plastic container or baggie in the diaper bag, thawing naturally until you need it. I loved knowing exactly what I was feeding my babies, and keeping all those jars out of the landfill. Big money-saver, too!

Amy Carol Webb, Miami, FL

One food prep lasts 12 servings – easy! (Gerber doesn't even make asparagus!) Meat proteins come next. Cereals are complex carbohydrates and harder to digest, so introduce them slowly. Dairy products should come last. Plain yogurt is ok, but milk proteins are very hard to digest and can cause the bowel to become irritated and bleed microscopically. Don't introduce cow's milk until at least 1 year, if ever. We are humans, not cows – no wonder so many people are lactose intolerant. And don't introduce sugar until her 27th birthday if you can help it!

Making a Mini Portion

I take a small portion of whatever vegetable we're having for dinner and puree it in a mini grinder, for the baby. This way, the food is always fresh, it's the perfect portion and rather than cleaning a big blender, the grinder wipes up easily.

Angela Perzow, Whistler B.C.

Parental Philosophy

Essential Life Skills

Over time, educators agreed to a collection of essential academic skills that children need to master at certain ages and grade levels. To make sure that happens, teachers work from a set of guidelines, an academic curriculum. Perhaps it's time that we Moms, being the primary 'Life Teachers,' should adopt our own program. (All will be described in depth at various places throughout this book.) Here is our essential syllabus:

Let's teach our children how to listen effectively: this means, how to listen without keeping up an internal running dialogue or preparing the next line in the conversation. Just listen and try to understand what the other person is telling you.

Most of us are listening for a chance to speak
instead of listening to hear what's being said.

Let's teach our children how to argue effectively: this means thinking through the opponent's side of the issue, understanding that position, deciding why your position is the best solution and articulating it clearly. This is the basis of negotiating, but that process goes one step further and ends (ideally) with both parties feeling like they got the best deal.

Let's teach our children that it's OK to say "No." You don't always have to please others. If it doesn't feel right, don't do it. If you don't have the time, say so. 'Please yourself' not in a selfish way, but learn to listen to your instinct and do what your heart dictates.

Let's teach our children that there is good stress, which motivates, and bad stress, which causes headaches, tension and anxiety. Use the good stress to get energized and accomplish things. Use the bad stress as a signal to exercise, meditate and relax.

Let's teach our children to exercise the brain just like any other muscle. Improving one's memory will have great rewards in school, in social situations and in life in general. There are memory techniques that are fun and easy to learn. Ask a librarian to help you find a program, start early - when your child is in kindergarten and learning is just a game. Board games like "Memory" are terrific, progress to brainteasers, crossword puzzles etc.

Let's teach our children that negative self-talk is poisonous. If you find yourself beginning to descend this self-defeating ladder, immerse yourself in a book or project. Learn to turn it off.

Let's have our children learn a second (or third) language. (European children learn several languages as a matter of course.)

Let's have our children learn about music and learn to play an instrument (but keep it fun.) Some studies show a dramatic link between music skills and higher math and science intelligence.

Let's teach our children about money. The whole world revolves around money and yet this most important subject is never taught in school.

- Ages 2 – 4: Help kids learn the difference between liking, wanting and needing everything they see advertised or see in store displays.

- Ages 4 – 6: Talk to your child about why things cost what they cost.

- Ages 6 – 12: Discuss the work ethic; teach money management through an allowance or with a small weekly job.

- Ages 12 and up: Use checking accounts, debit cards and pre-paid credit cards to teach children about credit and money management <u>before</u> they get to college.

Let's teach our children how to ask for what they need. Whether it is emotional or moral support, financial aid or help with achieving a desire, people should feel comfortable expressing their needs.

Let's teach our children that, unfortunately, bad things do happen, but we all have the capacity to handle hardship. Suffering results from only 2 types of misfortune: natural catastrophes and disasters of human behavior. 'Natural' occurrences such as illness, death, earthquakes, fires, hurricanes and the like are certainly terrible to endure, but when we help each other we can overcome and survive. But human disasters such as polluting and tampering with the environment, human apathy, religious intolerance, bigotry and warfare are all within our ability to change, and are therefore even more tragic. We can't just wish for peace and change, either personally or globally; we have to work for it.

Let's teach our children what to say and how to act when meeting someone who is grieving. Talk about death and explain the natural cycle of life. This is something that all of us will encounter, and knowing how to handle this situation is an essential life skill.

Let's teach our children _____. (Fill in your ideas here.)

Experience is what we call the accumulation of our mistakes.

Yiddish Folk Saying

Family Ties

Families are like intricate puzzles. In order to feel like one 'fits in' and to become 'whole' on one's own, a child needs to feel 'part' of a family. Emotional bonds (not biology) are the glue that makes individuals come together as an interlocking family. Strong bonds are forged with love and fun. Weak bonds made of mistrust or neglect, are temporary; they are quickly dismantled and fragmented as soon as they are able.

Self Esteem

Recently a "recovering jerk" confessed that he has come to realize that self-esteem doesn't come from having a well-stroked ego. His Mother was from the 'my-kid-can-do-no-wrong-tribe.' After a spending half his life with an inflated, conceited view of himself, he learned that true self-esteem comes from having a self-calibrating ego. He wishes his Mom would have pointed out his many weaknesses so he could have corrected them before reaching adulthood. Look for the best in your kids but don't ignore their faults.

Timeless Mom Questions

What do you want? - What are you doing?
Where are you going?
Who are you going with?
What's going on? - What have you done?
What are you thinking? - Who do you think you are?
Are you crazy? - What are you going to do?
Why are you doing that? – What do you need? – How is that?
What did you do? – How could you?
What do you think of that? – How did you do that?
What do you know?

There probably hasn't been a Mother in the history of the world who didn't ask these timeless questions. What's interesting is that over time the meaning of these powerful questions will change dramatically. Ask a ten year old "Where are you going?" and the answer will reflect his plan for the next twenty minutes – a bike ride over to Johnny's house. Ask the same question of an 18 year old and he'll rush to the mailbox looking for a college acceptance letter. Ask a 47-year-old man, "Where have you been and where are you going?" and chances are you might hear reflections on his life thus far and his hopes for the future. We Moms ask the most profound questions, don't we?

The essential Mom Questions will continue to shape our children as they grow and change throughout their lives. And hopefully we'll provoke our children to search for some great answers.

Facilitate

As a Mom of five children, (soon to be six) I have learnt to prioritize and let some things go. Having a large family is not always more difficult; I didn't have six children overnight. Together we have slowly grown into a large, close, loving and supportive big family. I depend on my older children to nurture, teach and support their younger siblings, and they receive a whole lot of love and companionship doing this. Being a Mom of a large family is different than being a Mom of one or two children. I see myself as more of a facilitator than a dictator. I teach my family how to care for each other, to help each another... and I do not micro-manage everything for my children, especially my teenagers!

Julie Riley, Newburgh, NY

A Family Statement

Stephen Covey (author of "The 7 Habits of Highly Effective People") recommends that families sit down together around the dinner table and develop their own mission statement. It should reflect a goal, shared values or whatever everyone will respect and work on together. Get everyone involved, be patient, and post your 'Family Statement' in a highly visible place once you have it.

Keep the Goal In Mind

Remember that the objective is to raise men and women... not boys and girls encased in adult bodies. In other words, teach sensibility, responsibility, sensitivity, generosity and a sense of humor.

Good parenting is not so much what your kids do while you are there, but what they do when you are not there!

On Loving

As Eric Fromm once suggested there are two kinds of love which we crave from our parents. We need to feel both kinds of love to become self-confident individuals. The first is "Mother love" meaning unconditional love, given from both parents. This is love given freely because "you are the flesh of my flesh, bone of my bone" – you are unique and you are mine. The second type of love is "Father love," and it is showered upon the child for what they have achieved. It is earned love born of pride, respect, honor and appreciation for the individual's accomplishments. Acknowledge your child for both who they are and what they do. You can spoil a child by giving her too many things, but you can never give her too much love. Ultimately, people need to feel that they can be loved and give love and make a difference in another person's life. Dean Ornish put it very well –"I used to feel I was loved because I was special. Now I feel special because I'm loved and I can love."

Don't threaten a child: Either punish him or forgive him.

The Talmud

The decision to have a child is to know that your heart
will now live outside your body.

We heal through loving connection. Every time we're hurt or feel like we can't go on, it's someone reaching out and connecting that makes the difference. And love – no matter how it's offered or when it comes – can build a bridge to something better.

Oprah Winfrey

And Promises To Keep

Keep your promises. If something comes up and you can't keep a promise you've made to your child, ask to be released. If you aren't released, change your plans and keep the promise you made. There isn't anything (whether in business or otherwise) that is worth losing your child's trust.

Catch 'Em If You Can

And the best advice I've ever gotten (though it can be hard to live by): try to make sure that your child hears positive reinforcement 2/3 of the time, and negative comments only 1/3 - or less! Catch 'em being good, and tell them you're proud of them, even if it's only for covering their mouth when they cough!

Sandy Cash, Beit Shemesh, Israel

Love is an act of endless forgiveness, a tender look which becomes a habit.

Peter Ustinov

Ages and Stages

Each stage of a child's development is temporary -- embrace it or grin and bear it!
Never compare your children to each other (or to someone else's child).

Even in the busiest of times, make sure to put a few quiet moments aside for your children.

Liz Jacques, Great Barrington, MA

Trust Your Instincts

Always trust your instincts. My daughter swallowed a penny, and everyone, including my pediatrician and the ambulance driver, told me she was fine, and that she would pass it. But I had a bad feeling. So bad that I got up at 11:00 at night, and ran with my baby to the ER. My husband fought with me the whole way there, telling me how wrong I was, how the doctor knew better, yadda yadda yadda.

Well, the Xray showed the penny was wedged in her throat sideways. Had I put her to bed in her crib, it would have tipped, and completely obstructed her airway. The surgeon told me I probably wouldn't have heard a peep. ALWAYS TRUST YOUR INSTINCTS. If you feel like something is wrong, it is!

Karen Tarolli, Denton, Texas

Parenting Styles

I am not a psychologist or family therapist. But looking around, I've noticed that there are basically three types of parenting styles: I call these styles 'bonsai, weed, or flower parenting.' This is what I've observed:

'Bonsai parents' dwarf their children by being abusive. They cut children down to size either by neglect, physical abuse, sexual abuse, verbal attack, criticism, constant teasing, emotional detachment or intimidation: they isolate, twist, pick on and prune their child's spirit in order to satisfy their own need for power. We've all witnessed this and wondered why anyone who endured this treatment as a child goes on to inflict the same mistreatment on their own children. If you came from an abusive background, you can stop the cycle by recognizing it and seeking out a good counselor to help you. If you had a genetic error that could be fixed, you'd do it to save your children, wouldn't you? Thankfully, the human spirit is amazing and people who want to, can and do rise above their tortured start in life. James Lipton, who has interviewed thousands of actors, has noted that about seventy five percent of them came from broken homes. Whether by divorce, illness, death or disinterest, they all grew up emotionally alone. As a result, they went into the profession of 'Hey, look at me! Look what I've done!' They are yearning to be recognized. I know a few very gifted artists who also grew up in this type of environment, (they too are in the 'look at me' category) and somehow ended up very OK in spite of it. They embraced life and now teach others by expressing tremendous compassion and a deep understanding for the importance of expressing love. But sadly, there are those who didn't find positive ways to say to the world, "Look at me!" They are the bullies, and the outcasts who commit violent acts in order to be recognized. They hurt, and so they hurt others. Hurt people hurt people.

Some parents adopt a very 'laissez faire' attitude. They never seem to organize their child-raising philosophy, have very loosely structured homes, and their children are left to more or less parent themselves. So long as they don't get run over in the street, it seems they are left pretty much on their own. With no rules, no limits and no directions they grow up like 'weeds,' taking hold and gathering nourishment and structure wherever they can find it. I have seen these kids grow up to be somewhat troubled and insecure. Often they get into trouble. Rarely did these kids hear the word "no" – and they grow up thinking that they are entitled to everything they desire. It seems that some people who were raised without limits develop insatiable black holes of need and often feel emotionally starved. Others found nurturing in other places – in their friends' homes or from role model teachers. And surprisingly, a few humans are so resilient, that they achieve amazing things seemingly all on their own.

Parents who cultivate their children are the 'flower gardeners.' They plan and do things carefully and thoughtfully. Their children have the advantage of parents who think through their decisions instead of responding with knee jerk reactions. They provide a nurturing, loving environment for their children, and sprinkle them liberally with all kinds of experiences... the best kind of life fertilizer! But I've noticed two subtypes of flower gardeners. First are the 'landscape designers.' Those who plan very precisely and try to control every bloom; they seek to govern every flower as they carve out mazes and clip every stray branch that wasn't in their original design plan. These parents have a tendency to go overboard. Some are strict and have many rules, others may try to manipulate their child's friendships or control their child's choices and decisions. They hyper-parent and hover like helicopters. Often they schedule too much of their children's lives. Is it really necessary to be busy or industrious every second of every day? It doesn't feel natural to me. Hobbies, music lessons and sports are only OK if they are fun and not taken too seriously. Some children, who were expected to practice their instrument (or sport) for hours a day say that they traded their childhood for their parent's dreams. Too much of a good thing is really not a good thing.

And then there are the simple, farmer type gardeners: those who cultivate, build sturdy crop rows, plant the seeds in rich soil, fertilize often, water systematically and watch their children's spontaneous growth with great joy, encouragement and enthusiasm. They lay down a few, firm 'ground rules' and engage in a 'beneficent dictatorship' – a friendly, flexible but structured management style.

Why examine parenting styles? Because you should actively decide what type of gardening style you would like to adopt. Sometimes we find ourselves going down a path by chance or by habit, and we might not recognize that there may be a better route. If you would like to change parenting styles, make a conscious decision, get help if you need it and change. Parenting is like any other art form. It takes practice and thoughtfulness, and the knowledge that there is never perfection in the art of art. You can't will a 'masterpiece' to happen.

Parenting skills are extremely important, but ask any experienced parent and they'll tell you - kids are hard wired with their own personalities from the get go. This would explain why children brought up in the same house with the same parents, same values, same opportunities – all grow up to be so different. If the truth be told, we can only steer and guide our kids; the rest is up to them.

> There are only two lasting bequests we can leave to our children.
> One is roots, the other is wings.

A Happy Home

A happy home, like a marriage, doesn't happen by accident. You have to make it happen.

Disagreements happen. That's normal. If they didn't you wouldn't be human or have human children. But once the children realize that you really are on their side, life gets smoother. As I always told my children, "Friendships, boyfriends and (in this society) even husbands come and go, but I'm going to be your Mom forever. You are my business, my only business. I have no ulterior motives. I have nothing to gain. I only seek your happiness."

When things got testy or we were disappointed with one of the girls' behavior, often we would write her a letter and leave it on her bed for her to read. This tactic has a few advantages. One, she can't answer back. Two, she can read it and reflect on what we're really saying, instead of focusing on our tone of voice or her defensive rebuttal. Three, she can read it again and again, later on. We used to leave letters but if I had to do it again, I'd have a special "life lessons book" where all of these quiet admonitions could be written in one place.

> Misery has enough company. Dare to be happy.

University of the Heart

Make your home the 'University of the Heart.' Expose your children to plays, music, art galleries, museums, travel and all types of international foods. (There's more than pizza out there!) Some of the most important aspects of education are never taught in schools today. What good is knowing some complicated aspect of calculus you may never be called upon to use if you have no appreciation for the world's greatest food, theater, literature, music or great works of art?

There are bargain art books available at bookstores all the time – buy a few and teach your children how to 'read' art. Look at the style, colors, composition, lines, forms and focal point. Understand what the artist was trying to express. Follow it up with a visit to an art museum and ask for a docent to give you a tour.

> Art washes away the dust of everyday life.   Picasso

With regard to music: In a recent article in the Miami Herald, researcher Donald A. Hodges told an audience of University of Miami students and faculty that "Nothing activates as many areas of the brain as music." On the screen above him, Hodges showed scans of the brain in the midst of musical activity. Both hemispheres were lit up, in Hodges' words, "like a pinball machine." He explained, a rich environment makes a difference: "The brain: Use it or lose it. The more education you have, the more the interconnections in the brain. Music changes the brain."

Parents who play Mozart for a baby - or a pregnant belly - with the long-range hope of an acceptance to Harvard should know that this project may not bear fruit, but exposing a child to great music - as a listener or as a player - will pay off in enjoyment and life smarts.

Travel too costly or not convenient? No matter – pick a destination and go there... without the luggage. Pick a country and have a theme day or week. Have the kids Google the language, customs etc. Watch a video about your destination. Libraries stock travel CD's and DVD's of most foreign countries. Get some recipes that represent the country and try them!

'Home' should be the ultimate refuge from the tumult of the outside world - a fun, warm, accepting and comfortable place to be.

> A person should hear music, read a little poetry and see a fine picture every day in order that worldly cares may not obliterate the sense of the beautiful, which God has implanted in the human soul.
>   Goethe

Establish Proxy Parents

We all goof up. Sometimes we make such major blunders that we're too ashamed to 'fess up and seek help. For kids, life mistakes are magnified by inexperience and the fear of parental repercussions. But they need someone who they can reach out to for help without fear of reprisals, someone who they are comfortable with and can confide in. So establish a 'proxy parent' they can go to for help when they can't face you. They need your assurance that whatever is discussed will be kept secret and not be divulged (to you their parent) unless they agree to it, and that this 'proxy parent' has been given the authority to act and make decisions on your behalf. The person you choose should be someone you respect, have confidence in and someone you feel will handle a situation as you would. Perhaps your sister, brother or your close friend might be a good choice.

On Parental Decisions

*I believe in explaining the mother's or parent's reason for the decision, allowing for a question or two to help the child understand, so s/he can learn from it. Then I believe the parent has to stick with the decision rather than get into an extended discussion or argument. And a mother should **never** say, "Wait until I tell your father!" or "Wait until your father gets home!" if she wants to command any respect for herself or her decision-making authority. It's OK to say, "I'd like to discuss it with your father," if it's a decision worthy of a joint evaluation of the situation. That sends a different message and should be reserved for the more weighty decisions.*

Mara Giulianti, Mayor, Hollywood FL

Tell Me Why

Of course we our want children to feel that they are secure and that we, as parents, have enough worldly knowledge to keep them safe from harm and answer most of their questions. But why do so many parents feel compelled to perpetuate the myth that they have all the answers? No one has all the answers - not the wisest teacher, not the most esteemed doctor or judge, not the president, nor the queen, nor the sheik, rabbi or pope. They are all just people, and just as fallible as anyone else. Life is a mystery, a journey, and a quest. If you don't know something – admit it! Wouldn't it be better to tell our kids that there is so much to learn in life, that we are still discovering all kinds of things? It's OK to keep looking, learning and enjoying the journey.

Mummy Mea Culpa - Being Big Enough To Say When You're Small

Don't be afraid to apologize to your children when you're wrong. They deserve it, and they will learn that being wrong isn't such a terrible thing and that it doesn't make you a bad person. The value of an apology can change your whole world.

We all make mistakes as parents. Mistakes are inevitable. But the biggest mistake is not being able to admit it. There are a lot of things I'm sure I do wrong but one thing I'm proud of is my ability to go back to the kids after I've screwed up and tell them, "Girls, I made a mistake. I was wrong and I'm sorry. Please forgive me." In so doing, I'm modeling good relationship skills, which I hope they will imitate in their future relationships. We ALL need to say "I'm sorry" as grownups. At least we're supposed to! (Which may account for the divorce rate being so high. Too many people DON'T or CAN'T apologize.) I find that my children are not only quick to forgive, but it relieves the pressure when they make mistakes, too.

Cary Cooper, Dallas, Texas

He who never made a mistake, never made anything.   Joseph Conrad

Whose Game Is This Anyway?

I read an article, written by Sandy Hingston, who had such an appetite for competitive athletics that she pushed her kids into playing sports, even though it was only she who was really gung-ho about it. In 'Confessions of an Ugly Sports Mom,' Sandy bravely admitted that her kids might have been the ones on the field but she was the one reliving her youth as they were running, dodging and scoring. She'd often pace on the sidelines and sometimes she'd even verbally confront 13-year-old players from the other team! When things went well she was very, very pleased. But when things didn't go well – well, that was another matter. Her kids were so embarrassed they would plead, "Could you please not scream at the officials?" To her kids, sports were 'that thing that makes Mom go berserk.' One day she finally realized that she was really missing participating in sports herself, so instead living vicariously on the sidelines, raging at the refs, she joined an adult volleyball league, and got her own game back.

Making Memories

I remember my sister once telling me that she was trying to do lots of fun family activities so that her kids would have happy childhood memories. Then one day she overheard one of her teenage daughters on the phone, describing her fondest memories to a friend. She was recounting all the wonderful times she had strolling around the mall!

One of my daughters would sometimes stop in mid-action and seem to 'freeze.' When we asked her what she was doing, she said, "Shhh... I'm making a memory!"

Then I heard Tim Russert being interviewed about a new book which examines family relationships. He was discussing a child's perspective of an aging parent and how, in reality, one's childhood is vividly remembered and deeply appreciated, from the child's adult point of view. So don't despair - they will remember! Keep the good times rolling. He also made the sobering point that in the end, when we are remembered during a eulogy, our entire lives are summed in one twenty minute speech ... what is said then is in your control now.

Facts + Emotions = Memories

We are the sum total of our memories.
Memories are our truths, whether they are true or not.

Sometimes all you can remember are things you'd rather forget.

Andy Rooney

Favorites

Why do people always ask, "Which one is your favorite?" Life isn't just one big contest! Things shouldn't be in competition with each other. If you like a color, a flavor, a song, a movie, a book, fine – enjoy it; it doesn't mean you have to elevate it to some higher plane and place other colors, songs, movies or books in an inferior position. Why do we ask our children to make these judgments? Let them enjoy things without getting into the habit of comparing everything, making some things superior. Sometimes you do have a genuine favorite, but I think it should develop spontaneously and not as a result of people constantly asking you to choose one.

Looking Inside

In 'The Seven Spiritual Laws for Parents,' Deepak Chopra outlines several techniques to help you and your children awaken spiritually and achieve a greater appreciation for the world around us. The guiding principles he outlines are: Everything is possible. If you want something, give something. When you make a choice, you change the future. Don't say no, go with the flow. Every time you wish or want, you plant a seed. Enjoy the journey. You are here for a reason.

After I read this brief book I realized that all these ideas have been explored and illustrated, in different ways and perhaps with a slightly different twist, by several contributing Moms throughout this book.

Words That Kill

We've all witnessed and cringed at verbal abuse hurled at children. Frustrated parents lash out at their children in the heat of the moment or say something without thinking. If you say "You're so stupid! You're such an idiot! Why are you always so bad? How dumb can you be? Fatso! You're such a cute, chubby little girl!" to a child, what do you expect her to think and feel? Parents need to know that children really do believe what adults (especially their parents) tell them. Children take what you say very literally. Children do not understand sarcasm or playful ribbing. Neither do they understand teasing. Even playful teasing can act as an acid, eating away feelings of self-worth. Harsh words sting for the moment and linger in the child's heart, killing their self-esteem, confidence, imagination and curiosity. Remember, the words you speak in anger may be the words that sear themselves into memory, and s/he may spend her/his life living your words and expectations. No matter how horribly your children behave, that doesn't give you license to say horrible things to them. They will never forget those harsh words; they may forgive, but they will never forget. There is never a good reason to yell at children. It's the rock solid mom who can whisper when she's really mad.

Words are the most powerful tools we will ever own
- use them carefully.

Remember too that sometimes it's the mommy who needs a 'time out.'

When a child makes a mistake, remember that's how we all learn. Point out the mistake. Remember that we accomplish nothing by doing nothing.

If you don't want to stumble, stand still.

Instead of belittling a child, just use "the look of disapproval." S/he wants to please you, and s/he needs to know that it's OK to make mistakes... so long as they aren't repeated too often.

It is OK to criticize the behavior, but not the person. Replace "Because I told you so" with "Because I love you."

Practice the Art of 'Positive Speaking'

Phrase your comments so that they project confidence in your child's ability to do the right thing or handle any situation.

When you catch your child doing something good, (as often as possible) make a habit of saying:

Thank you! You are so _____ (sweet/caring/thoughtful/good/clever etc.) for doing _____.

When you catch them doing something you'd like to change, try saying:

- You're a smart person who just made a mistake.
- For a person who is so organized and clean, your room is pretty messy.
- You are a good person making a bad choice/decision.
- If you are doing _____, you are doing the wrong thing.
- Next time, I know you'll stop and think before you act/speak.
- Oh my, whatever will you do? Oh, how sad for you.
- I know you can do it, I've seen your work.
- Take a minute and think again.

Parenthood is the art of bringing up children without putting them down.

'What' Is The Question

It's fruitless to ask a child "Why did you do that?" Do we ever really know why we did something foolish, or on impulse? Even adults often act first and regret later. A better approach is to simply ask, "What did you do?" Because when a parent asks, "What did you do?" they help their child think about their actions and hopefully learn from their mistakes. The next question should be: "What are you going to do about it?"

Priming the Prophecy

We tend to live up to the expectations others have of us, whether it's positive or negative. If we're told that we can achieve something and we choose to believe it, more often than not, it happens. Sometimes we are so primed for success that we absolutely cannot fail. Let me give you an example. There was a well-known fortune-teller in the city where I grew up. People would seek her counsel on matters of the heart, business, finances, and sometimes young girls would show up just for fun. One day a young man came to her door asking for guidance regarding postgraduate school. After a few minutes of polite conversation, she invited him to sit down for a reading. She told him that he would soon meet his perfect life mate. In fact she felt quite sure that this meeting was imminent. Then she said she had a vision – he was to be at a certain place, at a certain time on the following day. After the young man left she phoned her niece and told the young girl that she had a strong premonition that the man of her dreams was waiting to meet her. And even though the young girl was skeptical, she agreed to humor her old aunt and show up at the appointed coffee shop. Well, you know the rest. Within a year everyone was dancing at the wedding. This is a true story! When you prime the psyche with expectation and couple it with positive anticipation, great things can happen.

Words that Heal - "I Love You"

Being told "I love you" isn't merely an expression spoken to the ear; it's both magic and music for the human soul. You can never say this simple phrase often enough. Growing up, my sisters and I rarely, if ever, heard love verbalized. It left a gaping hole in my heart. It was supposed to be understood, a given. My parents were of the generation who never spoke their feelings; they kept their emotions bottled up and hidden. I know my parents loved me but it sure would have been nice to hear it. I think kids take the world quite literally. They hear what you say, not what you think. If you don't speak the words, the feelings you have in your heart may not echo as loudly as you think they do in your child's heart.

In my household we use the phrase "I love you" like most people use salt – liberally and often: at the end of every phone conversation, whenever we leave each other and sprinkled throughout our conversations. How wonderful to know that those who mean the most to you are always thinking of you in terms of love. I'm reminded too of a family who suffered a terrible loss when their daughter was killed. They were so comforted knowing that the last thing they had said and heard from her was, "I love you."

Show and express affection everyday - this is a basic requirement in close family relations. It's vital and should be mandatory!

> The sound of a kiss is not so loud as that of cannon
> but its echo lasts a great deal longer.   Oliver Wendell Holmes

A seed hidden inside an apple is an orchard invisible.

Walnuts and Rice

A story is told of a Mother who had a very different way of teaching. One year, as the holidays approached, all four of her kids were anticipating grand presents. But this wise Mom decided to give the kids 'the gift of understanding the importance of family.' You see the kids had been fighting and bickering a lot lately. They were not paying any attention to each other, and each seemed to be only concerned with their own selfish needs and desires.

When the holiday gifts were finally opened, each child found that they had been given only an empty glass jar, a package of rice and six walnuts. Confused, they poured the rice into the jar and then they tried to add the nuts – but there wasn't enough room and the walnuts rolled onto the floor scattering in all directions. Then the Mom explained, "The walnuts symbolize your loving family, your Dad and I, your sisters and brothers. The rice symbolizes all the other small, interesting but incidental things that fill your life. How you fill this empty jar is how you fill your lives. There's room enough for both, walnuts and rice. If you put your loved ones first, you'll find that you do indeed have room for it all." The children gathered all the nuts, put them in the jar first and watched as the rice filled in all the empty spaces... just as it should be. The four jars were full of lessons learned as they stood like silent teachers on the family mantel. Soon the spirit of cooperation and peace filled the home again.

You Are My Favorite

I have told each of my four children, secretly and in private, that s/he is the sweetest, best behaved, most dependable and most special child. Now each one feels favored and is eager to maintain that 'favorite' status.

Dawn Gacadack, Jacksonville, FL

Talk, Listen, But Never Be Silent!

So much to teach, explore, discuss, analyze, criticize... life is so complicated when you're maneuvering through the mechanics - and so simple when you look back in hindsight. Talk to your kids about everything – there is really no subject that should be taboo in a modern home; then be quiet and listen to their take on the issues - you'll both learn a lot about who you really are. Your discussions may be rowdy, boisterous and (hopefully) opinionated - and that should be your goal. If you disagree, that's OK. Our intent should never be to create intellectual clones of ourselves. And remember that youthful idealism is normal and a natural rite of passage.

Keep talking - even when your children disappoint you (and they will sometimes). But never resort to silence. Silence is the cruelest form of isolation and emotional punishment. I know someone who was shunned by her mother every time they had a fight. The silence dragged on as neither one wanted to be the first to speak. It became a battle of wills. Sometimes they would avoid each other for days and their animosity built. Their silence created an emotional rift which grew larger and deeper with each fight. Questioned years later, the Mom explained that initially she just wanted to show her maternal authority and gain the upper hand. But soon they fell into a grudge-holding pattern, and the pattern became a habit. She said that she knew even then that it was wrong, and she felt terrible but she just wouldn't relent and change their silent seething. I remember reading the tragic story of Dave Pelzer, "A Child Called It," the sad account of one of the worst cases of child abuse ever documented. When the authorities later questioned his mother, regarding why this poor child had been tortured, abused and neglected, she too recounted that one day he did something stupid for which he was picked on. After that, he just became the family scapegoat. He was an easy target and tormenting him became the family habit. Be mindful of how small things escalate.

Hearing is automatic. Listening is an act of will.

The Other Silence

Life is messy. Kids should know that. The actress Rosie O'Donnell wrote of the time when she was only twelve and her Mother died of breast cancer. But no one explained to her what was going on. Rosie became emotionally confused and conjured up her own internal dialogue, as children often do when suffering isn't explained to them. Children used to be protected from life's struggles, as they were thought to be too 'fragile' to handle the truth - but actually it was the parent's inability to cope with the truth. An adult is just a large child, after all. Often they project their own fears, holdovers from their own childhoods, and unknowingly pass them onto their children. Perhaps you fear your own mortality and a host of other unexplained unknowns. Break the cycle. Talk it out... Kids are smart. Kids are resilient. Kids can handle the truth.

Silence is denial - it's the loudest scream ever heard.

Real parenting is nothing like a sitcom.   *Rosie O'Donnell*

Expectations

"Never ask more of your children than they can handle." I continue to remind myself even now that the kids are in their late teens and twenties. If they ask for my help, I jump in and do whatever I can. Because if they can handle it on their own, believe me, they're out there doing just that. Another way of thinking of it is this: if your kids aren't living up to your expectations, maybe your expectations are too high. The important thing to remember is that if you've encouraged them and helped them to believe in themselves then they'll always be doing the best they can - which of course can be applied to the parent (me!) as well. We all do the best we can and sometimes we fail miserably. And then, the best thing we can do is to forgive ourselves, pick up the pieces and keep on going.
Lui Collins, Ashfield, MA

Aspire to inspire before you expire.

Surviving Adversity

When my Mother was only 26 years old and the Mother of two, she contracted (and nearly died of) bulbar polio myolitis. She subsequently suffered severe upper body paralysis, but miraculously birthed me 6 years later. She was a remarkable woman. As a toddler, because of necessity and her painstaking explanations, my able hands became "her" hands. As her hands, she taught me to find beauty and significance in the simple details of life, to celebrate every victory, no matter how small, and that my own life is proof positive that love truly conquers all. This story, 'Greta's Hands' is on the 'No Place Like Home' CD. (sonicbids.com/epk/epk.aspx?epk_id=35173)

Rosalee Peppard

Kindness is a language we can all understand.
Even the blind can see it and the deaf can hear it.   Mother Teresa

On Friendship

Your children will have lots of friends, but only one Mom. Be friendly but not at the expense of your maternal responsibilities. You must be honest and tell them what they need to hear; often what no one else will tell them. The clothes are too tight; the hairdo is unflattering, the bra doesn't fit, the makeup is too garish, the presentation screams junior hooker or wannabe kid from the 'hood (with pants pulled down and underwear parading). You are the Mother - tell it like it is!

Make sure you know who your child's friends are and whom s/he hangs around with. If you feel they are inoculating your child with the wrong values, make sure there's a course correction! S/he will yell, s/he will scream, s/he will slam the bedroom door and then stab you in the heart with the words, "I hate you!" But don't be dissuaded. Smile. Breathe in. Do what's best for her/him, not what's easier at the moment. Get her/him interested in a new group, club or sports team. Change schools if you have to! The fallen leaf flows with the river. If you allow them to hang out with mediocrity they will accept the same of themselves. Unfortunately, peer pressure is a tremendous influence, but ultimately we parents still have the power to push them in the right direction.

It's so hard to soar with the eagles
when you only hang around with a bunch of turkeys!

Ah, Motherhood. It's very much akin to the military adage:
You may be the commander but you aren't always in control.

If your children feel thoroughly loved and accepted at home, they won't have the need to go looking for it in all the wrong places.   *Maria Shriver Schwarzenegger*

A friend is a present you give yourself.   From a Chinese fortune cookie.

Be who you are and say what you feel. Because those that matter don't mind.
And those that mind don't matter.

Teaching Colorblindness

A little girl and her mother were walking in a park when they came upon a balloon vendor. The beautifully colored, helium-filled orbs swayed in the warm afternoon breeze. "Which color will rise the highest?" the little girl asked her Mom. "That depends on how much colorless substance there is inside!" came the wise reply. Then the Mom used this perfect metaphor to discuss how skin color doesn't measure or indicate a person's inner worth, intelligence or potential, either.

On Parental Worrying

When our boys were teenagers and I spent many late nights worrying if they'd arrive home safe and sound, I shared my worry and frustration with a friend of mine. She told me that she always kept a small bottle of baby powder next to the phone; so that when her teenage daughter called at 3 in the morning, (for the umpteenth time!) she would pause before reacting in anger, reach for the baby powder and smell it - to reminder her of the love they shared from the very beginning. It works!

Rosalee Peppard Lockyer, Prospect Bay, Nova Scotia

On Competent and Confident Kids

I grew up in a family of girls, but I enjoyed being a bit of a tomboy. Living out in the country, I would change my clothes immediately when I arrived home from school and head to the woods to build forts and climb trees, go rock climbing and run down the hills. As I jumped and stepped from one rock to another, I remember that my speed picked up and my concentration intensified. It was great fun, but I always stayed focused because a twisted ankle or a broken leg was just unthinkable.

When my son was little I resolved to never tell him, "Watch out! You're going to fall down!" He was a climber too. So sometimes with confidence and other times with my heart in my mouth, I made sure to only say, "Be careful. Take it easy." I felt very strongly that I didn't want to fill his subconscious with negative programming. I didn't want his inner voice to hear me saying, "Watch out - You're gonna fail!" The power of suggestion is so great. The best thing we can do is to encourage our children to trust their instincts, listen to their inner voice, and do what feels right. Giving your child a strong faith in his own ability to size up a situation and to make a good decision is a most precious gift.

As an adult he's worked as an electrician, become a sailor, a wind-surfer, and a hang glider. Now he's an engineer making things safe for others. I guess he's not afraid to take risks after all.

Alex Burroughs, Brevard, NC

Watching Them Grow

One of the things I've noticed is that 'growth' is a process of expansion and contraction: Kids venture out and then come back, repeatedly testing themselves and their capabilities, pushing the boundaries, then coming back to a safe place to rest and recoup. Growth and regression, if you will. And I love both aspects; watching them move out into the world, stretching themselves, testing the waters - it's awesome to see them being successful. And I love it when they check back in with me to make sure I'm still here, supporting them when they need it. I saw my two-year-olds doing this, and I see my twenties doing it still. It helps me to remember that no matter what age they are, no matter what complexity the issues they're dealing with are, each part of the cycle is a natural and necessary piece of their growth that I can celebrate.

Lui Collins, Ashfield, MA

As we say in the wetlands, "Ribbit-ribbit-knee-deep-ribbit," which means, "May success and a smile always be yours -- even when you're knee-deep in the sticky muck of life."
Kermit the Frog, Southampton College, Commencement Speech 1996

The First Time and The Last Time

Yesterday s/he jumped into my arms, today s/he's suddenly too heavy to pick up – how did that happen? 'The last time' came and went so quietly. First times shriek with delight, last times barely whisper.

Of course you relish every 'first' - first smile, first tooth, first words, first steps, first birthday, first day of kindergarten, first date, first kiss, first crush – and you even grin and bear it when s/he sits behind the wheel for the first time.

The second (fourth, tenth, last) baby is rarely the same as the first. Maybe a little bit louder, or a little bit worse... been there, done that... you carry on with very few jitters. So by the time your last baby begins doing all the 'firsts' something feels different – you're happy, you're nonchalant and you're strangely mournful too. Your mouth may be smiling but your heart is heavy, because deep down you know that these first times are going to be your Maternal last times.

First Two Wheeler © C.Stay, A.Quinn, B. Henson
Hear their great music at: frictionfarm.com

Don't be frightened, but I'm gonna to let go
Don't think about falling just let it roll
Keep pedaling steady, keep your eyes straight ahead
You'll be surprised how far you'll go.

I'm a bit frightened, please take it slow
I never thought about how far you'd go…
I'll try to remember
I'm the one who let go.

Now I'm filled with wonder at the way you've grown
You rode into the world and found a home
You learned how to be steady, how to get ahead
But even when you ride away – you never let go.

On Religion

I realize that we are cautioned never to discuss 'religion' lest we offend someone's beliefs, but I'm going to venture forth hoping that you will continue reading with an open mind. I certainly hope I don't offend you, dear reader.

According to an Encyclopedia Britannica researcher, there are 10,000 separate, distinct recognized religions in the world today. Fascinating! Each religion preaches that it alone is the one, true and unquestionable way to find 'God.' Each one holds that only its path will guide you to find all the answers to life's eternal questions. Can 10,000 different ideas all be right? And what about all the past civilizations who were equally sure that their deities and explanations were true and correct? We dismiss past civilizations so easily, as we think of ourselves as being so much more advanced and sophisticated, but I wonder if we really are … Interesting, how one man's faith is another man's fantasy…

When scholars study religion from an analytical point of view, they may define religion as superstition; a means to achieve a state of emotional euphoria; or a sedative for the masses; but, at best, religion is still a set of unproven suppositions. Isn't it sad to reflect on how many millions have been murdered in the name of peaceful and loving religions? So many ancient feuds and centuries-old discriminations are continuously taught and handed down to new generations as legacies of hatred, greed and jealousy. We may walk upright, drive fancy cars and communicate across the planet at will, but emotionally we haven't evolved very far, have we?

We owe it to our children to bear in mind that all religions were formulated long ago, before anyone understood the forces of nature, the laws of physics, quantifiable science or the equal power of women. Throughout history, humans have either attributed what they didn't understand (the sun rising and setting, the stars appearing and then disappearing) to a deity, or prayed for divine intervention (more rain, less rain) to make life easier for themselves, 'believing' that some entity would respond. Alas, tradition is the last bad habit. Praying for the sun to rise or the rain to fall won't make it happen. We know that now. Praying for cancer to disappear won't make that happen either. I don't completely understand how invisible teeny, tiny waves dancing through the atmosphere, allow me to see how someone thousands of miles away can talk to me on my phone or TV screen, but I don't feel the need to fabricate a story to explain it either. Today it is perfectly acceptable to admit to our children, "I don't know" and it should be equally acceptable tell kids that no one really knows how the universe began, when it began, what our purpose here is, or what happens to us after we die. "We don't know" is truthful and reasonable. So why do so many still ascribe to religious myth and conjecture?

We so often forget that we are randomly born into a religion, by virtue of fertilization roulette (a sperm and egg lottery) and then we are rigorously taught religious tenants long before we have the capacity to question anything that we are told. Doesn't it seem reasonable for us, as adults in the modern world, to think for ourselves and reevaluate the thoughts, folklore and superstitions of those who continue to speak and inform us from graves thousands of years old? Perhaps we could start by asking a few questions. It should always be OK to question anything we're taught. And if we're told that we are asking too many questions, we might wonder why the pious are always content to ask so few.

We all have a story, a reason for being where we are and for believing in what we believe – yet, it is these 'many truths' that provokes judgment 'against' each other... consistently. It is these very realities that separate (us) without exploration or explanation and are too often void of understanding and compassion.

Lori Lennox, Many Truths

A friend of mine likens all the world's various scriptures to countless generations of people playing 'broken telephone' over centuries of time. After all, the stories were all oral histories handed down verbally from fathers to sons, mothers to daughters. Each one adding a word here, a phrase there, an embellishment or a deletion, and every so often there was sure to have been a slight twist to the original meaning. Word of mouth. Generation to generation. Century after century. Then, one day someone wrote it down, in his own words. And later the stories were translated into many different languages each with its own subtleties and the translator's paraphrasing. To see just how fast a word of mouth oral history can change, try this exercise with your family; have one child memorize a long list of grocery items. All the ingredients (include 10 – 15 items) will be used for making dinner later on in the week. Have him tell the list to another sibling in a day or two. Remember - no one is allowed to write the list down! Then have the list retold to yet another child two or three days later. It is his/her job to go buy the groceries the next day. Rest assured it will be an interesting, albeit different dinner than you had planned! That should get you all thinking about the reliability of the religious tradition ...

I think most religions are taught as an 'IF - THEN' set of principles. IF you behave/pray/chant or repeat special words/believe/have faith/wear the prescribed dress code/abstain or eat certain foods etc. THEN – you will be granted the promised rewards after your death. Now consider this: There have been countless people all over the globe who relate similar stories when reporting their own, personal near death experience. Regardless of their upbringing, or whatever religion they may have practiced before their NDE event, they all describe the same message upon their return to the living! *We are loved. The next phase of existence is peaceful. And all is as it should be.* So, considering that the message conveyed by all near-death-experiencers is the same – that of love, peace, and harmony balancing the universe - perhaps this is all we really need to live, understand and teach our children. Because no one has ever come back and feared death again, or suggested that any hellish alternative exists, maybe we should let go of the religious practices which preach that kind of punitive ideology and replace it with a more universal, loving message. Perhaps the real, underlying message of the NDE is: there is no 'if – then' to worry about! Whatever your religion, may I suggest that we encourage thought and teach tolerance. If you learn to be honest, ethical, empathetic, generous, compassionate, kind and loving to those you know, (and extend those attributes to those you don't) does it really matter who directed you there? If you live a good life, that should be all the reward you need. If there is a heaven, let its promise serve as only a garnish on a cake already dripping with lots of icing. Life is as sweet as you make it - right here, and right now.

My friend John Flynn sings: Religion is like many fingers pointing up at the moon. But we spend more time arguing which finger is pointing more accurately than we do looking at the light of the moon. And how easily fingers curl into fists! We will only live in peace if we start holding hands rather than pointing our fingers.

When Woody Guthrie, one of the great fathers of American folk music, was being admitted to the hospital, an admissions clerk read off a long list of religions and then asked which one he believed in. He responded, "All."

When the Dali Lama was asked to describe the essential meaning and practice of Buddhism, he replied, "Kindness." As Mothers we could change the face of the world if only we all taught this one simple principle. As John Lennon famously said, "Imagine." Think about it – one guiding word, kindness: no stipulations, no exceptions, no dogma, no discrimination, no traditions, no rituals, no prayers, no prescribed practices and no rules. This wouldn't be a religious revolution so much as a spiritual revolution. Let us all teach our children the religion of 'kindness' and remind our kids that we all seek the same things - internal personal peace, inter-personal peace and international peace. If we just practice KINDNESS it would make a world of difference, and soon we'd have a different world!

As the saying goes, "Perhaps we are humans seeking a spiritual experience, or maybe we are spirits having a human experience."

We teach our children that 'seeing is believing' right? Why, then, do we insist that children believe in what neither they (nor anyone else) can see? If there is an omnipotent supreme being, why do we think S/He needs or wants our approval, praise or reverence? Why do we expect this entity to concern itself with each organism's life cycle, personal wishes for health or wealth, territorial claim for more space in the test tube we call earth, or the silliest of all - the desire for a better sports related outcome? Sound preposterous? Yes. But that's exactly what we see some humans do!

Anne Garth

There is also an added sense of urgency, a realization that what the planet and humanity need most is a shift in consciousness, a spiritual awakening. Without it, we perpetuate the insanity of the past (which we can see most clearly in the history of the 20th century) or, at best, we only treat the symptoms of the disease, not the underlying cause. The disease, of course, is the collective dysfunction of the egoic mind.

Eckhart Tolle

Einstein once declared his belief in Spinoza's God, "who reveals himself in the lawful harmony of all that exists, but not in a God who concerns himself with the fate and the doings of mankind." A God who might be "subtle but not malicious" and "does not play dice."

It's Ok to have questions. Even Mother Teresa was not afraid to doubt. As she said, "For me the silence and the emptiness is so great, that I look and do not see, listen and do not hear. The tongue moves but does not speak.... What do I labor for?"

The absence of evidence is the evidence of absence.   Christopher Hitchens

Be a light unto yourself.   Buddha

People who want to share their religious views with you almost never want you to share yours with them.
                                                                                      Dave Barry

I think that anyone who says he knows God's intention, is showing a lot of very human ego.
                                                                            Michael Crichton, 'Next'

Hope is the powerful filter that hides reality.   Henry Krantz

One God, many forms
One river, many streams
One people, many faces
One Mother, many children.   MA

There are two ways to live your life. One is as though nothing is a miracle.
The other is as though everything is a miracle.   Albert Einstein

When faith calcifies into hardened dogma, making independent thought brittle – watch out!

We went to church just enough to learn to love our neighbors, but not enough to start criticizing and putting down their beliefs.
                                                                              Cheryl Wheeler

And on a related note …

World Wide Motherhood, I call on you to forbid all our children from killing anyone else's child in the name of religion. Because, if you have to kill someone to persuade them that your faith is good and holy then perhaps you have missed the message. Aren't we all just drops in the same ocean?

Alone Down Here ©Vance Gilbert
Hear his great music at: VanceGilbert.com

**I hope that we're alone down here
And when we go to war down here
With all the fancy reasons we can give to come to blows
The winners and the losers and the dead lined up in rows
There never was a war without reason, heaven knows
And I hope whoever's watching is making room for those
If not, then we're alone down here!**

Your thoughts ...

Toddler Time

How To Really Love A Child

Be there, say yes as often as possible. Let them bang on pots and pans. If they're crabby, put them in water. If they're unlovable, love yourself. Realize how important it is to be a child. Go to a movie theater in your pajamas. Read books out loud with joy. Invent pleasures together. Remember how really small they are. Giggle a lot. Surprise them. Say NO when necessary. Teach feelings. Heal your own inner child. Learn about parenting. Hug trees together. Make loving safe. Bake a cake and eat it with no hands. Go find elephants and kiss them. Plan to build a rocket ship. Imagine yourself magic. Make lots of forts with blankets. Let your angel fly. Reveal your own dreams. Search out the positive. Keep the gleam in your eye. Mail letters to God. Encourage silly plant licorice in your garden. Open up. Stop yelling. Express your love. A lot. Speak kindly. Paint their tennis shoes. Handle with caring. Children Are Miraculous.

Sark

Mother Mindfully

Right from the get go, practice thinking mindfully about what you're doing. Try to foresee what your decisions and actions will mean to this little one. In other words, be proactive rather than reactive. As an example, I bit my tongue and held my breath rather than show any negative reaction as I watched my toddler's frequent spills, tumbles and falls. When she did fall down we got in the habit of cheerfully saying 'fall down' in a singsong voice. She never cried until the day she fell out of the crib. (Yes, I'm guilty as charged – I took my eyes off her for one second - a momentary lapse of judgment ... but thankfully the statute of limitations has now run out.) I had turned my back for a second to grab something, because my daughter was still lazily lying down after a nap. I was so shocked to see her on the floor that my heart practically stopped and I yelped - only then, when she registered my horror did her floodgates open! I learned to hold my tongue and think.

Think Lovely Thoughts

When your precious baby falls for the first time, instead of asking if she's OK tell her that she is, in a cheery voice. It cuts down on melodrama and you'll know when your child is truly hurt.

Simone Ryals, Lauderhill, FL

More On Autism

The Modified Checklist for Autism in Toddlers (M-CHAT) is another useful tool:

1) Does your child ever use his/her index finger to point, to indicate interest in something?
2) Does your child respond to his/her name when you call?
3) Does your child take an interest in other children?
4) Does your child ever take bring objects over to you to show you something?
5) If you point to a toy across the room does your child look at it?
6) Does your child imitate you? For example: if you make a face will your child imitate it?

A response of "no" to two or more of these items should warrant a referral to a psychologist or behavior specialist. Research suggests that although atypical development does not always signify autism, it does merit additional evaluation. If you do have an autistic child an excellent resource book is, Healing and Preventing Autism by Jenny McCarthy and Jerry Kartzinel M.D.

Language Development

When you've established real two-way verbal communication with your child, speak to her/him with an expanded vocabulary. Try introducing new words in a fun way – with a pronounced emphasis on the new word. We did it this way; "Madame, can I interest you in a refreshing beverage? Perhaps you'd prefer some cow juice to accompany your morning cereal?" Make a game of it – try asking her to use the new word a few times during the week "for 2 points!" English is our mother tongue, but lately you'd never know it. The use of our language has diminished and deteriorated. (And it's never too early to start SAT prep!)

They're Not Too Young To Get It

I found that speaking to my children and explaining everyday life to them (on their level of course) was a good practice. Children are capable of understanding so much more than they are given credit for, even 'adult topics' like finances! Because, life really isn't as complicated as we've been told. One day, when my daughter was about 4 years old we got into a discussion regarding the pros and cons of owning a home or renting. This led to a description of what mortgage payments are – and just at that moment my father-in-law, having just awoken from a nap, walked into the room – he was quite amused, thinking that he must be still dreaming or that I had gone completely crazy, but my daughter just thought our conversation was fun and interesting. She didn't think it was so tough to understand, she got it! We've laughed about this conversation for years.

Stuck trying to explain the economy to a child? 'Isabel's Car Wash' by Sheila Bair (the former Chairman of the Federal Deposit Insurance Corporation, the FDIC) describes how companies borrow money from investors, pay dividends and grow. It also gives a simple explanation of the stock market.

Attention Please!

When you read a book to your 3 year old, of course you're going to use the time to snuggle and enjoy each other; but there's one more important thing to do. Get his/her attention! Start training that little brain to focus and concentrate.

Passive learning occurs when you are the recipient of information. But if you know in advance, that you'll be expected to repeat, explain or expand on the story, you'll be much more involved in 'the listening.' Try this: after you're finished reading, ask your child to tell you the story while s/he turns the pages looking for visual cues. Or, s/he might want to repeat the gist of the story and add a new ending. Active learning is much more fun and enriching but it does require participation.

Two Languages Are Better Than One

If you have the advantage of knowing a second language pass it on to your baby right away, don't wait. There are several ways to do this. One parent can speak to the child in one language, the other parent in the second language. Or you can speak one language in the house (Spanish) and the other (English) as you cross the threshold and step out of the house. Don't worry about confusing the baby – children are so much smarter than we give them credit for! When it comes to knowledge, you can never get enough.

Get Out There!

Consider getting some "Mommy Business Cards" printed with your name, children's names, phone numbers and email address listed on it. It's easier then scribbling your name and number on scraps of paper, when you meet other Moms or you're dropping kids off for a play date. Some moms also list their children's allergies and alternate emergency contact numbers.

Encouraging Good Behavior

If my son is getting antsy, I'll ask "Do you want to jump and boing like Tigger?" Then I hold him beneath his armpits and help him bounce up and down. This has turned whining into giggles while in the Post Office line.

Hitting is never acceptable, but if you don't want to punish for the first time that it happens, try saying, "Were you going to give me a high five? You have to tell me first. High five? (And hold out your hand)."

To handle whining calmly say, "I don't understand whining. I don't speak 'Whine,' I speak English. Explain it to me in words."

Give clear guidelines for good behavior, and stick to them. If my son is misbehaving, I'll give him "three strikes". The first occurrence is a warning, where I explain what the consequence will be. The second occurrence is a second warning, and a reminder of the consequence. The third occurrence will be punished. It's important to follow through; otherwise they will perceive that you are not serious.

Meredith Knight, Boston MA

Searching for Meaning in the Madness?

When your little one is freaking out and mouthing off in the midst of a tantrum, bear in mind that s/he's only doing that because s/he simply doesn't have the word skills to tell you exactly what s/he's thinking. He's frustrated both with you and himself. Help him sort through it by calmly asking a few key questions. If he screams, "Get away. You're mean!" Don't add fuel to the fire. Gently say, "Tell me about that." or "Why?" or "Tell me more." Then listen patiently so you can both understand what's really going on.

Buckle 'Em Up

I used to sing to distract my son as I buckled him into his car seat. Now that he's three, I count to ten while he chooses either to let me do it or to do it himself. He usually picks the latter!

Catching A Runny Nose

Instead of chasing after your toddler's runny nose with a tissue, let him wear a soft bib to wipe his own nose with. Change the bib frequently and launder with a little bleach to kill the germs.

To teach a toddler to blow his nose, ask him to close his mouth, then hold a tissue over his nose and ask him to make it fly!

On Staying In Sight

Toddlers are notorious for wandering off and have no concept of remaining within your view. Try reversing the strategy by telling her to always make sure she can see you!

No More Tangles

If you have a daughter whose hair gets sleep tangles, replace her normal pillowcase with a satin pillowcase and banish the morning hair tangle blues!

On teaching address and phone numbers...

Use the tunes of familiar songs to help a toddler memorize your address or phone number. For example, Mary Had A Little Lamb works really well... sing: "To call home push (123) 456 - 7788." S/he'll catch on very quickly.

On "Mommy Please, Just One More Time"

When your toddler/preschooler wants you to read the same story again for the umpteenth time, or sing the song again, or have the umpteenth treat - I learned to say "One more and no more!" *Now they know their request will be filled but this time it's coming to an end.*

Touchless Shopping

When you take the kids into a store, ask them to put their hands into their pockets or place their thumbs into their waistbands and remind them to "Touch whatever you like - with your eyes only!"

Make A Date

Kids have such a hard time anticipating 'later', don't they? "Is it time yet? Are we there yet?" To make the day go by faster, decide on a specific activity or game that you will do together 'later' when you come home from work and daycare. Put the cards, board game, cake mix or book on the kitchen table to wait for your return. This visual cue will stay with him the whole day and silently reassure him that you'll spend time together. Something you both can look forward to!
                                                              Karen Young

The Next Best Thing To Being There

If you are going away on a business trip or on vacation, either make a video or audio tape of yourself reading the children's favorite stories. They can replay it as often as they like and ease their longing to have you at home.

Glimpse The Future

Pay close attention to how your two-year-old behaves – it's usually a glimpse of what the teenage behavior will be like!

Brushing Up

Some kids resist tooth brushing because they think regular toothpaste 'tastes too much' so consider getting kid-flavored toothpaste and encourage them to 'tickle their teeth!'

On The 3 W's ... Whispering, Warming and Warnings

Whispering in a fussy baby's ear works well.
Warm baths at 4 in the afternoon, a very fussy time, worked wonders.
My favorite bedtime warning was "Do you want to go to bed crying or not crying? It's your choice, but you ARE going to bed!"

Penny Greenberg, Dundas, Canada

Artfully Yours

Collect your child's 'art' and cut out the most artistic sections, then collage the pieces together and frame it. If she's too young to sign it, cover her hand in paint and apply her handprint.

Make It A Mulligan

Kids fall into bad habits so easily. If your child develops an irritating habit, discuss the change you'd like to see and the next time s/he slams the door/screams into the phone/forgets to put toilet seat down/etc., just say ' do over' or 'mulligan the door' or (after you've discussed the concept of the movie Groundhog Day) 'groundhog that.'

New Year's For Tots

When the children are too young to stay up till midnight but they still want to participate in the festivities, plan their celebration to coincide with midnight in another country. After all, it must be 'New Years' somewhere! If you choose an Italian New Year (6 hours ahead of Eastern Standard Time) serve pizza, if you pick China (approximately 13 hours ahead) serve lo-mein noodles! Invite some friends, do the countdown, make some noise and let the kids celebrate too!

How Much Is That Doggie In the Window?

Young dogs that don't have any manners yet can jump on and hurt young kids accidentally. I think adopting an older dog is an excellent idea... because you know more about the dog's personality.

Susan Wilson, Certified Dog Trainer. (WNC Parent/Feb 2008)

Preparing For Kindergarten

Our educational system has unrealistic and inappropriate expectations for our kindergarten children. Four year olds are not six year olds. That said, try having your little one listen for beginning and ending sounds of words. Interest him/her in reading by letting him 'read the pictures' of books to understand the story.

Read. You can never read too much. Repetition is the cornerstone of learning, so don't balk at reading the same book over and over and over. See if your child can fill in the blanks (leave out a word in the sentence) and recognize letters. Point out letters and numbers and encourage her to name them - in books, magazines, store shelves. (Give her a highlighter pen and have her find all the 'B's" and "8's" on the page of an old book or magazine.) Nancy Singer, who has a master's degree in reading and teaches kindergarten at Harlan Elementary School in Birmingham, Michigan, suggests teaching children letters by forming them out of Play-Doh, writing them in the sand, drawing them on the carpet or using pipe cleaners to form letters and create words.

Talk. The more you converse – in full sentences, the better. Increase his vocabulary slowly but surely.

Experience. Take him with you to the cleaner, grocery, library or zoo. Describe everything you see. The world is new and fascinating to this little human!

Write. Encourage fine motor skills with finger paints, crayons, scribbles and doodles.

Socialize. Kids need to get along from an early age, learning to share, cooperate and communicate.

Sounding the Alert

Point of information: 'Stranger danger' is a myth. Most sexual molestation occurs between children and people they know and trust – friends, acquaintances, relatives, or respected authority figures. (Doctors, coaches, youth group leaders and the clergy have all been in the headlines.) The abuser will almost always groom the child by gaining his or her trust first. Then slowly and incrementally he may begin the process of introducing physical play into their relationship. He may start to innocently massage his/her back or shoulders, roughhouse or tickle, casually place a hand on his/her thigh during conversations, etc. so that by the time he begins to make more overt sexual advances the child may hardly realize what is happening. Your child may be confused and embarrassed to bring this form of 'play' to your attention because s/he may be feeling guilty about actually enjoying the new sexual feelings s/he's experiencing. Remember, sexual pleasure is a physical sensation like any other and it feels good physically regardless of a person's age. Abusers admit that they strive to please their victims, and not cause them any pain, in order to keep the relationship and the secret going. Warning: If a male seems to be spending as much time hanging around the young kids, as he is with the adults – consider the red-flag-alert to be waving! Kids who are isolated, angry with their parents, or who desire more attention than they feel are getting at home, are most at risk for being seduced. Don't mistrust everyone you know but do be alert. Encourage your kids to tell you if someone makes them 'feel funny.' If your kids say something – listen! If your own gut tells you that something is wrong – it is!

And one more thing…

Child abduction is a very rare occurrence but it certainly grabs the headlines! The best advice is this: Teach your children that they <u>can</u> talk to strangers they just cannot go off with strangers. It's an easier lesson to learn and it will prevent your child from growing up paranoid and freaked-out. If you have a conversation regarding 'stranger danger' tell your kids the smartest thing to do if a stranger does try to physically pick him/her up and walk out the door with him/her, is to scream as loud as possible, "I don't know this person! Help me!" Practice yelling these phrases, talk about the right times to do this, and that it's okay to fight, bite and scratch while s/he's screaming to attract attention and get help.

Toilet Training

Ready or Not?

If your toddler wakes up from an afternoon nap with a dry diaper – it's time to start training!

The Naked Tush Technique

Wait (hold it!) - there's no hurry. If you start toilet training too early you'll both be frustrated. When your child is really ready the process should be fast and easy and is usually accomplished in just a few days.

I suggest you spend a couple of days discussing the issue. To empower her and guarantee her cooperation, I asked my daughter to decide which day (next week) she was going to start using the potty. Imagine the sense of power that a child must feel when s/he decides that the time is right, and then masters the physical signals to control his/her own body.

We stayed home for a few days, butt naked with the potty at the ready (as close to the butt as possible; it traveled wherever the trainee was playing) for the first day. OK, I did have a big advantage: I live in Florida so playing outside was easy, and the first day's accidents were quickly washed away with the garden hose. As the training progressed and awareness grew, the potty was moved a little further away, until it landed and remained in the bathroom. We made a big deal of each success, rewarded the achievement with a small reward (animal crackers I think) and downplayed the few 'missed opportunities' by cleaning it up together and vowing to try again. Lots of drinking led to lots of practice! When the time came for a diaper-less nighttime try, we layered the bed with 3 layers of plastic and cloth sheets for easy nighttime bed changes.

Charting the Progress

NO MORE DIAPERS for my 23 - month - old son! Most thought it would be impossible, but it was really quite simple. First we went to the dollar store where he picked out $40.00 worth of JUNK. We brought it home and placed the loot in a gift-wrapped box, with paper that HE picked himself. Next, we made a simple chart. We started with 4 boxes across the paper. In the 4th box we wrote the word 'PRIZE.' Each time he successfully used the potty we gave him a sticker to put on the chart. Once the line was filled (3 stickers) he got to pick 1 prize. We would empty the box on the floor in the living room and he went through each item until he picked the perfect prize. After a successful few days went by I made another chart, this one with 7 empty boxes across and one at the end for the prize. This went on until I had just enough space to put a little sticker in 15 boxes. If he made 'a pooh' he would be rewarded with 2 stickers. It took about 2 days for him to understand that the only time he'd get a prize was when the chart line was full. If he had an accident, we calmly explained that he hadn't earned a sticker. By the time all the prizes were given, he was dry all the time!

Heather Gibson

'Front and Center' Potty Training Technique

Place a rubber bath mat, covered by a towel, right in your family room (or wherever your family tends to congregate). Put the potty there, front and center, and let your toddler sit there while you're all watching TV. Explain what the potty is for and then leave him/her alone to do his/her thing with no pressure. If s/he hits the mark, praise profusely and give him/her a gold star or sticker. (Applied to 'the chart' outlined above, the potty seat or an arm or a leg ... whatever tickles the imagination of the child in question.) Kids love being where the action is, so they're more likely to 'succeed' if they don't have to travel to perform in the beginning.

'Make' Magic!

Keep a bottle of blue food coloring in the bathroom and add a few drops to the potty-toilet water. Have your toddler note the color. Then encourage him/her to be a magician, pee and see the color of the water change to green! (Or change red water to orange!)

Target Practice

A toilet bowl manufacturer in Ireland has a small fly etched into the side of their bowls, knowing that men (and boys) like to take aim at things. After I stopped laughing, I started wondering ... perhaps it might be an idea to draw your own (with a permanent marker) or affix a small, flat object to the side (with silly putty or crazy glue) of the training potty and encourage your little boy to aim for the target.

FOOD

Deadly Foods

Have you ever seen a child choke? It happens often and it's not pretty. The 3 foods that are most likely to cause choking (airway obstruction) are: grapes, hotdogs and peanuts. Hard candies and marshmallows (large and small) also pose problems. To avoid this crisis always slice round foods, such as grapes, cherry tomatoes, olives and hotdogs vertically in half, then into quarters. Even when children get older continue to cut these foods vertically, so they retain a half moon shape. An easy way to cut grapes (or small tomatoes) quickly is to corral a bunch of them between two plastic container lids, lightly press down to keep them in place, and then slide your knife through the middle. This simple precaution will eliminate the naturally occurring round shape as they are introduced into the mouth, and greatly reduce the potential to occlude the small windpipe opening should the food be swallowed whole.

Peanuts also pose problems because people have a tendency to 'throw them back.' If they are aspirated in whole or in part into one's lung, they cause particular problems which are difficult to treat because peanuts are an oil-based food. When the kids crave the taste of peanuts, dipping slices of raw zucchini or yellow squash into peanut butter is nutritious and fun.

And on a related note: Button batteries are not food but they are small and round, and they land up in kids mouths anyway. They are often used to power remote controls, watches, and children toys, and they are becoming increasingly problematic because they can cause serious internal corrosive burning before being passed out of the body. If you fear your child has swallowed one – go to the nearest Emergency Room ASAP!

Don't Start a Food Fight

'Food glorious food!' We may think so but toddlers don't always agree. Kids go through all kinds of crazy eating jags. One youngster I know would only eat red colored foods for a while! So there were lots of beets, tomatoes, red potatoes, hot dogs and plums on the menu... other things got a healthy slathering of ketchup! Eventually, it eased up.

One Mom complained to me, "My daughter has a thing about mixing foods; "Ich - my chicken is touching my peas! My potato is touching my tomato! I want the ketchup on a different plate!" And before I knew it, it took seven dishes to feed her dinner!" Yup, kids will drive you crazy if you let them!

I recently watched children at a restaurant eating macaroni and cheese with a side of French fries. Apparently this was their standard nightly meal. I overheard the Moms commiserating that it was just easier to let them eat what they wanted than to fight about it. No wonder our kids are overweight and malnourished. My kids loved mac and cheese too, but we saved it for 'The Saturday Night Special' when the babysitter came and they all enjoyed it together! Often

I'd mash up some tofu, add extra cheese and presto – it was instantly healthier, and no one was the wiser. Obviously delicious, secretly nutritious ... every Mother's credo.

I don't know a single Mother who hasn't threatened, cajoled or bribed her kids at some point to eat. I'm guilty. It must be a survival instinct to entice one's offspring to consume some nutrition. But I don't know of any child in recorded history who actually starved himself voluntarily, unless he was using this tactic to manipulate and get a reaction from his Mother. Don't make food an issue: Serve, allow 20 minutes for dining and remove. The next meal will be served in just a few hours; nothing bad will happen if the kids miss a few meals.

That said here are a few ideas you might find helpful:

Finicky Eaters

To entice kids who are reluctant eaters, try serving a scoop of ricotta cheese, (yogurt, cottage cheese, egg salad, tuna, chicken salad or anything else you can think of) in an ice cream cone!

Buried Treasure - to get the kids to eat yogurt, I'd 'sink' a few chocolate chips on the bottom of the container and tell them they had to eat their way down to the treasure. I must admit that the volume of chocolate rewards increased dramatically over the years, but the kids ate yogurt daily and have never had any intestinal problems.

To make bland-looking food a little more kid friendly, try adding a drop of food coloring to oatmeal, cottage cheese, tofu, etc.

Try a tiny dusting of rainbow sprinkles and watch the food disappear!

If your child (5 years and older) is underweight, a poor eater and you want to provide a very high-calorie, nutrient-rich supplement, try this:

Oh For Goodness Shake!

1-pint vanilla ice cream
1 small container 'Egg Beaters' (or similar egg substitute)
½ cup instant dry milk
¼ - ½ cup liquid (milk, juice or water)
Fruit, chocolate syrup or other flavoring

Combine in the blender and whip for 1 minute. Makes 2 – 3 servings. Reserve the rest in fridge.

My Family's Favorite Meal – The Quickest Lasagna on the Planet!

Sauce:
1 16 oz. container ricotta cheese
2 packages spinach, thawed and squeezed
(Or any other chopped veggie – broccoli, mixed veggies)

1 16 oz. jar of prepared spaghetti sauce
Spices and sugar to taste
(I use about ¼ cup sugar or sugar substitute, it cuts the bitterness of tomatoes)
2 cups water
9 – 12 uncooked lasagna noodles
Grated cheese for topping

This is a super easy recipe suitable for kids and/or company. Combine all the sauce ingredients in a large bowl and mix well. Spray a 9"13" baking pan with nonstick coating. Beginning with a scant amount, spread some of the mixture on the bottom of the pan. Layer the remaining mixture on top of <u>dry</u> lasagna noodles. (Any brand – and they don't have to be the no cook variety) Repeat 3 – 4 layers, ending with the sauce mixture. Cover tightly with aluminum foil and bake at 350' F for 1 hour. Carefully peel back and remove foil, allowing the steam to escape away from you. Allow it to rest for 5 minutes, then cover with grated cheese and return to the oven until the cheese is melted and golden brown. It's even better the next day!

Breakfast Independence

Teach young kids how to fix their own breakfast and entertain themselves in the morning so you can sleep longer. As soon as my three kids could pick up a light jug of milk and open a box of cereal, get the utensils and a bowl (I placed each on very low shelves!), I taught them to prepare their own breakfasts. It saved me a lot of time and taught them to be independent. They felt very accomplished when they learned to do things for themselves. I got a few hours of extra sleep every day, which is a rare commodity when you have toddlers... and now they all cook! (I still don't!)   *Ellen Bukstel, Southwest Ranches, FL*

Crazy Sammies

Make sandwiches more fun to eat by cutting them into shapes with cookie cutters.

The Eyes Have It!

When your kids start complaining "I don't like it!" remind them that their tongue doesn't have the only vote ... their muscles, bones, eyes and teeth need certain foods to stay healthy so they still need to eat that food!

Good Snacks

Use unflavored gelatin to make orange (or any other) 'juice Jello.' Follow the directions on the package but let it gel in Ziploc bags (to squeeze out of one opened corner) or make 'juice gel' in reusable plastic containers with lids, for a portable, wiggly, nutritious snack.

I have three kids under three, so I have a lot to keep track of! To make sure everyone snacks nutritiously, we keep magnetized "snack cards" on the refrigerator. The kids choose the snacks they would like to have during the day using the cards. They are learning that they can only have one high sugar (yummy snack) plus one fruit snack per day.

Meredith Knight, Winchester MA

Green Slime Freezee-Pops

Blend together some banana, spinach or cooked broccoli or peas; then add enough applesauce to produce a thick slurrie. Pour the mixture into several paper cups, place a Popsicle stick into each cup and freeze. Run the frozen pop under cool water for a few seconds to thaw and peel away the paper.

Go Bananas

Bananas contain three natural sugars - sucrose, fructose and glucose combined with fiber. A banana gives an instant, sustained and substantial boost of energy and is a natural remedy for many ills. When you compare it to an apple, it has four times the protein, twice the carbohydrate, three times the phosphorus, five times the vitamin A and iron, and twice the other vitamins and minerals. It is also rich in potassium and is one of the best value foods around. Maybe it's time to change that well-known phrase so that we say, "A banana a day keeps the doctor away!"

Banana Brain Power: 200 students at a Twickenham school (Middlesex, England) were helped through their exams this year by eating bananas at breakfast, break, and lunch in a bid to boost their brainpower. Research has shown that the potassium-packed fruit can assist learning by making pupils more alert.

Cook's Corner

To keep kids away from the stove while you're cooking but keep them interested in the process, give them small pots and pans, a spoon and some water. Let them get involved in the cooking and stirring up dinner.

On Eating Vegetables

According to Fruit Sticker (fruitsticker.com), the produce sticker code reveals some very useful information...

- Conventionally grown produce has a four-digit number on the sticker.
- Organic produce gets a five-digit number that begins with a 9.

- And produce items that are genetically modified also have five digits, beginning with the number 8.

Fake Fries:
When my new step-daughter told me she wasn't crazy about string beans, I told her to put some salt on them and pretend they're French fries. This apparently worked, as she has since done the same with her children.

Give 'Em A Pass:
I wanted our children to try everything, at least once -- so we gave them an out - ONE thing that they never had to eat. One refused to eat tomatoes, one refused to eat broccoli. They felt quite important when "their" vegetable was served, and could say, "I don't have to eat that!" but they did realize that they had to try everything else!

Linda Morris, FL

Counting Bites:
To get my daughter to eat her veggies, I'd say, 'You only have to eat three bites because you're three years old!' She counted and consumed – and we were both happy!

As the kids got older the rule became: To eat as many bites as their age plus one more bite for good luck ... this assured me that they were eating enough and that they always had a balanced diet! If they wanted a sugary snack in the afternoon they knew had to eat a carrot or celery sticks first.

The Taster:
I used to let my son "help" me to cook. He stood on a chair next to me at the kitchen counter. If I was making a recipe that involved cutting up lots of vegetables, I would always let him try a taste of anything he wanted. Result: he likes almost any vegetable you can name - but only if not cooked (hey - it's healthier that way!). I bet I have the only kid who told his family doctor that his favorite vegetable was cabbage!!!

Reality check - this did not work for my daughter (5 years younger), which I guess just goes to show that each child is unique.

Catherine Joyce, CT

Fun Eating

Make a summer surprise on a hot day. Set up a picnic table with all the fixings for ice creams sundaes. Nuts, chocolate syrup, fruit, ice cream, whipped cream, etc. My Mom probably actually did this only two or three times, but it felt like a wonderful occasional treat and it was so much fun!

On a few winter mornings she'd surprise us kids with vegetable soup for breakfast! It's an exciting and fun way to start the day, and it's a nutritious breakfasts to boot!

Jackie Savagio, Lennox, MA

When things get really ho –hum, in the dead of winter, make a picnic on the living room floor. Spread out a large flat sheet, turn on some music and shock your family into having some fun!

Stuff It

Stuff a miniature marshmallow in the bottom of a sugar cone to prevent ice cream drips.
Martha Stewart

Have A Dinner Exchange

Schedule a night off from the kitchen! Once a week make a double recipe of whatever gourmet meal you're preparing and deliver it to a friend or neighbor or co-worker. Arrange for her to do the same for you. That way you each have a day off from the kitchen and also have a great meal to look forward to! It doesn't really require any extra effort to prepare more, the costs will even out, and the surprise feast is terrific fun! Just exchange a list of family food allergies before you begin sharing culinary adventures.

Friendly Competition

If one child stubbornly refuses to eat something, try saying, "I see you're not eating your fish. Perhaps your sister would like it." Suddenly the competitive urge not to be outdone takes over and presto – the food will disappear.

Food Additives - Do They Cause Hyperactivity?

There is concern that food additives, such as tartrazine, sunset yellow, and allura red, either cause or increase behaviors consistent with attention deficit hyperactivity disorder. The study lends credence to such concerns, although it certainly doesn't tell us whether food additives are a major contributor to ADHD. (Source: Journal Watch General Medicine, November, 2007)

Nourish Naturally!

When you are making food choices for yourself and your family, consider this: if the food product wasn't available 100 years ago, don't buy it. If you can't grow it, pick it, gather it, hunt it, milk it or fish for it, don't eat it. In other words, any food which is processed or manufactured doesn't belong in the pantry, refrigerator or in the tummy.
H. Friedman, Brevard N. C.

Produce Protection

If you're concerned that serving fresh produce may be dangerous to your family's health, (you may remember that a few years ago, several spinach and lettuce fields were contaminated with e-coli) take a tip from 'America's Test Kitchen.' Simply combine 3 parts tap water with 1 part distilled vinegar in a spray bottle. Spray to wash any firm, smooth skinned fruit or vegetable such as apples, pears, tomatoes, melons, carrots or lettuce. An application of this vinegar solution will remove 98% of the surface bacteria. (Source: cooksillustrated.com)

The Dirty Dozen

Because these fruits and veggies are so thin skinned, eat them only from an organic source if at all possible.

Celery - Peaches - Strawberries - Apples - Blueberries - Nectarines - Bell Peppers - Spinach - Cherries -Kale/Collard - Greens - Potatoes - Imported Grapes

The Clean 15

These are OK to eat from regular produce aisle.

Onions - Avocado - Sweet Corn - Pineapple - Mangos - Sweet Peas - Asparagus -Kiwi - Cabbage – Eggplant - Cantaloupe - Watermelon - Grapefruit - Sweet Potato Honeydew Melon (Source: foodnews.org/walletguide.php)

The Nights of the Round Table

If you're shopping for a new kitchen table, and you have the space, buy a round table. It's much more conducive to family conversation and togetherness.

Talk It Up

Keep conversations going at the dinner table. The same old "What did you do in school today?" will probably be answered with the same old "Nothing." But asking everyone to show up to dinner armed with a joke or an interesting fact to share might put everyone in the right mood for real conversation. (Keep a dictionary, a book of trivia or volume of the encyclopedia handy – open to a random page and "discuss amongst yourselves!") To keep the conversation going try asking, "Tell me more..." or "And then what happened?" "And?" In our house we discussed politics, current events and humanitarian issues all the time. There wasn't a single topic we wouldn't tackle at our family table. We expected our children to voice their opinions and back up their arguments. It was terrific fun! (And they became quite articulate in the process!)

Family Dining

As I walked into my home after leaving my daughter at college for her first year, I had a flash of nostalgia and even regret when my eye fell on the dining room table. It is the one I grew up with, and it has carried the emotional life of my family in its essence. My regret is that I didn't set it for family meals more often, instead so often eating dinner on the couch together, or worse, on the fly. Wouldn't we have discussed current events more? Processed our days together more? Probably, and I wish we had. So heads up, younger parents; studies even show that kids who eat with their families get much better grades. A Columbia University study has found that teens who participated in family dinners five or more times a week were 42 percent less likely to drink alcohol, 59 percent less likely to smoke cigarettes, and 66 percent less likely to try marijuana.

Annie B. Bond, Executive Producer, Care2's Green Living

Quiet on the Set!

When you sit down to dinner, shut the TV, let the nuisance telephone solicitors listen to the sound of your answering machine picking up, put your cells and Ipods in their chargers and listen to the sound of – each other!

On Eating Out

When I eat out with my two-year-old, we split an entree like chicken or pasta. It helps us manage portions, and my son gets a healthier meal than the usual kid-menu choices of nuggets and fries.

Avoiding A Restaurant Riot

When you're driving to a restaurant, remind your children to 'B'have or You'll B'Gone.' Go over the rules and expectations. If the kids don't handle themselves properly, don't give them a second chance: pay your bill, get up and leave. Actions really do speak louder than words so put your words into action just once and you'll never have a problem with restaurant outings again... I guarantee it!

Restaurant Behavior

When we took our little ones to a restaurant they were allowed to "dip" one little finger into a packet of sugar (they need to lick their finger first to get the sugar to stick.) This was a very big treat, as they didn't get much sugar at home. The 'one finger dip' kept them busy until the food arrived. And neighboring tables were so happy not to have our two sons chasing around their chairs.

Laurie Marson

Rest or Rant at the Restaurant?

Would you like a rest instead of listening to the kids rant next time you visit a rest-au-rant? Getting the kids to give it a rest is easy if you keep a 'bag of tricks' in the trunk of your car. Equip it with colored pencils, coloring books, fill-in sheets of tic-tac-toe, hangman, connect the dots, maze puzzles, word searches and easy sudoku grids.

Temple, Church and Restaurant Manners

Reinforce the rules with this little rhyme:

> No running or tossing stuff around
> No loud voices, or wrestling on the ground.
> If anyone looks our way – it had better be to say,
> "You kids are amazing! Stay that way!" OK?

It's OK To Play Hide and Sneak

Sneak fruits and vegetables into like-colored foods. Add orange squash to macaroni and cheese. Pureed white cauliflower can be slipped into mashed potatoes. Pureed red beets can hide inside tomato sauce. You get the idea. For great recipes refer to 'Deceptively Delicious' by Jessica Seinfeld.

Let 'Em Eat Cake

Seriously! This recipe is so good these cupcakes will disappear in a flash. No one will ever detect the secret ingredient* or suspect that these yummy treats are actually healthy and nutritious. No eggs or oil ... Try it, you'll like it!

Valerie Landa, Nashville TN

Double Good - Magic Cupcakes

1 box Devil's Food chocolate cake mix
*1 can pumpkin puree
2/3 cup water
2/3 cup chocolate chips

Mix by hand until combined and moistened. Fill muffin liners ¾ full. Bake at 350 degrees for 10 -12 minutes. Allow to cool.

On Getting Kids to Try Something New

When my grandson was 3 years old, he just hated my homegrown tomatoes, so I enticed him to "just try it." But of course he wouldn't. So I suggested that if I peeled the tomato it might taste better - he tried, but still hated it. Next, I got the sea-salt grinder out and he added salt himself using the grinder. You could try parmesan cheese too. Voila- suddenly he just loved tomatoes and wouldn't stop eating them. And everyone was happy!

Sheila Sidline, Hatboro, PA

We used to joke that 'it' (the unwanted food) could taste like chocolate – but you'd never find out if you didn't try it.
Disguise 'leftovers' and regular food with exotic names … "Wolf stew" "squish" and "cow juice" made the ordinary much more fun to consume.

Bribing Taste Buds

As my daughter grew older she became more finicky and hesitant to try different foods. She would often say she "did not like" whatever, before she even tried it. It was frustrating. So my husband and I resorted to bribing her. If she tried a new food we would give her a quarter. If she liked the food and she ate a normal portion, we would give her five dollars. (Of course desserts didn't count!) She hit the jackpot one night at a casino 'seafood buffet!' She tried many different items and ended up liking them all. The payout was $30! We laughed at her windfall as we all thought it was a win - win situation.

Cindy Bowers, Asheville, NC

Munch and Crunch

People are often impressed at how my kids eat their vegetables. We started early, putting lots of crunchy things like carrots on the table, and having crunch contests. Whoever made the loudest sound, won! Of course, we exaggerated our reaction to the crack made by the bite... just to make it a bit more fun. Fresh vegetables also go down much easier when there's a choice of salad dressings for dipping. We sometimes put that out after school, which works like a charm.

Sandy Cash, Beit Shemesh, Israel

Wok It Up

Go to the store with your kids. Buy a ton of vegetables and some chicken. When you get home have the kids clean, chop, and season all the food. Then get out the Wok - getting the children involved in the whole process makes it fun. They love eating what they create - and I know that it's good and healthy. To this day, my kids ask for "stir fry."

Laura Gonzalez, Lauderhill, FL

Obesity Watch

Dr. Michelle May offers the following advice regarding a child's diet:

- Don't reward eating. Do not praise or bribe toddlers for eating extra food, as this can establish a negative habit. Similarly, do not offer rewards for a clean plate at the end of the meal.

- Don't focus on ideal weight. Instead, set modest, achievable goals for overweight children.
- Monitor, but don't control. Limiting dietary choices can be counterproductive, but focusing positively as a family on healthy foods produces healthier eating habits over the long term.
- Don't give up on healthy foods. Children may need to try a new food up to 10 times before accepting and enjoying it. CDC.gov/growthcharts will give you growth guidelines.

In addition I feel that nothing should really be off limits because human nature dictates that we always want what we can't have. (My Mother was the original self-proclaimed 'health food guru.' She never brought anything sweet into our house and as a result we kids were always going over to a friend's house seeking cookies, chocolates and desserts.) I would suggest that you don't buy junk food to keep in the house, but don't forbid it either. When you go out on the weekends, allow your kids to eat some junk so they have it to look forward to and they won't feel deprived. It's almost like (not) 'having your cake and eating it too'!

Close Your Mouth

When my daughters were young, it was difficult teaching them NOT to talk with their mouths full of food. For them, dinnertime was like performing - they had our full attention (as if they were on center stage) and they would spend more time talking than eating! When they did put food in their mouths, they couldn't stand to miss an opportunity to chime in on whatever anyone else was saying, so they would join the conversation with food chunks peeking out of their teeth. Just telling them to swallow their food before they spoke didn't work, so I finally created a rule that anyone who talked with their mouth full had to go into the bathroom and count to 25 before coming back to the table. Of course, they thought it was really fun at first, but they soon grew tired of losing out on those 25 seconds of dinner conversation - and attention - and it worked! They especially liked it when my husband or I would screw up and wind up banished to the bathroom ourselves. To this day, they are very careful not to talk with their mouths full.

Jane E. Johnson, Tallahassee, FL

Kitchen Cleaning Tip

To prevent harmful bacteria from accumulating on your kitchen sponge, microwave it for one minute every night after you've finished washing the dishes.

GO By The Rules

Kids can easily become constipated because they are either too busy to sit down when they need to, or they're in the wrong place at the right time. Many have developed an irrational fear of any toilet seat that's not in their own home (more on that later) or they just aren't eating what they need to. This aspect of life should never be 'hard' to accomplish – bad pun, sorry.

1) Eat lots of fruits and vegetables (OK, you knew that)

<u>Find Fabulous Fiber in Figs and Flax</u>

2) The best natural laxative (safe enough for infants 8 months and older) is figs. Simply boil dried figs in water, (add just enough to cover, add more water as necessary) until they are very soft, puree in a food processor and cool before storing in the fridge. Serve 1 teaspoon - 2 tablespoons, daily. Reliable, regular magic! (If it worked for my son - see 'Our Story', it'll work for anyone!) or…

3) Add ground flax seed into your diet daily. Flax is one of the safest, mildest, most economical, natural and healthful products on the market. It is a remarkable food! But because it is so inexpensive and because natural ingredients cannot be patented, there will never be a big merchandising or marketing campaign to tout all its health benefits. Flax provides Omega 3 fatty acids, essential for heart health, in addition to fiber. More information about the health benefits of flax can be found at (whfoods.com). You can buy milled flax seed or whole flax seed in bulk. I prefer to grind it myself in a coffee grinder. Once you grind it, store it in the fridge.

For children: Begin by mixing 1 teaspoon into applesauce (daily) or sprinkle on cereal or mix into a smoothie. Increase the amount of milled flax seed until you have the desired results.
For adults: Mix 2 - 3 tablespoons into applesauce, etc. Always drink a large glass of water with your flax to increase its effectiveness.

4) When you feel the 'urge to purge' GO! If you don't, your body will reabsorb some of the liquids in your 'solids' thereby making it harder (literally) for you to go. Your digestive muscles have a mind of their own. Once you swallow food, the digestive tract functions without your knowledge and generally does a pretty good 'job'! These muscles have their own timetable and they work best when you cooperate. Don't postpone going to the bathroom.

5) Stop worrying about toilet seats! Fact: you will not get sick or pick up an infection from a toilet seat. You are much more likely to pick up someone else's sickly germs just shaking hands, sharing toys or touching door handles. There are more harmful bacteria on your phone, handbag and toothbrush. Unless the toilet is really dirty and disgusting - cover the seat if you like, but sit down and do your thing! Over time, toilet seat anxiety becomes a real issue for lots of people - they've even coined the term "Safe Toilet (Seat) Syndrome" to describe it... another modern day disease! Gimme a break! People, relax and let it go!

Get paper toweling before you begin to wash your hands and use it to close the faucets. Why touch what you just washed off?

Concerning Childhood

Get involved with other Mommies. Join playgroups, Moms' groups, early childhood PTA's. When your child is young it's easy to establish a big support group.

Always keep a few little pocket size toys, crayons, mini games on key chains, something in your purse or car... to save your sanity.

Keep some food in your car: Cheese 'n Crackers, dry cereal, juice boxes or whatever doesn't need refrigeration.

Buy every kind of 'band aid' that your child might like, and dispense them freely. I've seen children go from full-on cry to happy face at the mention of a fancy Band Aid.

Karenia Tarolli, Denten, Texas

On Apologizing

Simply telling your child to say, "I'm sorry" after she does something wrong may not mean anything to her. Instead, ask her to say "I'm sorry for _____" and then have her name the transgression – so she links the words with the deed.

Dr. A. Lazare

Uh-Oh

When my children would fall or get bumps and bruises, I would draw the attention away from their boo-boo's by asking, "Did you put a hole in the floor?" Or, "Oops, did you bust apart the table?" If they weren't seriously hurt, they would soon forget their pain by concerning themselves with trying to fix whatever they thought they had broken.

Brittanny Craig, Asheville, NC

On Bathroom Breaks

Inevitably when I went to the store for anything, as soon as we would be in the middle of an aisle at the opposite end of the store, one of the kids would need to go to the bathroom - in emergency mode! So I made it a practice upon entering any store to, first and foremost, go to the bathroom and then proceed with the shopping.

Joyce Tritt, Atlanta, GA

One Mandatory Sport

I'm not the athletic type. Let's just say, I was 'the kid last chosen for the team' and leave it at that. As a result, though I encouraged my kids to play and have fun participating in sports, there was only one physical activity that I demanded they learn. Learning to swim was absolutely mandatory. It's a physical sport that has the potential to save your (or someone else's) life. Both my girls took Karate classes for the exercise, self-discipline and the skills they'd learn, but swimming lessons came first. No matter where you live, water is a fact of life. And every year when I hear that yet another child has drowned, I think of that Mother's sorrow and how easily it could have been avoided.

Private Time

When my husband and I wanted some 'private time' (if you catch my drift) we'd lock our bedroom door and tell the kids not to disturb us because we were very busy wrapping presents. When they heard that, they'd leave us alone immediately!

Karen McElveen, Dania Beach, FL

A Touchy Subject

Some Moms love their little boys – a little too much. Have you ever seen a Mom with her 4 – 10 year old son, either sitting on her lap or sitting beside her, as she absent-mindedly caresses Johnny by rubbing his back or by stroking his hair or arms? I'm not referring to a harmless thirty-second back or shoulder rub. I'm talking about continuous pleasuring. (I'm not sure for whose benefit.) I've seen this happen a few times and was disturbed by the unconscious message it must be sending the boys. These Moms seem to fall into a trance and don't seem to be aware of their quasi-incestuous behavior. In my opinion, hugs are fine but stroking is not.

Louise Elwood, St. Cloud, MN

Lice Advice

Don't panic. You'll live through it – I promise. There is no shame in getting head lice and nits. Shirley Gordon, director of the Head Lice Treatment Department at Florida Atlantic University, explains that lice actually prefer to live on healthy people and clean heads. Most kids transfer lice from one to another just by being in close proximity - a quick hug is all it takes! So don't be shy, call and inform all your child's friends Moms of your collective predicament. Unfortunately there are no miracle cures because lice have become resistant to many pesticide products. But lice can only survive 24 hours off the head so there's no need to go crazy cleaning. Wash the bedding, pajamas, blankets and hairbrushes. Throw the stuffed animals in the dryer for a while. Then turn your attention to carefully removing the nits. Nits are tear-shaped eggs which cling to the hair shaft close to the scalp. If you pass your fingers over a bump on the hair shaft and it doesn't move, it's most likely a nit. Experts recommend washing your child's hair, applying a conditioner without rinsing it out and then methodically combing through the hair using a special nit comb. You usually have to retreat one week later. Consult your doctor for other lice-killing product recommendations.

On Stopping Thumb Sucking

It's A Wrap!

After trying many methods to break the habit, one day I inspected the thumb carefully and announced that I had discovered the little digit had a small booboo, which needed time to heal. With that I proceeded to wrap the thumb with an exaggerated, enormous dressing. (Producing a bandage as big as her hand!) It worked like a charm, after a few days the habit was broken.

Miriam Mandel, Hollywood, FL

Sometimes just a small, irritating band-aid will do.

Give your child a small pocket toy and beaded bracelet to manipulate to help keep those little fingers busy.

The Kids To-Do List

To help my kids become more independent and responsible for their daily chores, I wrote all the various tasks, (I cut out some pictures of brushing teeth, making the bed, etc. too) mounted them onto stiff cardboard and glued a magnet onto each one. I bought a small magnetic white board and divided it into two sections: "To Do" and "Did It!" Now we had a visual reminder and check off board all in one. The kids got a real sense of accomplishment as the pieces moved over from one side to the other.

Maria Kales

On Dealing with Boo Boos

Keep a few darkly colored washcloths on hand to clean blood from scrapes and cuts. It will camouflage the blood and cut down on the goriness of the event. Follow up with a bag of frozen peas or corn, which mold nicely to any area of the body. Offer your child a Popsicle at the same time – it's hard to cry and enjoy a treat at the same time. Then apply antibiotic cream and lots of fun band - aids.

On Hand Washing

A serious message can also be fun. Have the kids wash as long as it takes for them to sing "Happy Birthday" twice! Or…

As one Mom suggested (on AOL) sing this song to the tune of "Winter Wonderland"

> *Little bugs can infect you*
> *Washing hands can protect you*
> *Your very best hope is water and soap*
> *Walking in a germy wonderland…*   *Mary L. Austin TX*

Hand-washing experiment: Put a few drops of cooking oil and a sprinkle of cinnamon, into your kid's hands. Have them mix the 'ingredients' together and rub it all over their hands. Then have them wash with soap, just like normal and then do a smell test – the amount of cinnamon aroma left on their hands is a good measure of how well they wash!

On Bath time

- *If you're out of town and want to bathe your toddler in a friend's bathtub, place an empty laundry basket on a rubber bathmat and fill the tub. The openings around the sides will allow the water to circulate, but you'll reduce the space around your toddler so s/he'll be less able to slip, but still have plenty of space to play.*

- A can of shaving cream makes wonderful 'finger paint' that lasts until the bath is over. Clean off the walls with just a quick splash!

- Add a couple of drops of food coloring to the bath water to make magic water!

Right and Left

Using a permanent marker, draw an arrow on the sole inside the shoe, pointing inward toward the other foot. (---> <---) Write a big "R" in right foot, and "L" in the left foot. When the *arrows are lined up and pointing to each other, s/he'll know they're aligned correctly. Over time s/he'll recognize the letters too.*

As you are putting on your child's shoes, tell him/her "this is the right foot, this is the left foot" to help them learn left and right.

Meredith Knight, Winchester MA

Sex Talk

It's almost never too early to start talking about sex. In fact, the earlier you get used to it the easier it will be! Far too many parents shy away from talking about 'The Act' but like everything else – practice makes progress. Give simple, age appropriate, factual answers to your child's innocent questions. Kids usually ask simple questions, so you only need to give them simple answers. "Where do babies come from?" "A special place in a Mom's body called the uterus." If s/he happens to ask at an inappropriate time tell your child that s/he's asked an important question that you will discuss later, at home. (Then thank your lucky stars that now you have a few minutes to mentally rehearse what you're going to say!) Be true to your word, don't be shy and supply simple answers. There are so many TV ads lately for male enhancement drugs that I often wonder how young Moms are handling questions about erections and intimacy.

Explain anatomical facts simply to children around the age 10, if they haven't already asked. Encourage discussions about sexual feelings, respect, love and intimacy with older kids. Arm yourself with simple anatomical drawings and rehearse what you're going to say. If you're totally tongue-tied and need some guidance check out the book, 'Everything you Never wanted your kids to know about Sex' by J. Richardson and M. Schuster.

As time goes on don't stop the conversation. Kids need to be told over and over again that contraception, and using condoms to ensure safer sex are mandatory elements of any premarital encounter. Don't worry – just talking about using protection does not encourage sexual activity. As we have seen played out on the national stage during the 2008 election process, preaching abstinence-only simply doesn't work. If you're going to talk, get real and make it constructive. Some teens think that it's acceptable if they 'only' have anal or oral sex, so they can technically maintain their virginity! And 'vows of chastity' don't seem to hold up to the heat of the moment either.

Check the messages your children see you living. Put a lock on your bedroom door and have your kids get used to the idea that you and your husband/partner enjoy 'alone time.' You two are their models for respect, love and healthy intimacy. Human beings are sexual beings. Let's educate our children to seek joy in all the healthy, essentials of life – good food, robust laughter, loving sex and anything chocolate.

Real Words Never Hurt Anyone

Let's get over our fear of the English language. Words are just words. They are descriptive vocal references used to communicate ideas, and that's all they are. There's nothing 'dirty' about them. They are just vocalizations. If you use a euphemism (cute or otherwise) for a body part or bodily function, you are signaling your child that it's embarrassing to be human, in spite of the fact that everyone knows exactly what you're talking about anyway. When speaking to your children you'd never hesitate to say, "Aw, you hurt your knee. Take your elbow off the table. Move your ass!" But you might just freak out if someone dared to say the words breast, nipple, vagina, penis, masturbation, etc. within earshot of your kids! Right? Sex therapists and psychologists all agree that it's less confusing and much healthier to just use real, factual terminology.

Match and Learn

When I fold laundry, I ask my two-year-old to hand me specific items. It's fun (and educational) for him to pick out the different colors and match the different types of clothes.

Guess That Shape

To get my kids to sit still and relax while I spray or apply sunscreen or lotion, I have them close their eyes as I trace a letter or picture on their backs, arms etc. They try to guess what it is by the way it feels.

Carol Miesner

Artful Deception

Let's face it – even Leonardo's and Picasso's Moms couldn't keep every scribble their kids drew. You can either toss the stuff when the kids are asleep or blame it on the housekeeper. When you do come across something worthwhile, either frame it (I have a piece my daughter did in kindergarten – it looks like I plucked it off the wall of the Museum of Modern Art!) or save it to use as a greeting card.

Limits and Rules

Imagine joining a friendly group and organizing a baseball game. But everyone wants to be well liked and be 'best friends,' so it's decided to suspend all the rules. Now no one knows what's expected and pretty soon it's hard to play, as you no longer know what the goal of the game is. So the older kids start to make up some rules as the game progresses and then they begin to change the rules at every inning. Chaos ensues – the game is now confusing, frustrating and anxiety provoking. Life and family unity are just like that. We all need a little structure. We need to know what the rules are!

If a child lives with approval, she learns to like herself.

Dorothy Law Nolte

A good parent pulls their child closer with one hand
and pushes him away with the other.   The Talmud

94

Communication

Remember that NO is a real word with a clear definition. Say what you mean and mean what you say. If you say NO, it shouldn't mean maybe, ask me again later, or keep asking me till you get your way...!

How do you want your NO, fast or slow?   Michael Todd

Your body language and facial expressions speak volumes
Try not to grimace.
Your words will be permanently inscribed on the subconscious psyche
Try not to scribble.
Your tone, whether in angry or in tender moments, will echo in the heart forever
Try not to mumble.

Tell Me Why

Curious kids can make you crazy. But curious kids are smart kids, so don't turn them off. And instead of having to constantly admit that you don't know everything (although there's nothing wrong with that...) try telling them, "Good question, but so far nobody's figured that out yet." Or, "It's unknown." Or "What do you think?" Or, "The world is so mysterious; nobody knows!"

Offering Positive Choices and Control

We believed in giving our children as much control over what they were doing as they could handle, based on their age, abilities and maturity. One of our tactics was to limit the times we made a given action mandatory, so they would realize that we weren't always trying to "control" them needlessly. Whenever possible, we would give them at least two choices. However, when giving kids a choice, you need to be careful and make sure that you can live with whichever choice they make.

For example: bath time. Obviously, if our child had become sweaty or dirty that day, a bath became mandatory. But most times, a bath could be given that night or wait till tomorrow. The usual reason for not wanting to take the bath was that he was having fun and didn't want to stop playing. To begin, we would give a warning, such as "two more minutes to play" (without mentioning the bath.) We did not want to connect taking a bath with the need to stop having fun. When playtime was over, we helped him put away the toys. If there was bath time resistance, we again offered a choice; "Do you want to take a bath tonight or go to bed now?" Additional playtime was not one of the choices. In almost all cases, our children liked to postpone bedtime, so they would choose taking the bath. Of course, once they were in the tub, we eventually had to give them another 'two minute warning' to get them out.

95

The important thing about giving choices is that you only offer choices that you are willing to accept. When you really believe that a particular course of action is necessary and it is the only acceptable choice, don't give any alternatives and be firm. Don't keep saying, "OK, just a few more minutes." Kids learn very quickly when they can "play" their parents and when they are required to follow instructions.

Doris Davidoff, Boynton Beach FL

Check Your Child's Marshmallow Mind

This experiment has been replicated many times in human development research centers. The aim is to see how well a small child can control his impulses and test his/her ability to exert some self-control.

Place a marshmallow (or chocolate treat, or gummy bear, or whatever the child likes) on a plate. Invite your 4 - 5 year old into the kitchen and have him/her sit down at the table in front of the treat. Tell your child that you need to do something for a few minutes. S/he can eat the one treat right now, or if s/he can wait till you get back, s/he can have 2 or 3! Then leave the room and busy yourself for 7 - 8 minutes. If you can set up a video camera to record his/her facial expressions while you're gone you'll be able to watch that little brain working overtime!

Your purpose is not to tease your child, but to gauge self-control. Studies show that a child who can exert self-control at this age and tuff-it-out, did better all the way through school and eventually showed an average 210 point gain on SAT scores! Why? Because these children were well on their way to becoming 'emotionally intelligent.' Even at this very young age, they had already mastered their 'instant gratification' impulse in favor of 'I'll wait for the bigger prize later.' Remember self-restraint is a learned skill, so please don't admonish your child for eating the bait. If your child ate the treat, that's your signal to teach some self-distraction techniques such as: singing a song, playing with your fingers, reciting a poem, doodling with your finger on the table, or looking around the room. Work on his/her self-control and try a similar experiment again the following year.

Conversations With Dad

Dads are notoriously shy and nonverbal. I'm not talking baseball stats, I'm talking real life. Encourage Dads to go out with the kids, one at a time - for a walk, an ice cream, or a car ride and start a conversation. "How do I start?" they ask ... some suggestions: "Tell me about _____." "How did it feel to _____?" "You know you can tell me anything, I'm your Dad and I love you. What's buzzing around in your head?" "What are you dreaming about? If you could do anything right now, what would it be?" To keep a conversation going, have the kids try this: Answer the question and then extend the conversation by asking another question of the person you're talking to. Reciprocating not only conveys interest in the other party, but it is the polite way to converse.

Becoming 'Instrumental'

A study of 237 second graders, by researchers at the University of California, Irvine, (2006) found that those who received music instruction scored 27% higher on a fractions test than those who lacked music instruction. In a recent analysis by the Texas Commission on Drug and Alcohol Abuse, band and orchestra members were less likely to smoke, drink, or experiment with drugs. When the Princeton, NJ, based College Entrance Examinations Board looked at SAT scores, they found that young musicians scored 57 points higher on the verbal portion and 41 points higher on the math portion of these exams. But the best reason to learn to play an instrument is because it's fun, rewarding and will yield a lifetime of pleasure.

Expose kids to all kinds of music - from the Beatles to Bach, from birth on. By age 3-4 most kids can handle formal music lessons. Begin with the Suzuki method, which has a child learn to play what they hear much the same way we all learn to talk. Choose an instrument that's easy to master - a recorder, a violin, or a keyboard. Do you know that in Japan, every single kindergarten student in the country learns to play the violin! As a result the entire country has an appreciation of music, as well as the skills of focus and concentration which lead to learning and superior math skills. Decide on a regular time for practice - 10 minutes is enough to begin with. Practice should always be fun - if it's fun the session will grow longer all by itself. Ask older kids if they want to practice; if they don't, that's ok - they'll learn the consequences by themselves when the teacher is disappointed with their performance.

Adopt the expression, "Practice makes progress!" – Not perfection!

When your child is practicing their instrument and you don't think you can stand it anymore, repeat: "Oh, That was lovely honey, play it again."   *Andrea Grossman, Cranbrooke, B.C.*

Without music, life would be a mistake.   Nietzsche

Simple Division

Whenever there is something to be divided between two kids, one child should cut or divide it and the other child should choose his/her piece first. The real lesson is that in being fair to someone else, you will be fair to yourself equally; but if you are dishonest and cut or divide unequally, then you are the one to end up with less.

Pat Kracht, Homestead, FL

Only The Best! Why 'The Best' Isn't Always the Best Idea

We've all seen parents who insist on buying 'only the best' for their children (whether they can really afford it or not). The best clothes, the best toys, the latest gadgets and technology... But is it really the best thing to do? Let's say you decide to buy your daughter a ring for her birthday. Would you consider buying her a diamond ring? No, of course not. Why? Because diamonds are the 'best' rocks on the planet and we reserve this 'best' for a special time, place and person, to bestow it. In the same way, people need to have things to look forward to, to work for, earn, and to receive when they are really ready. As parents, we should learn to provide, but not indulge.

The happiest people don't necessarily have the best of everything;
they just make the best of everything they have.

Setting Goals

Rather than setting New Year's resolutions, try writing down a 'Gunna do it goal.' Begin by writing down one statement, which begins with "I will..." and the date you want it accomplished. Start by giving yourself one short-term goal - say 2 weeks. Once you have the satisfaction of having reached that goal, go on to a second goal.

Eye Contact

Making eye contact is so important whether you are speaking with one person or to a group. Eye contact forces people pay attention and focus on you and your message when you're talking. People will see you as confident, honest, assured and trustworthy when you look them straight in the eye. Children who are shy may find it difficult but it's a very valuable interpersonal tool to master.

Seeing Eye To Eye

I made it a habit to get down to eye level when speaking to my children so we could look each other in the eye. Even when angry I never stood over them. I didn't want them to be afraid of me no matter what I had to say. Being on equal footing, must have made me seem approachable because they have always come to me with all of their problems. Now both of my children are taller than me and things have come full circle. When my (six foot, one inch tall) son comes to talk to me, he sits down instead of standing over me! I guess he doesn't want me to feel intimidated!

Pointing In the Right Direction

My daughter remembers my shaking my pointer finger and lowering my voice instead of yelling or hitting when I was angry. We could be in a group of a hundred people and I would just shake my finger across the crowded room, and she knew that she was doing something wrong. It would stop her in her tracks.

Terms of Endearment

Using endearments and little rituals always helped then and now. I have nicknames for both of my children and still kiss them on both cheeks, even though they're all grown up.
Barbara Schwartz, Pembroke Pines, FL

On Taking Turns...

My neighbors and I have a great way of teaching our kids to take turns. If all of the kids want to play with a certain toy we get a timer and set it for 5 to 10 minutes. When the timer goes off the child playing with the toy knows his/her time is up, and the next child takes his/her turn. This practice has pre-empted so many arguments!

Joanna, Florida

On Discouraging Tattling

When your child comes to "tattle" on his/her sibling, listen intently to the story and then say, "So?" Usually the child will repeat it or give another version, to which you listen and say, "And?" If you continue to say "so?" or "and?" the child will eventually tire, get bored and hopefully cope with, or solve the situation herself. Obviously if your child is describing a potentially serious or dangerous situation, such as bullying or abuse, YOU NEED TO GET INVOLVED.

Linda Lentin, Hollywood, FL

Following Directions

Ask your kids to <u>direct you </u>in the car. This will not only make them sit up and pay attention, but cut down on the back seat hassles.

To further their brain organization skills: teach them to sew! It refines small finger coordination, has them focus on the task at hand, and has them follow a defined list of directions. Start with a simple pattern for an apron or tool belt. If the boys balk, remind them that Tommy Hilfiger, Armani, Ralph Lauren and Gucci all started with a needle and thread too - there's nothing sexist about fashioning cloth to fit human needs.

Once they're old enough to negotiate the kitchen, let them follow a cake box recipe, then gradually increase the degree of difficulty – encourage them cook from 'scratch.'

I Am Here

If you travel often for work get a large map of your territory, and show your children where you will be. This helps them feel that you are not quite as far away as it had first appeared.
Tracey Harris

Map Quest

To help your kids learn about geography and understand that there are different cultures all over the world, hang up a large map. Every time you meet someone new ask him/her for his/her city and country of origin. When you get home, find it on the map and mark it off with a high-lighter pen or sticker. We meet so many people from all around the world it won't take long for the kids to fill up the map.

Pen-Pals

I just read of a Philippine boy who maintained a pen-pal relationship with a Finnish girl for more than 35 years. How wonderful! Do kids even know how to construct a letter anymore? There is something to be said for the fine art of handwriting a letter, addressing an envelope, applying the chosen stamp and posting it. Then anxiously awaiting the response from someone who is around your age, who comes from a different culture and lives in a far distant land. The return stamp is always exotic, the paper and envelope design fascinating. Of course e-mail is less costly and yields the instant gratification of real time communication - but doesn't that, in and of itself, lose some of the pen-pal allure? Call me old-fashioned, but I still get a thrill when the 'post-person' delivers a piece of written correspondence addressed just to me. It's private, it's personal and it's prized.

When The Tooth Fairy Forgets

Have a crumpled dollar bill hidden in your hand as you pretend to look around the bed. 'Find it' on the floor... blame the misplaced prize on your child's moving around in bed!

Or come out of your room holding the dollar in your hand and explain that the Fairy got mixed up and left it under *your* pillow!

Or, explain that sometimes even tooth fairies run into traffic, have family emergencies or just don't get their 't-mail,' and that she'll surely come tonight ... then don't forget to deliver the 'under the pillow prize' with an apologetic note, perfumed and sprinkled with glitter!

I Can't Wait!

It's often very difficult for children to understand the concept of time. Especially when they're anticipating that something wonderful is going to happen. So whenever an 'event' is looming on some future horizon (a birthday, a trip, a visitor coming) try counting the 'sleeps' instead of the 'days.' Days seem to take forever to pass, but sleeps just fly by.

On Traveling

When traveling, keep a bag of "surprises" handy. When the child gets restless and fussy, pull out a surprise and the child will settle down and be a good traveling companion.

Children can enjoy museums, art galleries, concerts, etc. as long as you are cognizant of their needs. Teach the child about some of the art they are going to see or the music they are going to hear. Then, when they have had "enough", tell them how much you enjoy sharing that time with them and take them home, or to a park, or for a pizza. Children will enjoy culture as long as you know when they have had enough.

My son, at the age of 11, ran me all over Paris because his art teacher had turned him on to Van Gogh and he wanted to see every piece he could find. He taught me about art!

Enjoy every age because no matter how difficult you think the present stage is, it's going to get harder!
Betty Friedrichsen, Miami, FL

Avoiding Airplane Hysterics

Tell your kids that after you check in and get to the gate, they must run 10 - 20 'airport laps.' Find a relatively quiet area around the gate and have them run some laps between the rows ... the idea is to tire them out, of course, to release some energy before they get on the plane and are expected to sit quietly for hours. Hopefully they'll fall asleep once on board and the 'airplane brat' people sneer at won't be yours! Bring plenty of coloring books, CD's, cereal snacks and finger fruits (orange sections or dried fruits) for the ride. Expect to use 4 activities per hour plane ride.

- If you are going to be in an airport, dress your child in a very bright or fluorescent colored shirt – kids can get lost in the crowd and this will make it easier to spot her/him.

- If your child has a tendency to wander, consider getting Velcro handcuffs to keep her connected to you. Once you're on the plane, put them away.

Birthdays

Parties

Make birthday parties at home! When my little one was in the younger grades, I would make a carnival party, with stations. I set up games at the stations, like fishing for a prize, tricycle races, etc. Then I'd get the older kids to run the party. Little kids much prefer listening to other kids than to a shrieking Mom! The kids are still talking about these parties, and much prefer them to going out bowling (which I've also done!)

Wendy Chai, Toronto, Canada

A Dangerous Decoration

Every year a few children choke to death on balloons, but you rarely hear about it. Obviously balloons can break very easily, and if they burst 'in your face' – it can be disastrous. Once a small piece of plastic is jettisoned into the mouth, the force and speed of the plastic can completely occlude and seal off the airway. Unless one is prepared to surgically slash the child's throat to open the trachea and allow air to enter the lungs, the child will die within minutes. I hate balloons! Even the (slow to act) Consumer Product Safety Commission has regulations that ban balloons from being displayed with other toys, as a subtle way of informing the public that these decorations are not toys. Go with the crepe paper twists, and skip the containerized air.

The BD Ritual

Make your own family rituals for everyone's birthdays. We hang up signs all around the house and sing 'HB' at every meal, all day long. We also make a scrapbook page with a tracing of their hand and a picture of them to add to their book. (As long as you get their handprint within the year...it counts.) Use the book to write down some of the really funny things they say. When you look back and read over their funny sayings, it brings you right back to that moment.

Nikki Glantz, Ft. Lauderdale, FL

We always decorated the BD person's kitchen chair with crepe paper and bows, and had a small present waiting to be opened at breakfast. That started the day's celebrations in style! (What did we do before the advent of Dollar Stores?)

Re - Card

Recycle your birthday or holiday cards by cutting out the cute characters and gluing them onto colored construction paper or card stock.

Interesting Party Ideas

1) Do it yourself party - let the kids make their own decorations and sandwiches.
2) Cooking party - let the kids prepare a frozen pizza (add jazzy toppings), a salad and a cake mix. Presto – it's a party!
3) Come as a _____ party: (pretend you're a genius/a chemist/a retailer, etc) then organize games around your theme.

Interesting Birthday Presents

- Instead of the usual birthday present, try giving a one year magazine subscription. It's different; it lasts a long time, insures pleasure reading and it might just spark an interest in something new!

- Buy the child a beach or bath towel that features their favorite action hero. Pair it with beach toys or bath products.

- Buy a sleeping bag coupled with glow-in-the-dark stars ... then s/he can sleep under the stars any night!

The Stash

When you find interesting gifts on sale, buy them and keep them tucked away. Then you won't need to go hunting for every occasion or birthday party.
Jeanne Djaballah, Montreal Canada

The Gift of Time

Instead of giving a tangible gift, try granting a wish. Perhaps a day at the beach, a theme park, an aquarium, the zoo, a trip to the museum or a day looking around art galleries might be fun.

Going to Camp

There are things children can only learn on their own, from their peers and away from their parents. When your child is old enough (usually around 10 years old), consider sending her to sleep-away camp during the summer.

Spend some time discussing all the great things that she'll have the opportunity to learn and do at camp. And prepare her for some new feelings she may experience.

She may feel homesick – explain that it is natural to feel the loss of the familiar and the comfortable. But this anxious feeling is, of course, only temporary. As parents, we may understand that this discomfort may actually be a valuable immunization for the future. Life is full of loss and unaccustomed, difficult circumstances. Camp is a safe and controlled experience, with friends and staff to help her learn to handle these feelings.

Getting along with others, learning to compromise, becoming a team player, accomplishing new skills, becoming self reliant, and fitting in to a new and challenging environment are only a few of the valuable lessons kids learn when they're immersed 24 - 7 in this mini society. Camp is a good thing!

The Great Smoke Out

When my son was about 8 years old, I caught him and his friend sneaking puffs from a cigarette. I said, "If you want to smoke, let me help you. I'll teach you how to do it the right way!" I lit up two cigarettes and passed one to each child. Then I instructed them both to take huge, long, deep puffs. Of course they started to hack, cough, choke and feel sick to their stomachs. They only wanted to hand the smoking sick sticks back to me, but I said, "No, you really have to smoke the WHOLE THING to get it right." I sat there as they choked and coughed, getting sicker and paler by the minute. From that day on neither boy would ever come near a cigarette again. More is less ... a great lesson!

Betty Holland, Driving a Mobile Home around the USA

A Little Tipsy

A Bar Mitzvah (Bat Mitzvah for a girl) is a Jewish celebration, which marks a 13-year-old child's coming of age. First s/he studies the Hebrew language in order to read from the Torah (the five books of the Bible.) Friends and family are invited to the service and the child is called upon to either lead the service or take part by reading several blessings and that week's Torah portion. This ceremony allows one to be counted as an adult and accept the responsibilities of carrying on the religion.

We lived in a close community. When the first boy was ready to participate in the tradition, everyone from our neighborhood was invited to the service and the party later that evening. It was very exciting! At the party, cocktails were being served to the adults. More than a few Moms thought that we girls might enjoy 'tasting' a little whiskey sour, an apricot gimlet or a screwdriver … by the time the night was over I was more than a little drunk! When I awoke the next morning my head was spinning, I felt nauseous and wobbly. Soon my brain wanted out of my skull as it pounded and throbbed. This was my introduction to the delights of alcohol, and I was not impressed. Although no one had the slightest intention of teaching any lessons that night, I learned that drinking wasn't for me, and I've never even come close to being tipsy again.

When I see kids binge drinking and hear reports of alcohol-induced deaths, I wonder if my early experience wasn't a great blessing in disguise. The French have always included wine on their family dinner table. Children grow up drinking small amounts of (diluted?) wine routinely, and the French don't have any problems with teen alcoholism. Human nature seems to dictate that we always want what we can't have, and 'forbidden fruit' seems to be just too alluring. Maybe we should take a lesson from our French cousins and let them sip, so there's no novelty later on.

On a related note: There have been parents who provided beer and alcohol for their teenage kids' parties. After the party, when the teens were involved in drunk driving accidents the parents were rightfully charged with aiding and abetting a crime. If you provide the means, you will be held responsible. Teen drinking is a serious problem – don't encourage it.

A Sip of Wine...

As a first generation Italian-American I have early memories of drinking homemade wine mixed with orange juice at Sunday dinners. At family parties we were allowed to have a drink. As a teenager I watched my friends go to great lengths to acquire alcohol and then proceed to get falling-down-drunk or terribly sick. When I became a mother I did for my son what my parents did for me. Today I seldom drink and now my adult son never bothered with drinking as a teenager.

From: Newsweek, Letter to the editor. Linda Gennari, Cambridge, MA

Decorating Your Child's Room

We furnished our kids' rooms, with lovely pastel painted walls, matching bed linens and window treatments – very pretty and in accordance with 'Home and Garden TV' guidelines to be sure. But, if I had it to do over I might do one thing differently… I would consider painting one entire wall with blackboard paint and use it to print inspirational quotes, math equations, new vocabulary words, funny jokes, interesting facts, a picture of the solar system etc … and encourage the kids to "see the writing on the wall"!

I have included inspirational quotes and additional "Blackboardisms" throughout this book but there are scores of interesting and fun facts to be found everywhere.

Good Doggie?

Caution your children to steer clear of unfamiliar dogs. Many dogs look friendly but aren't - always ask the human caregiver about the dog's temperament before petting any canine, no matter how cute it is.

On Listening To Your Child

God gave us two ears and only one mouth for a good reason. So we could listen more and talk less. Kids really want your attention. Turn off the TV, computer, etc. It's not just about being in the same house, or same room, it IS about being present... Play! Play cards, play dress up, play ball, but PLAY. Be with them. Time is really shorter than you know. Listen to what they have to say. Don't put YOUR spin on it...really listen to their experience. Don't always tell them your story... let them tell you theirs. Elyse Brunt, Hollywood, FL

In The Mind of A Child

Kids are kids - what do they know? They exaggerate the smallest detail of an experience or snippet of a conversation and cling to those images for life. Of course we can't watch every word we say, nor can we orchestrate every scenario, but we can be conscious of the fact that our childhood lingers in our personality everyday of our adult lives. People tend to blame all their personal shortcomings and failures on childhood experiences. So be mindful of what you say and how you handle your children's mistakes. Remind children that we all make mistakes - but just like in the movies, when they film a scene over and over again, (and call it "take one, take two, take twenty three") we too get to repeat the experience (the mis-take) and hopefully get it right.

One way of getting 'it right' is to recognize the connection between actions and consequences. Alert to kids to the power they have choose between right and wrong when they are tuned in to the 'about to' moment. As soon as they feel they are about to lie, about to misbehave, about to talk back, etc, they have the power to stop, and change their actions.

Remind kids that life is like a coloring book - we all get the same colors, but what we draw and create is entirely up to us.

Over-Scheduling Kids

Sometimes we should adopt the Buddhist way of thinking and suggest to our children that they - 'Don't just do something, sit there!'

The Ten-Minute Warning

A 'ten-minute warning' that a major activity is coming to an end soon will prevent all sorts of tears.

Andrea Grossman, Cranbrooke, British Columbia

They Just Don't Know What They Don't Know!

When my son would ask why he couldn't have something he didn't work for, sometimes I would say, "No. There's no free lunch." or "There's no free ride." When he looked at me with a blank expression, I realized that he had no idea what those expressions meant! We discussed them and many other valuable old expressions too. Today he's proven that he understood the lesson of the work ethic - he worked hard enough to become a neurosurgeon!

Donna Jacobs, Weston, FL

More Proverbs to Ponder

It takes two to tango.
One man's loss is another man's gain.
Actions speak louder than words.
Silence is golden.
To err is human.
Seeing is believing.
Like father like son.
Home is where the heart is.
A rolling stone gathers no moss.

An apple a day keeps the doctor away.
A penny saved is a penny earned.
Finders keepers, losers weepers.
A penny saved is a penny earned.
A stitch in time saves nine.
It never rains it only pours.
In for a penny, in for a pound.
Curiosity killed the cat.
There are none so blind as those who will not see.

The MOMMY Test

I was out walking with my 4-year-old daughter. She picked up something off the ground and started to put it in her mouth. I quickly took the item away from her and I told her not to do that again. "Why?" my daughter asked. "Because it's been lying here outside and you don't know where it's been and it's very dirty and it has lots of germs," I replied. At this point, my daughter looked at me with total admiration and asked, "Wow! How do you know all this stuff?" "Uh..." I was thinking quickly, "All Moms know this stuff. It's on the Mommy Test. You have to know it or they don't let you be a Mommy."

We walked along in silence for 2 or 3 minutes, but she was evidently pondering this new information. "OH...I get it!" she beamed, "So if you don't pass the test you have to be the daddy."

"Exactly." I replied back with a big smile on my face and joy in my heart.

Let Them Make Their Own Mistakes

Of course you can't let your kids "learn" by experience not to stick a fork in the toaster, but there are lots of lessons they can learn on their own. You don't need to teach your children not to eat sand. The only way a child will end up eating sand twice is if you make a fuss and the child sees it as a way to get your attention.

When my son was 4 years old he inherited some pajamas from his girl cousins. He decided one pair of pajamas was a Spider Man suit. He wore these pajamas around the house constantly. One morning he showed up at the breakfast table and announced that he was wearing 'his suit' to pre-school that day. I told him he couldn't wear pajamas to school. He got very agitated, insisting it was a Spider Man suit and not pajamas. I finally had to tell him that in fact, they were Wonder Woman pajamas. I told him if he wore the PJ's the kids would make fun of him. This didn't dissuade him at all. He got even more adamant. "This is my Spider Man suit and I'm wearing it to school!" There are some things you don't need to fight about, and I decided this was one of them. His carpool arrived and away he went. At noon a much more subdued little boy returned home and said, "You were right, Mom... It's Wonder Woman."

He was much more trusting and interested in my advice after that.

Anne Feeney, Pittsburgh, PA

On Teaching by Pretend Example

When my daughter wanted to climb a tall fence I'd caution her not to by saying, "I know a little girl who tried that and she ended up with a broken leg, poor thing couldn't go swimming for a long time." I'd use this "I know a little girl..." tactic to dissuade her from doing things I'd rather she not do. One day she said, "Mommy, you sure know lots of little girls!"

Patti Glick, Hollywood, FL

Why? Why? Why?

When I was at that age when everything was "WHY" my Mom would say, "I really don't know because I had on a paper dress and it started to rain and I had to go home". At this point she would just turn and continue on another chore --- leaving me wondering why she "had on a paper dress". A thought provoking statement for a little two or three year old!

Connie Howard, Gainesville FL

On Child Psychology

Once when my son was very young and wouldn't eat his dinner, we nonchalantly removed his plate, divided it between us and ate his dinner. He must have thought we would continue to eat all his food - because getting him to eat was never a problem again!

When he tried coming into our bed at night, we applied the same psychology. We would lie down and spread out all over him, crushing him slightly and crowding him. When he complained, we told him that's just the way we sleep - he went back to his own bed and never ventured into ours again.

Donna Jacobs, Weston, FL

Honest Competition

Whenever we played checkers, cards, backgammon, chess or scrabble we all played to win... for real. We never 'let them win.' If the kids won it was fair and square and they knew it, which made the winning very sweet. Kids have built in radars – they always know when you're faking it.

They Do Run, Run!

When my two girls were eight and four, their 'big brother' Sam (our upstairs neighbor) graduated from high school and was heading off to college. His going away party was about to begin in the backyard when out of the blue my older daughter announced that if he was leaving, so was she. She was running away! We stopped what we were doing and talked about how much she would miss Sam, but that he'd be coming back to visit soon. First I tried to joke with her, then I tried to distract her, but it was to no avail. She got out a little suitcase and began stuffing her things inside, all business.

We live in an urban neighborhood, not far from a major thoroughfare, and I couldn't really let my eight-year-old go wandering off alone, suitcase in hand, to 'walk it off.' Suddenly I had inspiration - I just knew what to do: I calmly told her that it wasn't safe for her to run away by herself. If she absolutely had to leave, her little sister and I would just have to come with her. I let her finish packing and the three of us headed out of the house – 'my little runaway' in the lead. I didn't know how long this was going to take, but at least I'd pre-empted a power struggle and I didn't need to worry about her safety. We made it down the front steps and headed toward a nearby park. We hadn't packed any food nor were we equipped for a night out on the ground. I could see that she was trying to think on her feet but she was getting exasperated. Things clearly weren't going according to plan. Soon she sat down for a moment of quiet contemplation, then stood up announced that this wasn't going to work. We quietly filed back into the house, marched through to the backyard and joined the party in progress.

Deborah Silverstein, Cambridge, MA

This Too Will Pass

There were many months when I was tucking my son into bed at night wondering if Charles Manson's Mom had thought that he was just a little "high-spirited." Quite a few people thought I ought to medicate my rambunctious, extremely active son. I figured that as long as

I could get him to sit still to listen to a 1/2 hour bedtime story every night that there was no way he was truly hyperactive.

But then I remembered a wonderful story of a man who returned a Stradivarius violin to the shop. The shopkeeper said, "Sir, why are you returning this fantastic violin?" The owner replied, "I've tuned it and tuned it but the thing just won't stay in tune!!!!" Kids are like Stradivarius violins. Priceless and perfect in their own way, although they still require a lot of maintenance and fine tuning!

Anne Feeney, Pittsburgh PA

Powers

All kids believe that their parents are magical, omniscient and all powerful. When my kids were hurt, sore or had a headache, they would come to me and ask for my "powers." Slowly and methodically I would close my eyes, take several cleansing breaths, clap my hands together 5 times and then rub my hands together vigorously. The heat created would then be applied to the ailing part for several minutes. The ritual would be taken very seriously and with great reverence. Soon enough the soreness would dissipate or the headache would dissolve. Was my power magic or was it the power of love? Either way, it never failed to work.

The Mind Is A Terrible Thing To Waste

The mind is a terrible thing to waste – but we do it all the time. Teach your kids to trust their instincts and believe in themselves. In addition, teach them to respect and use the power of their natural, 'mind body connection.' I have reviewed hundreds of studies and authored a clinical study myself, which proves beyond any doubt that we can and do exert tremendous influence over our bodies by what we think, how we feel and what outlooks we chose to adopt. Our Mothers used to say that 'you are what you eat,' but it is much more accurate to say, 'you are what you think!' It has been clinically proven that 90% of all disease processes are stress related.

Together with your children, learn this simple meditation exercise:
Sit with your hands gently resting on your lap. Inhale slowly, with a relaxed belly. Feel your belly pushing out as you listen to your incoming breath. Exhale slowly while your belly flattens, and listen to your breath leaving. Perhaps you'd rather repeat the word 'good' (or 'peace,' 'one,' 'gentle,' 'calm' or any pleasant sounding foreign or made-up word.) You might imagine the personal space around your body as a bubble which you can contract or expand as you wish. Breathe into it and know that no one can ever pop or enter your sacred bubble without your permission. Be consistent, and invite your kids to join you and practice this mindfulness exercise daily, for just 30 seconds, or maybe just one minute initially. After a few weeks, when sitting still, deep breathing and quieting the mind have been mastered, slowly and gradually increase the time you practice to two minutes. Suggest to the kids that they can watch a clock and sit for as long as they are comfortable beyond the two minutes.

After a time, you may choose to let go of the key word and focus only on the breath: notice its differing quality when you feel stressed or at peace. It won't take long for you and the kids to notice several benefits; better focus, less anxiety, less fidgeting, and better health, to name just a few. After several weeks of practice you may notice that anytime you breathe mindfully, you will instantly feel at peace because you have linked the cues together in your deep subconscious mind. This is a very valuable technique for children to learn, because it will help them to remain calm during the stressful situations we all encounter throughout life.

In her book 'The Mindful Child' Susan Kaiser Greenland suggests we teach this mindful practice: Whenever we feel sadness or anger we should articulate the facts that provoked the anger/sadness and the accompanying emotion. I call it 'the why and the what.' Why am I mad? What do I feel? Put the situation into words. "My toy broke and I feel very disappointed." Immediately follow that statement with 2 or 3 things that you are thankful for or happy about. This teaches kids to recognize what is really happening and how it impacts their feelings. It also stresses balance and that not everything is negative, even when one thing goes wrong. What a terrific lesson to learn and carry throughout life! Remind your children that painful emotions are like unwelcome visitors; they maybe irritating for a time but eventually they will leave.

Another technique: When we feel down or frustrated, it's helpful to take a minute, enter 'our personal bubble' and imagine the breath swirling around the body like an eddy in a river, churning away illness or bad feelings, filling in those spaces with energy (or calmness) and happiness.

Sleep Ease

All Through the Night

Kids need more sleep than either you or they think they do. Jodi Mindell Ph.D., associate director of the sleep center at the Children's Hospital of Philadelphia, recommends the following: Preschoolers need 11 – 13 hours of sleep, not just bed-time; 5 – 12 year-olds need 9 – 11 hours, and all the rest of us kids require 8 – 9 hours of serious, brain refreshing sleep. Additionally, human growth hormone is released primarily at night, so tell your kids they must get to sleep if they want to grow!

Never put a television or telephone in your child's room, ever. I have never allowed a TV into the master bedroom either!

How to have your child go to sleep

Develop a ritual. Bedtime routines should be short and sweet – 20 minutes from 'toothbrush to tuck-in.' Once the child is tucked in, you need to control yourself and don't give in to whining, coming out, crying etc. Every child needs to learn the art of self-calming in order to fall asleep.

Say good night, reassure them you'll see them in the morning and leave the room. Then don't intervene!

Have a set schedule. Make bedtime early and be firm about sticking to the time. Children need a lot more sleep than they think they do. If s/he does come out of the room, march her/him back without any talking, put her/him in bed and leave. You can repeat this up to three times, then ignore her/him – completely! No amount of crying or carrying on should cause you to even look in her/his direction. You'll have to control yourself, but if you don't give her/him the attention s/he is seeking, s/he'll stop and go to bed. Remember – it takes two to tango – don't join the dance.

We had just such a phase … and miraculously we all lived to talk about it!

There are times when, just like the adults, children really do have a hard time falling asleep. That's when we used the "picnic sleep" method. Offer a 'sleeping potion' – a warm glass of milk with an added teaspoon of honey. (Do not give honey to children younger than one year old.) When you warm milk, the honey stimulates the release of tryptophan, (an amino acid used by the body to make the neurotransmitter serotonin) which promotes sleep. But over time the body can develop an immunity to tryptophan, and its sleep-promoting properties dissipate, so don't make this a nightly routine. (Don't forget to have her/him rinse her/his mouth with water after drinking the sleep potion.) Then prepare a picnic area: place a comforter and pillow on the floor, cover the child with a blanket and – bingo - s/he'll be asleep in no time. Sometimes just a change of venue, like sleeping with your head at the foot of the bed will do the trick. Or you might try giving her/him a soothing back rub with a 'secret sleeping lotion.' (Lavender scented body lotion.)

Walk softly into my dreams
And wake me not
Speak gently to my heart
And leave but a kiss upon my thoughts
Write words of comfort upon the wall of my soul
And leave as you came
And wake me not

Dennis of Ozyan Harman

To get my little one to stay in bed, I read her a story, then leave and have her to recount the tale to her favorite bedtime cuddly toy. I remind her to be very quiet afterwards so her baby can fall asleep.

Give Them A Pass

If you have a child who keeps coming out of bed, try giving him/her a 'one time pass' that s/he can use one time per night, to come out for an extra kiss, hug, drink, etc. Once s/he hands over the pass - that's it till tomorrow!

More Bedtime Magic

If you are having a little trouble putting your child to bed, try a little reverse psychology. As you leave the room, say, "Now I'm coming back to check on you and you better not fall asleep!" I would say this half seriously and then I would come in and if she was still awake I would say, "That's good, keep it up!" This way she never resisted going to sleep and we had a good laugh, rather than a fight at bedtime. We both learned that it's much harder to try and stay awake, then to try and fall asleep!

Marilyn Lerner, Toronto, Ontario

Lullaby and Goodnight

Some of the most wonderful times I experienced as a mother (of seven children and grandmother of twenty four!) were the bedtime moments when I sang my children to sleep. It was especially important when the day was very hectic or stressed. My children, all grown-ups now, still talk about those special memories and songs. The most wonderful question ever came from my grandson who once asked, "Granny, can you do this for me, forever?" Sadly no, he is now 6' 5" tall! But what better joy could a child, mother, or grandmother have? So I'll just keep singing (and rocking as long as they fit in my arms ...)

Jean Wenz, Newburgh, New York

Rock On

We would always rock our babies to sleep. Both my husband and I made this our priority. We never believed in kids crying themselves to sleep and we always cherished this time. We really believe in this calm, quiet time together at the end of the day. Kenny Loggins' 'Return to Pooh Corner' is our absolute favorite lullaby CD!

Julie Riley, Newburgh, NY

Happy Rituals for Bedtime and Naptime

Even when our boys were babies, my husband and I were sure to make bedtime a happy time. It was reassuring and comforting. We loved having the baby in the cradle next to our bed for the first four months and then we moved the baby into his own room.

The bedtime ritual included a bath and fresh pajamas, a story on our bed (usually "Goodnight Moon") and then Daddy would scoop up the baby and start saying 'goodnight' ... first to Mommy with a big hug and kiss and then the cats and the dog, then all the family members, wherever they might be. "Goodnight Grandma, goodnight Grandpa," we'd would walk around the house and say good-night to the rooms and the stuffed animals and then we'd stand in front of the window with the baby say good-night to the beautiful day. We always took our time, mindful of being calm and quiet...holding the baby close.

Usually the baby would literally fall into the crib...so HAPPY for bedtime.

As the boys got older... (3 - 6 years old) our once quiet ritual morphed into a playful game of "Taking out the trash!" Daddy would announce, "It's time to take out the trash" at bedtime. We'd take our son's favorite blanket and lay it out on the floor. Our little boy would jump onto the blanket and lie down...squealing with delight and anticipation, as we would gather up the corners of the blanket, pick up the giggling bundle, carry him upstairs and dump him out on the bed!

Sloan Wainwright, Ketonah, NY

On Staying Put - In Bed

I went through a phase of awakening in the late evenings when I was little, and it took quite a while for me to get settled back into bed. My Mother, who had 3 children in a span of 36 months, was exhausted at the end of the day and frustrated that her only quiet time was being interrupted. One day she gave me a children's magazine through which to browse, and in it was a picture of a Bride Doll. I instantly fell in love with its white gown and veil, etc. I asked my mother if I could pulleeze have the doll. She seized the opportunity. The doll was $13 and took 3 weeks for delivery. (Times and costs sure have changed!) If I could stay in bed and sleep through the night for three whole weeks I could have it. We marked the calendar each day with a big red "X" after I had slept through the previous night. Three weeks seemed like a long time but those red X's added up! Mom had ordered the doll the day I asked for it, and when three weeks had passed she gave me the doll I had earned. She got her relaxing evening time back; I learned about the calendar, delayed gratification, and good sleep habits!

Jackie Salvaggio, Lenox, MA

On Nightmares

With your firstborn, every 'first' is a learning experience and very often you just wing it. When my oldest son was 3, he started to wake up at 4 am in sheer terror. After 4 or 5 nights of the same disrupted sleep pattern (his and mine), I thought I had better give him the tools to deal with his terror. Before bedtime, we did a monster search, looking under the bed, behind the curtains, in the closet while verbalizing aloud our warning to any monster that might be lurking that he had better vacate the premises or face the consequences of our monster sweeping broom. After we had done a clean sweep, I told my son that the monster would not be back but he would now be equipped to handle it. That night I instinctively awoke at a few minutes before 4 am, but my son slept soundly through that night and never had night terrors again.

Nancy Engels, Montreal, Canada

Party With The Bad Guys

When my son was young he occasionally struggled with "scary dreams." Just before he went to sleep I'd sit with him and say, "Now close your eyes and picture those folks you were afraid of walking towards you... raise up your hand & say, STOP... I'm having a PARTY! Come with me, let's have some FUN!" I would then describe in detail the party scene and have him picture himself and all his new buddies sitting at one big picnic table, laughing, joking and eating ice cream. I'd tell him, "You're not afraid, you're having a blast... can you feel it?" He'd awaken the next day saying, "It worked- it worked!"

Annie Wenz, St James City, FL

School Days

Pre-School Smarts

It seems that lately our educators have unrealistic expectations of children. They expect 4 year olds to behave like 6 year olds. They want the children to enter school ready to sit still and have all the pre-reading skills they used to teach. Children are expected to know much more, much earlier. So be prepared. Kids should know colors, numbers and recognize all the letters in the alphabet before they step foot in school, so education must start at home. When you teach letters and numbers, make the lesson come alive. Numbers and letters can be exciting if they are attached to something tangible and tasty. For example, discuss the fact that there is 'one pickle on the plate' to illustrate 'one' and 'p'... talk about the meaning of 'one' and the taste and sound of the 'p' in pickle and plate. Use all the senses to reinforce the lesson; have foam letters and numbers to manipulate and see. Have large bold print numbers and letters written down, so the child can trace it over and over with her/his finger. Once s/he's really familiar with the shape of the symbols give her/him a highlighter pen to pick the number and letter from a page of large-print random letters and numbers (which is easy to prepare and print on a computer). When s/he can find the symbols easily, see how many 1's and P's s/he can find on a magazine page or newspaper page... kids love games. Go slowly, master one number and one letter (upper and lower case) a week.

Sandra May, of Boynton Beach, FL, has found great success using sign language to teach her kindergarten students alphabet skills. She wanted to find a way to reach kids who didn't respond to verbal or visual lessons alone. Now they have the additional benefit of 'speaking' a new language.

Starting School

Spend time talking it up, let kids know it's OK to feel nervous. This happens whenever we start something new, and it happens to everyone - even adults too! Bring kids to visit the school in advance. Tour and make note of the most important landmarks - the bathrooms, the playground, the lunchroom and their classroom. Begin the school wake-up routine one week before the actual first day of school. Have everything well prepared for the big day. Clothes, lunch, book bag, supplies, and the 'kindergarten keepsake.' If possible, arrange for kids to make friends and play with new classmates right away - being armed with friends will certainly reduce fear and anxiety. Send particularly anxious kids to school armed with an 'kindergarten keepsake' or 'anxiety amulet.' This can be a photograph, a small toy that you've smothered with kisses, a locket necklace ... anything that will keep a little piece of 'you' close by!

Have A Pick-Up Plan

Emergencies happen. As we saw, many children were in preschool, kindergarten and elementary school on 9/11/01 and their parents were unable to pick them up. Of course the schools did not have a plan in place for such emergencies either, at that time. Do you have a plan with your kids, schools and families if you cannot reach each other by phone? If you cannot return to your home, have a safe-place alternative plan ready. If you cannot get to your child's school, do your children know who to call, where to go and what to do? They should have a trusted neighbor's phone number, and a preplanned 'safe place' to go.

Secret Security Stash

Get (or sew) a small cloth change purse and safety pin it to the bottom of your child's backpack. Put a few dollars and emergency phone numbers in it, just in case.

Homework Buddy

I noticed that my son did his homework without any of the usual whining, complaining or procrastinating if he had a friend with him after school. Once I made that little discovery, I made sure that he invited friends to come over 'to play' at least two days a week. They seem to do their homework so much faster and easier when they're together and - miracle of miracles - the effect has spilled over to the days when he doesn't have anyone over!

Emily Chappell, Baltimore, MD

On Truancy

When your kids scream and cry, and carry on because they don't want to go to school, tell them " IT'S THE LAW!" ... and if they don't go, their Mother will go to jail!

Laura Morse, Bethlehem, NH

After School

The majority of modern families have both parents in the labor force, and three-quarters of Mothers are in the labor force these days. Yet after-school care and programs haven't caught up with the modern reality of working families. Did you know that each school day 40,000 kindergartners are home alone after school, and a total of more than 14 million children don't have any place to go after the final school bell rings?

MomsRising.org 7/31/07

In light on this astounding statistic perhaps you might consider organizing a playgroup and hire a high school student to supervise for the time you're still at work. Share the cost and rotate the home each week.

Homework Help/ Safe and Fun Internet Sites

A good informational Internet site that includes an encyclopedia, an almanac and a dictionary is: infoplease.com

Educators have created a directory of fun websites at: kidskonnect.com

Picking School Clothes

Arrange your child's closet so that there are two clothing bars. The top one should hold clothes for special occasions such as holidays, parties, Church, Shabbat, etc. The bottom bar should hold all the clothes the child can pick from. My daughters liked party dresses and fancy shoes. I went to an inexpensive children's clothing store and bought a bunch of party dresses and Mary Jane shoes. My daughters chose their clothing but I still exercised some control.

Another hint for having children wear clothing you feel is appropriate for school or dress - up is for the parent to pick out 3 acceptable outfits and ask the child to choose the one s/he wants to wear. Now you are empowering your child by allowing him/her to make the decision, but you have controlled the choices.

Ellen Adelman, Hollywood, FL

Dealing With A Bully

Kids should know that bullying is all about power - if you can retain your own power, you take theirs away. And once the bully's power over you has weakened s/he'll have move on to the next target. If your child has a run-in with a bully, discuss how best to handle and diffuse the situation. Explain that when we are challenged, it is human nature to either run or fight. But fighting doesn't mean making fists and punching; it can take a proactive and more positive form. It will be better for everyone if you can handle the situation with tact and humor... here are a few suggestions:

Befriend the Bully

If your child agrees, invite the offender and his parents over to play on the weekend. You can't be enemies if you're friends, and if your parents become friends it will be impossible!

If you want to learn to love better, you should start with a friend who you hate.
Nikka - age 6 (We need a few million more Nikkas on this planet.)

The more you shine your light on others, the brighter you will be.

The One-Word Solution

Practice these one word retorts in front of a mirror to get the desired effect: Say, "WhatEVER" or "Yeah." "Riiight." "Sure." "Wow" or "What?" in a very exaggerated, very sarcastic, very bored manner, coupled with an eye - roll. This subtle comment will diminish the offending verbal sting and show the offender that s/he's definitely not dealing with a wimp.

Buddy Up

Have your child team up with a friend to walk to and from school. Kids are rarely picked on when they present a strong presence.

If the Problem is Yours

If your child is the bully, don't shrug it off. Take this display of aggressive behavior seriously. Some parents might prefer to think that their child is just showing signs of leadership, but in fact this child is really demonstrating a need to dominate, intimidate and exert power over others which is obviously not healthy. Interestingly, it has also been demonstrated that some children who bully, do so because they incorrectly read the facial expressions of others. They often (mis)interpret other people's facial attitudes as menacing or leering so they react in a defensive, bullying way. Whatever the cause, the effect needs to be addressed.

Sibling Success!

A Brand New Baby!

When I was born my father took my brother to the hospital, stood him in front of the display window of the newborn nursery and said, "Pick one! She'll be your darling little sister." Once I, the new baby, came home and he started complaining about having to share time, toys and space with me, my parents would remind him, "Don't complain, you picked her!"

Shirley Apteker, Emerald Hills, FL

From Me to You

To ease the introduction of a new sibling and all the attention that tiny bundle will demand, buy the older child(ren) a gift and present it as a present from the new baby. Write a card expressing his/her dreams of having tons of fun, growing up together and sharing lots of memories. Sign it from the little one. The gift might be a camera to document their lives together, a stuffed toy or a T-shirt that reads 'Now I'm a big sister/brother!'

Evening Out the Sibling Joy

Consider keeping a few extra inexpensive gifts (books, puzzles, etc) tucked away to give the older kids when well-meaning (but forgetful or unthinking) visitors arrive, bearing gifts for the newborn baby only.

On Dealing With a New Sibling

My younger daughter was born with a dislocated hip, which required hospitalization and much attention to casts, braces, etc. My older daughter was already 7 and quite used to being an only child. Not only was there now a sibling, but a handicapped, demanding one. In order to give her some private 'Mommy time,' once a week we would "lunch" out and discuss a book that we both had read during the week. Talking about the book often opened up doors, so she could express her feelings about the changes in our family.

Marilyn Levy, Boynton Beach, FL

On Sibling Fights

When kids age 4-14 squabble with their sibling(s), don't attempt to mediate/facilitate/place blame. Take away any item over which they're fighting and have them immediately sit down on the floor facing each other (but not able to touch each other!) Set the timer for a minimum three-minute 'no-talking-allowed' time out. Three things are achieved:

1) The squabble is stopped immediately, and they quickly come to understand that when they fight they BOTH lose whatever they were fighting over.

2) Squabbling cannot be used as a tool to get your attention - you've set the timer and walked away.

3) No kid can sit motionless for long - my two began giggling, toe touching and their fighting turned in to a highly positive "bonding" experience! During one time out they named each other's big toes - and mentioning those toe names now still sends them into paroxysms of giggling!

Ask A Bystander For Help

If you need advice and you see a gray-haired old lady smiling fondly at your kids, while you're in a crowd or waiting in line -- ask her advice!! Tell her that yes, you know that "time flies, that they grow up fast, that you have to tell them you love them" (those are the pieces of advice I got very consistently). You'll flatter her greatly by asking her help with a specific problem or situation -- AND you'll have your problem solved! Listen to the voice of experience.

Susan Sweeney, Davie, FL

Stop Scuffling and Sing

When my children just couldn't stop fighting or bickering with each other, I had them stand on one foot with their hands behind their backs and standing face to face, they had to sing "The Star Spangled Banner." One usually fell over, and their argument seemed to get lost in the silliness of what they were doing. Now they both tell me that at the time they thought this punishment was so dumb and they really hated it, but in retrospect it actually worked quite well.

"It's Not Fair!"

When my kids were about 8 and 6 they started down the "It's not fair!" trail, and I found myself constantly giving long explanations about growing spurts and individual needs. I tried to explain to them that treating kids exactly alike would actually be unfair. One day my son had ice cream and cake at a birthday party and my daughter felt that I should make her a cake because "it wasn't fair that she didn't have any." I sat both kids down and told them that from that moment on, they were going to be treated exactly alike. They would wear boy's clothes one day and girl's clothes the next, including underwear. (That got their attention!) When one of them yawned, they both went to bed. When one was dirty, they both got a bath. When one needed a shot from the doctor, they both would get one. If one were sick, they would both stay in bed. If one of them did something wrong, they both would be punished. I hate to admit it, but seeing the horror on their faces was a little gratifying. I went to their bedrooms and laid out boy's clothes for the next day...that's as far as it got. They both agreed that being treated exactly alike wasn't at all what they had in mind. I never had to go any further. Now they truly understood what I had been trying to tell them. We had a long and meaningful talk about how treating someone according to his or her needs was a lot fairer. I never had that problem again. Once or twice, one of them started to say something 'wasn't fair' and immediately took it back!

Anne Hawn Smith, Fernandina Beach, FL

Pass Me Down Clothes

I know my older sister loves me because she gives me all her old clothes and then she has to go out and buy new ones.
Lauren - age 4

Each One Teach One

The best way to learn something is to have to teach it. Encourage the kids to help each other learn the ABC's, multiplication tables, spelling, etc. This sets the stage for the big sister/brother to shine, so look for the younger sibling's area of expertise so that s/he can be the 'authority' too sometimes.

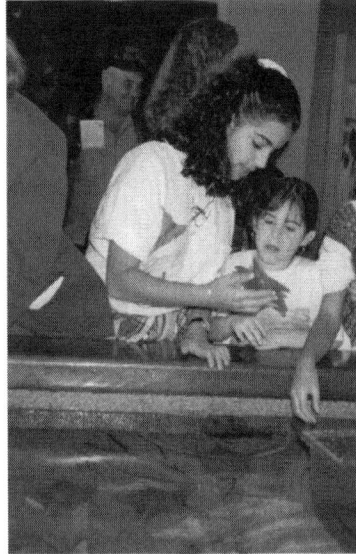

Birth Order Considerations

We always hear people say, "How come three kids all come from the same household and end up so radically different from each other?" Well, while they may be living under the same roof, their experiences are all different. Each child's environment is different because, as more children are added to the family, they change the dynamic. And of course, parents become more relaxed as they gain experience. More responsibilities and expectations are typically placed upon oldest children, so they may end up being the 'take charge organizer,' 'the responsible one' or 'the authoritarian, strict, bossy type.' Middle children generally receive less attention and are stuck in the middle of things. As they are often even-tempered, they typically are the 'pleasers,' 'good listeners' and 'peacemakers.' Youngest children usually receive the most babying at first, but the most freedom later. Sometimes, in an effort to overcome the perceived 'baby' designation, they become 'risk takers' in order to prove that they can be bigger than the others. Only children who spend a lot of time with adults often have more extensive vocabularies coupled with more mature opinions at earlier ages. Birth order doesn't guarantee that children will exhibit certain characteristics but it may accentuate traits that a child already possesses.

In a recent study, Professor Leong of Ohio State University demonstrated that birth order may play a role in chosen adult occupations. "One of the strongest findings was the fact that only children and first-born children tended to have more cognitive and analytical interests, while later-borns were more artistic and oriented to the outdoors." Dr. Leong says, "Parents typically place different demands and have different expectations of children depending on their birth order. For example, parents may be extremely protective of only children and worry about their physical safety. That may be why only children are more likely to show interest in academic pursuits rather than physical or outdoor activities. As they have more children, parents tend to become more open and relaxed, and that may allow younger children to be more risk-taking. If the first-born or only child wants to be a poet, that may concern parents. But by the fourth child, parents may not mind as much."

Your Child's IQ and You

A recent study revealed that firstborn children tend to have a slightly higher IQ than their younger siblings. However, if the oldest is removed from the household (due to death or relocation) then the next in line (who then becomes the eldest child) tends to score as high as if s/he were the actual first born ... "It is the social rank not the biological rank that counts," said Peter Kristensen of Norway's National Institute of Occupational Health. Which begs the question: Do we invest so much more in our firstborn children that we can actually influence intellectual development? Think about this ... especially when you tell subsequent sibs that you're too busy, too tired, or too occupied to pay attention to them.

Together Kids

Once a year challenge your kids to work together on a team-building project. You might give them a box of straws and have them build a bridge worthy of carrying a (predetermined) toy car. Or, give them an unlimited amount of newspapers and masking tape with which to build a house large enough to fit them all - complete with a roof, windows and a door. Give them a weekend or a rainy-stay-at-home afternoon to complete the project. You might want to have the kids repeat the same exercise several years in a row and note how their creations grow and become more complex. These exercises foster team work, spatial 'out of the box' thinking skills, innovative cooperation, compromise, fun, giggles, and best of all - great memories.

Life Lessons

Expectations

Expect your child to fit into the world.
Don't expect the world to adapt to her.

It's just not reasonable to expect the world to adapt to the presence of every new human who pops into the planet. Children need to learn to adapt, whether it's in your own home, a movie theater, a plane, a classroom or a restaurant. But how do you impress this lofty philosophy on a 3 day old? It's easier than you might think - just integrate your baby into the world from the get go. Don't insist on hushed voices. Continue to run the vacuum. Allow the doorbell to ring. Keep the TV on at a normal volume. Play some music during the day – and let the baby learn to filter it all out. Everyone has to learn how they belong and immerse into the bigger picture – taking their place, making a contribution and learning to accept from others – that's how we live. It's a general philosophy that can be taught from day one.

Expect 'truthiness' when s/he tells you a story... most of the time! And understand that lying/fibbing/confabulating is a normal part of the human psychological condition.

Expect honesty when s/he deals with others.

Expect your child to obey you. Don't "wish, whine or want" your child to pay attention to you – have him/her stop what s/he's doing and get his/her attention. Tell him/her what you want – to set the table or do the dishes, and make sure it happens – now, not later. Expect even your young kids to actively participate in family chores. We used to fold laundry by turning it into a matching game. Participating is contributing, and contributing is an essential part of feeling valued.

Expect generosity. Teach your child to be giving of him/herself and to give to others who are less fortunate in the community and the world. Get involved in a community project such as feeding the homeless and actively participate on a regular basis. This is particularly important for teenagers; kids who are actively engaged in doing something worthwhile that makes them feel important, while getting them some attention and positive recognition, probably won't get into trouble!

News Update: "The Helper's High"

The ABC TV program 20/20 (11/06) did a story highlighting people who donate their time, money, energy and 'give something back' to society. Scientists have now tracked the brains of those who were actively engaged in contributing and helping others. They discovered that these individuals' brains actually secreted more dopamine and endorphins, causing them to 'feel good' and wanting to continue to do good work. Brain structures are activated when you either receive a reward or give to others. "It's a spiritual buzz!" the scientist reported.

The smallest deed is greater than the grandest intention.
Quoted by Patti Labelle

Expect her to 'do the right thing.' Take every opportunity to help others, no matter how small the deed and soon it will be automatic.

On the other hand – do not expect a perfect child. Accept mistakes, imperfections and occasional stupidity.

Do not expect perfect grades, singing, piano practice, athletic ability or speech. Ask only that your children do the best they can.
Ellen Becker, Vancouver, Canada

Children are likely to live up to what you believe of them.
Lady Bird Johnson

Learning to Handle a Personal Crisis

Teach your child to expect the unexpected.

We never expect difficult situations to happen to us, but tragedies happen all the time, without warning, without reason, and they happen to everyone. The most difficult questions to answer are: Why did this happen? Why did it happen to me and/or my loved one? What meaning is there in this terrible tragedy?

I struggled with this myself and found some comfort in thinking about the balance in nature, the balance that makes the whole world perpetuate and the balance that makes up each of our lives. The yin and yang of life … There are hills and there are valleys. There are oceans and there are deserts. There is day and there is night. There is a time to plant and a time to reap. There are times of more and times of less. There are good times and bad, successes and failures. It's the price of life; for everything there is an opposite, just as all light must cast a shadow. Being human also means that to know great joy you must also know some sadness. I am a reluctant expert. (see: Our Story)

Kutenla, a Tibetan monk explains*: "We are born with the seed of joy. Every human being comes into this world wanting happiness and not wishing to suffer. The lotus grows in the mud. The lotus is the most beautiful flower, whose petals open one by one. But it will only grow in the mud. In order to grow and gain wisdom, first you must have the mud – the obstacles of life and its suffering. The mud speaks of the common ground that we humans share, no matter what our stations in life. Whether we have it all or we have nothing, we are all faced with the same obstacles: sadness, loss, illness, dying and death. If we are to strive as human beings to gain more wisdom, more kindness and more compassion, we must have the intention to grow as a lotus and open each petal one by one. All you need is the intention and the wish to be happy and it will be so."*

You never know what's around the next corner in life.

Remember that sometimes what happens to you, may actually happen for you.

While we may feel sad, angry and anxious about whatever situation we are faced with, the best we can do is:

- Face it. Don't deny the lump! Don't retreat into a darkened room.
- Grieve for your loss and know that you will continue to grieve, sometimes loudly and sometimes quietly, on and off for a long time, and that's OK.
- Seek advice and counsel from friends and the best professionals you can find.
- Seek out second opinions. Mistakes happen.
- Take time to digest the information.
- Do what your heart tells you.
- It is important to feel the support of friends and family; accept their gifts of love and listening. Accept help from the people around you. People want to help but often they just don't know what to do. Ask for what you need and allow them to help you just as you would want to help them if the situation was reversed. It's a 'mitzvah' - the Hebrew word for obligation or good deed.
- After the crisis has past, use the experience to make something positive happen.

If you are helping someone else through a crisis, learn to be a sounding board, a good listener. Be there for them. Listen to them talk and cry and validate their feelings. Just be there.

Never tell someone:
"God only gives you what you can handle."
"You're a special person who was given a special mission."
"Everything happens for a reason."
"Be strong for your family."
"You need to get over it."
"You need to find closure."

None of these statements are true. They don't help or comfort anyone who is in pain. In fact, they only make the individual feel targeted. Remember that even when people say dumb things, they are really striving to say something helpful. These phrases have developed over time and have become accepted, but when you are in pain you would much rather hear:

"You talk - I'll listen."
"Cry – it's ok. Crying washes your soul."
"I can't imagine how this feels."
"Whatever you need help with, please ask me."
"What can I do to help you?"
"I'll drive. I'll come with you to the doctor."
"I'm so sorry this happened to you. You don't deserve it."
"I'll help you get through this."
"My heart is with you."
"Take as much time as you need, hurt doesn't heal in an instant."

"Time doesn't remove the pain, but thankfully time dulls the pain."
"Whenever something hurts us in life, we have a choice to make.
We can become bitter or better."

There was a four-year-old child whose next-door neighbor was an elderly gentleman who had recently lost his wife. Upon seeing the man cry, the little boy went into the old gentleman's yard, climbed onto his lap, and just sat there. When his Mother asked what he had said to the neighbor, the little boy said, "Nothing, I just helped him cry."

What comes from the heart goes to the heart.   Yiddish saying

People will forget what you said, people will forget what you did, but people will never forget how you made them feel.   Maya Angelou

And one of the things we need to do as parents is let our children handle their failures – be there to support them, but let them handle it, because that's how they build the ability to go out on their own and face obstacles.   *Gray Whitestone*

Don't cry because it's over; smile because it happened.   Dr. Seuss

We're not human beings. We're human becomings.   Rabbi Irwin Kula

Life is forever in motion after all, never stopping, never resting, always moving.
                    Dr. Wayne Dyer

The best emotional advice for what we can't get over, or won't get over…
…Sometimes we have to cherish the past because it is the past.

I know someone who is afflicted with a cruel, debilitating disease. He is watching himself slowly deteriorate and become more and more dependent on others to look after him physically while his mind remains perfectly intact and alert. When asked how he manages to cope with this horrifying illness he said, "All of us are on a journey. I just have a better, more detailed map."

We are all wounded creatures, and we should recognize that scar tissue is often stronger than skin.

Strength is not absence of weakness but how we wrestle with our weakness.
                    Noah benShea

Talking About Death

Kids are not afraid of the unknown – they only fear what they're taught to fear. Have an open discussion and ask them what they think happens after life is over – you may be fascinated by their answers.

Sooner or later a death will happen... a goldfish, a dog, a friend, a grandparent. Life, as they say, is a terminal condition and ain't none of us going to get out alive.

Be honest and tell the kids that no one knows exactly what happens to someone's spirit after death just like we don't know where we were before our birth. Tell them that a body is just like a machine and that it can't go on working forever. Sometimes the parts break or wear out. Explain that although the person's body will stop working their spirit can live on in your heart, mind and memory. Your actions and those you touched will continue to touch others, just like all the people who came before us shaped our family and the world we have today.

Never tell children that death is like going to sleep – they may start thinking that going to bed every night is like playing a life or death roulette game. If someone close to them has a serious medical condition, don't tell the children of the impending death too soon. People can sometimes live far longer than they are expected to. So even though you want to be honest and up front, telling them too soon leaves the children anxiously watching and waiting too long. Better to wait until the death is imminent and they can clearly see that the message matches the picture they see in front of them.

We should be more interested in life before death than life after death.

Richard Gere

Looking Ahead - To When We Go

It's a fact - we're going to die, all of us. Some will know well in advance, some will go out to the corner store for milk and never come back. One day will be our last day. Dying is the easy part; being left to mourn a loved one is the hard part. Universally, most people wish to have had one last day or even one last hour to say good-bye, right a wrong, forgive or be forgiven. Most of us don't get this opportunity. So don't wait, sit down TODAY and handwrite a letter to each child and/or all of your loved ones. (I audio-taped my thoughts; you may want to videotape yours.) Share your treasured memories, remind them of their own special traits and how proud they made you, give gentle advice that they can carry with them and treasure forever. And remind them that you'll always 'be there' in their hearts. Put these sacred keepsakes in a safe and secure place and tell a close friend where to find it when the time comes.

You don't get to choose how you are going to die. Or when.
You can only decide how you're going to live. Now.

Joan Baez

What you leave behind is not what is engraved in stone monuments, but what is woven into the lives of others.   Pericles

And one more thing...

Now that you're a parent, you have a duty to act responsibly. There are three things you must attend to *now:* (1) Have a will prepared. (2) Fill out a 'medical directives' form also known as a 'living will.' (3) Seek the permission of those whom you would like to assume parental authority for your children should something catastrophic happen to you. These subjects were probably never mentioned in your childbirth classes, but it behooves us as responsible parents to look out for the welfare of our children in the event that we fall seriously ill, are in an accident or die suddenly.

Suze Orman also suggests that if you have a life insurance policy it should be left to a 'living revocable trust' where someone is named to look after the money for your child/ren. Because, as Suze reminds us; minors cannot inherit any money.

Nobody said parenting was going to be easy.

"For me, that's part of showing them love. It's taking care of them whether I'm here or not."
Diane Sidovnikov, a Mom dying of cancer, on finding adoptive parents for her daughters.

Raising kids makes most people, including me, grow up - at least a little.
                                                                                           Madonna

The most important thing you can give your children is - wings. You won't always be there to bring food to the nest.
                                                                                           Elizabeth Edwards

Using Pain and Sorrow

Remember that pain and suffering are inherent in the human condition. Because no one can escape being hurt, try to embrace it, make friends with it and ask, "What meaning can I derive from this? What can this pain teach me? Can I use it to plant the seed of compassion in my heart and soul? Can I allow it to help me grow and become stronger?"

Tragedy flows like a river, it takes a strong swimmer not to drown.

Life is a series of contests.   Andy Rooney

ARE YOU A CARROT, AN EGG OR A COFFEE BEAN? A teaching story.

A young woman went to her Mother and told her that she was tired of life's struggles. Every day, endless problems made her feel angry, frustrated and worn down.

Without a word, her Mother took her hand and led her into the kitchen. There, she filled three pots with water. Into the first pot she placed some carrots. In the second she placed an egg and in the third pot she placed some ground coffee beans. After twenty minutes of boiling, she turned off the burners. Then she scooped out and placed the carrots in one bowl, the egg in another and the coffee in a third.

She turned to her daughter and asked, "What do you see?"
"Carrots, an egg and coffee." the girl replied.

"There's much more." her Mother explained, "There is a great lesson to be learned here. Each of these objects has endured the same hardship - the boiling water - but each has reacted differently. The carrots were at first strong and unrelenting, but after facing adversity they became soft and weak. The egg had been fragile, with a thin, hard outer shell to protect its soft liquid interior. But after sitting in boiling water, its insides became tough and hardened.

But the ground coffee beans were unique .... They changed the water!"

When you face a challenge, ask yourself...

Am I the carrot that seems strong, but with pain and struggle do I lose my strength?

Am I the egg that starts out with a malleable heart, but changes when the heat gets to be too much? Does my shell look the same but am I bitter with a stiff spirit and a hardened heart on the inside?

Or can I be like a coffee bean - using the hot water to release its fragrance and flavor - do I use the circumstance to make something good happen? When the hours are the darkest and my trials the greatest, can I elevate to another level?

Author Unknown

Mommy Guilt

Jenny McCarthy describes 2 types of maternal guilt: 'Nine - Five Guilt' because you have to or have chosen to go to work, when you really feel that you should be at home. 'Choo - Choo Guilt' because you are staying at home but feel that you are going bonkers playing kiddy games and you'd give anything to escape. And then there's what I call, 'Flesh of My Flesh Guilt' stemming from having an autistic or otherwise ill child.

Regarding 9 – 5, and Choo-Choo guilt: if you have chosen to work or to stay at home to facilitate accomplishing a greater goal, then accept your decision and stop second-guessing yourself. If you want to change your mind about a decision you've made, then free yourself and change your circumstance!

If you have a sick child ... I do know exactly what you're feeling. People have asked me if I ever felt guilty (see 'Our Story') and the truth is - I did. But not because of anything I actually did or didn't do. Just because... I carried my child, birthed my child and gave life to this child; therefore I shared the scar of his affliction. Just like any proud parent who 'kvells' over their child's achievements and secrets a piece of that accomplishment in one's own heart forever... "My son is a doctor! My daughter is a lawyer!" Don't we all beam with pride when the little darlings do something great? And don't we all cringe with embarrassment and will the ground to open, so we can hurl ourselves into the abyss when our disappointing delinquents do something stupid? "My son got involved with the wrong crowd, sold drugs and got arrested." Then why isn't it obvious that we can feel equally, if not just as unreasonably responsible for their diseases, genetic imperfections or acquired illnesses? We had no hand in causing it, but we take ownership no matter what... 'guilty' as charged. It's irrational but it's natural.

Mommy guilt seems to be written into the job description, albeit in invisible ink. Let it go! It's OK to feel what you feel for a while, but ultimately it's more important to think rationally. Recognize the randomness of all our circumstances - "there but for fortune go you or go I." If you stop 'thinking' you are guilty, in time you can force the feeling to give up its power.

<u>Our Story</u> - Featuring a 2 wheeler, a 3 wheeler and a 4 wheeler.

This section was tortuous to write and it might be just as difficult to read. I debated whether or not to include this painful, private chapter of our life into this manual, but I will share my story with you to illustrate how easily life can surprise you and change your path in an instant. My purpose is certainly not to frighten you, but rather to give you a tiny glimpse into one heartbreaking aspect of parenting I pray you never experience firsthand. One day when your kids are driving you crazy, you may remember reading this and appreciate the precious, normal aggravations of parenthood.

Some stories begin with, "Once upon a time..." and end with "happily ever after" but that's not the way all stories end. May I suggest that you pause and go get a tissue? I think you're going to need one – or two.

As we walk the journey of life our personal stories unfold. So often we start out following a carefully chosen route, sure of our destination. We plan, we pack and we pore over maps. We learn the lingo, study the customs and anticipate the adventures to come. We set the GPS, turn in the right direction and trust we'll end up exactly where we intended to go. But for some of us, in spite of our careful preparation, we end up in a very different place. Because sometimes, in an instant, without any warning, things go awry and the road of life just crumbles beneath us - washed out by a sudden, unexpected flood. That's what happened to us. The road swerved, took a sharp turn and our family landed in a place no one ever chooses to visit.

We had a beautiful, healthy daughter and life was grand! She was sweet and bright, and we were a very happy little family. As we felt that three years was the right amount of time between siblings, we planned for and became pregnant easily. I felt wonderful and attended exercise classes, ate just right and took advantage of our glorious Florida fresh air. The main industry in Florida is tourism so there aren't any smokestacks belching chemicals around here. Everything was fine. At one point I did have a bad cold and remarked that the baby seemed to have stopped moving a lot, but the doctor said not to worry.

My delivery was right on time, quick, natural and easy. Our little boy was a good weight, pink and healthy. Just another ordinary, everyday miracle. We were delighted. But he was having difficulty breastfeeding as he didn't seem to have an adequate suck reflex. The doctor said not to worry.

We took him home. He cried a lot and was losing weight. I felt that something was wrong. I repeatedly took him to the doctor and pointed out his poor weight gain, his lack of muscle tone, his continued perinatal reflexes, his high-pitched cry – they did tests and told me not to worry. I was a Registered Nurse with many years of experience in neonatology, and I knew that these were the hallmarks of serious pathology. Weeks went by, and I kept going back to the doctor, my fears escalating with each visit. There were more tests and more doctors, and each one told me not to worry. But I knew something was very wrong even though all the tests came back 'normal.' It took almost two hours to feed Jordan; only gravity drained the bottle and feeding him solids was like taking one step forward and two steps back, because he had a tongue thrust which made swallowing difficult. He wasn't holding up his head. He wasn't turning over. Strangers would remark that he was "such a good baby" because he didn't move around or throw toys out of the stroller. And he was so cute! As time went on he became exceptionably beautiful, which may have contributed to all the doctors discounting my fears and continuously telling me not to worry.

When Jordan was almost a year old we went up to the Boston Children's Hospital. There, a team of specialists redid all the tests and although they too could find no reason nor give us any definitive diagnosis or prognosis, they did confirm our worst, and most dreaded fears – our son was indeed profoundly retarded and severely handicapped. The catchall diagnosis "Cerebral Palsy" is just an umbrella term meaning "brain injury." Well you didn't need a medical degree to figure that out; as the kids would say – "duh." The assembled medical staff was so caring and so gentle, but their poisonous words pierced our eardrums and hearts like shards of glass dripping with acid. We had spent the past year weeping throughout each day and sobbing ourselves to sleep each night but that day we cried so long and so hard that every cell in my body was shrieking in agony and burning with searing pain. And I remember feeling that my heart was actually breaking apart as it pulsed with sorrow and splintered with each beat. Whatever thin mist of hope we struggled to keep alive suddenly evaporated into the whirlwind of reality and despair. We would of course, lovingly care for our child but we also had to reconcile that nothing would ever be coming back – no response, no interaction, no snuggling, no hugs, nor any kind of demonstrable love, and no hope that anything would change, ever, in his future. Perhaps if you pause and think about this for a minute, you might feel what it's like to have a piece of your heart shatter inside you. It was like experiencing a sudden death. All our hopes and dreams for his life were dead, but our child was still breathing... he was caught, stuck in a life he couldn't live. The worst thing in the world had actually happened – to him, to us - How? Why?

Looking back, I realize that before we could accept what our son's situation really was, we first had to accept who he couldn't be, so we spent the next two years fighting his 'involvement' intensely. The medical community often uses the term 'involved' as a strange euphemism for significant levels of disability. We loved our beautiful little boy so much we nearly wore him out trying anything to make him better. All our tender hugs and kisses couldn't heal his boo-boos. There were no pills, potions or drops we could give him. No surgery that could cut away his problems. So we tried all kinds of other therapies: hydrotherapy 3 times a day in the pool, and countless hours in between spent doing physical therapy, speech therapy, spinning therapy, play therapy, patterning, and a form of behavior therapy developed by a doctor who claimed his method could rehabilitate people with serious brain injuries. And, there were always more doctors' appointments. I was lucky to have help. I cooked all of Jordy's food from scratch, confident that organic food would certainly help. Laundry was unending, as there were so many towels from the pool therapy and Jord's continuous drooling. We went to healers: some conventional, some not – several nutritionists, an iridologist, a couple of psychics and a rolfer - we were desperate, we would try anything. (Rolfing is a system of soft tissue manipulation, with the objective of realigning the body structurally and harmonizing its fundamental movement patterns.) We were also trying to be somewhat normal for our daughter, but we were failing. At one point I added up all the man/woman hours it took to look after our little boy – it came to 34½ hours a day! The stress and tension were unbearable. We were struggling with life. We were sad all the time. We had been sucked into the deep, black hole of despair. Someone described life in a similarly devastating circumstance like living inside a black balloon. It is the perfect analogy because while you can dimly see the world outside through the dark haze of your existence, you feel that no matter where you look your life has become dark, stale, stifling, claustrophobic and endlessly circular. You're trapped, totally encased, sealed off from normal happy life with no way to escape.

Sleeping was no relief either. All night I would endure nightmares as debilitating as our tortuous days. I remember one dream in particular… Jordy was standing beside our bed, wearing glasses, hair tousled from sleep but neatly dressed for school. He was whining and telling me to get up, complaining that there was a test today and he didn't want to be late… It was so ordinary, so mundane, so real. I thought, "Oh, thank God, I was only dreaming that there was something terribly wrong with him…" Then the cruel sun forced my eyes open and the tortured reality of my waking life began anew. I was exhausted.

We were disappointed, diminished, drained, devastated. We were living in a state of constant crisis. Sadness had become our new normal. If tears drops were dollar bills, we could have fed the hungry, clothed and sheltered all the world's homeless and still had enough left over to buy the crown jewels. David lost 40 pounds from his slim frame and he couldn't focus on work. Most people thought that surely he must have cancer. My spirit had been frozen and buried under an avalanche of pain. The stress hormones circulating in my body eroded fifty percent of the bone mass in my jaw, and my perfect teeth were at risk of falling out! I never knew that could happen. We were lucky that we had a very long, strong history as a couple and we were able to weather this tragedy together. Most relationships tear under the constant strain of this situation, and divorce is very common.

All parents want their children's boo-boos to heal quickly, painlessly and to leave no scar. But whatever had happened, however it happened, our Jordy's brain injury was obviously not going to get better. We began to realize that this injury was never going to heal, and that neither our devotion nor any known therapy could cure him. We were exhausting him with our efforts and disappointing ourselves. So much time and attention went into Jordy's care. We came to realize that he was going to need this type of intensive care around the clock, every single day, for the rest of his life. We also knew that our little sweetheart daughter was being short-changed. It wasn't fair. Slowly we began to face the fact that he simply wasn't going to get better no matter what we did, or how hard we tried. We started thinking about the unthinkable. Hesitantly we made the anguished, heartbreaking decision to find a permanent residential placement for our son outside our home. It was the hardest decision we would ever face as parents. It wasn't easy but eventually we found a wonderful care facility near Orlando. It was 4 hours away, but there just wasn't anywhere nearby that was suitable or could look after his medically fragile and substantial needs. Residential services are essential for individuals like Jordy, who have profound developmental deficits, uncontrolled seizures, severe spasticity, and profound cognitive impairment. They are totally dependent on others for everything, including their quality of life. The day we left him in the loving hands of others was the worst day of our lives – we felt utterly defeated. For the next 5 years we visited often and would call the facility every day. One day they asked us to give them a break and stop calling so often – but it was hard. Like a good friend of ours sings:

With You, Without You
© 1996 Amy Carol Webb (ASCAP)
Hear her great music at: amycarolwebb .com

I am with you even when I am without you
From afar I feel everything about you
Be still and you will feel my arms around you
For I am with you even when I am without you
Neither miles nor time,
Can keep your precious heart far apart from mine
For I am with you - even when I am without you.

Jordy's cognitive and developmental level was said to have been around 2 months old. According to the strict definition, he was in a vegetative state: unable to relate or react to the world around him. He could never lift his head, turn over, sit by himself, crawl, stand, eat, drink or communicate in any way. He didn't know us as his parents; he didn't seem to have any memory as we think of it... he lived quite literally 'in the present moment.' He was a true innocent. When he was young he would smile and laugh. He enjoyed music and would rock back and forth – especially to Elvis! And he seemed to be attracted to blondes! Go figure! He had the most beautiful hands. Long thin fingers that were meant to play the piano or violin – anyone could see that. And he had the most fabulous hair... It was dark brown, straight and shiny, thick and full, and it had the bounce and body that every hair commercial promises will come flowing out of their bottles. So we grew his hair long and donated his 12-inch ponytails (we did it twice) to the Locks of Love Foundation. His gorgeous hair would be Jordy's contribution to the world, proof that everyone has something to give. He had an easy demeanor and rarely cried unless he was in pain. He was exceptionally beautiful too, and in the profoundly involved segment of the disabled population beauty is a real rarity. The nursing staff fell in love with him, and they would often take him home - on their days off! It was as if he had been blessed with 40 part-time Mothers.

We resisted the physiotherapists' pleas to measure him for a wheelchair. Instead we kept buying larger strollers; but the day came when we had to give in – and that day I watched a piece of my husband's spirit wither and crumble, and disappear like dust in the wind. I have searched, but there's no way to capture in words the excruciating torture of a parent's conquered, anguished soul. Jordan was to be forever bound to his 4 wheeler.

Ultimately, after years of providing Jordy with superb care that wonderful residential facility decided to close its doors. Luckily a new, equally excellent care campus had just opened south of us. Instead of bi-weekly weekend visits, we could now see our 'sweet boy' anytime – he was only an hour away.

We needed to invest in life again and renew our spirits – we needed to feel joy again. We needed to laugh again: we had hardly even smiled in three years. We needed to have another child. We felt it would have been unfair for our daughter to feel as if she was an only child. I once read a greeting card that said: Courage doesn't always roar. Sometimes courage is the quiet voice at the end of the day saying, "I will try again tomorrow." So, we tried "not to worry" as we held our breath and had another daughter. I was OK until the day after her delivery. Then I fell apart … what had I done? What was I thinking? How could I have taken such a huge risk? Then, even as she began to accomplish normal developmental milestones, I was just a little apprehensive waiting for the next marker to be achieved. Not until she took her first steps across the kitchen floor was I finally able to really relax – she was fine! Not to worry…

Jordan died when he was 22. He lived a very long, short life. He suffered from seizures and was easily startled. He endured several complicated surgeries throughout his life; operations on his hips and legs, which necessitated wearing a body cast for months, and the eventual insertion of a feeding tube. His was not an easy or comfortable life. He died of pneumonia, which is common for individuals who don't move or exercise their bodies and lungs. We had been to the hospital, which was an hour away from our home, twice that day. About midnight the staff encouraged us to go home and get some sleep. They said it could take up to two days for the end to come. The emotional pain took physical form as the tension gripped my neck and shoulders in tight, painful knots. As I lay in bed reviewing Jordy's life and all that we had been through together, sobbing into my pillow like so many nights gone by, a familiar heaviness pressed down across my shoulders. And then, quite suddenly, there came an unexpected, spontaneous release. The vice-like muscle cramping and heavy weight that I had been shouldering all that day rose up, hovered above my head for a few seconds, and left. I glanced at the clock – it was 3:25 am and I knew deep in my soul, that our sweet Jordan had died. I said out loud, "It's OK. We love you sweet boy, go in peace." David had finally fallen asleep, so I got up and went to look through some photo albums waiting for the phone to ring. It did. Just like Amy's song, "I am with you even when I am without you. From afar I feel everything about you." The end came quickly, and he didn't suffer. And even though we had been preparing ourselves for twenty-two years, we weren't really ready. It was still a great shock and we found that we still had many, many more tears to shed. For a long time we mourned the son who should have been. Now we mourned for the son we had. We didn't choose this journey, but life had led us down the 'road rarely traveled.' No one signs up for misfortune. Medical science isn't as advanced as we think it is. People still don't believe me when I tell them that we never found the cause of our son's condition. It wasn't genetic or caused by a stroke or some exotic metabolic syndrome. All those tests never yielded any answers. In fact, he was reevaluated and retested when he turned twenty but still they found nothing. The doctors were clueless.

We did learn many things along the way. Like others who have faced tragedy, we learned that the best way to go from hurting to healing is to turn pain into purpose and focus your energy helping others. We have used our insights and energies to help other families coping with similar challenges. We were instrumental in a legal case which forced the state of Florida (for a time) to deliver much needed care to thousands of disabled citizens who were languishing on 'waiting lists' for service. We also established two statewide organizations and we continue to advocate on behalf of the mentally retarded and developmentally delayed. We made Jordy's life matter.

I learned a lot about myself during this period, and I also learned about how others respond. Some friends and family were amazing, open to listening. I know it wasn't easy to hear, to bear witness to our pain. Our real friends allowed us to cry while they held our hands and hearts. We soon learned that many people shy away from lending their support during difficult circumstances, just because they don't know what to say. They lack the essential human skills of just being there for you, listening and validating your heartache, offering you their love and quiet support. Some friends and even close family faded away. Disappeared. Were mute. I'd like to give them the benefit of the doubt and think that it wasn't for lack of compassion, but for lack of good communication skills and confidence. For them it was out of sight, out of mind. It was almost as if they could deny what was happening by not acknowledging it. But for us, the silence was deafening, and that was very, very painful. It took time to forgive them. Forgive – yes; forget - no. Because, when you've been seriously injured a scar remains, even after the wound has healed. It's just a natural part of being human. At the time we felt abandoned and isolated, almost shunned, because of other people's inability to cope with our tragedy.

Looking back I can see that we did go through some of the five stages of grief while our son was alive. The doctors participated too, as they were the ones in 'denial.' Then we took over – first experiencing anger, then bargaining and depression. Acceptance isn't really the correct word, as the human spirit always keeps a tiny glimmer of hope in the inner recesses of a broken heart. 'Magical thinking' is more accurate; maybe one day Jordy would fall, hit his head and be OK... Truth be told, you just get used to your situation but you never really accept it. And then, after the physical death, there's a rarely discussed sixth stage of grief: it's reserved only for parents of very ill or severely disabled children, and all the survivors of various types of abuse and neglect. It is also experienced by anyone who has witnessed a loved one suffer severe intractable pain, and all those who have lost someone due to various forms of dementia, as well as those who have endured years having someone's mental illness wreak havoc with their whole family's life. This quiet stage is called 'Relief.' To be honest, we were relieved to be released from our pain too, thankful that all our suffering was finally stilled. And we were relieved that, although our daughters would have gladly stepped in if needed, to look after Jordy's needs when we are gone, it wouldn't be necessary. Not to worry.

It may seem like an oxymoron but sadness and sorrow taught me to be happy. Let me explain. I recently met a lovely lady at a musical production. After an hour of conversation and getting to know each other, she (a psychologist) said she had rarely met a person as happy as I appeared to be. I told her my happiness was acquired at a steep cost. When I told her of our family tragedy she was astonished. I explained that I feel after you have endured a prolonged and severe trauma, all of life's petty disappointments pale in importance. It wasn't that I had become numb to life. It's just that life really isn't worth sweating the small stuff, and after 22 years of life with Jordan, I realized that almost everything is pretty small stuff. You also have a choice to make – you can become bitter or better. I chose to be happy. I chose to cherish every ordinary moment ... that's my big secret! Choose to be happy and enjoy life! You may have to fake it, at first. But somewhere along the line, happiness becomes a habit and a very good friend.

Jordan silently taught us to have patience, to accept (or at least stop fighting) what you cannot change, to rejoice in every human sense and sensation, and to jump in - participate in life! Help those who need help, and remember that you're only one breath away from needing help yourself. Life is a mystery, and we don't always find the answers we seek. And all those times that I was told, "not to worry" – no one taught me that lesson quite the same way Jordy did: no amount of worry would or could change anything. Most of the time, worry is a total waste of time and human emotion. Let it go.

The columnist Leonard Pitts Jr. wrote: *"Life is a dance on the high wire above mortality. It unfolds in the shadow of tragedies past and tragedies yet to come. There's nothing you can do about it except use the time in between to laugh, sing, hug, read comic books with your grandkids as often as you can. And try to forget that you are a wisp in the wind."*

Celebrate life. Appreciate all that you have. Love. Lighten up. Live it up. Laugh a lot. Learn to let things go. Love some more.

Our kids ride 2, 3 and 4 wheelers.

For those families, who like us are forced to travel down roads you never chose, in lands you never wanted to visit, I wish you strength, a path to peace and a way home.

Resource Guide For Special Needs

The Oxygen Revolution, Hyperbaric Oxygen Therapy,
Paul G. Harch, MD and Virginia McCullough
Describes a complementary treatment option for autism.
On the web at: hyperbaricmedicalassociation.org

Miracle Flights for Kids arranges transportation for children who must travel to find appropriate medical care.
On the web at: miracleflights.org

MUMS (Mothers United for Moral Support)
A parent-to-parent organization, to enable parents to share and exchange medical information, as well as the names of clinics, doctors, resources, research and regarding rare conditions. 1-877 - 336 5333
On the web at: netnet.net/mums

Exceptional Parent Magazine
This comprehensive magazine addresses the parents of special needs children. On the web at: eparent.com

VOR
This is a national organization to advocate on behalf of retarded, intellectually disabled citizens and their families. On the web at: vor.net

Making The Best of It

On Nov. 18, 1995, Itzhak Perlman, the violinist, came on stage to give a concert at Avery Fisher Hall at Lincoln Center in New York City. If you have ever been to a Perlman concert, you know that getting on stage is no small achievement for him. He was stricken with polio as a child, and so he has braces on both legs and walks with the aid of two crutches. To see him walk across the stage one step at a time, painfully and slowly, is an awesome sight. He walks painfully, yet majestically, until he reaches his chair. Then he sits down slowly, puts his crutches on the floor, undoes the clasps on his legs, tucks one foot back and extends the other foot forward. Then he bends down and picks up the violin, puts it under his chin, nods to the conductor and proceeds to play. By now, the audience is used to this ritual. They sit quietly while he makes his way across the stage to his chair. They remain reverently silent while he undoes the clasps on his legs. They wait until he is ready to play. But this time, something went wrong. Just as he finished the first few bars, one of the strings on his violin broke. You could hear it snap - it went off like gunfire across the room. There was no mistaking what that sound meant. There was no mistaking what he had to do. We figured that he would have to get up, put on the clasps again, pick up the crutches and limp his way off stage - to either find another violin or else find another string for this one. But he didn't. Instead, he waited a moment, closed his eyes and then signaled the conductor to begin again. The orchestra began, and he played from where he had left off. And he played with such passion and such power and such purity, as they had never heard before. Of course, anyone knows that it is impossible to play a symphonic work with just three strings. I know that, and you know that, but that night Itzhak Perlman refused to know that. You could see him modulating, changing, re-composing the piece in his head. At one point, it sounded like he was de-tuning the strings to get new sounds from them that they had never made before. When he finished, there was an awesome silence in the room. And then people rose and cheered. There was an extraordinary outburst of applause from every corner of the auditorium. We were all on our feet, screaming and cheering, doing everything we could to show how much we appreciated what he had done. He smiled, wiped the sweat from his brow, raised his bow to quiet us, and then he said - not boastfully, but in a quiet, pensive, reverent tone - "You know, sometimes it is the artist's task to find out how much music you can still make with what you have left."

What a powerful line that is. It has stayed in my mind ever since I heard it. And who knows? Perhaps that is the definition of life - not just for artists, but for all of us. Here is a man who has prepared all his life to make music on a violin of four strings, who, all of a sudden, in the middle of a concert, finds himself with only three strings; so he makes music with three strings, and the music he made that night with just three strings was more beautiful, more sacred, more memorable than any that he had ever made before, when he had four strings. So, perhaps our task in this shaky, fast-changing, bewildering world in which we live is to make music, at first with all that we have, and then, when that is no longer possible, to make music with what we have left.   This came as an email - author unknown

Gratitude can turn a meal into a feast, a house into a home,
a stranger into a friend.

Building Good Character Traits

Your "good name" is the only thing you will ever really own.

Make A Mench

The Yiddish word "mench" describes a person who is kind, generous and righteous... someone who does the right thing. We need more of them!

Rabbi Joseph Telushkin has written a wonderful book outlining qualities which build good character traits. I have listed his principles and added the predictive strengths which The KIPP (Knowledge Is Power Program) NYC Academy, Riverdale Country School, as well as Dr. Angela Duckworth, Dr. Chris Peterson, and Dr. Martin Seligman have outlined for their students. You and your child might refer to this list as a guideline to nurture character and help him/her develop a strong inner core of principles. This checklist is like a blueprint for a strong, moral code. Like the army motto "Be all that you can be!" if s/he can "BE" most of the attributes listed below – Wow! S/he will be a pretty confident, loving and wonderful person.

Becoming a strong, self reliant, good person involves the ability to ...

Be Spunky. Live zestfully! Approach life with excitement and energy! Participate enthusiastically, invigorating others to be engaged and activated along with you.

Be positive. Recognize that everyone has strengths and weaknesses. Try to improve shortcomings, but focus daily on positive attributes. It's easy to criticize, but catch yourself (or someone else) doing something right and praise the accomplishments and kindnesses.

Be respectful. Treat all people with respect and expect the same in return.

Be ethical. If you find that your 'ethics' conflict with your 'values' – do the ethical thing. For example, sometimes it's OK to 'tell on someone' when they are placing themselves or others in danger. Additionally, we all understand that it was perfectly acceptable for people 'to lie' during the Holocaust in order to hide and save Jews from certain death.

Be a fair person, and judge others fairly. Practice putting yourself in someone else's position and understand his point of view.

Be Optimistic. Expect that 'the best outcome' will happen in the future and work to achieve it. Get over frustrations and setbacks quickly. Believe that neither education nor any life experience is ever wasted, and every effort will improve your future.

Be courageous... and have the guts to do the right thing. This is a prerequisite for having good self-esteem.

Be honest. In the Midrash, it is said that when you get to heaven the first question that you will be asked is, "Did you conduct your business affairs justly?" Because if you dealt honestly in business with people you probably didn't know personally, then you were a truly honest person.

Be grateful. Becoming aware of and thankful for all the opportunities that one has, is both an art and a prerequisite for happiness. Develop the capacity to look around and inside yourself and genuinely feel grateful for all you have. Stop and think before you start complaining. Verbalize 'the positive' to counteract all the negativity that constantly surrounds us in our society. Recognize and show appreciation for others. Be emotionally generous by sharing in the stories, accomplishments and happiness of others a regular basis.

Be in touch with yourself. Learn self-control; regulating feelings and actions, as well as being self-disciplined. In school this is demonstrated by coming to class prepared, paying attention and resisting distractions, remembering and following directions, and getting to work right away instead of procrastinating. Personally, self-control involves remaining calm even when being criticized or otherwise provoked, allowing others to speak without interruption, being polite with everyone, and keeping one's temper and emotions in check. Learn to delay gratification. Work for what you want; you'll appreciate 'the prize' much more when you have earned it.

Be mindful and use common sense. Stop and assess the situation before acting or reacting in haste.

Be Curious. Take an interest in new experiences and learning new things for its own sake – the world is truly fascinating. Be eager to hear different music, taste exotic cuisines and explore new things, ask and answer questions to deepen your understanding, and actively listen to others.

Be honest about your shortcomings. Admit when you've done something wrong or hurt someone. Don't justify wrong deeds or rationalize. Don't call it a mistake - take ownership of the injustice, learn from it and then forgive yourself. When you argue, restrict your anger to that one incident and learn to exclude the words 'you always' and 'you never' from your arguments.

Be Sure to Cultivate GRIT. Grit is a combination of persistence and resilience. Finish what you start. Complete whatever you set out to do despite obstacles. Grit requires continuing your work even after experiencing some failure and working independently, with focus.

Be forgiving. We all get hurt, sometimes by life or circumstance but mostly by other people. This is understandable when you consider that we are all novices in life – and we keep learning as we go along. Remember that *pain is inevitable but suffering is voluntary.* By allowing one's inner voice to ruminate and repeat the injustice, we only compound the hurt, building hostility and resentment. Usually the person who hurt us is either completely unaware of their action or your reaction to it, or they don't care anyway. Even if they truly intended to hurt you, you are the one giving them the power, by focusing on their words or deeds. When you forgive someone, you don't have to have a verbal exchange with them, forget their actions, or treat them with unwarranted respect; you only have to release yourself from the grip of anger and sorrow they have planted in your heart and mind. It's as if you are removing a psychological rock from your shoe. No one else ever saw it, it only had the power to hurt you and now you've eliminated the irritant. Some say that true forgiveness is when you stop wishing the past didn't happen, or when your heart can say "thank you for giving me this experience because it made me the person I am today." Everything, no matter how horrible it was to live through, has a lesson - a gift hidden inside it. It is the sum total of our experiences that makes us who we are.

Be Socially Intelligent. Become aware of the motives and feelings of other people and yourself. Develop the ability to reason and find solutions during conflicts with other people and between groups. Demonstrate respect for the feelings of others. Know when and how to include others.

Be empathetic. Develop the ability to think and verbalize what it must feel like to walk in the other person's shoes, because we are diminished when we fail to evaluate another's plight.

Be patient with those who aren't as quick as you are either physically or mentally.

Be ready for change for change is the only constant there is in life.

The best index to a person's character is:
how he treats people who can't do him any good, and
how he treats people who can't fight back.
Abigail Van Buren, "Dear Abby"

Try not to become a man of success but rather a man of value.
Albert Einstein

No act of kindness, no matter how small is ever wasted.

Values are the main shield you carry throughout life –
they will protect you.   Queen Rania, of Jordan

Your take ...

BEHAVIOR

Words of the Wise

The following lists of incantations are extremely potent and powerful mind cultivators. Commit these words and phrases to memory. For best results, use these words and phrases liberally and at every opportunity. (Note: No ill side effects have been reported. Individual results may vary.)

Great!	Wow!	Well done!
Remarkable!	Fantastic!	I knew you could do it!
I'm proud of you!	Nice work.	Looking good! Beautiful.
You're catching on.	Bravo, you figured it out.	I love you.
Good for you.	How nice.	Brilliant!
Hurray for you.	Neat!	Way to go!
Super!	You're special!	Outstanding!
You're the best!	Excellent!	You're terrific!

Actions Always Speak Louder Than Words

Blah, blah, blah... sometimes we talk so much our kids don't hear a word we're saying. Often the clearest messages we send are not verbal at all - we teach by example. Model the behavior you expect to see in your children. Be happy, busy, engaged, honest and kind.

If Mama ain't happy, then nobody's happy. Fill the well of your heart, mind and soul. You can't give what you don't have.

Christiane Northrup, M.D.

Sometimes Words Hurt

Every time one of my boys said "I hate you!" as they were growing up and testing boundaries, I chose to hear "I love you!" It was hard to hear but I knew they didn't really hate me; they hated whatever restriction I was trying to enforce. Now, years later, they see the wisdom of Mom's actions and thank me with "I love you's" I don't have to translate.

Lisal Kayati Roberts

Happy Is As Happy Does

An obvious but often overlooked truism is that when we feel happy and comfortable with ourselves, we smile easily, behave and cooperate with others. However, if we feel unhappy, frustrated or uncomfortable, we sulk, throw temper tantrums and don't get along with anyone. Knowing this might help you to untangle some angry energy. Simply put, people who like themselves, behave themselves. Kids are people, so if they like themselves, they will behave themselves.

It's Not The Thought – It's the Deed That Counts!

So often we hear the adage 'it's the thought that counts' but I couldn't disagree more. 'A passing thought' doesn't amount to a hill of beans. Let's teach our kids that it's not good enough to think about it, or talk about it. In order to help someone, recognize someone or change something, one has to make an effort and do something! Lip service doesn't cut it. One of my children was always saying, "I meant to buy you a birthday present. I thought I would vacuum for you. I was going to do the dishes. Etc, etc, etc." But if nothing ever gets past the thinking stage … it doesn't really count, does it? We are judged by what we do, not what we think we are going to do.

Karen Jackson

Thank You

Every time we line up at the cash register, swipe the plastic and hand over 'the toy du jour,' we teach our kids to say 'thank you!' Half the time they say it automatically, without any understanding that it took an hour of (our) real work to earn that little toy/chachka/bauble. More often than not, we forget to teach gratitude for all the things in life that are truly priceless. Do we need to wait for Thanksgiving to get a break from the "Gimme, gimme 24/7 boogie"? Show and tell the kids that the most important things in life are not things at all. We can all do with less stuff and more time with each other.

The greatest things in life aren't really things at all.

Attitude Is Everything

The longer I live, the more I realize the impact of attitude on life. Attitude, to me, is more important than facts. It is more important than the past, than education, than money, than circumstances, than failures, than success, than what other people think or say or do. It is more important than appearance, giftedness or skill. It will make or break a company … a school … a home. The remarkable thing is we have a choice every day regarding the attitude we will embrace for that day. We cannot change our past … we cannot change the fact that people will act in a certain way. We cannot change the inevitable. The only thing we can do is play on the one thing we have, and that is our attitude. I am convinced that life is 10% what happens to me and 90% how I react to it.

Charles Swindoll

In German concentration camps during the Holocaust, there were a few men who always gave away their last morsel of food to other people. Perhaps it was an effort to prove that you have the freedom to choose your attitude in ANY set of circumstances, to control the only thing you can ever control in life - YOU!

You've heard it said a thousand times in a thousand ways, but it's true. We are what we choose to be. Kids may have a hard time understanding this concept. From a child's point of view, it must appear that they are totally powerless and just victims of circumstance. Children need to know that we all have the power to change our lives and what happens to us, any time we want. Of course some people are born into easier situations than others, but that doesn't necessarily mean that they'll be happier or more successful in the long run. We make choices every day, all the time and we can change the choices we make at any given time. Just walk away, hang up the phone, make new friends, join a different group, snuff out the cigarette, lace up your sneakers and go for a walk, eat right, read the book, order a soft drink instead of the beer or alcohol, stop the negative self talk and decide that you deserve to be happy. Life is not that complicated. Attitude is everything... it's all up to you.

What is not possible, is not to choose.   Jean Paul Sartre

You're not a bad person. You're a good person that bad things have happened to.

'Sirus' / Harry Potter

Food Can Feed the Fire

If you feel your child's behavior is becoming a problem, begin by looking at the fuel that feeds the fire. Nutritional diets which eliminate all processed sugars, wheat and dairy products have dramatically changed behavior in children, even those diagnosed with debilitating disorders such as autism. One such diet is the 'Gluten Free Casein Free' diet. Changing a child's diet is easy to implement, doesn't require a prescription or costly intervention, but you might consider consulting a nutritionist to make sure you are providing an adequate diet and adding vitamin supplements if necessary. You have nothing to lose but the tantrums or serious behavioral problems. Information at: gfcfdiet.com

Medical Update
September 10, 2007 — Artificial food color and additives commonly found in children's food increase the mean level of hyperactivity in children age 3 to 9 years, according to the results of a community-based, randomized, double-blind, placebo-controlled food challenge study published online September 6, 2007, in *The Lancet*.

Ultimate Success

Pop quiz! Are you ready?

What is the leading predictor of someone's life success? or relationship? or career or business success?

a) S/he seems to get all the breaks. S/he's just very lucky.
b) S/he gets along well with others.
c) S/he has a college degree (or equivalent) and is reaping the rewards of high academic achievement.
d) S/he really smart. S/he was born with an innate intellectual superiority (high IQ).

Well, this is quite interesting. When researchers looked into the personal histories of (many) different company's CEO's, they found that the great majority got there as a result of hard work, a certain amount of brains and luck, but most important of all was that they were very nice, likeable people. (If you answered 'b' you get a gold star!) To be sure there are some miserable, egotistical, power-driven bosses, but of those who started at the proverbial bottom (maybe in the long-lost mail room) and worked themselves up the ladder – they were helped along because their peers and employees revered and respected them. Why? Because these people are 'emotionally intelligent.' They have mastered the art of controlling their emotions, rather than allowing their emotions to control them. If a problem should arise they don't blow up, insult or belittle people; they resolve disputes with consideration and calm; they explore and respect the opinions of others and they make decisions thoughtfully. They don't necessarily have a PhD, or high IQ, but what they do have – we can all learn.

Clinical psychologist, Dr. Daniel Goleman suggests that we can teach the vital skills of becoming 'Emotionally Intelligent' to our children, and these abilities will pay off handsomely in many ways throughout their lives. (Check out his book Emotional Intelligence) Here are some of his ideas.

1) Optimism: The main difference between an optimist and a pessimist is what you tell yourself during moments of stress. The optimist sees the flaw in the circumstance. (e.g. "There were so many good people trying out for the part, I know it will be hard for the director to choose just one person.") The pessimist sees the flaw in himself. ("I stink at acting, no wonder I'm never chosen for a part.") But the good news is that if we point this out to our kids, they can learn to think like an optimist. If your child starts complaining that the glass is half empty, explain the better mental approach and when s/he understands the difference, ask him/her to change his/her statement by reframing it. The brain is extremely malleable and you can really 'change your mind' but (like everything else) this skill must be practiced in order to become second nature.

2) Empathy: Empathy is the root of caring and getting along with others. It's the human emotion that keeps us from hurting each other. When we identify with another's pain we learn to consider their plight. So, it's important to encourage our children to show understanding and nurturing towards their siblings, pets and friends. Even smart kids need to learn this skill

because there is absolutely no relationship between understanding something (intellectual intelligence, IQ) and understanding someone (empathy).

3) Social Skills: Every interaction with another person yields either a good, nourishing feeling or a bad destructive feeling. We all have the power to make each other feel better or worse. A person who is happy within will treat others well. Happier people are also healthier people, because the brain directs the whole show!

4) Handling Stress: Stress doesn't come from things that happen in life – stress comes from how you react to it. So learning to handle stress is vital. To handle stress you can; change the circumstance, change how you see the circumstance or learn to handle the situation differently. Goleman sites two studies, which point out that today's kids are more anxious, depressed, disobedient, angry and lonely. Apparently there has been a steep decline in emotional intelligence (EI) over the last two decades. How sad. But luckily, 'EI' skills can be learned and mastered, and because we know that repeated experiences actually physically reshape the brain, we can help our children train themselves to think and feel better. How? Point out the emotions the kids display. ("I sense that your feelings are hurt, which is making you feel angry and upset.") Suggest a cooling off period. ("Why don't you go play for awhile and we'll talk about it later.") When the child has had some time to regroup by him/herself, discuss the events and brainstorm ideas to remedy the situation. This scenario can even be taught to young children if you liken the process to a traffic light: Red – don't react, just stop and cool off. Yellow – proceed with caution, and think about the situation. Green – go and talk about the best way to handle it. These steps are the key to good impulse control. It has also been demonstrated that children who adopt this technique (now being taught in a few forward-thinking schools – hooray!) have much better academic outcomes. Why? Because these kids have been taught how to stop, focus, think through a problem and come up with a resolution. Of course this carries into other areas of life. They resolve conflicts, so they worry less, are more positive and get along better with their peers and teachers.

The Knack of Nagging Nicely

It's true: you attract more bees with honey than with vinegar. It's also true that dogs, kids, budgie birds and husbands can all be trained to listen (and act) if you offer them a few positive rewards and speak gently. Try using small incremental steps when teaching obedience "Put all your toys away and then we'll cuddle up and read a story together!" Then begin to decrease the verbal suggestions until all you have to say is, "Toys." Or, try using audible prompts: when you catch your kids (or husband) doing something right, reward them by making loud smoochy kissing noises ... they'll get the message loud and clear. Often we make the mistake of thinking that our families are mind readers; they are not, so if you want something done, be specific. "Take your sneakers to your room and put them in the closet." Using humor and visual aids often speaks louder than words do. A note or picture of what you want accomplished, left in an unusual place like a breakfast bowl, attached to the toothbrush or stuffed into a shoe, will make a much bigger impression than anything you could possibly say again (and again and again!). So instead of nagging, do the Mary Poppins thing, give 'em a spoonful of something ...

Learning to Focus

Attention Deficit Disorder may be a real, physiological problem for some – but for the majority of our kids, the problem is that they don't know how to focus. Like most other things we do, learning to concentrate takes energy and skill, and it has to be cultivated. Begin by asking your toddler to complete one task. Give one instruction and see that s/he accomplishes it. "Bring the ball to me." In time, you can progress to two-step requests. "Put your toys away and then choose the book you want me to read." Slowly build the complexity, allowing her to have to remember the sequence of steps she has to accomplish. Get her attention, tell her precisely what you want her do and **then don't repeat your instructions**. 'Focus' means zeroing in. Concentration means focusing, then listening, understanding, remembering and following through; devoting oneself to completing the task at hand. Make a conscious decision to let her do it on her own.

Concentration can also be encouraged by engaging in certain types of play – stringing beads, connecting the dots, finding the way out of a maze pattern with a finger or crayon – there are lots of skill builder toys. Always buy 'brain active' rather than passive toys.

Focus leads to concentration. Concentration leads to self-discipline. Self-discipline is the key to success – in school, in work, in life.

Consider "can't" a four letter word (and teach that to your kids). Amazing things can happen if you focus. With focus comes success.   M. Roizen M.D.

If your mind is scattered, it is quite powerless.   The Dali Lama

Try It! You'll Like It!

Momma said, "When in doubt, do the positive." A life of doing is better than one of regretting what you didn't dare to do.
                    Jeanne Marie Laskas

Some people spend their lives on the sidelines, watching other people actively living. If you try something and you don't like it, you don't have to do it again, taste it again or experience it again. My Dad used to say, "Nothing ventured, nothing gained." I say, "Jump in! Life is not a rehearsal." In the end you only regret the things you didn't do.

On Encouraging Independence

In my experience (I am step-mom, next of kin mom, childcare provider and soon-to-be adoptive mom), children learn through independence and frustration. Sounds strange but it works. Allow your child to continue to work out a problem (whether it's tying shoelaces or putting on his/her own clothes) even if you see him/her getting frustrated. DON'T intervene. Eventually s/he will learn to work out all these problems and become more confident and self-reliant in the process.

Additionally, if you jump in and 'help' you are silently screaming, "I don't think you are smart enough to handle this. I don't trust your ability to succeed."

When Bad Things Happen

Tragedy is both universal and random. Bad things happen. Life would be so much easier without the heartache. But wishing it doesn't make it so. If we Moms were granted one magical protection for our children, I think we would all want to shield them from pain and hurt feelings. But alas, the good fairy's power doesn't cover everything and so some pain is certain to enter our kid's lives. Therefore, the best things we can give our children are the tools they will need to deal with the inevitable.

If something negative happens to your child (or to you), it shouldn't be allowed to take over his/her thought process, fester and ruin his/her life. Too often we live out our entire lives haunted by negative childhood images. Ultimately, no matter what happened to us, we are still responsible for our choices and our own happiness. The first step is always choosing to overcome the trauma. Once we do that we can proceed. Here's a suggested roadmap to recovery...

Sit down and talk it out together. Explain that whatever happened, happened. No matter how terrible the experience may have been, try to keep in mind that it was a one-time ordeal and if you keep repeating it in your mind, you are in effect continuing to injure yourself long after the real perpetrator has gone or the incident is over. Ruminating is the worst psychological poison there is. It's like drinking the poison and expecting your enemy to die.

In order to heal oneself, you must make a decision: How are you going to allow this to impact your life, negatively or positively? Are you going to become better or bitter? Understand that it was not your fault. You didn't invite this misfortune and you aren't responsible for anyone else's actions but your own. The only way out of a bad situation (or crisis) is to go through it. Begin your healing by letting yourself feel what you're feeling – don't deny the pain. Never try to 'put it behind you' by burying your feelings. (Those repressed feelings may very well manifest themselves as physical problems later on; low back pain, intestinal problems, hypertension, migraine headaches etc.) Scream, cry and grieve for what happened. Then decide to overcome it, let it go and move on. Once you heal you will have gained something precious: a deep sense of control and self-reliance that will carry you through all the rest of life's hardships.

Sometimes what happens to us actually happens for us.

Research shows that if you can dissociate the negative image from your heightened emotions you can truly overcome the trauma of the event. To do this you need to change your internal movie of the incident; the things you see and hear in your mind. Our memories are much like Jello: while it's setting we have the power to make the memory stronger or weaker depending on how much adrenaline (which acts like a bonding agent) is pumped into the brain system. Try to block the rush of adrenaline immediately following a traumatic event, in order to

149

dissociate the memory from the feelings of the memory. Do whatever you can to distract yourself from thinking about the event: read or put headphones on and immerse yourself in some happy music.

In the days following, reduce the experience to its core, reframe it to find a positive lesson and rethink it from that point of view. Think, "The bullying/fire/accident/injury/assault/rape was terrifying but I thought quickly and I survived – I am so smart and so strong! Now I know I can overcome anything!" Focus on the positive and repeat your mantra "I'm OK now and I can overcome anything" over and over.

When you are ready, try recasting the original frightening image by imagining the characters involved as cartoon characters acting in bizarre and funny ways. Replay this new, non-threatening visualization and repeat the story/scene/memory on your mental movie screen, 50 - 100 times in rapid succession, until all traces of the hurtful emotions are gone. It is much the same as repeating a single word 50-100 times; it tends to lose its original meaning and it just sounds like gibberish - try it!

Step out of your history and into your present. Don't define yourself by one life event or one incident or one terrible 1/2 hour. If you get stuck in a bad head-scene, you will be robbing yourself of lots of good fun and pleasurable feelings, here and now. Learn to let it go.

Forgive the offender and acknowledge your newfound resilience. Then let it go.

This may sound simplistic but many say it really works. If you've tried to help your child (or yourself) and can't seem to get over the trauma, then seek professional help. A therapist will talk and listen patiently until the client heals himself.

A Mother is only as happy as her saddest child.

Sadness is a shadow sewn to happiness. It is life's inevitable garment, clothing all of us. And this is a truth not a reason for sadness.   Noah ben Shea

One thing always stays with me: the way a trauma in childhood – though the memory is so blurred and disjointed – can affect us deeply without our even realizing it.
                                                                                                Kate Winslet

Creating Competence

I always encouraged my kids to "do for themselves" and I made sure that they understood how things worked … from household appliances to cars. My daughter helped me change all the toilet tank hardware when she was six years old. Both kids were dressing themselves at 3 or 4 years of age. The more skills they had, I reasoned, the more confidant they would be. And it seems to have worked. Children who have no skills are much more easily influenced by others.

When my son was 4 he asked me "Why don't my clothes match?" The Mother of one of his nursery school friends had made a comment about how my son's clothes never matched. I showed him how to match his shirts and pants. Once he realized that he owned "matching" clothes, he made no effort at all to match them. He preferred to make his own (mis)matched duds. Competence and skills immunize kids from peer pressure.

The mystery of life is not a problem to be solved, but a reality to be experienced!
Vanderlou

Most things are difficult before they are easy.

Pin One On

Humans rely on visual cues all the time. The army bestows medals to be displayed as visual reminders of bravery. Wedding bands signal commitment. Uniforms signify position. Teachers use gold stars and stickers. Because visual cues can help motivate or serve as silent reminders, here is an idea that you can adapt to help your family speak and act in more positive ways. Buy 3 packages of (red, white and blue colored) plastic clothespins. Explain to your family that each time they complain, gossip, say something negative or rude, they will have to wear a blue clothespin for the weekend. After 3 offenses, the accumulated blue clothespins (worn on their shirt collar or sleeve) are replaced with the dreaded red clothespin. If they say something positive, they are rewarded with a white clothespin. The person who accumulates the most white pins might win a 'chore vacation,' an extra dessert or whatever you deem appropriate. The purpose of this exercise isn't really to win a prize, so much as point out how often we complain, say and do negative things without even realizing it.

Billie Lister, Swannanoa, NC

Loop a Love Chain

Once your kids become aware of their negative behavior, try going in the opposite direction by pointing out the positive. Keep a pen and a stack of 1" x 6" strips of colored construction paper in a designated area. Everyone in the family can choose his/her own (different) color. When someone does something nice, volunteers, compliments another etc. record 'the deed' on their color strip and loop it onto the 'chain of honor.' Hang the paper chain prominently around a chandelier, in the kitchen, or around a bathroom mirror – somewhere everyone can admire it for awhile. It probably won't take long for the competitive spirit to provoke cooperation, goodness and acts of loving kindness.

Decision Making and Making Choices

It is really important that children learn to make decisions for themselves. Growing up I was not given this opportunity and I had to work extremely hard as an adult to gain a sense of confidence. Even when my children were little, I would give them the power to choose. Whether it was what book they wanted me to read or what they wanted to wear, I tried to give them a choice. I found this worked beautifully, although I remember sometimes having to bite my tongue! My daughter tells me that she remembers never feeling frustrated because she always felt that her opinion counted. We rarely argued, never had to endure the "terrible twos" or had a rebellious teen phase in our home. When things went badly and they had a rough time - perhaps because of an argument with a friend, or a problem with a teacher - I was very conscious of not placing blaming. I tried to help them work it through in a way that would not compromise their convictions. I was blessed with intelligent, kind children but I do think that my giving them choices helped them to become independent and confident people. Children must know that they too have a voice and what they say matters.

Lindy Meshwork, Toronto, Canada

When Grandparents Visit

When grandparents, aunts, uncles or friends came to visit, I always insisted that they play with the children for a good long while before any 'gifts' were distributed. Discuss this with your visitors before they arrive, and ask them to leave the presents in their car until the appropriate time. Children should never associate 'getting something' as an expectation when meeting someone. Forming a relationship and learning to value the time spent with this person should be the priority. Introductions and welcoming hugs should not be a prelude to acquiring a new toy.

Nature or Nurture?

Why do people behave as they do? We've all seen this scenario play out a thousand times: Many kids, same parents, same household, same values, same upbringing – totally different personalities and outcomes. One explanation is birth order, another cites environment and then there's our genetic makeup - DNA. Forget what the scientific name is, my translation is Donated Nutty Affectations! Some time ago I realized that the strangest things are genetic. Weird things seem to be hard-wired into our human psyches. How else would you explain children who share the same (irritating) habits, voice inflections, mannerisms and idiosyncrasies as grandparents or relatives they hardly, if ever, see? Often these quirks skip a generation, so if your child is driving you crazy look around and see if you recognize a familial pattern. There is actually some evidence to back up my crazy theory. Consider all the research, which documents so many cases of twins separated at birth who end up choosing the same professions, marrying very similar personality-type spouses and then choosing the same names for their children. So often they live very similar, parallel lives. It happens too often to be chance so many of our thought processes must be hard-wired.

Which leads me to question some other personal thoughts and feelings. How much do we really understand about our deepest selves? If you have ever known a gay, lesbian or trans-gendered child, they will leave no doubt in your mind... we are all hard-wired (from birth) to be just the way we are.

"Birds do it, bees do it, even educated fleas do it." So go the lyrics penned by songwriter Cole Porter. In his day "the birds and the bees" generally meant only one thing — sex between a male and female. But, actually, some same-sex birds do 'do it.' So do same-sex beetles, sheep, fruit bats, dolphins, orangutans and virtually every other animal species. Zoologists are discovering that homosexual and bisexual activity is not unknown within the animal kingdom. "The homosexual behavior that goes on is completely baffling and intriguing," says National Geographic Ultimate Explorer correspondent Mireya Mayor. If you want to explain this phenomenon to children, the book "And Tango Makes Three" by P. Parnell and J. Richardson, relates the true story of two male penguins living in the Central Park Zoo, who loved and cared for each other and then hatched an egg together, becoming the zoo's first two-dad family!

This information begs the question; if same-sex attraction and homosexual behavior is normal in the 'natural world,' why are we so surprised that some humans behave just as 'naturally'? Sexual orientation is no more a choice than one's eye color. Playing with dolls will not make a boy gay anymore than playing softball will make a girl a lesbian. Kids know 'who they are' in their hearts early on. As an example, our neighbor's adopted son insisted on wearing his mother's slips and clothes. Even as young as 3 or 4 years old, whenever he was asked what he wanted to be when he grew up, he'd emphatically reply, "A woman!" He wasn't kidding or mimicking anyone (his father was a minister); he was just speaking from his heart. If you have a difficult time embracing 'the different' child who came into your life, remember the serenity prayer; Accept what you cannot change. As one Mother said, "You don't lose the child but you do lose the dream. If you love the child and want them in your life, find a way to accept what they didn't choose."

Hello!

Kids (and husbands!) have a burning need to talk to you as soon as the phone rings – ignore them! Maybe you'll succeed. I have told my family that unless the house is burning, they are hemorrhaging or having a heart attack, they can wait. (But alas, I've had to repeat this for the past 25 years!)

If the kids can't wait to get your attention, teach them to come over to you and signal you by touching your arm instead of screaming or whining. Then place your hand on top of theirs to show that you recognize they want you and you'll be with them soon.

The quickest way to get a child's attention is to
sit down and answer the phone!   Ginny Unser

Attention shoppers, problem on aisle seven... Dealing with Bad Behavior

When a child kicks up a fuss, is negative, nasty or uncooperative:
- Ask her to stop the behavior and tell her the consequence if she doesn't.
- Remain calm and quiet; be matter of fact in your approach.
- Remove her from the situation; physically pick her up or hold her hand firmly and leave the store, birthday party, sandbox etc.
- Do not give her 'a second chance'! (This is an invitation for escalating bad behavior!) Remember that it's not good enough to stop the bad behavior for a short time, when you really want to alter and change the behavior forever. Short- term pain will lead to long-term gain if you follow this advice. Do this correctly once and you'll never have to do it again. I promise.
- Turn your ears off and drive home in silence no matter how loud the crying gets. (It might even burn off some of his/her negative energy.)
- Once you are home calmly explain, "I'm very disappointed with your behavior. You were throwing sand even though you were told not to. Now sit here and think about how you may have hurt someone. Next time, I expect you will behave differently."
- Expect an apology with an explanation. "I'm sorry that I threw the sand, it may have hurt someone's eyes."

As psychologist Mira Kirshenbaum put it; expect an AAA - an Apology, Affection and a promise of Action. You say you're sorry for what you've done, or said, or hurt, or how you have disappointed someone. You immediately offer a hug, a kiss or a gesture of warmth and pledge to do something to make it right.

If you are trying to pre-empt negative behavior, try explaining what will happen if your wish isn't acted upon immediately, and then start counting backwards, slowly. ("If you don't start brushing your teeth by the time I get to 0, there will be no bedtime story tonight.") 5-4-3- .... I never got to 1 … sometimes I didn't even announce the consequence, I just started counting and PUFF - Thy will be done!

Remember that guilt and regret are necessary self-correctors. They are the roots of 'conscience.' So don't worry about causing your darling little delinquent some psychological pain, consider it a positive ego investment.

The trouble with our children is before they grow up...
And after they grow up.   Honest Henry Kranz

The Behavior Formula

"DGPPL" - stands for Discuss the Goals, Praise or Point out problems, but always Love them. Or you might think of it as 'Develop Good Personal Powers for Life.'

Here's how it works:

Discuss the desired behavior or goals together.

Goals: Have your child write down his/her goals, stated in the present tense. (Ex. "Finishing my laundry chores will help my whole family.")

Praise: When the task is completed, praise the effort and the deed and reinforce the accomplishment. Express your love.

or

Point out the problem: If the task is not completed, (or something is not done as you had expressly outlined, or you want to point out poor behavior) get your child's undivided attention. Look directly into his/her eyes and hold his/her attention. Eyeball to eyeball, slowly express your feelings verbally and make him/her feel pinned with discomfort beneath your glare. Point out how you feel, what you think and the consequences his/her actions will have on others. (For example, say; "I am feeling so mad and disappointed with your behavior. I'm seething with anger because you didn't finish doing the laundry and your sister really needs that sweater to wear in the play. When you are irresponsible, you make it difficult for everyone.") Hold your gaze - let that uncomfortable, distressing feeling sink in! Let him/her squirm for a while and struggle with remorse. Tell your child that s/he can, and needs to do better. Remember that a healthy dose of embarrassment and humility are good for the soul: They are the human vitamins that build character and conscience!

Love: Remind him/her that even though s/he 'did the wrong thing' that you trust that s/he has learned from this experience, and you know s/he'll 'do the right thing' next time. (Make sure there's a next time shortly after this experience, to reinforce the lesson and give him/her an opportunity to make amends.) Always end the praising or confrontation the same way - with a hug and tell him/her that of course you still love him/her.

S/he should walk away feeling badly about the behavior, but still good about him/herself.

_5, 4, 3, 2 ... 1_

When we hit the number 1, something that was 'thought' to be very important (video games, bike, TV show, etc.) was taken away. But I have never taken something away that made them 'feel' comforted. My 8 year old has slept with a Pluto dog since he was 3 months old. He believes he CANNOT sleep without his beloved "Doggie." One time he tearfully asked, "Mom, are you going to take "Doggie" away?" And the fear in his voice let me know that if I ever did take the beloved stuffed animal, it would be very traumatic ... and that is not something that I would ever want to do. So, even though I may have been tempted, I would never take that 'comfort zone' away from him. Your kids should not be afraid of you. You are the most important role model and teacher in their life. You are also the foundation of your family. Without a strong foundation, how will they be strong enough to build their lives?

Laura Gonzalez, Lauderhill, FL

1 – 2 – 3 ...

Counting worked well with my girls. When I asked/told them to do something and they didn't, I would start to count, slowly: "one... two... three..." I never made it past three. I don't know what they thought would happen when I reached five, for I also don't know what would have happened...but they did whatever had to be done.

When they deserved to be 'punished', rather that send them to their room, where there were toys to play with, they had to sit on the stair for several minutes, until they had thought about the situation. The stairs were a rather boring place to sit.

Sharon Fitch, Ottawa, Canada

... On The Other Hand

Expecting and recognizing good behavior sets the stage for a 'self-fulfilling' prophecy. If you speak the language of 'positive expectations' you may be surprised by the response because, deep down, all kids really want is our attention and approval. Think of it as making a connection rather than trying to control your child. For example, try saying, "I know you'll remember to walk the dog as soon as you get home from school. I am relying on you!" instead of "Don't forget to walk the dog, because if he has an accident it'll be your fault!"

On Discipline

My first child was a sweet little boy who rarely misbehaved and needed only a slight reprimand to correct his behavior. When I saw other people's children being unruly I complimented myself on what a good Mother I was. My third child corrected this misconception on my part by being very defiant and unruly despite my best efforts to control him.

I was raised in a "spare the rod and spoil the child" environment and this child definitely seemed like a good candidate for the rod; but, through trial and error, I found a hug and some love were much more effective for stopping a tantrum.

Graciela J Moses, Cooper City, FL

In my opinion, punishment doesn't work. It causes more bad feelings and damages relationships. What does work are 'natural consequences.' I highly recommend the (small, quick read) book "Helicopters, Drill Sergeants, and Consultants" by Jim Fay. It says it all. Time out and punishment don't work. I mistakenly used them on my eldest, who is now incredibly critical, rigid and a real perfectionist. He might have been anyway, who knows? I tried a different approach with my youngest. I have never punished him nor used a time-out. When he makes a mistake, as we all do, there are natural consequences that happen. For example, if he breaks something, he replaces it. If he does something to damage his relationship with me (e.g. lying or stealing -which haven't happened much) we talk about it and he is asked to make a repair - to do something meaningful for me; besides apologizing, he needs to 'make it up to me.' The same goes for others. If he needs money, he earns it. He is expected to contribute to the general running of the household without payment. Do I have to remind him and keep on him? Of course! But he does it whether it's mowing the lawn or helping with laundry.

Some people still believe that they can determine their children's abilities, interests, even personalities - that they are presented with a 'blank slate' and we have only to write their destinies upon it. Not so. It is important for a parent to learn their child's temperament and to work within that framework, according to his or her abilities and interests, rather to try and squish the poor little guy into some kind of mold, be it "Soccer Star" or "Prima Ballerina." My son loved guns and I deplore violence so that was out. However, I could not stop him from pretending to fire a gun, making pretend ones out of sticks, etc. But he also loved playing with "Goop," a cornstarch and water mixture, which forms a fun colloidal. And baking, so we did lots of baking.

One of the most important things parents can do for children is to help them to learn how to make decisions and to problem solve - which means allowing them to make mistakes (make the 'wrong' choice, if you will) and to live with the consequences of that mistake. This is what the real world is like. When parents 'make it all better' all the time, kids don't learn that there are consequences of their behaviors. They don't learn how to make decisions, and they don't learn how to solve problems.

Caryn, MA

I have learned that success is to be measured not so much by the position one has reached in life, as by the obstacles which he has overcome to succeed.

Booker T. Washington

How Rude!

"Manners" are what we as a society determine is a reasonable way to behave. For the last couple decades we have allowed 'casual Friday' to become casual everyday! Our society has become casual to a fault. Not only in our manner of dress, (take a look around the mall, people, we are downright sloppy!) but also in the way we treat each other, the way we expect to be treated and in the way we carry ourselves, use table manners and conduct our conversations. Because we've forgotten how to carry ourselves with dignity, we as Americans tend to laugh it off. But our lack of good grooming, manners and poor etiquette is no laughing matter. When did 'Please' and 'Thank You,' 'May I ___?' and 'Hello Mrs. ___' go out of style?

Manners Monday

Every Monday, at an elementary school in NJ, students enjoy lunch at cloth-covered tables, set with china and cutlery. The goal is to teach etiquette, and hopefully, the lessons learned follow the students home, into the classroom and onto the playground. Very civilized!

On Learning Self-Control

I had 2 little ones, only 19 months apart. I wanted to foster a loving relationship between my daughter and my son. What I didn't want was for them to learn to hit each other when they were angry. So we had "Drop Fist Drills" to teach them self-control before they got angry. Totally apart from a stressful situation, I'd ask them to act like they were really mad at each other and raise their fists (a real kiddie drama!). Then I'd say, "Okay, DROP YOUR FISTS!" The children would quickly let their fists drop to their sides and giggle. We had several training sessions, and it worked. I can't remember their ever getting into a knockdown, drag-out fight. Train your kids in obedience and self-control! You'll be glad you did! A peaceful home is a true treasure.

Kate Carpenter, Callahan, FL

The Grandmother's Rule

I think the one thing that worked best for me as a Mother and as a classroom teacher as well, was using what I called the 'Grandmother's Rule.' I used this long before I was a Grandmother or before I learned that it's called the Premack Principle. It goes like this:

"If (or when) you do _____ (something desirable), then we can do _____. (Something my son or students wanted to do.) "

Donna Ellis, Tallahassee, FL

Getting Comfortable With Being Uncomfortable

We need to teach our kids to get more comfortable feeling uncomfortable. So often we want to protect them and shield them from life's hurts, but it just isn't realistic. Feeling uncomfortable is just part of the human condition. Chances are that everyone will feel disappointed, frustrated, angry, sick or annoyed, pretty often – we may as well get used to it!

Susan May, Atlanta, GA

On Respect

Children seem to rule their parents today – a total role reversal. We must teach every generation to understand parental authority and to respect adult authority. Expect your children to call adults Mr. or Mrs. _____, or Aunt/Uncle _____. Do not permit your children to interrupt during a phone call or personal conversation unless it is an emergency.

Macki Feinstein, Hollywood, FL

Anger

We all feel angry from time to time – that's normal. A burst of pent up feelings erupt onto the surface of our psyche, and suddenly a torrent of words come gushing out of our mouths. Children who are taught to 'stuff' their emotions usually end up 'acting out.' If this becomes a pattern, in later life they may develop passive aggressive personalities. Children should learn that expressing their emotions (without hurting others with their words) is a healthy way to release their hurt feelings and they should never be punished for it.

Too many children never learn the art of self-calming. If anger becomes an issue, and your child is old enough to discuss matters, sit down and talk. Explain that no one else really has the power to make you angry. Anger comes from within and is a choice. Because before you can feel anger, you generally have to feel something else first: It may be frustration that something has not gone your way. It may be fear – perhaps something has scared you or you are worried about something. Or it may be that you have hurt feelings. If someone hurt you, you might want to hurt them back, but it doesn't work and rarely satisfies. If you can figure out what's really bothering you – frustration, fear or hurt – understand and deal with that, the anger you feel towards others will usually magically melt away.

Anger is a self-administered poison.
Try not to take a daily dose.

"Afraid" is a country with no exit visa.   Audre Lorde

Quelling the Fire: Learning to Control One's Temper

- Watch and become aware of what triggers your personal emotional fire.
- Try to imitate the calm, thoughtful behavior of someone you admire. Act as you imagine s/he would act in this circumstance.
- Notice the signals your body is sending you. Are your hands shaking? Are you experiencing nervous sweating? Is your gut getting agitated? Are your muscles tight with tension? Is your breathing fast or heavy? Mindfully dial back your response.
- Stop your internal fireworks. Calm yourself. Count slowly from 1 – 10. Breathe slowly and deeply. Say to yourself, "Relax and think about this."
- If you're still fired up - repeat these steps.

A Nail In The Fence (a teaching story)

There once was a little boy who had a bad temper, and he would say terrible things in the heat of the moment. His mother gave him a bag of nails and told him that every time he lost his temper, he must hammer a nail into the back fence. The first day the boy drove 37 nails into the fence. Over the next few weeks, as he learned to control his anger, the number of nails hammered daily gradually dwindled. He discovered it was easier to hold his temper than to drive those nails into the fence.

Finally the day came when the boy didn't lose his temper at all. He told his Mother about it and the Mom suggested that the boy now pull out one nail for each day that he was able to hold his tongue and his temper. The days passed and the young boy was finally able to tell his mother that all the nails were gone.

Then the Mom took her son by the hand and led him to the fence. She said, "You have done well, my son, but look at the holes in the fence. The fence will never be the same. When you say things in anger, they leave a scar just like these holes. If you stab a man with a knife and then pull the knife out, it won't matter how many times you say "I'm sorry," the wound will still be there." A verbal wound is as bad as a physical one.

Author Unknown

Trust Your Gut

Scientists have actually mapped the neurological pathway from brain to gut. So, if you feel 'a gut instinct' it's a very real 'mind – body' connection. Pay attention to it! Children are truly our experts in this area because they haven't learned to second-guess themselves. Let's persuade them to respect their intuitions and hunches, and listen to their feelings. If their hair stands on end, if they get goose-bumps or feel that something's just not right – it's our human alert system sounding the alarm! Trust yourself, go with it!

Worry

Stop worrying! We're safer now than we've ever been in all of human history. Lions and tigers and bears, oh my! Burglars and murderers and kidnappers, oh my! Food borne illnesses, viruses and swine flu, oh my! Killer bees, plane crashes and terrorists, oh my! Is it just me or are we being frightened to death? It's silly, it's sensational and it's irrational! None of these things are waiting to attack you or your children. The media hypes these anomalies to grab our attention and force us to keep watching. Let's face it – bad news sells, good news pales. We're becoming, no, we ARE a paranoid nation. Worry is only worth the energy if it serves as a preventative measure – a wake-up call to motivate us. If you discover a suspicious lump, don't sit there worrying; get to the doctor! If you need to worry, worry about things that really do endanger your children: car crashes, (statistics prove that more than 100 people die in car crashes every day due to unsafe driving practices like speeding, talking on a cell phone or texting, writing notes, or fixing makeup while maneuvering a 2-ton piece of equipment) smoking, drinking, poor eating habits, lack of exercise and medical errors. These are the real dangers. They cause more harm to more people than all the other implied threats. And you can actually do something about them... so take control!

Worry is like praying for something you don't want to happen.

Irrational worries and phobias regarding spiders, black cats and heights, are things that rarely hurt anyone - yet these things terrify people. Toxic worry paralyzes. So if you have (or are) a 'worry wart' try using some of these techniques:

Worry Proofing

Put A Lid On It! Keep a pad of paper, a pencil and a jar in a designated spot. Write down the 'concern' and think about it for a minute. Then stuff the worry into the jar, close it up and forget it. Or, use a similar technique called "The Worry Tree.' Allow the worrisome slips of paper to hang outside and let them disappear into the breeze.

Go With the Flow. If your child is a control freak, allow him/her to feel a bit of frustration when things don't go as planned. Which you can plan to have happen 'accidentally-on-purpose.' Respond with, "Oh well, it's fine just the way it is." Or "Good enough!" Practice imperfection... it's what we humans do best!

Start With the Ending. Look at the worst-case scenario, face it, develop a plan and (thereby) diminish the anxiety.

Let 'em Be Choosy! When we say, "I should..." aren't we really saying that we should do something because it's what somebody else wants us to? But when we say, "I choose to..." we are taking control, doing what pleases us for all the right reasons, so the words themselves become empowering. Words are powerful, so have your child get in the habit of owning their decisions by stating what they are choosing to do.

Go Exploring. When your child has a small worry, ask, "So what?" Let him explore what alternatives solutions there might be or what the big deal would be if things didn't work out so well.

Stand In the Flood. Begin by stating your fear out loud and repeat it 100 times. "I'm afraid of cats." Then escalate the statement by saying, "I want to hold a cat and be licked by a cat." Repeat this statement 100 times. Practice 15-30 minutes a day. Repeating the thought may actually make it less frightening because you get bored and acclimatized to it.

> Worrying is as effective as trying to solve an algebra equation
> by chewing bubble gum.   Kurt Vonnegut

> A day of worry is more exhausting than a day of work.   John Lubbock

Fear

FEAR = False Evidence Appearing Real. Simple, right? Yet, when we're in the grip of fear, the logic (or illogic) of it is completely beside the point. Fear cripples us. It fills us with the quaking, heart-pounding, voice-shaking inability to move. And sometimes it undermines us in very subtle ways.   *Debra Russell and Wendy Keilin*

All children under the age of two are afraid of sudden sounds, strange new objects, the loss of physical support and pain. These fears are hardwired and universal regardless of culture or ethnicity. They are inborn and disappear spontaneously after the age of two. Older kids tend to be afraid of dark places, high places, strangers who appear to be angry or menacing, sudden noises and snakes. But most of the time these fears also dissipate with time.

Good fear means 'listening to your gut' and reacting accordingly. If you feel instinctively that something isn't right – it isn't. Kids should know that it's ok to pay attention and run from the situation or person. This is teaching kids to be street smart: becoming aware of one's surroundings, determining what people's true intentions are or judging the safety of a situation.

Most other fears are generated from our imaginations. The emotion is usually based on some real or observed situation, TV show, book, conversation or implied event. The threat becomes magnified in our minds and if left unchecked, the fear can become paralyzing. Try to show your child that his/her fear is unfounded and then have him/her face it. There is a marvelous children's book "Harry and the Terrible Whatzit" by Dick Gackenbach that teaches this lesson very effectively. It involves a young boy who was afraid to go down into his basement for fear of the monster who lived in the clothes dryer. When he finally confronted the monster it shrank and shrank until the only way it could survive was to go live in someone else's house. The moral being things are rarely as bad as we imagine them to be and once we face our fears head on, we can control them. Our fears only have the power we give them. Fear is an emotion. Courage is a skill. Perception is indeed reality. And while it may be impossible to be completely fearless, it is certainly possible to fear less!

My mother used to say, "Yesterday no tears, tomorrow no fears."   Dan Rather

Courage is not the absence of fear, but rather the judgment that something else is more important than fear.   Ambrose Redmoon

Eleanor Roosevelt suggested that you do something that scares you every day. Fear gives us the gift of wisdom. It makes us work harder than we imagined we could.

Offer Positive Choices

Humans pride themselves on their ability to think and exercise free will. As parents, we often try to channel that 'will' to conform to our idea of what we would like our children to do. Sometimes this leads to conflict – starting at around age 2, when children figure out that they too can think! Kids, like adults, don't like to feel challenged. A tug of wills can be easily avoided if you develop the habit of offering easy, positive choices. "Which dress would you like to wear today, this one or that one?" "Do you want a pony tail or braids?" "Would you like a bath now or in 5 minutes?" "Are you going to do your homework or clean your room before dinner?" Either answer will suffice, and the decision is theirs, so there's no fight. Easy. Using this method, one of our kids slept through the 'terrible two's' one afternoon and the other stamped her foot for a couple of days.

Habit Control

I am your constant companion.
I am your greatest asset or heaviest burden.
I will push you up to success or down to disappointment.
I am at your command.

Half the things you do might just as well be turned over to me,
For I can do them quickly, correctly, and profitably.
I am easily managed, just be firm with me.

Those who are great, I have made great.
Those who are failures, I have made failures.
I am not a machine, though I work with the precision of a
machine and the intelligence of a person.

You can run me for profit, or you can run me for ruin.
Show me how you want it done. Educate me. Train me.
Lead me. Reward me.
And I will then...do it automatically.
I am your servant.
Who am I?
I am a habit.

The author of the above is unknown, but the words are right on target. If you set out to develop good habits, they will help you. But like the weeds in a garden, bad habits can take over your life.

Breaking Bad Habits - The D and C Method

A habit is a repeated action which supplies some comfort or satisfaction. But as we all know, once a bad habit is acquired it's very tough to lose. Tough but not impossible! The best way to stop a bad habit is (of course) not to start it. So if you see your child doing something you'd prefer not to see continued, get him involved in a different activity or action. If the habit is already entrenched (thumb sucking, nail biting, hair twirling, blanket clinging, etc.), the best we humans can do is replace a bad habit with a new, better or healthier habit. The D and C Method: Distract and Change. As a hypnotherapist, I have helped many clients break habits by counseling them to change several things relating to the action and not to focus on just the one behavior.

For example - for nail biters: Begin with a discussion of how hands speak for a person and how we should value all the things our hands and fingers do for us. Name 5-10 things and write them down. Discuss the consequences of not stopping the bad habit. For example: stubby looking fingers, bloody, jagged, painful cuticles, and possible infection. Talk about how we should look after and prize our hands and fingers because they are our most important human tools. When your child agrees that s/he wants to stop nail biting, take action; use brightly colored nail polish, lots of heavily perfumed hand lotion and allow one fingernail only that can still be chomped. It probably won't be, but allowing 'a safety hatch' nail relieves the pressure. Adorn several fingers on both hands with rings. Visual cues are important reminders that fingers are beautiful and special and need to be respected. Compliment her on her resolve, willpower, maturity and lovely hands! This method works equally well for boys, just use clear polish and have him wear a bracelet on each wrist, or rings on his index fingers and thumbs. Then encourage a replacement behavior: knitting, crocheting, doodling or sketching, whittling or manipulating beads or a bracelet, anything to keep those fingers busy for awhile.

Sometimes you need an additional verbal reminder, so agree on a catch phrase or word or hum a tune to signal 'stop doing what you're doing.' Don't bug - just use your auditory reminder. Don't expect success overnight: it takes only 7 – 10 repetitive actions to develop a habit but much longer to suspend or replace it.

Good Habits

Not all habits are bad. In fact some habits are well worth cultivating. Put your keys, purse and glasses in the same designated spot each and every time you come home. Get your kids to put their backpacks, books and homework in the same place all the time. This cuts down on last- minute search parties! Brush your teeth and your kid's teeth (start as soon as you see the first one) 'only as long as you want to keep them,' as every dentist office's plaque says. Take a multi-vitamin everyday whether you need it or not. Go to bed at the same time every night. Do good deeds, no matter how small, as a matter of course.

See it, do it, nothing to it!

The Aladdin Principle

In their book 'The Aladdin Factor,' Jack Canfield and Mark Victor Hansen point out that so often children are told to: "Sit down and be quiet! Stop asking so many questions! Stop announcing your feelings. Stop being so demanding!" As a result we unwittingly teach our children to stifle their natural instinct to ask for what they need and want. Why do we do this? We all need each other's help everyday at home, in school, in business, in friendship and in love. Whether we need a hug or help with homework, housework or heartbreak, needing help is part of being human. Perhaps we need to learn and teach our children the art of asking. Here are the steps:

Ask for what you want, not what you don't want. Ask specifically for exactly what you want in a friendly, positive manner. Express your need in a way that assumes you'll get it.

If it's something you want to achieve, establish a goal. Write it down. Visualize yourself doing it. Do 2 things everyday to get you closer to your goal. Ask others to help you achieve it.

Ask in a way that provokes a positive (yes) response. Here's a foolproof method:

Let's say you need one child to stay at home and 'keep company' (nothing worse than a 10 year-old hearing the word 'babysitter'!) with another sibling on Saturday night. Here's an approach the experts recommend. You might try a conversation that goes like this...

Mom: Parties always seem to be planned for Saturday night, aren't they?
Teen Tom: Yeah, sure seems that way.

Mom: So if you were invited to a party, you would expect Dad and I to stay home with your little brother, wouldn't you?
Teen Tom: Yeah - nobody makes parties during the week.

Mom: That's right. Saturday night is party night. As a matter of fact, we've been invited to a party for that young couple who moved here to work in Dad's office so they can make friends and meet people. You can understand that, can't you?
Teen Tom: Yeah. Moving to a new city is lonely I guess.

Mom: Our regular sitter is busy, so I need you to stay home and keep Billy company. I'm sure this party will help to make them feel more welcome here, right?
Teen Tom: Yes...

Mom: Besides, when you spend some time with your little brother Saturday night, it will give you guys some time to catch up and play some net, won't it?
Teen Tom: Yeah, it's been awhile. All right, I'll cancel my plans.

Mom: Thanks Tommy. I knew I could count on you. You're the best!

Goals and Dreams

Some people know exactly what they want, they set out to achieve a dream and do it. Others talk, daydream, (which is OK for a while) but they never seem to get past the planning stage.

First conceive it
Then believe it
If you want to achieve it!

1) Know what you want. Your goal may change before you achieve it, but a destination is necessary to find a direction. Write down your desired goal.

2) Motivate yourself. Envision all the positive effects of being successful. If you want to change a behavior, review the negative and painful consequences of maintaining the same unwanted behavior.

3) Change: Do things radically differently from what you were doing before, even if it feels uncomfortable at first. Change your visual images and the way you feel about things. This is the 'scrambled egg approach' - once you mix things up, it's impossible to go back. Example: If you are used to smoking a cigarette while drinking coffee and talking on the phone; doodle on a scratch pad, drink orange juice and hold the phone in the opposite hand.

4) Model someone else's ideal behavior.

5) Repeat pleasure. Recognize your progress, no matter how small. (Wow! I haven't smoked in 1 hour!)

6) Reward yourself! Set small goals and reward each small step of the road to success. Like follows like; one smokeless day (or 1 less pound or 1 mile walked) at a time.

Goals are dreams with deadlines.   Anthony Robbins

Nothing happens unless it's first a dream.   Carl Sandberg

But I Neeeeed It!

Advertising and societal pressure being what they are, today's kids feel that they need to keep up with 'mini Joneses' down the street. When the whining becomes pleading and the latest consumer fad is a "I gotta have it or I'll die!" scenario, it's perfectly OK to say, "We can't afford it." It may feel a little awkward but it puts things into perspective right away. Children are not entitled to everything they see and want, even if you can afford it financially. It's not a lie if you think about it this way; "We may be able to pay for it with money, but can we afford to teach them the wrong values?" You may satisfy them with the item for the moment, but you may be (unwittingly) laying the groundwork for a lifetime of crippling consumer addiction. Again, it's easier to avoid forming a bad habit than it is to break one.

Liar, Liar, Pants on Fire!

Lying isn't a good thing, but it's normal and let's face it, we're all guilty to some extent. Psychologists tell us that: Young children (ages 4-5) often make up lots of stories. This is considered to be normal because they enjoy hearing stories and then exercising their own imaginations. Little kids don't always understand the difference between reality and fantasy.

Some kids between the ages of 11 and 15 seem to be chronic liars. So no, your son is not the only ten-year-old who could be Pinocchio's understudy. Lying is practically a reflex at this age, because kids of this age group are particularly insecure, afraid of messing up and sometimes regard their parents as 'the enemy.' Point out the consequences of lying. Be the model of honesty yourself and watch out for your own 'little white lies,' because kids love to catch their parents in hypocritical moments. Don't forget to thank him/her and reward your child's honesty just as you would punish your child for lying.

And teens, of course, tell self-serving lies to avoid doing something or deny responsibility for their actions. Try to respond to these instances of lying by talking about the importance of 'truthiness,' honesty and trust... but it may not be easy!

If you know something's up and you want to get at the truth, try this approach: Say, "I want you to tell me what happened at school, (or at the park, at the store, with Jimmy, etc.) But I want you think to about it first and then we'll talk about it in 20 minutes." Let your child organize his thoughts, and remind him that we all make mistakes, but that honesty is always the best policy. This cooling-off period works well because, if you put kids on the spot they're more likely to lie in order to end the conversation quickly, avoid getting into trouble or to save face. Sometimes your own emotions may be bubbling hot with anger and disappointment, but try to stay cool and calm as you tell him that lying only compounds the problem, lessens your trust and never fixes anything.

Teenagers feel that lying is acceptable in certain situations - such as not telling a boyfriend/girlfriend the real reasons for breaking up, which is understandable. Or they may want to protect their privacy, or they may want to feel 'independent' by denying that they sneaked out late to be with friends.

Lying isn't a good thing but it is part of life. And before you get totally bent out of shape, remember all the lies, fibs and half-truths we adults perpetuate: The Tooth Fairy, Santa Claus, a few drops of oil lasting the eight days of Hanukah, and all the other religious folklore handed down to us. Depending on your motivation there's a very fine line between fibbing, lying and story-telling.

If you suspect the kids are not telling you the truth, chances are you're right. Trust but verify!

Tell Kids the Truth Or Face Some Unintended Consequences!

THE GOOD NAPKINS... ah... the joy of having girls...

My Mother taught me to read when I was four years old (her first mistake). One day, I was in the bathroom and noticed one of the cabinet doors was ajar. I read the box in the cabinet. I then asked my mother why she was keeping 'napkins' in the bathroom. Didn't they belong in the kitchen? Not wanting to burden me with unnecessary facts, she told me that those were for "special occasions" (her second mistake).

Now fast forward a few months.... It's Thanksgiving Day, and my folks are leaving to pick up my uncle and his wife for dinner. Mom had assignments for all of us while they were gone. Mine was to set the table. When they returned, my uncle came in first and immediately burst into laughter. Next came his wife who gasped, then began giggling. Next came my father, who roared with laughter. Then came Mom, who almost died of embarrassment when she saw each place setting on the table with a "special occasion" Kotex napkin (a bulky feminine pad, about 10 times the thickness of panty liners) at each plate, with the fork carefully arranged on top. I had even tucked the little tails in so they didn't hang off the edge!! My Mother asked me why I used these and, of course, my response sent the other adults into further fits of laughter. "But, Mom, you said they were for special occasions!!!"

Isn't it easier to just tell the truth?   *Author Unknown*

On Holding A Grudge (Another teaching story)

One day, two Zen monks met a beautiful, young maiden at the side of a river. "I cannot swim and I am so afraid, could you please find a way to help me get across?" she said. One monk quietly picked her up and gently carried her safely to the other side. Then the two monks continued on their journey in silence. That night by the fire, the second monk said, "It was wrong of you to pick up that fair young girl; we have taken a vow of purity." "Oh her, I put her down at the side of the river, but obviously you have been carrying her all day."

Author Unknown

Teachable Moments

I am a strong believer in 'teachable moments.' You can't teach children to walk, talk or do math before they are ready – but when they are ready, they learn quickly and easily – your job is to be aware and be ready to seize the moment. Don't push kids too early, you'll only frustrate both of you and delay success. Successful accomplishments are essential to building self-esteem.

> You can't push a wave onto the shore any faster
> than the ocean brings it in.   Susan Strasberg

You don't have to be better than anyone else. You don't have to win. You don't have to be number one or number 27 or any other number. Give yourself permission just to be.

Wayne Dyer

Teach by Example

How many times do you see people begging on the street? They are usually carrying a cardboard sign asking for food or money. Once, when the kids were young, we came across this scenario. We began to discuss how humiliating it must feel to have to beg, and in a country as rich as ours – we should be the ones to feel embarrassed. My husband's actions spoke louder than our words when he quietly turned the car around, headed into the first fast-food drive-through and bought two full meals. Then he silently delivered the food to the needy man. Now we all follow suit.

> We don't know why and we don't know when
> But we're all part time angels every now and then.   Johnsmith

Carpe Hug 'Em

Research has shown that human beings need 4 hugs a day to survive, 8 hugs a day to maintain health, and 12 hugs a day to stimulate growth. Physical closeness is necessary to boost the immune system, foster emotional closeness and is a vital part of close relationships. But a good hug can do so much more...

Does your child need a self-confidence booster? A behavior modifier? Or an injection of family values? If so, grab your kid, hug 'em tight and say, "I simply don't know what this family would do without you!" What could possibly be more motivating? How could s/he even dream of doing something dumb or foolish after this burst of enthusiasm? This endorsement of his/her self-worth? Consider it a painless shot in the arm!

Is It Really Praiseworthy?

"Good job" is a bad expression. Kids don't have jobs – at least until they get to school. Then, school is a child's fulltime job. Better to say, "Wow! You tied your shoes by yourself!" Recognize what the child actually accomplished, but don't praise him just because he can breathe the air!

During the 1980's, the popular psychology was to praise children profusely at every opportunity, to bolster self-esteem, 'they' said. This led a lot of kids to falsely assume that they were 'great' and that their every deed was worthy of applause. Red pens were banned from the classroom because the educators wanted every child to feel like 'a winner' all the time. Wrong answers were just 'less right' than they should be. Trophies were handed to everyone even if you lost the game because ... 'You're still a winner!' This conditioning proved to be very debilitating – the constant need for positive reinforcement and endless praising has made a whole generation (now dubbed the 'millennial generation') feel very apprehensive if they don't hear cheers and adulation from their bosses or professors in the 'real world.' As a direct consequence of yesterday's pop psychology, employers today are stymied by 'twentysomethings' who think the world owes them a living, and who are so primed for success that they only know how to take 'yes' for an answer! They are a generation of 'praise junkies'. It's quite disappointing to suddenly find out that the world isn't as nice as you were always led to believe. Ouch! Good intentions are not necessarily good ideas. It's tough out there and kids need to learn that not everyone will always be rewarded for just being alive – you need to actually do something to be rewarded!

Whether you believe you can do a thing or not, you are right.   Henry Ford

Don't Plead or Bargain

I had a neighbor who would tell her child to "Pick up the paper please. (10 seconds later) I said pick up the paper. (10 seconds later) Did you hear me, I asked you to pick up that paper. (10 seconds later) Pulleeeze pick up the paper. (5 seconds later) (yelling) Pick it up! (whining, 10 seconds later) Pick up the paper and I'll give you a candy – don't you want a candy?" Within one minute she went from parenting to bribing. And what she really taught her child was: the tail can wag the dog. He learned it only pays to listen when you want to; you can control your Mother by ignoring her.

Ask ONCE, then stand there and deliver "the look" until the task is done. Do this once or twice and you'll never have to do it again.

I had a grade school teacher who could make you feel very, very, very uncomfortable with her laser-focused glare. One glance in your direction and that sneer would have you holding your breath. Not a word was uttered, but you got the message loud and clear. (So did the rest of the class ... oh, the embarrassment!) Develop 'the look of disapproval' – it's the emotional equivalent of 'a picture's worth a thousand words.' And once 'the look' is imprinted in your child's mind – you can silently get your point across, forever!

No More Begging

When I hear a mother say to her 2-year-old, "PLEASE don't smash that other person's glass, PLEASE!" I just cringe at the stupidity of begging a child. It is crucial to not give (or pretend to give) a ridiculous amount of power to children. Be sure and set limits for your very young child and assert a level of parental control. Remember, if you cannot control your 2- or 3-year-old, how will you handle things when they are teenagers?

Laurie Marson

On Incentives

When my three youngsters were small they always wanted to get on their bikes and go to the park after supper. I told them that if they placed all their toys in the correct boxes and had the house all cleaned up that they could go to the park as a reward. BUT, if one didn't do his/her chores then that would ruin it for the others. I told them that they had to work as a group. After a few tries they finally got it down pat. Responsibility and cooperation paid off.

We reinforced the same theme when they did errands and chores around the house every week. When they were all finished doing what they had to, then they'd get allowance money.

Barbara Davidson, Sheffield, MA

Just Do IT

All day long, I sit in my office and I see Moms threatening their children, hoping that this will make the kids behave. But the kids realize that these are idle threats and their Mom is not going to do squat. What's going on? These parents appear to be afraid to discipline their children. Tell the child once and then take action.

Mary Martha, MA

The Verdict's In – The Chicken Came First!

I don't know how successful I was/am at mothering, but I always tried to remember that my kids came to live with us, not the other way around!

Pat Shays

Consistent Consequences

This may take some effort and work but you will be rewarded with well-behaved children. Whenever a situation arises where you have given a warning regarding poor behavior, be consistent and deliver the promised consequence. This may sound easy and logical. However, if you are in a restaurant and your child is acting up and you say, "Do it one more time and we are going home!!!" you really have to get up and leave the restaurant when s/he acts up again! It may not be convenient but you must follow through! (We have learned to it think over before we warn our children about the next consequence.)

The payoff is that after only a few times of following through with consistent rules and consequences, your children will understand that you will do exactly what you say you are going to do. Therefore, they trust you. With trust comes safety, structure, good behavior, guidelines, and in the end, a pretty well behaved and confident child.

Nikki Glantz, Ft. Lauderdale, FL

Havoc Can Become A Habit

"You can make your life as simple or as difficult as you want." When you choose to make it difficult then you have to deal with the resulting havoc you create. Havoc can become a habit and ultimately make your life a struggle. My 19-year-old nephew just learned this the hard way. He let his dog run loose around the yard. First the dog broke her leg running through a wooded area that resulted in the leg having to be amputated one year later. Then the dog got pregnant, leaving him to care for 8 puppies. If he had fenced an area for the pooch (which I had suggested earlier) surely it would have eliminated all the subsequent problems. The vet's bill for the broken leg and amputation cost $4,000.

Although he had heard me say it many times, he now realizes that it is true. Havoc does indeed become a habit. So stop the cycle while your kids are young.

Donna Magadov, Burnside, TN

An ounce of prevention is worth a pound of cure.

- words become actions – actions become habits –
- habits become character – character becomes destiny -

Motivation

Sometimes you need to motivate children the old-fashioned way - with a threat! I tell my (teenage) son to clean up or lose the iPod 'till it's done!

Mala J., Manchester, NJ

Advice from a river...
... go with the flow – immerse yourself in nature – slow down and meander – go around obstacles – be thoughtful of those downstream – stay current –
the beauty is in the journey...

On Listening to Yourself

When my daughter was born at home, I thought I had to nurse her and be there for her all the time. Although this is a good idea in principal, the result was that my daughter did not sleep for more than about 2 hours, for almost 2 years. If I was up I nursed her and when she did sleep, I got up to express my milk for the next day. Every day for a year I sat in the bathroom at work and ate my lunch alone so I could express more milk. I was alone, often miserable, and exhausted. But I was doing what I thought I was supposed to do. Later in life, a counselor asked me why I continued to do that even though I was so unhappy. I shook my head and said, "Because I thought I was supposed to. It never really occurred to me to do it another way." Now I know better. When something doesn't feel right, and what you are doing is because you feel you "have to" and not because you want to, nor from the place of "love"... LISTEN TO YOUR HIGHER/INNER VOICE!! Don't keep doing what doesn't work for YOU. Ultimately, your sleep, and your well-being are crucial to being able to nurture your child. Don't do what doesn't feel right, because it only builds silent resentment. If you read something in a book, it might have been good for the author, but if it doesn't work for you, throw the book away. Just listen to yourself; your instinct is better! My daughter and I have a great relationship and we are really close. I know this isn't because of breastfeeding but because I finally learned to listen to myself and to her.

Elyse Brunt, Hollywood, FL

Trust yourself

The most important parenting secret is: If you hit on something that works for you and your child — no matter how unorthodox — just do it. The neighbors might think you're nuts because they see your five-month-old sitting in a high chair, right there on the driveway – but who cares? When she's cranky, a simple change of scenery and some fresh air might just do the trick!

Mary McLaughlin, Fairfax, Virginia

On Patience

The thing that has kept me going through any difficult time of parenthood (infancy, the "terrible twos", all the way to teenager-hood) would be to remember that each stage is just that - a phase; and this too shall pass!

Enjoy each of the many moments of discovery that your child will bring to your life; they too are fleeting, and if you don't stop and notice them all along the way, they'll be gone before you know it!

Riki Lerner Green, St. Catherines, Ontario

Teaching Kids the Art of Decision Making

When my daughter brought a dilemma to me, I usually asked her what her options were. I then asked her what the consequences would be if she went with Option A and what they would be if she went with Option B or C. We discussed pros and cons of each option and possible ramifications. When all was said and done, if she hadn't already figured out what she was going to do, I told her to pick one. If it turned out well, then that was good. If it turned out badly, then she learned a lesson and I would be there to help her pick up the pieces. Fortunately, these kinds of discussions went on before she reached an age where the consequences were more serious. By then, she was making pretty good decisions most of the time. Some consequences provided some pretty serious lessons and fortunately none were life-threatening. I really like who she became - she makes good, sound decisions for herself and she has an excellent sense of self.

Robby Greenberg, Pembroke Pines, FL

On Treating Your Children As Equal People

When my children were very young, in the early 60's, children were considered 'children' as opposed to 'people'. This bothered me when friends would visit and exclude my children from conversations or activities. On average, this was the attitude toward children - they were to be seen but not heard. In our house, I always made sure that my children were part of everything and stood my ground to make sure they were heard. They may have lacked maturity, but their views and opinions were always important. This is important in building a child's sense of self worth. They need to be made to feel important even though they may be smaller than the adults around them.

Brona Rosen, Toronto, Canada

Life is Like a Multiple Choice Test

One day, my son was trying to hide a mistake from me. When I asked him why, he said he was embarrassed that he didn't make the right choice. I sat him down and explained the following:

Pretend you get a question wrong on your midterm exam. Do you think you would choose the same answer again on the final exam, if you found the same question? If you chose 'A,' the first time, now you know it is wrong. So you might choose B, C, or D. Well, life is like that too. As a teenager, you are not supposed to know all the right answers. Sometimes you learn the right answers by first choosing the wrong answers.

Sometimes you guess. If you already know A is wrong and B is probably wrong, you have C and D to choose from. Sometimes you get it right and sometimes you don't. Choosing the wrong answer is part of growing up.

It is a parent's job to give you the tools to help you choose the right answer. Don't ever be embarrassed that you were wrong or to admit that you made a mistake. If you make the same mistake twice, then you need to pay more attention so that you can really learn from your mistakes.

Joan Sheinwald, Plantation, FL

On Building Self Confidence

In order to have confidence in one's self, one must be convinced of one's self worth. To feel worthy one must do something worthy. This is best achieved when you contribute something of value to your family, your friends or to your community, and then be recognized for your contribution. Achieving academic, sports-related or musical proficiency can lead to feelings of success, but they do not speak to 'who I am' as much as 'what I've done.'

When one of my daughters was in kindergarten, the popular psychology was to have the children repeat, "I love myself!" as a self-esteem building exercise. I didn't approve of this narcissism and would follow up with, "That's good. We love you too, because you are a giving, friendly person."

When we instill confidence in our children, it is as if we are recording directly onto the continuous loop of unconscious internal dialogue that they will hear throughout their lives. If we fill this inner voice with positive messages, we will virtually guarantee inner peace and good self-esteem. Imagine hearing and feeling that you are thought of as great, capable, strong, worthy, sweet, good natured and able to achieve whatever you set your mind to do. You'd have a good chance of "being all that you could be!" Tell your children who they are – or someone else will … and it won't always be what you'd like them to hear.

Girls especially need to be told often that they are beautiful. They need to know that they are wonderful, beautiful people, both inside and out. And that they are fine just the way they are. Our silly society has kids measuring their entire self-worth based on air brushed, manipulated photographs of malnourished models. I never allowed celebrity worship in the form of magazine pin-ups on bedroom walls for exactly this reason. Surrounding themselves (literally) with cosmetically reconstructed good looks would only encourage them to idolize 'fake reality.' The rule was: you can hang as many posters and celebrity pictures as you like - inside your clothes closet!

Remind your daughter that she was born with the potential to be great. But it is up to each individual to develop oneself or not. All the great people of the world simply said 'yes' when others said 'no.'

The book and DVD 'The Secret' produced by Rhonda Byrne, describes The Law of Attraction. The same concept has been described many times throughout history. The basic idea is that whatever you consciously (or unconsciously) desire will be exactly what you attract. You actively choose and attract people, opportunities and circumstances by what you expect from the universe. This is the power of positive thinking. Simply stated, if you think you are undeserving you will be and your life will not change. If you think, feel and emanate positive energy, you will attract good, positive energy and people. Briefly, the outlined steps for acquiring positive flow are: Ask (yourself and the power of the universe) for what you desire, and walk in that direction. In other words, if you want to achieve something it's not enough to want it and expect your wishful thinking to deliver the desired outcome. You have to actively work for it. Believe that you will achieve it. Put in the effort required and receive it. It is as if a universal power is saying, 'Whatever you set out to do, good or bad, it's up to you... permission granted.' Energy flows where attention goes! This is quite a powerful message to teach our children!

Believe in your children more than they believe in themselves.

Don't ask children WHAT they want to be when they grow up but rather, WHO they want to be... a generous, knowledgeable, caring person.

The real measure of your wealth is how much you'd be worth if you lost all your money.
Bernard Meltzer

The best way to show your children a positive sense of self is to feel it yourself.

A woman who radiates self love and self acceptance vaccinates her daughter against low self esteem.
Naomi Wolfe

A Word About Getting Divorced

If you've gone for counseling and have determined that there is no possibility of saving your relationship, and you've decided to get divorced, then (and only then) you need to tell your children. Tell them together, on the weekend, two days before the actual separation. Plan ahead and have a prepared, well-rehearsed talk which explains that they, the kids, are not the cause. Explain that sometimes one's life changes and things don't always work out as we plan or hope for. Be honest and tell them why you are splitting up. You don't need to give details, just explain, "We weren't honest with each other," or "We didn't get the help we needed before our small problems became too big for us to fix." If you don't explain things the kids will confabulate (a fancy word for filling in the blanks you don't understand) and often they'll blame themselves. The way you handle this discussion may dwell in their minds forever, so be careful of what you say and how you say it. According to child psychologist Dr. Gary Neuman, you only have about 45 seconds before the kids are overcome with emotion and cease to hear what you're saying. Don't place blame and NEVER say you don't love each other anymore – kids may interpret that to mean you can stop loving them too. Reassure them that you will always love them even though life may change a little. And even though you may no longer be husband and wife, you will always be Mom and Dad. Let them know where they will live and where their other parent will live. Don't spend longer than 5 minutes in the initial conversation and then let them express feelings. Expect them to have strong feelings – their hurt is understandable. Tell them that even though you know they want you to stay together, that this is your choice and your decision and that after a lot of thought, this decision is final. Your children don't need two parents who live under one roof. But they do need two parents who will put the needs of their children ahead of their own.

Once this conversation has taken place, suggest that everyone take a break to think about things and disperse for an hour. Then, I suggest that you plan to have dinner ALL TOGETHER. Yes, all together! This family dinner is so important because it will set the tone for future family harmony. Of course, you and your husband need to plan and agree on this dinner arrangement ahead of time.

And once we're on the subject, please always remember that you once loved and chose this person to be your spouse. Your hopes and dreams may be shattered. You may feel frustrated, hurt, betrayed, etc. but speaking with disrespect about your ex only reflects negatively on you – not on him/her as you intend. It is never constructive and only invites reciprocal disrespect and escalating venom. Your 'husband' is now your 'was-band.' You were in this relationship together and whatever happened to cause you to separate is over and done. As hard as it is to admit, it is never only one person's fault that relationships falter. You tried to resolve your differences but you could not. Rise above it, let it go and move on.

Remember – in every life some pain is inevitable
but suffering is always voluntary.

Your kids need to be able to vent their feelings too, so go for a drive, pull out some playing cards, start a board game, cuddle in bed – do something together, but side by side and not entirely focused on 'a discussion' (that's the ultimate kid turnoff.) Gently slide into a talk sideways by mumbling..."You seem upset/angry/mad/sad..." Continue your parallel play as you listen. Try to hear things from a kid's perspective. Don't negate what s/he's saying by trying to defend yourself or your husband's words/feelings/actions. Let your child vent, spill and cry, even if it hurts you. You may feel guilty and responsible for causing their pain so it's natural to feel defensive but don't say a word. Just listen and validate what s/he's feeling. Apologize for causing so much pain; let him/her know (again) that it's not his/her fault.

You can't stop the rain but you can open an umbrella.

After a good long year has passed and you begin to venture out into the dating world (take your time!), include your kids in your decision to date. Don't ask their permission, but don't keep it a secret either. Don't discuss your private life or your dates with the kids. Just say you had a nice time, the person was interesting etc. Only introduce your children to someone if you become seriously involved and when you are both ready for a committed relationship. Your children should not have to guess or hope or wish that every boyfriend might be 'the one.' When you're ready to introduce your 'someone special' be casual about it and plan a fun family activity (bowling, fishing, hiking) so everyone can get to know each other gradually without a lot of pressure. If there are other kids involved (and your families become blended), don't expect instant cohesion. The kids are just kids – they need time to figure stuff out. If you do remarry, remember that these 'other kids,' are not sisters and brothers … and they won't necessarily 'feel the love,' just because you want them to. Your kids still want and need you (just you) to themselves sometimes. So reserve one night a week just for them – go out alone, even if it's just for a drive – give them some private time.

Your feelings...

Discipline – Life's Little Calibrator

Be of One Mind

Now that you are parents, sit down together, discuss and decide how you feel about discipline issues. Formulate a plan – don't react to unwanted bad behavior with a knee-jerk reaction. Develop a calm and quiet approach. Learn to respond rather than react. Above all, the number one rule to keep in mind is:

Do not feed negative behavior.

Keep in mind that you are the parent, not the friend. Be the boss in a warm and loving way. Adopt a benevolent dictatorship style of domestic administration!

Controversy is a fact of life. Any seasoned parent will tell you that it is essential to pick your battles carefully, but when you do choose a battle it is essential that you win it! Think it through, stand firm and don't set yourself up for failure.

Don't worry about causing your child to feel frustrated because s/he's not getting her way. And if you catch yourself 'giving in' because it feels easier than fighting, you are doing the wrong thing. All you are really doing is setting yourself up for repeated, escalating battles. I believe it may actually be healthy for children to develop a tolerance for feelings of frustration, thereby building some immunity to it. We all face frustration in the real world almost every day, so it follows that we should learn to take it in stride and move on.

If you find your child is developing behavior problems, try to remove yourself from the equation. In other words: Let the child own the problem and allow the consequences to be the mediator. The law of unintended consequences is an excellent teacher! For example, if being on time to leave for school is becoming a problem, buy a kitchen timer. (Every household should have one.) Explain to the child that s/he alone will be responsible for getting ready. Set the timer for 45 minutes and leave the child to accomplish all the tasks s/he needs to do on her/his own - getting up, dressed and fed, books ready and at the door at the appointed time. If s/he's not ready take her/him to school as s/he is. No breakfast? No problem – s/he'll just be hungry. Don't hound her/him or remind her/him of the time, let the child own the problem and deal with the consequences. If s/he accomplishes everything s/he's supposed to – don't make a big deal of that either, you'll only be feeding the original fire, which was to push your buttons and get some attention. Never feed the negative behavior.

Don't allow the sound of your child crying to weaken your parental resolve. If your child is frustrated because s/he isn't getting his or her way, and has an emotional, vocal outburst, just consider it an investment in his/her personality fund. S/he is learning. That's a good thing. Over time small deposits will yield and mature. Don't worry, just repeat your mantra, "Never feed the negative behavior."

Reserve spanking for the most extreme circumstances. (I never did, but I would have in a life-or-death situation such as running out into the street.)

The 'time out' or the 'naughty chair' technique seems civilized; it teaches self-discipline, delayed gratification and doesn't feed negative behavior. You might want to reframe the phrase 'time out' and call it 'take a calm moment' or 'rest and rethink.' Consider having the child spend time facing into the corner … why? Because every room offers four of them, so no matter where you are they are always available! Time out rule of thumb is: one minute / year of life. So, a 4-year-old should sit/stand for 4 minutes, in a place where there's nothing to do but sit or stand there. The idea is to think about the bad behavior, not to be entertained by you, the TV or the environment.

Keep in mind that people (children included) will always rise to meet your expectations. Whatever your verbal and nonverbal communication demands of people, (be it performance or attitude) that's exactly what their behavior will mirror.

Discipline is not about controlling your child, it's about teaching your child to control him/herself.

Eye-lock, Talk, then Walk

Do you want to spend the next 18 years nagging and badgering the children to set the table? Get the homework done? Take out the garbage? I didn't think so. The only requirement for getting children to pay attention - is to expect them to!

Here's the magic formula: Get their attention. Tell them what you expect to be done. Let them do it. But it is essential to enforce the 'once only rule.' Say it once, turn and walk away. Remember that 'eye-lock, talk, then walk' is all you need to do.

If the kids don't comply adopt a strategy of calm control. Simply do not provide the next expected perk-of-the-day. Don't get angry - get even; by which I mean remain even-tempered and pleasant but explain that because A didn't happen, neither will B. Let the consequences teach the lesson. Adopt the cliché 'actions speak louder than words' as your new child-rearing motto. If this seems too difficult, or too easy to be true, remember that the fastest way to change someone else's behavior is to change your own.

Yes and No

'Yes' is such a wonderful little word!' Yes, we all love to hear it. That tiny monosyllable is the quickest way to satisfy, reap instant praise or hear your child say, "Oh thank you, Mommy! I'll take such good care of it…" Yadda, yadda, yadda! But, when your kids are whining or they ask you for something else they don't need, just think of saying "No" as if you are putting money in the bank; it may take time for the interest to accrue and compound, but you'll all be so much richer in the end.

There are times when "Because I said so!" is appropriate. Kids should know that your word is THE WORD. So don't be afraid of the word "no." "No" does not mean "I don't love you." "No" should be used like a good thunderstorm – not all the time, but whenever necessary. Not everything is worth a tug of war but when you say no – mean it, and if you put a lot of love behind it, your kids will hear it loud and clear. If you later decide that you made a mistake don't be afraid to admit it to your children – they should understand that you are only human and subject to the same frailties as they are. Moms and Dads are not perfect - they make mistakes also. Show that you can laugh at yourself and recover from your mistakes. There's something quite comforting in knowing that your parents are honest enough to admit their mistakes, and you can be sure that your children will more readily admit to their own. Kids will forgive your mistakes. But they'll never forgive your 'sins of omission.' You need to be involved with them. Play with them and express your love, support and enthusiasm.

Make sure that 'no means no.' NO exceptions. And, of course, parents should NEVER contradict each other, especially in front of the kids! If you do disagree about an issue, discuss it later and handle it differently next time. But stand united and you'll avoid having the children learn to play one of you against the other.

Be consistent. If you say 'No' today, the same should apply tomorrow. If you do change your mind about an issue, be sure to explain why you've changed your mind.

The Power of 'Yes'

Remember too that not everything is worth a fight. Just as "No" is a real word, so is "Yes." Pick your fights carefully. Allow your children some autonomy by letting them make decisions, too. When my daughter wanted to start shaving her legs at age 10, I thought she was a bit young, but I said yes and showed her how to do it. (I remembered when my Mother had said "No" I did it anyway and promptly cut a two-inch gash in my leg. I still bear the scar.) By denying her request, I'd only be delaying this inevitable rite of passage for a little while at best. Once her request was maternally sanctioned, somehow the idea lost some of its original urgency and appeal. I learned that sometimes "yes" can be as much of a deterrent as "no."

A simple life lesson … say yes much more often than you say no.
Frances Ford Coppola

Say what you mean, mean what you say, and do what you say you're going to do.
Susan Moss, Pembroke Pines, FL

Just Say YES

My daughter was one of the most strong-willed toddlers I have ever seen. In consultation with the rest of the family, we agreed to try to avoid all confrontations with her by implementing a "Just Say Yes" program for one week. It turned out we only had to do it for one day. Drawing a line in the sand with this child had led to unpleasantness, and it was clear she brought more determination to 'battles of will' than we did, so we agreed to try to do whatever she wanted.

She arrived home from pre-school and demanded to play with the toy her big brother was playing with. "Okay," he said, and got up and left it to her. After a few seconds she was bored with that easy victory so she came into my office and demanded we make cookies. "Okay," I said, and shut down the computer. We were baking cookies when she then demanded to go to the pet store to buy some fish. "Okay," I said, taking off my apron, and I put her into her car seat. At the fish store she wanted so many fish that I said, "If we put this many fish into our small tank they will die because they won't have enough surface air." She insisted, so I went ahead and bought the fish. I figured when the fish died she would learn something (and if they didn't die, I would learn something). As we were standing at the counter paying for the fish, she announced that she now wanted the store's parrot. It had an $800 price tag. I said, "We can't buy something that expensive without talking to your daddy first." She threw a complete tantrum -- legs and arms flailing, screaming. I paid for the fish and carried her out to the car screaming like that. I calmly reminded her that we had made the cookies, that she had gotten to play with whatever toys she wanted, and that we had just bought some nice fish. She picked up the bag of fish and threw it at the windshield screaming, "I don't want fish! I want a PARROT!!!" The bag exploded and suddenly I've had two dozen fish flopping all over the floor of the car. I drove home with the fish gasping.

At the dinner table that night, Amy burst into tears. She couldn't quite explain why she was so sad, but I think it was because she learned that having her own way wasn't quite as much fun as she had thought it would be. I won't say we never had another moment of trouble with her, but she was a changed little girl after that day: much more considerate and aware of others' feelings. Today she is extremely thoughtful, and that maddening stubbornness has transformed into an admirable sense of persistence and loyalty.

Anne Feeney, Pittsburgh, PA

Temper the Tantrum

Tantrums are only good if they play to a receptive audience. Whenever a tantrum was brewing, I just isolated the screamer in his room (it's not as much fun to scream by yourself.) I was not interested in negotiating with a terrorist! Talk only when the screaming has subsided.

Realize that your kids might fight like crazy when you're there, but as soon as they're in camp together (or somewhere else where you are not present) they hug and kiss and love each other! Go figure!

The punishment should always fit the crime, so don't go overboard. Teach self-reliance... for example, if milk is spilled or something is broken, have the child mop it up or pick up the pieces. Do it together.

Wendy Chai, Toronto, Canada

The Squeeze

Most people respond to the calming sensations of deep pressure - like body massage and long, deep, encircling hugs. And it has been found that kids who act up or act out respond well to the feeling of firm pressure surrounding their body. So, if your child is experiencing behavioral problems and tantrums, try taking some large pillows to envelop him/her and then apply some firm hugging pressure to settle the child down. This tactile approach seems to works quite well with kids who have emotional disturbances. Some kids discover this method themselves and self soothe; by burying themselves deep inside heavy sofa pillows. So if you see your youngster cocooning like this, s/he knows what s/he's doing - just leave her/him be.

Punish with a Pen!

When my husband was in grade school he had a propensity to call out the answers before the teacher called on him. He was smart, impatient and he demanded to be heard... alas, nothing has changed! (And I know this because I sat in the seat in front of him all throughout grade school. Yes, we've been together since we were 5 years old... but I'll save that story for the next book.) More often than not, his exuberance resulted in after-school detentions. Not wanting to waste his time, but still needing to keep him quiet, learning and mastering a skill, his (British-educated) teacher found a punishment that aptly fit the crime. She would open the Funk and Wagnall's dictionary to a random page, and with ink pen in hand, he would have to copy every word with perfect penmanship! Without divulging just how many times this happened, suffice it to say that he has a _very_ extensive vocabulary and handwriting that looks like computer generated calligraphic script. Not to mention excellent SAT scores! Try this punishment option when you want to make a real impression – it gives a whole new meaning to the adage, 'the pen can be mightier than the sword.'

Your ideas...

Getting and Staying Organized

Avoiding Injuries

According to the National Safe Kids Campaign, unintentional injury is the leading cause of death among children ages 14 and under, with 45 percent of those deaths occurring in and around the home. Additionally, more than 4.5 million children ages 14 and under are treated in U.S. emergency rooms each year for injuries that occur in the home. Well that got MY attention!

• Install fire and carbon monoxide detectors, and replace the batteries every New Years day.
• Insert plastic outlet covers into all outlets.
• Install locks on windows and exterior doors. If you're replacing windows, choose windows that open from the top, not the bottom, to help prevent children from falling through loose screens.
• Shorten cords on window blinds to prevent strangulation hazards.
• Post all emergency numbers next to the kitchen phone.
• In the bathroom: put nonskid bath treads in the tub, put all medicines and chemical cleaners out of reach. If you use green/non toxic cleaners, you won't have to worry.
• In the kitchen: Install child safety locks on the inside of each cabinet and drawer. Remove all harmful chemicals from lower cabinets and move them to locked areas out of reach. Remove all potentially dangerous items, like knife blocks and toasters from countertops. Cover oven knobs with plastic safety domes that prevent them from being turned.
• Outside: Keep potentially dangerous items, such as tools, lawn and garden equipment, outdoor chemicals and grilling accessories, out of the way of children. If you have a pool or hot tub, purchase a hard cover and install a locked gate around the perimeter. Install an alarm that will alert you if the water surface has been disturbed. Make sure that the pool's vacuum return has a safety cover so that children's hair can't be sucked into it.

Creating Order

I found that a loosely structured chore list, scheduled over the whole week, worked best for me. Nothing was set in stone and we could change our routine easily, but the house ran more smoothly when everyone knew what was expected.

Clearly Zipped

To keep toys together use the clear, zippered bags that blankets and sheets come in. They are perfect for storing games, puzzles and art supplies, as they don't fall apart like the boxes do. You can easily see what's inside, and they make clean up simple.

The Cool Secretary

To keep your appointments straight: Glue a magnet onto the back of clothespins to make separate appointment cardholders for each member of your family. Personalize them with a photo or nameplate. Keep them on the fridge to hold all your appointment cards, neatly and organized in plain sight.

Hook It and Hang It

If you have kids' after-school activities planned, hang 7 hooks, each labeled with the days of the week. Hang a bag on each hook with all the activity equipment needed for that day. Ballet slippers in Monday's bag. Football pads in Thursday's bag, etc. When you come home – hang the bag on the appropriate peg and it will be ready for next week!

Rotate Your Recipes

To organize meals plans: Develop 10 – 15 favorite recipes and rotate them every 2 or 3 weeks. This makes planning easier than figuring out a different menu every night.

Try this: Cook your regular recipes 4 nights a week, leave one night open for a new idea, one night for 'someone else' (husband or kids) to cook, and one night for take- out/dine out.

Toothpaste Tricks

Rub your fingers with a little toothpaste to get rid of the smelly residue from garlic or onions.

Remove tough stains from both clothing and carpets. For clothes, apply some toothpaste directly to the stain and rub briskly until the spot disappears, then wash as usual. Note that some 'whitening' properties in the paste may bleach the fabric. For carpet stains, apply toothpaste to the stain, scrub it with a brush, then rinse.

If a baby bottle develops a sour-milk smell, use some toothpaste and a bottle scrubber to clean away residue and deodorize it. Be sure to rinse the bottle very well.

Kids love to write or color on anything and everything besides what they are supposed to. Am I right, Moms? If there is pen, pencil, crayon or marker on something, use adult toothpaste on a baby-wipe to clean it off.

Laundry

I worked when the kids were in school, so I got a head start on the laundry by throwing it into the washer before I left the house. When I came home I tossed the load into the dryer and after dinner we'd have a folding party. One day we did whites. One day we did darks and on the weekend we'd change the sheets and do the towels. This way we never had a big accumulation of laundry and everyone was involved.

The Great Stain Cover-Up

Spills happen! Cover up stains on the front of shirts by printing out a picture of your child's favorite fiction/action character onto heat-release transfer paper. Then iron the picture (or store bought transfer) onto the shirt to cover up the stain. Not only will you save the shirt but you'll also have a top s/he really loves.

Cardboard Car Central

Keep a cardboard box in your car for storing loose car toys, an extra supply of diapers and wipes, cereal snacks stored in plastic containers, etc.

Dishwasher Indispensable

Take a plastic container and cut holes all around the sides and top. Use it as a dishwasher basket (top rack only) to clean nipples, teething rings, small toys, pacifiers, contact lens cases, etc.

Very Funny Wrapping Paper

Instead of using wrapping paper for birthday presents use the comics or have the kids color over some newsprint pages.

Napkin Notes

Use the napkin in your kids' lunch bag to write notes on – love notes, multiplication tables, history test notes, doctor appointment reminders, and lots of notes of encouragement.

Halloween Hurray!

After years of accumulating fast food meal toys, birthday-party-take-home loot, carnival fair toys, books the kids had outgrown, balls of all types, CD's, tapes, video's, etc, I started recycling them as Halloween giveaways. The neighborhood kids loved getting "stuff," and I got to clear out a lot of old toys.

Have a Go-Go Holiday

After years of seeing our play room fill up with toys that seem to be played with for a short time then put aside, I knew I had to change my children's ideas about the holiday (tradition of receiving gifts). I wanted them to realize how lucky they are to even get gifts, when so many children go without - even during the holidays.

Nikki Glantz, Hollywood FL

So Nikki established the 'Go-Go' (Get one - Give one) tradition of holiday gift giving, first in her own family and then extended the practice throughout her community. When holiday time rolls around have the children choose gently, but seldom used clothing or sports equipment, toys or books from their collection to donate to less fortunate children. Once the selections have been cleaned and wrapped, involve the whole family in the giving process; have the children deliver the presents to your local homeless shelter or community center for distribution.

File It

Always save your receipts. To find the receipt easily, write the item you purchased on the back of the receipt slip and file the receipts by store name in an accordion file. It is much easier to return items when you have the receipt in hand.

Major Clean

Once in awhile when we all had accumulated too much stuff I'd call for 'a major' room cleaning. Everyone got two garbage bags: one for donations to the local homeless and family shelter and one for the local garbage dump.

Of course there will be times when messy teenage rooms get completely out of hand. I tried not to be a total 'neat freak,' but I too had my limits. When the occasion did arise, I decided not to get into a verbal conflict but still get my message across 'loud and clear.' As I passed a construction site I asked the foreman to give me several yards of their yellow "CAUTION" tape. My daughter came home to find her room completely barricaded by zigzag ribbons of tape barring her entry with an eviction notice attached! Once she made her way inside she found two roses with a note that read, "Roses among the ruins." Later that day, after she had cleaned up, she revised the note to read, "Restoration" to which I had to write, "Redemption - Rejoice!" We had fun instead of resorting to harsh words and angry tempers. Whenever possible, persuade rather coerce.

Bag It

If you're a working Mom, you might want to try laying out school clothes on Sunday for the entire week. Make five packages, including an outfit, underwear and socks, and slip each day's outfit into a plastic bag. Then your child can select which package of clothing s/he wants to wear that day...ah, hassle free mornings - precious!

Or buy 5 tops and pants that are all color coordinated and interchangeable, then no matter what s/he selects s/he'll always match!

Or better yet, persuade your school to adopt a 'uniform' policy. I firmly believe that this is better and less costly for everyone. A common uniform puts every child on an even playing field psychologically. Standard dress attire not only eliminates the competition of 'dressing up' in the latest fashion, but it helps to promote feelings of belonging and being part of the whole school body, which is so important. Perhaps, if our children were encouraged to feel more a part of a school family, we would have a little less bullying and violence in our schools.

The Lost

Kids can get lost in the blink of an eye... at the beach, in the mall, at the circus, in an arena ... one second they're there and the next - poof - they seem to evaporate into thin air. Can you spell PANIC? Preempt the whole event by reviewing the 'if you get lost' procedure every time you set out, and reinforce 'the rules' before you get out of the car. 1) Pick a meeting place. 2) Tell your kids to trust another Mom (who they see interacting with her own kids) to help.
3) Don't be afraid to ask a police person for help.

Be Ready For Anything

I'm not suggesting that we all becoming survivalists but it might be a good idea to build a preparedness kit for emergency situations. The Red Cross recommends having enough food and supplies on hand to last at least seven days. With the exception of the water, store your supplies in a sturdy, easy to carry, water resistant container such as a backpack or (if you are packing a lot) use an outdoor trashcan on wheels. Include:

Water – 1 gallon per person per day
Food - energy bars, ready-to-eat canned goods, dry cereals, peanut butter etc.
Flashlights – and extra batteries
First Aid kit
Matches in a waterproof container
Medications & Band Aids, hand sanitizer, and antibiotic cream, Pepto Bismal
Battery operated radio – with extra batteries.
Tools – a loud whistle, a manual can opener, canvas gloves, a screwdriver, a hammer, a knife, duct tape, plastic sheeting and garbage bags.
Clothing – including sturdy shoes, T-shirts, hats, gloves and underwear.

Personal Items – extra eyeglasses, copies of important papers (birth certificates, passports, social security cards, living wills, insurance info etc.)
Photos of family members. (On the back write their name, date of birth, date the photo was taken, height and weight, medications they need, allergies, address and phone number.)
Sanitary supplies – Diapers, toilet paper, feminine supplies and disinfectant bleach.
Cash – in small denominations ($1, $5, $10 and $20 bills)
Emergency phone numbers and a map of your area.
Pet supplies
Books or coloring supplies for the kids

Double – For No Trouble

As soon as you recognize that your baby or child has developed a 'gotta have it' favorite item, go out and buy extras. The same advice goes for bras, lipstick and nail polish, too! As soon as 'they' find out you love it – poof – it's off the market! If your child falls in love with a special toy, blanket or T- shirt, buy three identical ones and rotate them.

The Kid's Drawer

We kept one low kitchen drawer stocked with plastic cups and plates for the kids to access on their own. This system worked so well, we still use it and our kids have long since left the roost!

Car Magic

I keep a package of small paper bags and stickers in the car for long trips. When the going gets tough, I get the kids to make some bag puppets and put on a back seat play. Or you can turn old socks into car puppets – they'll keep kids amused for miles. I also store some small unbreakable hand mirrors in the car – they always seem to fascinate the kids.
Debby Perry

Keep kid-friendly CDs in the car.

Keep a complete change of clothes in a ziplock plastic bag in the trunk of your car. Spills, mud and accidents happen!

Try creating your own "Never Ending Story." It's a brainteaser, as well as being lots of fun. Start a story with one silly sentence. Have each person repeat the sentence and add on to the story by adding his/her own line. This can get quite involved and funny!

Stuff Happens!

Don't 'supersize' your personal or household inventory... get in the habit of throwing stuff out. Take control and simplify your home, your wardrobe, your kitchen, your car and your life. It seems the more we have, the messier life around us gets. The messier it gets, the harder it is to clean it up. The harder it is to clean it up, the more confusion it creates.

Control your clutter or it will control you. I had a single friend whose house was so congested with stuff that she was literally caught in the clutter. She wouldn't have anyone over because she was too embarrassed by the mess, but the mess served to insulate her in a self-isolating vicious circle.

Hint: if you have to rent a 'personal storage locker' you have too much stuff! People become emotionally attached to items that represent people and memories. Don't pay someone else to warehouse your memories. My advice: take a picture of the treasured item, keep the memories and toss the stuff.

The Gift

It happens to all of us – your child gives you a gift and although you're smiling on the outside, you're grimacing on the inside. If it's an article of clothing wear it once (to a movie?) and then give it away, but tell the kids that the cleaner ruined it. If it's something like a vase, keep it out for a while, then give it away and lament that it broke. If it's your child's handmade, one-of-a-kind 'work of art,' love it and cherish it no matter how abstract it is!

On Cleaning Up

You Go (Green) Girl!

There are four inexpensive, readily available, low-impact cleaning products that will keep your whole house sparkling safely! Interested? Almost all of the usual store-bought cleansers can be replaced by baking soda, vinegar, castile soap, and hot water. These are much less expensive, eco-friendly and do their job/s just as well as 'store bought' cleaners. Baking soda has scouring and anti-fungal properties. Vinegar is an acid that counteracts bacteria and mold. Soap cleans up dirt and you know all about the hot water. If you'd prefer, there are a variety of 'clean green' products now on the market. Check these out online: simplepureclean.com, shaklee.net, simplegreen.com, seventhgeneration. com, cleaningpro.com

Chore Challenge

I am so looking forward to built-in, multi-suction, self-vacuuming floors; self sanitizing sinks, bathtubs, shower stalls and toilets. Too bad the future isn't here yet and our current household chores are still lifelong activities. That said our kids need to learn how to do all the mundane tasks of life and pitch on a weekly basis. When they squawk about it, just remind them that even the future king of England, Prince William has scrubbed toilets and mopped floors while on volunteering assignments. Of course doing chores can be more fun if you just turn up the music, challenge the kids to cleaning contests, or have them 'choose a chore' from a bag filled the written cleaning must-do's of the week.

When the Kids Burn the Pot

Just to be clear - we're talking about a cooking pot here. It's going to happen - someone will forget to stir or watch the pot. To minimize the need for elbow grease, fill the metal pot or pan with water 1/4 of the way, bring it to a boil and add 5 tablespoons of baking soda. Turn off the heat and let it sit for a few hours. The caked-on mess should slide right off.

If your glass or ceramic casserole dish gets caked with food, just fill it with very hot water, add a squirt (or sheet) of fabric softener and let it sit over night. The grime should lift off easily.

If The Pot Is On Fire

Shut the stove. Leave the pot in place. Never add water to a flaming pot. Calmly, wet a dishtowel and carefully drape it over the top of the pot covering the flames. Leave the wet towel in place.

Wipe It

I keep an extra package of wipes in both our cars to use for spills, sticky hands, spots on clothes, etc. Wipes are amazing at getting anything clean, not just tushies!

Beat The Clock

To get your kids to help you clean, set a timer for ten minutes and challenge your kids to clean up before the bell rings. Stick to the ten-minute rule or your kids will start to mess up what you've just cleaned. As the timer ticks away, they'll love helping you beat the clock.

Play I Spy

To get my kids to clean up, I say, 'I spy something red (or noisy or soft) that needs to be put away.' My kids compete to find the right thing and then run to put it away.

Categorize

If the play area is scattered with lots of toys, assign one toy category to each child. Ask one child to put away the books and another to put away the dolls or action figures, etc. This way everyone knows exactly what his or her responsibility is and the job is accomplished quickly and easily.

Try Pavlov's Principle with Music

Pick out one particular CD and reserve it just for 'clean up music'. As soon as the kids hear it, they'll know that it's time to put away their toys. Sometimes they can have more fun by: racing against the music, or trying to beat their own 'clean up record,' or being faster than you.

Top Shelf Toys

To clean small plastic toys, load them into a lingerie bag and place them on the top shelf of the dishwasher.

Freeze!

Do you know that every ounce of household dust carries 42,000 dust mites? Yuk!
If you are concerned that dust mites might be the cause of your child's allergies, Dr. Myles Bader suggests that you gather up all the stuffed animals, put them in plastic bags and place them in the freezer for 24 hours, once a month.

Off the Wall

Crayon on the wall? Rub it with a stale piece of bread or make a thin paste of water and baking soda and apply it to 'the masterpiece' with an old toothbrush. The "art" should scrub right off.

Gummy Hair

Getting the gum out of your child's hair is easy. First massage it with cooking oil or a glob of peanut butter. As you work it into the gum, the mess will release from the hair. Use a large toothcomb to ease the gum out. Wash and warn the kids to be more careful next time.

Multi-tasking

Most multi-taskers think they are accomplishing more in less time, but in reality they are doing less and taking more time. "It's almost inevitable that each individual task will be slower and of lower quality," says James C. Johnson, a research psychologist at NASA's Ames Research Center.

This is true for the general population, but here's a little studied phenomenon: Moms are exempt from this particular law of physics.

Multi-tasking Moms actually do become highly proficient at breastfeeding the baby, while answering the phone, stirring the culinary pot, watching the neighborhood children at play, planning a board meeting, and simultaneously answering email. As I said, Super Moms are exempt from the natural laws of the universe!

A Note on Maternal Attention Deficit Disorder, MADD: Sometimes you'll find yourself asking, "Where was I? Who am I talking to? What am I doing?" So, while you actually may be doing several things at once, don't expect them all to come out well! Of course, there are people who suffer from real ADD, but for most Moms, MADD is not a disease - it's a self-imposed lifestyle.

Home Office Organization Tips:

Email: Follow the rule of 4 D's - **d**o it now, **d**elegate it, **d**esignate it for follow-up or **d**elete it.

Your desk: Clean it up! Having an uncluttered work area makes it easier to unclutter your brain as well.

The disease of the Internet age is "Continuous Partial Attention." We're so accessible we're inaccessible. We can't find the off switch on our devices or on ourselves. We want to wear an iPod as much to listen to our own play-lists, as to block out the rest of the world and protect ourselves from all that noise. We are everywhere — except where we actually are physically.
Linda Stone

I'm finding this age of interruption overwhelming. I was much smarter when I could do only one thing at a time. I know I'm not alone.
Thomas L. Friedman

Family Fun

Rituals

Rituals are fun – they bring a family together and make lasting memories. We always ate together as a family, almost every night. But on Friday nights I'd light the candles, say the blessings and go around the table kissing everyone on the forehead. As I usually had on lip-gloss, there would be grunts and groans and complaints of getting 'shellacked,' but nobody ever moved an inch or tried to evade 'the kiss.' Even the kids' friends would look forward to and enjoy the messy smooch! It was, and still is, a treasured family ritual. Family rituals are the experiential scaffolds that bind you together; they don't have to be elaborate, they just have to be yours - unique and meaningful.

The Talking Stick

Consider holding monthly (or weekly) family meetings. Don't wait until there's a crisis. Use these meetings to produce new solutions for family problems or develop plans for vacations, parties, projects, etc. A worthwhile tool is the use of a traditional Indian 'talking stick.' This could be a spoon, a decorative stick, a branch, a stone, a stuffed animal or whatever you choose. When one holds the stick, they have the floor. No one can interrupt, ask a question or divert attention from the speaker. The person holding the stick speaks until s/he feels heard, accepted and understood. S/he accepts questions and comments only when s/he is ready. When you give up the stick to someone else, you remain silent and attentive while you listen to that person. This changes the dynamic from being defensive to being open, attentive and cooperative.

Backwards Day

Once a year I'd make a backwards dinner. Cake first, soup last – it was fun and livened up a humdrum week.

Shower Power

Shower time was always a blast when the kids were young. The two girls and I would jump in the shower together, laugh and play. Quite often we'd play 'geography' and get extra points for naming places we had been to or if we knew someone who lived there. The kids would holler and yell "ding, ding, ding!" when someone hit this great jackpot. Made the hair washing process a lot easier too!

Family Night

Set aside one night a week for 'Family Night.' Go bowling, go skating or swimming, make popcorn and watch a movie, bake cookies and play charades or board games. Make this a sacred family ritual. Our family decided to lighten up on 'organized' activities (like little league and soccer) and instead we spent the time together. It helped our kids develop strong bonds, enhanced sibling relationships, and now we all have memories of riotous laughter and sharing.

Plant a Garden

A study conducted for Britain's Royal Horticultural Society (RHS) has found that encouraging children to learn gardening boosts their development by helping them become happier, more confident, and more resilient. Gardeners tend to be hopeful and philosophical people who look forward to future seasons, enjoy the present and become more accepting when things are not perfect. Planting seeds and watching them grow helps teach patience and allows kids to develop a sense of empowerment when they sit down to taste the bounty. Perhaps they'll even discover for the bigger lesson: how a little effort now earns big payoffs later.

The Kitchen Elf

Kids are intrigued with stories of fairies, elves and the promise of magical events. Knowing this, at dinner one night I mentioned that I was going to try an experiment. I was going to try to conjure up a kitchen elf that would magically appear and clean up the nightly kitchen mess. I made some exaggerated arm movements, spoke a silly incantation and announced that I was going to lie down for a bit - hoping that an elf would come to my rescue. A minute later the kids were busy cleaning and holding back the giggles! Even though doing the dishes became one of their daily chores, they themselves would sometimes wish for own relief- kitchen elf. Magically, Daddy would show up to give them a break!

On Eating Together

Time together around a table is more than a way to pass time. Too soon the plates will be taken from the table. Too soon the seemingly endless clatter of dishes and conversation will end, like a dream dissolving not for lack of light but because of it. Children grow up, move on and break bread with their friends. Whenever you sit around the dinner table don't table your emotions or your memory. Pass the love.

Noah ben Shea

Sunday Dinner

Once a week on Sunday afternoons my parents would let us "make dinner" and it was so much fun! My sister made a simple meat loaf with ground beef, an egg, and breadcrumbs. My brother "made" the vegetable, usually fresh green beans (I think he boiled them, now I would prefer a steamer!) And I had the simple but 'tres' important job of making baked potatoes! I recall scrubbing them and piercing their skin before putting them in the oven with my sister's meat loaf. We were careful not to start the beans too soon, and it was an easy supper to prepare. When everything was ready, my mother and father came into the kitchen and sat down at the table, and in single file we presented our dishes to them. They made such a big deal out of what a delicious dinner we made, and then, treat of all treats, my parents cleared the table and did the dishes, which was our job when one of them cooked! So it was fun all the way around. My mother especially LOVED not having to cook, and it was warm and sweet family time during which we all felt good about our contributions and established great attitudes about cooking and pitching in with household duties.

Jackie Salvaggio, Lenox, MA

What a cool way to bring your kids together, foster independence and teach cooperation.

A Rose and A Thorn

Once a week, at a family dinner, go around the table and listen as each one shares one thing that s/he is grateful for and one thing that s/he'd rather be rid of from that past week: a rose and a thorn. This way you get to support and appreciate what happens in each other's lives.

Rabbi Tizrah Firestone

Yes You Can - Explore Beyond Our Shores

We were very fortunate to be able to travel with our kids and explore different countries and cultures. But there are so many opportunities to explore the world that we often forget to look in our own back yards, no matter where we live. Find a local farm and arrange a visit. Bring the kids to 'pick your own fruits and vegetables.' Go visit the national parks – they always have educational and fun activities. Go fishing. Go hiking. Go rafting. Go sailing. Sleep under the stars, even if it's in the back yard! Get out there and have a good look at nature!

Our kids are becoming more and more clueless about the world around them. I bet most of them would think that just going to a mall in the next county would qualify as a great adventure. The good news is: You don't have to be rich to see the world anymore. You just have to be curious. For just the price of an airline ticket, you can visit another country for weeks! Simply join a 'house and car exchange club.' Go explore the world! Check out these and other online sites: 1sthomeexchange.com, homexchangevacation.com, homelink-usa.org

Visualizing the Future

On New Year's Day gather up all of last year's magazines, some colored paper, poster board (or cut open grocery bags to be used as a backing) get some glue sticks and scissors. Have your family cut out pictures of things that interest them or images that show something they'd like to achieve in the coming year. Have each person assemble a personal collage and post them where each person can see his/her visual dreams. This powerful motivational tool works well for everyone. Pictures really are worth a thousand words!

Your suggestions...

Playtime

Toys and TV

TV may have started out standing for the word 'television' but now it stands for Tranquilizer/Vacuum. TV is an addictive electronic drug. It is a sedative, which sucks creativity, dulls the senses and destroys imagination. It has virtually no educational value and is mildly entertaining at best. As time goes by, it is rarely even informative anymore. I never allowed a TV in any bedroom - certainly there are better things to do in there! TV watching should be very limited. We restricted our kid's 'watching' (more like zoned-out gazing) to 3 hours a week, to be viewed on the weekends only. Occasionally there were some exceptions when a 'children's special' was being presented, but thanks to VCR tapes I could regulate what the kids could see and when. Even "Sesame Street," always touted as the gold standard, is of questionable value. Kids can learn numbers and letters from many other sources. As the kids get older they may want to watch a certain show so that they are still 'in the loop' with their friends. That's fine, just include it in the three-hour allotment.

Have you ever wondered why so many kids are being diagnosed with "Attention Deficit Disorder?" Just watch the never-ending series of rapid-fire scene changes in any TV production and the answer will be obvious. Scenes and sequential conversation are rarely longer than 5 - 15 seconds – we are actually training our kids to lose the ability to pay attention!

TV's only redeeming feature is that you will have some quiet time whenever it is on.

Theater is life.
Film is art.
Television is furniture.   a T shirt inscription

To make matters worse our children are being 'screened' from the real world. Consider this: our kids watch movie screens, TV screens, video screens, computer screens, and telephone or hand-held screens all day, every day. No wonder they have trouble paying attention to reality, whether it's the teacher, following an in depth discussion, or focusing on real world activities. It seems that if it's not in 2-D, it's becoming more difficult for our kids to relate to the real 3-D world.

The Tools of Childhood: Toys
The Essential Few

Alphabet letters and shapes
Blackboard and Chalk
Backgammon board
Balls of all shapes and sizes
Books
Binoculars
Bug inspection containers
Camera (age appropriate and inexpensive)
Cash register with lots of real change and play dollar bills
Cardboard boxes
Checkers
Chess set
Child-size reading chair and lamp
Construction toys (Lego's, Tinker toys etc.)
Dolls or action figures, plastic animals
Dress up clothes and costumes
Flashlights (for exploring, making shadow animals on the walls and
making scary monster faces!)
Hand and finger puppets
Magnifying glass
Memory and other board games
Microscope
Music – CD player.
Plastic measuring cups, pots and pans
Paper, pencils and crayons, watercolor paints, finger paint*, glue, scissors
Play Dough
Playing cards
Plastic water bucket and 2" paintbrushes
Puzzles
Scrabble set and dictionary
Wooden blocks (one or two boxes)
Work/Play area, with appropriate sized writing table and chair

*Add a few drops of dish detergent to finger paints, for easier clean up.

Toys

Have you ever noticed that kids who have too many toys have decreased attention spans, limited imaginations, lack spontaneity and creativity? They don't know how to play. They only know how to manipulate objects – big difference! My kids had plenty, but still fewer toys than their friends so they just became more creative with the stuff they had on hand: they invented and ran three pretend corporations: a Veterinary Clinic, a Candy Store and a Dance Tech Studio. These enterprises had price lists, business plans and accounts payable records (all of which they took very seriously)! Their friends would come over and play for hours.

I suggest that you limit the number of toys available at one time and never introduce more than one new toy at a time. After a birthday party, sort the presents and have the 'birthday person' choose two new things to play with ... put the rest away for another time.

Less is definitely more.

The Best Toys

Like most babies, my son was not amused by commercial toys. He preferred playing with everything else, like pots, pans, Tupperware, paper bags, cardboard boxes and my husband's tools. So we said, "If it won't hurt him, let him play with it." We were careful, because the simplest things can hurt kids. The kitchen was usually dismantled, but he always seemed to be entertained.

Peggy Solomunsen, Sweden

Toys That Stereotype

The messages we send to kids as they are growing up have the power to influence the rest of their lives. And (these) toys do send a message about the roles of women and men in our society. Through the world of toys, girls and boys are given separate dreams to follow. Girls are prepared for a future of looking pretty, keeping house and taking care of babies. Boys are given a pass on that domain, and instead pointed toward the outside world of challenge, physical development and achievement.

A lot of this has to do with making money, I'm sure. After all, if girls and boys don't share toys, families with kids of both genders have to buy twice as many products. But it's also about promoting difference between the sexes. Our society, heck, the whole world, still isn't ready to give up the standards that define gender and all the rules and customs that go with it.

Women will never be fully equal until we, and all of our society, stop restricting our children's aspirations based on their sex, and constantly directing them toward predetermined roles. It starts with pink and blue baby clothes, then dolls and trucks. Next thing you know, boys and girls are being segregated into separate classrooms and schools because they "learn differently." Then, they enter the workplace with an outlook that can only perpetuate division and derision.

Girls and boys both will benefit if we offer them limitless options. They will grow up to be more fully developed people if we give them the freedom to discover who they are, without the stress of tightly patrolled gender borders.

Kim Gandy, President, National Organization of Women (12/21, 2007)

Taming Testosterone

I'd rather my boys read or watch Playboy™ than let them play with guns and swords!
Judy Kaufman, Maggie Valley, NC

It's Sickening: Our Toys and Food May Be Killing Us!

In 2007, more than 25 million toys were recalled because they either had small, loose pieces that could become choking hazards or because they were tainted with toxic lead paint. Eighty percent of these toys were made in China. That's not only startling and terrifying for parents of young kids - it's outrageous! Yet the agency responsible for the safety of more than 15,000 products has only 15 inspectors at ports nationwide! U.S. imports from foreign countries have nearly doubled since 2000, but compared to when it opened its doors in 1973, today's Consumer Product Safety Commission (CPSC) has only half its original size in both staff and resources! Which, if you do the math, means they only had 30 inspectors before... obviously protecting our kids has never been a big priority. Who knew?

You can find out about recalls and safety issues from: healthytoys.org

or call the U.S. Consumer Product Safety Commission 1-800-638-2772

on the web: cpsc.gov

or: consumerreports.org/cro/babies-kids/school-age-kids/toys/toy-buying-advice/index.htm

or: for general health and product safety go to:
http://www.cosmeticsdatabase.com/

These websites let you sign up for email alerts about recalled toys:
toysrus.com/safety or kbtoys.com/safety

If you think your child may have some of these recalled toys in his collection, take them away. Ask your child's doctor about a blood test to measure lead levels. Your child can be treated if blood lead levels are too high. (Source: Healthy Life Letter, 12/2007)

Meanwhile, the Food and Drug Administration manages to inspect only one percent of all our food imports! With so little enforcement, companies that want to risk importing shoddy, unsafe products and food grown using polluted water and unsafe chemicals know they can get away with it.

We must demand that our representatives force these agencies to do better. Much better! Get involved - tell them 'they're making us sick!' (Source: Consumers Union Advocacy and Mom'sRising.com)

Beware of Kiddy Bling

Little girls love to dress up and wear some glam, but kid's costume jewelry is becoming dangerous because of the inclusion of cadmium.

Cadmium is a soft, whitish metal that occurs naturally in soil. It's perhaps best known as one half of rechargeable nickel-cadmium batteries, but also is used in pigments, electroplating and plastic. Lab testing organized by The Associated Press shows that it also is present in children's jewelry — sometimes at eye-popping levels exceeding 90 percent of the item's total weight. And kids think nothing of putting stuff in their mouths.

"Just small amounts of chemicals may radically alter development," said Dr. Robert O. Wright, a professor at Harvard University's medical school and school of public health. "I can't even fathom why anyone would allow for even a small amount to be accessible." Recent research by Wright found that as cadmium exposure increased, the kids were more likely to have lowered IQ's and learning disabilities. Be careful of the bling. (Source: anh-usa.org)

On Creativity

In our house, if a toy or gift came in a box or some type of wrapping, what was 'outside' was always more interesting to my kids than what was inside. Cardboard boxes became all kinds of houses and hide-outs, bubble-wrap paper was like finding gold, and strings, ribbons, and bows went a long way in the creation of many masterpieces.

Kathy Zuckerman, Montreal, Canada

The List

Whenever we were out shopping or if we went to the toy store, the kids naturally wanted to buy 'something' to take home. I developed a strategy which satisfied them for the moment, taught delayed gratification and had the kids evaluate what they needed from what they wanted.

I kept a little notebook in my purse and when they said they wanted an item, we ceremoniously wrote it down on 'the list.' When we returned to the store to actually buy the toy, it was only after we discussed the stuff on the list and the value of the toy in question. Then we made an informed, rather than impulsive, purchase... it worked really well! It also saved a lot of money, whining, yelling and tantrums, because if a fuss was made, the desired item was instantly crossed off the list! The list can be applied to junk food, junk cereal, junk movies and junk in general... definitely the most useful child-rearing tool to ever pop out of my mouth! But in order for it to be truly effective, you have to occasionally, really buy something that's on the list.

The Best Play Dough

2 cups flour
½ cup salt
2 tablespoons oil
1 tablespoon alum (ask the pharmacist for this powder astringent)

Stir all ingredients together. Slowly, add 1¾ cups very hot water (with or without food coloring). Knead until you reach the desired consistency. This makes very soft, pliable dough that will last a long time.

Baking Soda Clay

1 1/4 cups of water
2 cups of baking soda
1 cup of cornstarch

Mix ingredients together for a non-toxic modeling clay. Add a dash of food coloring for extra fun.

EDIBLE PLAY DOUGH

Peanut Butter Play Dough

1 1/2 c. peanut butter
3/4 c. powdered milk
3 tbsp. honey

Mix all ingredients together. Form play dough into shapes. While you play with it, you can even eat it!

Lactose Intolerant Peanut Butter Play Dough

1/2 cup peanut butter
1/4 cup honey
4-6 oz. corn flour or corn meal

Mix the peanut butter and honey together. Add the corn flour until it reaches the desired consistency.

I came up with this idea after finding recipes only using dried milk. I had a very lactose intolerant child in my class. In my opinion this recipe tastes better than the recipe using dried milk. Note: Corn muffin mix (like Jiffy-Mix) can be substituted for corn meal.

Tricia Dalaba

A Puzzling Conversation

When the kids are in elementary school, set up a card table and keep a family puzzle going. While everybody works on it at their own pace, you'll probably notice sibling cooperation and conversations happen quite spontaneously... amazing!

Pre-Picasso Painting

Being a Mother of four very peppy and close-in-age children, I had to keep them busy at all times. My best summertime game was a real hit. Early in the morning before it got too hot in Memphis, we played a game which would last for hours. I gave each of my little darlings a brightly colored plastic bucket filled with cool water and a clean, new 2" paint brush. They proceeded to 'paint' the back porch and steps. As the sun dried their efforts they'd paint it over and over again. It kept them busy and cool for hours, as I sat under my magnolia tree sipping sweet tea, and watching my budding artists at play.

Saralyn Singer, Plano, TX

On Play

Kids now have cell phones, video cameras, digital cameras and an array of interactive video games, which are geared to entertain from infancy onward. No doubt this has the potential to send parents into paroxysms of worry, and for good reason. Hours in front of the screen means less time in social interaction. Pushing buttons on a control translates into fewer push-ups and exercises. And constant visual stimulation – well, that can only exacerbate our already short attention span.

Overdeveloped thumbs might turn out to be the least of our worries. We may wind up raising unimaginative, asocial, overweight children who don't know how to sustain eye contact. But don't blame the kiddies.

Toys reflect the culture, and we are a juiced-up society that can't unplug itself. We've forgotten how to be quiet. We don't know what it's like to be bored. We hate to be away from the constant stimulus that promises to keep us connected 24 – 7.

And in the end it's that loss, that inability to be alone with ourselves, that should concern us most.

Ana Veciana Suarez, Miami Herald Columnist

Sharing Toys

When you're over at someone's house and the kids start to get upset about sharing their toys, I say to the host child, "I promise that we will leave everything here that was here when we came. Remember, my son/ my daughter only gets to play with these toys while s/he is here – you get to play with them anytime."

Meredith Knight, Winchester, MA

It's New Again!

Every few weeks, I go into the kids' playroom, put half the toys in a bin, tidy up and leave clean, orderly shelves. A few weeks later while the kids are sleeping, I do it again, thereby switching the bulk of toys. I'm always amazed how excited the kids get about their 'new stuff!' Occasionally I add in something from the 'birthday stash' waiting in the closet.

A Whole New You!

Often children only see their parents as authoritarian figures and it's hard for them to see you as you really are - a whole person. To change their perception look for something to do together that either gets your entire family participating as equals, or find an activity that involves parents and kids on a whole different level other than the usual parent - child relationship. Perhaps you can find an interest that allows you to be equals first; become students together so that you both take direction from someone else. Or find hobby that allows your family work together as a team; hook a rug, write a book, paint a family masterpiece, quilt a blanket, play music together, learn to sing and harmonize, learn a new language before heading off to a distant land, plant a garden or get involved in a (noncompetitive) family sport ... team bowling, boating or sailing.

Play-ing Together

Find something that you and your child(ren) can do together. For me, the experience of performing in a local play with my son was incredible. Not only did he get his first chance to be on stage, I got the opportunity to build something creative with him (and be a co-worker/colleague instead of just a Mother.) It was wonderful.

Sandy Cash, Beit Shemesh, Israel

'Ending' the Opposition

So many video games seem to have one thing in common: They involve solitary play, and in order to 'win,' you 'the player' are asked to tackle, dominate, eliminate or 'kill' the opponent. There may be many varieties, but it appears to me that most of the video and computer games are the essentially same, albeit with different characters or scenarios. They seem to encourage an aggressive approach and teach the player that this is acceptable, if not the only way to win. When computers were relatively new and my kids played one of these relatively innocent games, I insisted that they referred to the elimination of the opposition as 'ended' rather than 'killed.' They thought I was nuts, but I felt (and still do) that if we allow our kids to become desensitized to these words, their feelings about these words will soon follow. We live in an age of drive-by shootings, nightly news telecasts describing murders, war and mass genocide... we are already visually desensitized, as we listen without flinching to these reports. If we allow our children to control a 'game' whereby they are enabled and encouraged to 'kill' something (even innocuous Pac Man!) – it can't be a good thing!

Update – Dr. Vincent Mathews, professor of radiology at Indiana University School of Medicine recently explained the results of a study; "After playing a violent video game, these adolescents had an increased activity in the amygdala, which is involved in emotional arousal. At the same time, they had decreases in activity in parts of the brain which are involved in self-control." The findings were to be presented at the annual meeting of the Radiological Society of North America. (Source: HealthDay News 11/28/06)

Playtime and Exercise

There's no substitute for good old outdoor play. As a child I never knew anyone who was diagnosed with 'hyperactivity.' In fact this diagnosis didn't exist until kids became more housebound. We walked to and from school twice a day, as we came home for lunch. We played outside after school almost every day, riding our bikes around the neighborhood or skiing, ice skating, playing hockey, building forts or igloos in the snow, rollerblading, playing baseball or swimming, etc – and all on our own – no leagues, no organizations – just kids playing together! What a concept... Then there were small household chores, homework, dinner, maybe one TV show, bath time and bed. Who had energy to be any more active? We were pooped! Hyperactivity...? There was no such thing. Get your kids out there, moving more and sitting less ... there's no drug that can compare.

A Balancing Act

Eat right and exercise in front of your children. My kids have asked me, "Do you really like eating that?! Do you really like all that running?" I tell them, "Life is not necessarily about what you want, it's about what you need, and this is what a body needs." I explained to them that their grandparents never exercised, and perhaps this is why grandma has aches and pains, and limps when she walks. I remind them that both grandpas died at early ages – they smoked, and didn't take care of themselves. While they are outside playing, I'll often go running. When they see me 'coming 'round the mountain' for a 2nd mile, they cheer me on! My son (begrudgingly) has begun running (1 mile) on the treadmill at least 3 times a week. My daughter started eating more fruits and fewer sweets for dessert. If they eat right and exercise, it's ok to have a piece of cake or an ice cream over the weekend. Life is about **balance.**   *Jeanette M. Barceló, Boca Raton, FL*

Run For It

I have always been a fitness nut, and I wanted to make sure my kids stayed fit as well, but that grew to be a challenge during the summer months when they weren't involved in school sports. So, in order to earn their allowance, I would create a list of chores for them to do each day around the house, and I would include 30 minutes of some type of continuous exercise. If they didn't do the exercise, they didn't get their full allowance. As much as they would protest, once they started moving, they almost always wound up running, biking or swimming for even more than 30 minute mandate. They have both continued to work out regularly!

Jane E. Johnson, Tallahassee, FL

On Rainy Days

My Mother used these two of her 'aces up her sleeve,' when she had just "had it" with us 3 kids, stuck inside on a rainy day: She would throw a blanket over the dining table and give us flashlights, playing cards, and just a toy or a game, and we played under there in our own private "apartment" for hours, as she emphasized, "Without any fighting!" I guess we were thrilled with our own space. Sometimes, when it was raining my Mother would "let us" go play in the back of our station wagon while she watched us from her blissful silence indoors, through the window. She, of course, never gave us the keys and she never let us out of her sight, but she had an hour of two of quiet time and we were delighted to play "pretend" in the car. Oh, 1958!!!

Jackie Salvaggio, Lenox, MA

On Education

School Education

It's no secret that our educational system is inadequate. Our kids are really being shortchanged. But there is quite a bit you can do at home to bridge the gap. There's a marvelous set of books, which begins in kindergarten and continues through 8th grade entitled "What Every___ Grader Needs To Know." I found that this series fills in a lot of world history and culture, which sadly is not taught in our school system. I was disappointed when I realized how Ameri-centric the curriculum is. American history is taught over and over again. And now that I've read "Lies My Teacher Told Me" by James W. Loewen, I realize that the texts teach whitewashed half-truths, sanitized, revised American history lessons at best. Most children don't have any idea that ancient civilizations are responsible for developing math, science, physics or the arts. Our neighboring countries of Canada, Central America and Mexico remain undiscovered mystery civilizations. Our children can't find any major countries on a blank map! Our kids are oblivious. They just don't know what they don't know - and the rest of the world has so much we could learn from! Our children have the false impression that we know everything because they are always being told that the USA is "the greatest country in the world." Yes, we have a lot, but America is still a preteen in comparison to European countries. As technology brings us closer than ever to the rest of the world, wouldn't it be wise to give our children a more global education? Our children should learn about other cultures and religions in order to understand how we fit into the world. We need to discontinue the impression that the world revolves around us. Our children need to feel that they are 'global citizens' because only then will we have a world where we all work together, solving our global problems. This change will happen when global Moms push for a shift in the collective mindset, from 'me' to 'we.'

And another thing…

When I was in grade school I was told that soon we would be learning 'Esperanto' an international language. What a fantastic idea! One language linking every citizen on the planet! Can you imagine everyone freely communicating without any linguistic ownership, cultural bias or poorly expressed translation? It made too much sense – it never happened. But Esperanto is an easy-to-learn living language! I suggest that we strongly urge our school boards to include its teaching in the curriculum. Talk about a global peace initiative - within one generation we could do more to enhance global peace, (from the bottom up) than if all the world's leaders sat together in room for a year.

And one more thing…

When I see the world in chaos, as it is today, I wonder if there's really any value in mandating the study of history. As I understand it, the traditional explanation for the inclusion of history class in the curriculum has been "you have to understand the past in order to move forward, or you'll be doomed to repeat it." Well, lately when I want to assess any given idea, I've learned to ask one simple question: 'Is this approach working?' Too often we just go along to get along. We accept the same old, same old, just because it's always been done that way.

Consider this: The study of 'history' really means; who killed who, who reigned over and controlled who, who took another's land, riches and property, when and why... all through the ages. Aren't we just setting our children up to believe that fighting and killing are acceptable ways of dealing with conflict? Are we legitimizing 'the sand box mentality' I described in 'The Testosterone Problem'? And isn't it always 'his – story' that is taught? Not a word about the women and children... as if the only thing worth learning about is male dominance. Perhaps we'd all be better served if we strive to achieve a worldwide, collective amnesia – because in spite of the old adage, we really haven't learned anything from studying the world's mistakes. In fact, the only thing we have learned from studying history, is that we haven't learned anything from studying history. We just keep on repeating the same mistakes. The world has behaved very badly, and our kids should know that. I'm not suggesting that we try to sweep our collective dirty secrets under the carpet. But I am suggesting that instead of glorifying war, which is usually some form of religious or ethnic persecution, let's inform our children of the brutality, give them brief descriptions of various wars and the cruel insanity of the Holocaust, but let us not dwell on the negative year after year. Teaching history as we have been only carries forward tribal mentality, ancient bitterness and perpetuates legacies of hate. Look at today's wars – has anything changed? Religious persecution and ethnic hatred abounds. Genocide remains a current issue. (And if we're not stopping it, then aren't we part of the problem?) Insanity is 'doing the same thing, expecting a different result.' So let's stop doing the same thing. Instead of allowing our schools to be tools of indoctrination and perpetuating 'group think' perhaps we should insist that the curriculum be revised to teach creativity rather than the study of cruelty. If we want to evolve we must change! What can we change? Only what we feed into the hearts and minds of our children.

We need a paradigm shift. So here's one idea. Perhaps we could better use the 'history' time period to teach our children about peace initiatives and conflict resolution strategies. As well we should celebrate the positive achievements and beautiful (historical) contributions from all the world cultures. Which civilizations are responsible for inventing algebra, geometry? (No, we're not going to declare war on those societies, children!) Who first explored astrophysics? Who has made the most significant medical contributions? What inventions have different civilizations given to the world and what impact do they have on our lives today? Trace the roots of electricity, refrigeration, and modern medicine. What do the great works of art and music have to teach us about a particular time period? Memorize the names and explain the accomplishments of Nobel laureates, philosophers and scientists. Wouldn't this approach stimulate thought and advancement better than having our children memorize dates and facts about battlegrounds and a lot of deceased generals?

When we evaluate our educational system and what it plants in our children's hearts, we need to decide: Do we really want to plant the seeds of old, and teach our children to remember hostilities? Do we want them to believe the often biased worldview portrayed in so many textbooks? Or, do we want them to think creatively and be positive about the world and themselves?

How do you feel about this? If we Moms band together and demand this one little change, maybe we could affect world peace faster than all the world's politicians, diplomats and dignitaries.

A brave heart is a powerful weapon.   Rudy

Let Real Life Be the Teacher

My mother-in-law gave me a very important lesson. She said: never let school stand in the way of your child's education. Given the choice between being in school and taking a family trip where a child can have new experiences, the trip wins hands down. I wouldn't advocate pulling an older kid out of school during final exams, but for the younger ones, there's almost nothing that can't be learned later.

Sandy Cash, Beit Shemesh, Israel

Learning Diffabilities (no I don't have a lisp)

When I was growing up I had a severe disability. To the outside world I looked perfectly normal, but inside I was quite sure that I was retarded and fought to keep my secret to myself. My friends were quite bright, and it seemed to me that *they all* got very good grades. And there I was, so dumb I couldn't even read. I struggled and tried so hard that my eyes would hurt, my stomach would knot up, I'd get nauseous and my head would pound. I hated school and feigned illness several times a week. I dreaded whenever the teacher announced it was time for 'spelling' or 'reading out loud.' I could do neither, and I was so embarrassed, I wanted to escape and disappear. There was no word for my problem in those days – I was just dumb. Then came the day my deepest fear became a reality. The principal came to my house. He and my parents told me that I was going to be held back. All my friends were moving on to the next grade but I would have to repeat the year. There was no hiding my secret now – I was so humiliated! I wished the earth would open and swallow me up. I was nine; could there be anything worse?

My parents found a college student who was willing to work with me; she was writing a thesis on learning disabilities. We met several times a week in the clinic area of a hospital, furthering my belief that something was really wrong with me. Gradually we found a way to conquer my dyslexia. Through the use of color, we created a system to correlate letters and sounds into meaningful words and phrases.

I still read very slowly and it takes a lot of energy to garner the meaning from written text. As with any obstacle, one finds that there are many ways to accomplish everything in life. The blind read with their fingers, and I prefer to read with my ears!

There are many gates into the garden, but to enter the
garden you need only pass through one.

I've read hundreds (maybe thousands) of books on tape and CD's – and since I began listening attentively something strange and miraculous has happened. My memory has improved dramatically! It appears that my brain spontaneously rewired and reorganized itself after about six months of daily attentive listening. Both my husband and I noticed a remarkable, sudden difference. Whereas before, I had an average memory, now I have instant recall of all sorts of information – trivia, long-term memory, minute details of events and almost total recall of complete conversations. We later learned of a study which scientifically documented this phenomenon as many people have been sharing this experience. Reading with one's eyes may be traditional, but I would urge you to get some children's books on CD, climb into bed with your youngster and use the audio books for your ½ hour bedtime reading ritual.

If you discover that your child has any type of learning disability, I prefer 'diff-ability,' because there's nothing dis' about different abilities, please reassure her over and over again that she is not stupid or dumb or retarded and that there is absolutely <u>nothing</u> wrong with her. *Different doesn't mean damaged!* Some people are right-handed and some left-handed. Some people can run fast, draw nicely or sing on key. We all have gifts and we all have weaknesses, and it has nothing to do with being smart. It is only a matter of finding out how your brain works and learns best. If you still think that difficulty reading might mean that your child won't ever accomplish much, consider this list of dyslexics: John Irving, the author; Charles Schwab, the investment banker; Sir Richard Branson, founder and president of Virgin Records and Virgin Airways; Wendy Wasserstein, the Broadway playwright; Ted Turner, founder of CNN; Jay Leno, host of the Tonight Show; and Walt Disney. The list is a very long one, but this will give you some idea. There are many doctors and lawyers who have learning diff-abilities, too. You really can achieve anything. Find an alternate way to achieve what you want to learn, focus on your talents and make it happen.

Nobody's Perfect

As the Mother of four kids with a generous assortment of developmental problems, an important piece of advice: don't wait for your suspicions to blow over, and don't be afraid to push for educational or psychological testing. The earlier you get the help your kid needs, the sooner he'll be experiencing a more level playing field, free of the crippling frustration that can make a kid depressed and angry.   *Sandy Cash, Beit Shemesh, Israel*

Work It!

To quote the character Tyler Durden, from the movie 'Fight Club,' "We've all been raised on television to believe that one day we'd all be millionaires, and movie gods, and rock stars. But we won't. And we're slowly learning that fact. And we're very, very [ticked] off."

… Which points out how important expectations and self-perceptions are: Starting in the mid 1990's, a team led by psychologist Carol Dweck did a series of experiments over a 10-year period, focusing on fifth-graders. One fascinating study compared two randomized groups of children in a classroom setting. Researchers told one group of students that their achievements were due to their effort, and the other group was told their achievements were due to their intelligence. Those who were praised for their hard work, it turned out, were more likely to attempt difficult tasks and performed better than those who were praised for intelligence.

Why? Because children who were told that their innate intelligence was the key to their success were less likely to expend a lot of effort and take risks, perhaps because they were trying to maintain the image that the outcome was not under their control. But the kids who were told that their initiative and persistence led to their achievements were much more likely to 'work it.'

On Encouraging Early Reading Skills

The book "Goodnight Moon," by Margaret Wise Brown and Clement Hurd, is very popular at bedtime. On every page printed in color there is a mouse hidden somewhere in the picture. Have your child search the page for the mouse. Try it yourself, too!

Laura Johnson, Boston MA

Read to your children, even in the womb. Get a bookshelf that is "child height" so your child can pick out the books. When my son started to be able to identify objects in the story, I started to have him "fill in the blanks" so that he is reading the story along with me. He loves books now.

My son will often pull out the same books night after night. To keep it interesting for both of us, I leave out key words and have him fill them in.

For example, when we read Goodnight Moon, I will read, "In the great green room there is a _____ (telephone) (pause and you can point to the telephone if he or she needs prompting) and a red _____ (balloon) and a picture of a _____ (cow) jumping over the _____(moon)." This type of "active reading" helps children develop literacy skills.

Another reading trick is to point to different objects on the page and ask, "What is this"? Once your child gets good at that, you can up the ante by asking, "What on this page do you put on your feet?" (Shoes, socks, slippers) "What do you wear on your hands?" (gloves.)

Encouraging Early Math Skills

When you see things in groups, count them. If your child says " Fans!" I say, "You're right! I wonder how many fans there are, one... two... three?"

Meredith Knight, Boston MA

On Reading

Of course being able to read is a very big deal. I think it's certainly the most fantastic human trick of them all! Reading is, after all, a manmade invention for passing on information, and no doubt reading is the key to one's future. As a teacher once told me – first we learn to read, and then we read to learn. As soon as your child can pick out and read a few words, make a big celebration of it! Make a huge deal out of going to the library and getting her very own library card, take out some beginner books, go home and bake an "I can read" cake. Celebrate big time – leave no doubt in her little mind how momentous and special this milestone is. The more impressed she is with your enthusiasm, the more she'll want to tackle the books.

I recently heard of a Mother and daughter who started a 'book of the month club,' with a bunch of her friends and their Mothers. They started during the fourth grade and continued the reading club until all the daughters left for college. How fabulous, to bring girlfriends and Moms together for an intellectual and fun shared experience! Librarians helped them choose books that were age-appropriate, challenging, funny, or led to discussions about life's common problems. Read a designated book and then either meet at someone's home on a Sunday afternoon to discuss, share stories and snacks, or once in awhile, go out to a restaurant all together.

A child is not a vase to be filled, but a fire to be lit.

Some Teachers Rule!

Most everyone can think of a standout teacher who, often without ever knowing it, helped to shape or change your life. (Keep in touch with them if you can!) We have a friend (DavidRothmusic.com) who is a national touring artist, a musician. He sings of an elementary school teacher whose music class inspired him ... and how once, upon returning to his childhood home, he sought out this aging man in order to thank him. The teacher, having devoted his life to his students, never married. He didn't have children of his own and he was soon ready to retire. "Thank you for the music, Mr. Ryan. You'll never know how much it's meant to me," he told his teacher some 35 years later. "Thank you for the visit, my child," said the teacher, "you'll never know how much it's meant to me!"

One day my daughter came home and said that she needed to select an additional course to fill in her high school schedule. She looked through the syllabus and even though she already had keyboarding skills, she thought that by taking 'typing' she would to learn to type her term papers faster. As I looked through the selections, I was fascinated by all the interesting courses offered. I explained that, in time, practice would speed her fingers, but taking a 'philosophy' class would open her mind to new and challenging ideas. She didn't know what 'philosophy' even meant, but she signed up for it. That class changed her life. That teacher was inspirational - he stimulated her love of learning, as he encouraged his students to explore new thoughts and concepts. Because of one quick conversation and that chance course change, a terrific teacher gave her a dexterous mind instead of nimble fingers. Celebrate the teachers in your child's life - they turn on the power!

The Troubling Teacher

Our son's first grade teacher wasn't 'kind and nurturing.' In fact, she continuously hounded our little boy regarding his failed efforts to color and print. After numerous meetings with both the teacher and principal, it was decided that he needed "testing." A request was put in and after many, many months the school psychologist finally showed up. After receiving the results and learning of our child's learning disabilities, we decided that it would be best for him to go to a private school the following year, but until then the teacher would "leave him alone." Unfortunately, she simply refused to let him be and she continued to berate him in front of his peers. She just wouldn't leave this struggling little boy alone! I was hurt and angry, and I was at the school - constantly speaking with the principal. I learned to be an advocate. Always, always, be an advocate for your child. Be there. Go to school and make yourself very, very aware of what is going on. Speak up. And if necessary, be a pain in the neck! Nothing is more important than your child's heart and education.

Mom Acing Advocacy

Switching Out

Let's face it – we just aren't going to get along with everyone in the world. The same is true for our children. If there is a strong conflict between the teacher and your child, sometimes the only answer is to separate them. If you've tried to work things out; had a parent-teacher meeting, a parent-child-counselor meeting and a parent-principle meeting, and the personality clash is such that your child cannot learn well in this particular classroom environment – then it's time to take action. If you want to move your child into another class, ask the principle, "What is the policy and criteria for getting a child moved into another class? What is the procedure?" In other words, try to approach the problem and get the appropriate solution, right out of the school policy and procedure playbook. Go with their flow! If you go along with their criteria they will be less defensive, and almost unable to say "no" if you are willing to fit into the standards that they themselves have set.

On Test Taking

Point out that there are good strategies to adopt when taking tests.

Read all the directions before doing anything. Decide which portion of the test is worth the majority of points. If the last section requires an essay and is worth the most points, then plan to avoid spending too much time on a 'true/false' section and devote most of your time and effort to the essay. Quickly devise a schedule that will enable you to cover all areas of the test. This usually takes less than one minute. Then stick to your game plan! When your predetermined time is up, move on. Try to leave a few minutes at the end to look back over the test and check your answers. A few moments of checking can eliminate a lot of careless errors. Do not spend too much time on any one item. If you are stuck, just keep moving on! Do not leave blanks. If you have no idea what the answer is, guess. When in doubt, answer 'true.' Generally speaking, it is easier for teachers preparing 'true/false' sections to write 'true' statements. The odds are therefore in your favor if you answer 'true.' Look for 'give-away' words and phrases. In 'true/false' as well as multiple choice tests, such expressions as 'always,' 'never,' 'without exception,' 'in all cases,' and 'only' tend to signal a 'false' statement. Look for answers within the test. It is difficult to write a good test without including some of the answers.

Proper preparation prevents poor performance!   Nancy Pelossi

Type It

All children should learn to type now that computers are so much a part of our lives. It is vital to learn to type quickly and articulately. Hunt and peck typing is not adequate. An added perk - typing is the great penmanship equalizer!

Confession of A Science Fair Mom

I was an overactive Science Fair Mom. I'm guilty. I confess. I loved 'helping' with my kids' school projects. All that construction paper and glue, designing, layout and mounting ... it was 'our' once-a-year foray with an arts and crafts project. But I did too much. The kids always did all research and most of the writing, which I edited. But in the spirit of coming clean, I have to admit that I produced most of the artwork in the presentation. And I was rewarded for my efforts, too! 'My kids' usually got a place ribbon, or at least an honorable mention ribbon! This meant that their projects ended up at the Mall where they were judged against the entries of other students entries, from around the county. But as we strolled along the aisles, one thing that I couldn't help but notice was just how well organized and artful the other students' work seemed to be as well. It was plain to see that I was not alone. Either we have a lot of 8th - 10th grade students' who have very professional, graphic design skill sets, or we have a lot of parents competing for ribbons. Is it cheating to help your kids? Should we parents have to sign affidavits, declaring that, "_____ do solemnly swear that _____ did all the work on this project"? In retrospect, I wonder, would it really have been better to let kids compete against the other parents on their own? Or was I justified in lending 'a helping hand' after all?

Still Too Shy to Give My Name

Support Their Dreams

Steven Spielberg's parents gave him a cheap movie camera when he was very young. Albert Einstein did poorly in school, landed a job as a file clerk while he spent his time daydreaming - lucky for us! Edison was probably told to "go fly a kite" ... playing and dreaming are the essential links to greatness. Encourage it!

No matter what your kid says he wants to be when he grows up, believe him. Talk to him as if he really can do it. Strategize about the skills he might need to acquire. Although that particular ambition might fade away, he'll always remember how you supported his dreams.

Sandy Cash, Beit Shemesh, Israel

People often say to me that motivation doesn't last. Well, neither does bathing ...
that's why I recommend it daily.   Zig Ziglar

Your vision will become clear only when you look into your heart. Who looks outside,
dreams. Who looks inside, awakens.   Carl Jung

People often say that this or that person has not yet found himself. But the self is not
something one finds, it is something one creates.   Thomas Szasz

Not everyone can earn a PhD, but most can earn a PhDo!

On Mentors

If you have a child who needs advanced mentoring, do not choose educators based on their degrees, charm, performance skills, fame, connections, reputation, or how their prestige might have a positive effect on your child's career or college application. Choose a teacher because you genuinely like the person. Then, assess their credentials as an artist. Ask yourself, "If we met outside this of situation, would I like to be a friend of his/hers? Do I respect his/her life choices? What are his/her priorities? Does it match what I want for my child?" Because without a single conversation, your child will learn so much about life from this person. Children emulate their mentors. Lessons start young. It's about relationships. Those who teach the lessons - music, drama, voice, baseball, it's doesn't matter what - are as influential as you are in many ways and they will leave an indelible imprint on your child's life. If a teacher is going to be with your child over an extended period of time, then it's certainly worth your time to investigate and find the right one (even if it means you might be doing some extra driving).

I speak from experience. We were a fully committed Suzuki family for over ten years; three kids, six instruments, hundreds of master classes, courses, group lessons, institutes, parent lectures and thousands of private lessons, specialty camps, programs in alternative string, jazz and folk genres. My son, my eldest, has gone on to receive great acclaim. He has won many awards and has recorded his first CD to rave critical reviews. Nice, I know, but it didn't happen by magic. My husband and I were not musicians ourselves but we believed that children can do wonderful things with love and attention. We simply followed our son's interests and became more knowledgeable and involved as his needs dictated. Yes, my two younger kids fell into the vortex of music too, but now they have different things that they enjoy as well as music.

We didn't know that our son was a unique talent until we took him to a conservatory when he had just turned ten. The teachers drooled over him. They also barked at him, "Work hard! You need to dedicate hours and hours each day to practice!" He balked. He wanted to travel, play soccer and continue to attend little league. We listened. We too wanted him to have his childhood. If he wanted to be a musician later on, he could decide that later on.

At sixteen he has now decided that the world of music is his calling and we respect that as a mature decision. He has been around artists from every genre and he has seen firsthand how their lives have played out. Because we talk about everything honestly, he is learning to make good judgments on his own.

So, choose carefully who your children will spend thousands of hours with. It's a marriage between student and pedagogue. They teach your kids about life and values. Choose a great person and your child will learn far more than notes and rhythm. It's the best lesson we ever learned.

Tami Weiser, Westport, CT

Freedom Is Not Free

I once heard Richard Dreyfuss, the actor, speaking about the need to teach our children the fundamentals of democracy. Sadly this, too, is being neglected by our school system. He reminded the audience that our democracy is only 300 years young and it is truly a modern-day miracle. Historically, similar attempts to sustain democratic governments ultimately dissolved into theocracies, monarchies or dictatorships - and ours can too, if we aren't vigilant. We must teach our children that in order to enjoy civil liberties we must expect and demand our civil rights, and be dedicated to securing these precious protections. The 'tools' of democracy he mentioned were reason, logic, clarity, dissent, civility and debate. We must find the time and creativity to teach these ideals of western civil liberties or we may end up, as so many others in history, the oppressed victims of religious fundamentalists, stupidity, intellectual darkness or political fear tactics. *"When we observe one person ruling over people, dictating to the entire state,"* wrote the philosopher Jacob Klatzkin, *"we are really watching a large group of human beings conducting themselves with fear. But whom do they fear? In reality, the slaves are immeasurably superior to their master in terms of power. But each slave sees himself as one against all his fellow slaves. If they desire to rebel they are afraid of one another. It is not the ruler who is the source of the fear, but the army of slaves who follow his orders. Or, if you will, they fear themselves. Their weakness is an imagination, a slave's error. All great revolutions are really the correcting of this misconception, an error in the minds of the enslaved."* The social norms we live by today were once ideas that were socially unacceptable. The British did not see the American Revolution as an act of heroism or bravery. The idea that "all men are created equal" was a completely revolutionary idea. What any ruling party fears most is an individual who will stand up and dare to tell the truth - just like the child who said, "The Emperor has no clothes!" The Western ideals of opportunity, mobility, and freedom of thought and expression can all disappear if not protected by educating our children to expect these rights. We must also teach them to exercise critical thinking, question governmental power and verbalize their dissent if need be. It is our duty as citizens of a democracy to safeguard it.

Liberty – use it or lose it!

Practicing Civil Obedience

Every four years we have an opportunity to show our kids how 'the system' works. Discuss democracy, the ideology of the parties, the way the parties elect a representative to run for president, and the ensuing process. Encourage the kids, especially our girls, to get involved in the political process by working for a campaign. Even though kids can't vote until they're eighteen, they can certainly fill out their own personal ballot at home, come with you to the polling station and watch you vote. On election eve make sure they stay up to watch the TV and see the process unfold. We're always interested in something we get involved in, right?

Have Patience Please - a teaching story

A man found a cocoon of a butterfly. One day a small opening appeared. He sat and watched the butterfly for several hours as it struggled to force its body through that little hole. Then it seemed to stop making any progress. It appeared as if it had gotten as far as it could and it could go no farther.

Then the man decided to help the butterfly, so he took a pair of scissors and snipped off the remaining bit of the cocoon. The butterfly then emerged easily. But it had a swollen body and small, shriveled wings.

The man continued to watch the butterfly because he expected that at any moment the wings would enlarge and expand to be able to support the body, which would contract in time. Neither happened! In fact, the butterfly spent the rest of its life crawling around with a swollen body and shriveled wings. It never was able to fly.

What the man in his kindness and haste did not understand was that the restricting cocoon and the struggle required for the butterfly to get through the tiny opening were Mother Nature's way of forcing fluid from the body of the butterfly into its wings so that it would be ready for flight once it achieved its freedom from the cocoon.

Sometimes struggles are exactly what we need in our life. If we were to go through our life without any obstacles, it would cripple us. We would not be as strong as we could have been. And we could never fly.

What makes this story so touching is that the man was trying to do the right thing. The man had the highest intentions. And they were wrong. His good intentions were his failure. In much the same way, too often we try to sort out or preempt our children's problems. Make your children responsible for their own actions. Don't clean up their messes. Let them get themselves out of hot water and solve their own problems, while you stand by their side. It will save both of you later on....

Everything that happens to you makes you who you are. Helen Keller said, "Character cannot be developed in ease and quiet. Only through experience of trial and suffering can the soul be strengthened, vision cleared, ambition inspired and success achieved."

Author Unknown

Experience is a hard teacher.
First you have the test and then you learn the lesson.

The Easy Way and The Hard Way

Whether s/he's doing homework, a science project, cleaning her room or learning something new, impress on your child that there are usually two ways to do anything: the easy way and the hard way. The easy way involves working on one thing at a time, doing it diligently, concentrating and putting in all the effort the task requires to accomplish the job at hand. The hard way is doing it with half the effort necessary and then having to do it all over and over again! Put another way, you could say, short- term pain leads to long-term gain. Do it once, do it well and move on.

Inch by inch, life is a cinch.
Yard by yard, life is hard.

On a related note: I went to a conference regarding time management skills. The speaker recommended a similar approach for adults. As an example: When you pick up your mail, DO NOT put it down - walk over to the garbage can immediately, and toss the junk. As you sort the rest, select mail that you'll read and deal with <u>right now,</u> then place the rest in the calendar slots of an accordion file, to be dealt with on the appropriate day. Touch each piece of mail a maximum of twice: once when you receive it and once when you look after it – then you should be done with it! Don't keep moving it, making new piles and rereading the same mail. Haven't we all done that?

Sometimes the fastest way to get where you are going is to go slowly.

Noah benShea

Do Your Best?

So often we hear people say, "Do your best!" but is it really reasonable to expect that we can always perform at our best? None of us can always be on task, alert and 'in the zone' all the time. If we tell our kids that this is what we expect of them perhaps our expectations are too high. Maybe it would be better to ask our children what they think they want to achieve and what their goals are. Then trust them to decide when to do their best.

One Mom told me, that she would impress on her kids that most of the time good enough IS good enough. Pursuing perfection only leads to frustration and problems.

The Right Words at the Right Time

My son just reminded me of something I did for him when he was in high school. He always did everything to the best of his ability and he always strived for "perfection." But when you're competing in sports, perfection is a lofty goal. Once, when he went to play in a national finals playoff and I couldn't go with him, I placed an envelope in his suitcase with a few extra dollars and a note that read, "Remember, you're close enough to perfect for me." That was almost 20 years ago! He recently told me how much that note meant to him and that he intends to send the same message to his children one day.

Nancy Williams, Tallahassee, FL

Creative Thinking

Listen and Learn

Some kids have a real struggle trying to learn anything by rote memory, but most children learn song lyrics quite easily. Try making audiotapes for them to listen to using familiar tunes. If you can rhyme it, so much the better – but if not, using nonsense words to rhyme the endings works just as well. List country and state capitols, multiplication tables or anything that just requires repetition to learn.

an idea expressed by Elinder Martin

Memory Helper

Memory is all about making associations between what you already know and something you want to recall later. When you have to memorize a bunch of facts for a test, try this: Pick a room in your house that you can visualize perfectly in your mind's eye. Close your eyes and see it clearly, e.g. let's say you're trying to memorize the Presidents in order. Choose a starting point and identify 20 – 30 items, in the order they usually appear around the room. Now, visualize all the same articles: the couch, pillows, windows, window shades, coffee table, TV remote, pictures etc. being used by the people you are trying to memorize. See George Washington sitting on the couch, leaning on a pillow that has John Adam's face on it. There's Thomas Jefferson staring in the window, while James Madison is fidgeting with the remote. If you run out of furniture and knickknacks before your list is finished, move your mind into another room! The funnier you make the mind movie, the easier it will be to remember.

Practicing Active Listening

There's more to listening than hearing the words. Active listening skills include reading body language and nonverbal cues, withholding opinions until all the facts are in, and learning to discern when someone wants to hear your opinion vs. just wanting to vent. Some of these skills will take hold immediately; some will take decades to sink in. However, this is why we plant seeds. Some will bloom right away, while others take time to germinate.

A Mom who wrote into "Dear Abby"

Thinking Out of the Box

Looking for new and innovative answers is sometimes easier if you...

- Look for a similar situation that already has a solution and apply or adapt that idea to your problem.

- Flip the problem by asking 'why not.' For example: kids used to run around the grocery store, often getting in the way and causing havoc for the cleanup crew, until someone thought of two great solutions. Why not make grocery shopping a fun activity? Give older kids their own scaled down version of a shopping cart to navigate, give younger kids a fun place to sit and take a ride.

Where Does Stuff Come From?

Here's a fun way to get kids to think about all the products we consume. See if you can trace the origins of each of the following items. Discuss each component of the article: whether it was derived from an animal, vegetable or mineral, chemical or synthetic source. Discover how the product was assembled and where.

A wool scarf - Shampoo - Chocolate milk - Sneakers - Plastic bags – A garbage can
The newspaper – A CD player and CD's – Your house - Kitchen dishes – Carpets
- A telephone – Styrofoam cups – An oil painting – Woven basket

Explain that when you buy a product you are "voting" in a sense, and endorsing the company that markets the item. You are rewarding that company with your dollars and support. Empower your children to become savvy consumers. Discuss child labor laws, or lack thereof, in other countries.

Explain that there are lots of hidden costs, which other people pay, for every consumer item we have. A wonderful teaching tool can be seen at: thestoryofstuff.com

And while we're on the "where does stuff come from" subject ...

Childhood Sex - Ed

Don't wait. As kids ask simple questions you only need to give them simple answers. "Where do babies come from?" "A special place in a Mom's body called the uterus." Explain anatomical facts simply to children around the age of 10, if they haven't already asked. Encourage discussions about sexual feelings, respect, love and intimacy with older kids. Arm yourself with simple anatomical drawings and rehearse what you're going to say. If you're totally tongue-tied and need some guidance check out the book, 'Everything you Never wanted your kids to know about Sex' by J. Richardson and M. Schuster.

The Art of Happiness

Happiness is a relatively new concept. For millions of years the human objective was to eat, stay warm, keep out of trouble and procreate. Then came equipment, entertainment and the electrical energy to run them both. That has yielded time to think and time to pursue pleasure. There are actually people who are now studying this new phenomenon! They have determined that the ability to feel happiness is similar to one's having a body weight 'set point.' Each person may have his or her own happiness threshold, which seems to set at around age sixteen. So if we can provide a happy childhood for our children perhaps we can insure they'll be happy at heart.

Is that glass of apple juice half empty or half full? Of course that depends on which child you ask. Research shows that pessimists may actually do better and be happier if they mentally prepare for negative circumstances, plan concrete actions and practice constructive worrying. Optimists tend to have an expectation of positive outcomes. And it seems that life events may actually be determined by one's outlook – because like attracts like. Perhaps this explains the expression 'We make our own good luck.'

Personally, I think that if children see and feel their parents actively enjoying life, they will simply imitate them. Give your kids the gift of a happy example.

Happiness is an attitude.
We either make ourselves miserable or happy and strong.
The amount of work is the same.

Steps to leading a happier, more fulfilling life:

1) Give people more than they expect and do it cheerfully.
2) Marry a man/woman you love to talk to. As you get older, their conversational skills will be as important as any other.
3) Don't believe all you hear, spend all you have or sleep all you want.
4) When you say, "I love you," mean it.
5) When you say, "I'm sorry," look the person in the eye.
6) Be engaged at least six months before you get married.
7) Believe in love at first sight.
8) Never laugh at anyone's dream. People who don't have dreams don't have much.
9) Love deeply and passionately. You might get hurt but it's the only way to live life completely.
10) In disagreements, fight fairly. No name-calling.
11) Don't judge people by their relatives.
12) Talk slowly, but think quickly.
13) When someone asks you a question you don't want to answer, smile and ask, "Why do you want to know?"
14) Remember that great love and great achievements involve great risk.
15) Say "bless you" when you hear someone sneeze.
16) When you lose, don't lose the lesson.
17) Remember the three R's: Respect for self; Respect for others; and   Responsibility for all your actions.
18) Don't let a little dispute injure a great friendship.
19) When you realize you've made a mistake, take immediate steps to correct it.
20) Smile when picking up the phone. The caller will hear it in your voice.
21) Spend some time alone.

In a nutshell: The five simplest rules for happiness: free your heart from hatred, free your mind from worry, live simply, give more, expect less.

Here are some "Happiness Homework" ideas:

- Turn off the TV and DO SOMETHING. Socialize, exercise or meditate.
- Take up a hobby. Lose yourself in the experience and feel the 'flow' – become so engrossed in the moment that you lose track of time.
- Keep a weekly journal. Write down, in detail, what you're thankful for.
- Do something nice for someone else. Pick several good deeds and vary them.
- Set goals and try to achieve them, be persistent even if discouragements occur.

The happiest people don't necessarily have the best of everything, they just make the best of everything they have.

Now and then it's good to pause in our pursuit of happiness and just be happy.   Guilliaume Apollinaire

A Warning About 'Warnings'

We live in a time of uncertainty, jealousy, political polarization, religious zealotry, corruption, and crime. We can't escape the constant barrage of 'doom and gloom.' While the outside world is in an apparent state of chaos, within our homes we try to create a haven of peace and refuge for our families. Of course, we have an obligation to teach our children how to navigate through the world, become 'street smart' and watch out for dangerous situations. But consider all the warnings we cast, while still wanting our children to live free, open and carefree lives: The environment is unsafe, so watch out for toxic pollutants. They warn us that too much exposure to sunshine will give us skin cancer but recent studies show that people who have the lowest blood levels of Vit D3 – the vitamin we make from the sun's rays, actually have the highest rates of cancer overall! Be careful which toys you give to children! Be mindful of global warming! Be wary of people and never talk to strangers; they can be burglars, kidnappers, pedophiles, rapists or murderers! Cars are dangerous places so lock the doors immediately upon entry and always buckle up! There are hidden hazards everywhere so always wear a helmet for bicycle riding, motorcycle riding, snow- boarding, skate boarding, skiing! Read every package carefully and be aware of the warnings relating to their contents! Don't smoke, don't use drugs, don't binge drink, don't drink and drive! People can't be trusted so be careful in school and report anyone 'suspicious' looking, be wary of stalkers and bullies; be careful on the Internet – there are predators hiding behind aliases! Be careful of leaving plastic bags around – they are hazardous! Be popular with your peers but wary of peer pressure, bullies and backstabbing, venomous gossip, date rape and date rape drugs that can be surreptitiously placed into a glass of punch, or a can of soda! When you choose to become sexually active remember that the act comes with the threat of life-threatening viruses and/or cancer! Relationships may also be perilous – so watch out for boyfriends who may become physically, sexually or emotionally abusive! The list is endless... Imagine if aliens landed, checked into a motel and watched TV, plugged into the net and listened to the radio for a few days – they'd wonder why anyone on earth would dare leave their homes! You could certainly understand why E.T. would want to go home!

Of course we want our children to feel safe and secure, but we're always warning them of the dangers that lurk. Yes, bad stuff happens – but not all the time and not to all people. In fact, really terrible things happen rather rarely. Our world forces us to plant these seeds of caution, and we can only hope that these ideas don't germinate into feelings of fear, distrust or paranoia. As we try to protect our children with the armor of warnings about the world, we should also insulate them with a thick layer of humor to survive it. And remind them that in spite of everything, most people are good and life still pretty safe. Stop worrying. Get out there and have some fun.

Your impressions...

Medical Issues

The human body is designed to be a self-regulating, self-cleaning, self-protecting and self-healing organism. It is my belief that when we humans try to outsmart and mess with Mother Nature, sooner or later She will mess with you. (I concede, once in a while the great Mother needs a tiny helping hand – that's why we invented plant irrigation and make-up.) Consider the devastating effects that we have thrust upon the natural landscape, and the global crisis we are facing because we failed to respect our air, water and forestry resources. When we take advantage of Mother Nature's good nature, she teaches us the lesson of unintended consequences. In the last 60 years the medical establishment has sought to manipulate normal physiology and now we're beginning to see the damage caused by either good intentions and/or financial incentives.

I am not alone in my belief that we have undermined our very health by tinkering too much with the natural world. More and more, research is forcing the medical establishment to recognize that the epidemic diseases of our time (cancer, asthma, superbugs, auto-immune diseases, neurological and psychiatric illnesses) are the price we pay for a civilization built without any regard to the consequences it will have on human health. We must reconcile ourselves to the notion that Newton was right: for every action there is a reaction, whether we're talking about environmental or personal physics. 'Garbage in' will yield 'garbage out.' If we insist on breathing, injecting or ingesting pharmaceuticals, drugs, chemicals or synthetic foods, we shouldn't be shocked when our bodies rebel. A headache is not a Tylenol deficiency, a cough does not require suppressing and a baby is not born to become a human sponge – artificially pumped full of vaccinated pathogens.

If we stick to a wholesome, varied diet, breathe clean air, drink clean, unpolluted water and allow our bodies to function as they were designed to, we will be healthy. If we try to trick or outwit Mother Nature, we will get sick. It's just that simple. I can hear you thinking, "What about viruses, bacterial infections and disease?" Yes, we do have to contend with occasional illness, but for the most part if you have a healthy, functioning immune system, you won't get sick! Your body will rid itself of most disease and cancer cells, various infections, etc., if it hasn't been compromised, by inadvertent tampering. We will be better off if we allow our bodies to work without suppressing our natural defenses. I think that cough suppressants, fever-reducing agents, too many antibiotics, vaccinations and various other drugs are making us even more vulnerable to disease.

There are naturally occurring epidemics and pandemics which have plagued the world from time to time, and although I do feel sorry for the people who suffered through them or died, we need to understand that nature ebbs and flows to keep the world in balance. Diseases and plagues used to die off on their own accord. If they didn't, none of us would be here! But we are here because natural selection primed our genetic code and strengthened our immune systems over centuries of time.

We in the modern world have been quietly led down a radically different road during the last century. We have allowed the 'health care' industry (which should really be called the 'disease care' industry) to determine that no matter what ails us, our bodies cannot deal with it adequately – doctors need to intervene and drugs are always required! There isn't a sniffle, restless leg or sexual organ that doesn't need something! What are we thinking?

I think I speak for many when I say that I'm disappointed with the medical establishment. They are too slow to admit their mistakes. They allow questionable clinical studies funded by their benefactors, the drug companies, to go unchallenged. And when questioned, they treat even very well educated people with an air of condescension. A megadose of humility is in order. Medical errors kill the equivalent of four jumbo jets' worth of passengers every week! According to the Health Grades Hospital Quality in America Study (2011), the rate of medical harm occurring in the United States is estimated to be over 40,000 harmful and/or lethal errors each and EVERY day.

Perhaps the next time you ask a doctor about drug safety issues and s/he gives you that look, you might ask him or her to consider the following few recent examples highlighting our doctors, drug companies and FDA debacles: Pregnant women were given Thalidomide for morning sickness, causing thousands of deformed infants to be born. (More on that later.) Vioxx and Duract, they assured us, were very safe painkillers until they had to be pulled off the market due to patient deaths, which undisclosed study data would have foretold. The drug Rezulin was widely prescribed for diabetics, but it led to liver failure and also caused a number of deaths. Not until there were serious life-threatening illnesses did we discover that Fen-phen and Ephedra were very unsafe weight loss products. Adult antidepressants prescribed 'off label' to children and teenagers led to tragic suicides. The allergy and asthma drug Singulair is also being linked to suicide. Zocor, Zetia and Vytorin are drugs sold to control cholesterol, but are now found to be contributing to plaque laden cardiac arteries – the very thing they were supposed to alleviate! The much touted hormone replacement therapy (HRT) prescribed to tens of millions of healthy women was subsequently shown to dramatically increase their risk of breast cancer! Trasylol, used to control bleeding during heart operations is thought to have injured many hundreds of patients, although two far cheaper and safer drugs are widely available. (Source: 'One Thousand Lives A Month' 60 Minutes, CBS News, 2/17/08) And, oh yes, now we learn that Viagra may cause blindness... a minor price to pay for a little pleasure and a multibillion-dollar profit, don't you think? The 1990's rotavirus vaccine (rotavirus can cause infant diarrhea), had to be quietly pulled off the market after the vaccine caused several infant deaths. But recently the FDA and CDC have put it back on the vaccine schedule! (Source:cbsnews.com/blogs/2008/03/06/couricandco/entry3913875.shtml) And what about the inclusion of mercury, a known neurotoxin, into some vaccines and medicines for the sole purpose of enabling the drugs to be delivered in multi-dose vials? (See: mercury-freedrugs.org) Gardasil (the HPV vaccine) has also been implicated in dozens of deaths, convulsions and paralysis. VAERS is the FDA's Vaccine Adverse Event Reporting System. A recent VAERS report of HPV vaccinations shows more than 24,000 adverse events and more than 3,200 serious events. As of August 13, 2012, the VAERS report included 9,889 emergency room visits, 2,781 hospitalizations, 517 life-threatening adverse events, 894 reports of permanent disability and 119 reports of death following this 'safe' HPV vaccination. There is compelling evidence that the Ortho Evra birth control patch has been linked to a high rate of heart attacks, strokes, and deaths due to venous thromboembolism. And, Avandia (prescribed to diabetics) has been shown to have caused thousands of cases of heart attacks and cardiac failure. Sadly these are not isolated incidents. This is just a tiny sampling, and with the addition of more and more and more vaccines, well – we'll just have to wait and see what horrific iatrogenic incidences happen next.

The lesson? The 'studies' used to approve all these drugs aren't as scholarly or conclusive as we all thought. In fact it has come to light that negative trial outcomes are routinely deleted, so 'peer reviewed' studies are not the gold standard they are said to be. If you have the opportunity to use a natural remedy, try it first. And don't allow your doctor to be dismissive of anecdotal evidence either. Which would you rather rely on, a peer reviewed study with falsified data or 4,000 years of anecdotal evidence, from millions of people supporting the use of safe botanical and herbal remedies? And keep in mind, when it comes to anecdotal evidence, doctors do it all the time - they are more than happy to rely on reports from just a couple of their friends or colleagues when it comes to prescribing a drug for off-label use. Talk about a "do as I say and not as I do" double standard!

I was trained in the (western) allopathic tradition of medicine, the first tenant of which is the Hippocratic oath, 'primum, non nocere' or 'first, do no harm.' Apparently that dictum is just so quaint and so yesterday, it's now totally disregarded. Western medicine has become nothing but a vehicle to do endless diagnostic tests, promote drugs, chemicals, and surgical interventions. There was a time when a prescription drug was taken without a second thought. Doctors would prescribe and trusting people would dutifully swallow. But that was twenty years ago when modern medicine was still considered a source of miracles. Too many of our present day potions, end up being prescriptions for poison. Even the American Medical Association notes that prescription drugs kill as many as 198,815 people annually and put another 8.8 million in the hospital. (That means that only cancer and heart disease kill more patients than drugs!) With all the recalls listed above I urge you to wake up and embrace the I-age (information age). When a doctor prescribes a drug, ask if there's an old, tried and true treatment that will help you because very often, new is not better. When it comes to your health, question everything - even what I tell you. If the pharmaceutical fix is relatively new, the first thing to do is consult your computer, (Blackberry, iPhone, and Google, Ask.com, Safari, etc.) and quickly access a complete, unfiltered description of the drug and with all the associated risks, before you even pick it up from the drug store. Since 'safe until proven harmful' is the pharmaceutical, government, FDA and medical establishment's new standard, it behooves us to check-it-out for ourselves. Evaluate the risks, physical side effects, monetary costs and determine if the real benefit is truly greater than the placebo control. Quite often it isn't much different.

Modern medicine is great if you're bleeding, have acute appendicitis, a broken limb or a seriously infected skin laceration. But before you swallow any chemical mixture I urge you to let your body work – before it forgets how! If you eat good, wholesome food you will activate your own internal pharmacy, and if you allow your immune system to function - you will awaken the doctor within!

Be careful about reading health books. You may die of a misprint.
Mark Twain

The cardiologist's diet: If it tastes good, spit it out.

Too Much Fluoride Can Harm Young Children

Although touted as an essential part of daily tooth care, fluoride can harm some children, according to Health Canada. If children under 6 years old ingest high levels of fluoride while their teeth are forming, they can develop dental fluorosis, which causes very white areas or brown stains to form permanently on the teeth. This may also damage the tooth enamel, causing tooth pain. In addition, scientists at Harvard and Dartmouth universities have found that fluoride overexposure contributes to thyroid disorders, bone decay and memory loss, as well as multiplying the dangerous effects of lead tenfold. To minimize risks, parents shouldn't give fluoridated rinses to children under 6, and they should monitor the amount of toothpaste their child uses. Children should use a pea-sized amount of toothpaste and avoid swallowing it. Parents should brush the teeth of children under 3 years old without using any toothpaste. The risk of fluorosis decreases when children reach the age of six since their teeth have finished forming. (Source: Health Day News, 2005)

Spotting Speech Disorders

Speech disorders often result from abnormalities in development of a child's lips, teeth, tongue or soft palate. They can also be caused by hearing problems or by neurological conditions that impact speech. These conditions may include difficulty pronouncing certain sounds or combinations of sounds, or disorders such as a lisp or stutter.

The Children's Hospital of Cincinnati says it's important to diagnose and treat these problems early. These warning signs could signal a speech disorder:

If your child can speak in complete words or sentences, but consistently leaves out letters or sounds from words.

If your child substitutes a sound or letter for one that is more difficult to say, such as substituting a "w" sound for an "r" or a "w" for an "l."

If words are distorted, elongated with extra syllables, or are slurred.

By age 2-3 months, if your child is not trying to make sounds and or is not making vowel sounds.

By age 6-7 months, if your child is not trying to make consonant sounds, especially b, d, m and n.

After 18 months of age, if your child is still only able to mostly make vowel sounds.

By age 3 or 4, if your child's speech is still very difficult to understand, and there are certain sounds that he or she cannot make.

On Doctor Visits

If you have questions to ask, go ahead – there are no dumb questions. Write your questions down and ask them during the exam, not as your doctor is leaving the room.

Instant Replay - Instead of "What did S/He Say?"

It's extremely helpful to bring a small recording device to doctor's office visits, especially if you have a seriously ill child. So often we ask questions and, because we're nervous, anxious and trying so hard to focus on the answers, we don't really absorb the information we're given, or we get it wrong. Doctors should welcome you recording what they have to say. Additionally, if you have to see another specialist, you can have them hear the initial doctor's opinion firsthand. If recording is not possible, bring a trusted friend into the visit, someone who can listen objectively with you and for you. Have the doctor write down what s/he's telling you, so you can review it later.

I Don't Wanna Go...

Whenever we went to the doctor or we did something that my child did not want to do, I always made sure that there was something to look forward to later on that day. If we were going food shopping, he could pick out his favorite food and we would buy what we needed to make his favorite cookies that night.

Sunny Burdman, New York, NY

Sunshine in Your Eyes

Now that we've blown holes in the ozone, we need to protect our delicate eyesight. Keep infants younger than six months old away from direct sunlight. After that, do your best to shield your children's eyes from dangerous UV waves. Wide-brim hats and sunglasses still offer the best protection.

Eye Exams

If your child is having difficulty reading or focusing, and complains that words seem to be jumping off the page, or experiences a pulling sensation around the eyes, ask the ophthalmologist to screen for *convergence insufficiency disorder.* This condition is often missed and can be easily treated with visual exercises.

Your Pediatrician and You

MDs practice = 1 part art, 1 part science, 1 part experience/educated guess,
                1 part Bottom Line.

Parents insuring their children's health = 1 part trust, 1 part caution

Fact: Doctors are just people. Most are wonderful, caring individuals but there are a few psychologically imbalanced, pedophiles mixed into their ranks. It isn't as easy as one might think to discern who is trustworthy, that's why pediatrics is the perfect profession to procure prey. Always err on the side of caution and NEVER leave your child alone with a doctor, no matter what reason they may offer.

Fact: Doctors are only human. They make mistakes, individually and collectively. We've all seen it - one day they write a prescription, the next day the drug is taken off the market. One day 'they' tell you to do this, the next day they advise you to 'call your doctor' and stop doing that!

Case in point – a cautionary tale. Fact: *Thalidomide first appeared in Europe in the 1950's. It was used to treat morning sickness in pregnant women. However, between 1956 and 1962, some 10,000 children were born with severe birth defects (missing and deformed limbs) as a result of their mothers having taken this prescribed medication. (Source: Health Day News, Nov. 2007.)* It took ten thousand severely deformed, disabled children and over 6 years for the medical establishment to concede there was a problem! Lesson learned? When it comes to your child's health, ask lots of questions, ask for data, don't be afraid to ask hard questions or to ask for a second or third opinion. I'd rather be a pain than have my child suffer a life of pain! That said, let's talk about vaccinations.

Regarding Vaccinations ... The good, The bad and The We're Not Sure.

Buckle up – I'm joining a group of concerned Moms who are vigorously rocking the boat...

It is commonly believed that vaccinations are the single most important thing you can do to keep your child healthy. Most doctors and the lay public think that mass vaccinations are solely responsible for wiping out most of the diseases that killed thousands in the past. But a review of the data proves that those diseases were actually waning and dying out on their own accord, so perhaps those vaccinations may not have been as powerful as we have all been led to believe.

And yet, in spite of the data, the vaccination schedule recommended by the Centers for Disease Control and Prevention (CDC) and the American Academy of Pediatrics (AAP) has become extremely rigorous. Your child can receive up to 32 combined vaccinations by the time s/he's 2 years old and as many as 6 shots in a single doctor's visit! Doctors continually assure the public that this practice is safe, but to my knowledge they have never done any routine, double blind studies to back up this claim. In spite of the medical establishments' attempts to vaccinate and eradicate disease, it is also true that we presently have some of the sickest kids in the world. Consider this: As we have dramatically increased the number of vaccines, we have also seen simultaneous explosions in the rate of juvenile diabetes, childhood cancer, bowel disorders, asthma, allergies and autism.

The following quote was taken from a news release issued by the Children's Hospital of Philadelphia, wherein Dr. Paul Offit said, "A baby's body is bombarded with immunologic challenges - from bacteria in food to the dust they breathe. Compared to what they typically encounter and manage during the day, vaccines are literally a drop in the ocean." *(Jan 10, 2002)* He cites studies that show, in theory only, that healthy infants could safely get up to 10,000 vaccines at once. He recently revised his estimate to 100,000 vaccines! Really?! That's not the way I see it. Once again, let's defer to Mother Nature and take a lesson from her. She does not jab and inject micro-organisms into a newborn infant. In fact, she offers highly evolved protections from the environment in the form of salivary and stomach acid, nasal and bronchial mucosa and cilia. Then she adds a thick external coating (known as skin) onto which she invites a host of healthy bacteria to take up residence and defend against harmful organisms. She goes very, very slowly, introducing environmental challenges gradually. She insures that a baby, any baby, anywhere on the planet, is given twelve months to assimilate into his/her environment. This naturally takes the immature immune system through the four seasons, with all the accompanying allergens, viral and bacterial immune challenges. And assuming that the baby is breastfed, (as Mother Nature intended) all the immune protections available from the Mom are transferred to the infant via the breast milk, for as long as the breast milk is offered. While I have no scientific data to back up my concern (only because there is no data to research!) my Maternal instincts and common sense tell me that burdening a young, immature immune system with multiple vaccinations is not advisable. Look at it this way... would you expect an infant who was afflicted with 3, 4, 5 or 6 simultaneous, serious diseases to survive? No? Neither would I. So why do we inoculate a baby with those same pathogens (which, let's not forget, replicate disease!) and pretend that it's perfectly normal and safe? I repeat, there are NO DOUBLE BLIND STUDIES which show the efficacy of any vaccination.

Dr. Offit's contention that vaccines cannot cause autism is inconsistent with what even Dr. Julie Gerberding, the former director of the Centers for Disease Control (CDC), has said:

Dr. Sanjay Gupta: "Are we ready to say right now as things stand that childhood vaccines do not cause autism? "

Dr. Gerberding: "What we can say absolutely for sure is that we don't really understand the causes of autism. We've got a long way to go before we get to the bottom of this." (CNN, March 30, 2008)

I offer one simple question: What is the big hurry? Measles, mumps and rubella are not life-threatening diseases. In fact, I had them all, as did most of my friends – we're all alive and none of us has suffered autism, juvenile diabetes, ADD, ADHD or the other devastating illnesses so prevalent today. What's different now? The introduction of more and more vaccinations at earlier and earlier ages, which, you may not know, do NOT offer lifelong immunity to disease, nor is any vaccine 100% effective. Fact: A vaccination is the introduction of a weakened organism into the human body with the intention of provoking an immune

233

response, thereby assuming that this will eliminate the disease from plaguing that person in the future. But it's not true. Some people still do get the disease, even though they have been vaccinated! Vaccination by injection makes an unproven assumption that artificially provoking an immature immune system will yield immunity. Obviously that can't be true if 'booster shots' are necessary. Vaccination does not mean immunization! Fact: Measles is currently coming back, 'breaking through' in spite of all the vaccinations and boosters. So what's the medical establishment's reaction? Vaccinate with a third dose! Fact: Immunization can only be achieved when the body interacts with the actual disease. Here's a little history: Vaccination policies were put into place when there were only a handful of vaccines for children. Up through 1975, children received only oral polio and diphtheria, tentanus toxoid and pertussis (DTP) vaccines. In 1978 measles, mumps and rubella (MMR) were added, although they are self-limiting childhood diseases and at that time, the three illnesses combined caused only 17 deaths per 100,000! (17:100,000) Compare that to the rate of 1:88 children who are now being diagnosed with the lifelong disability of autism! In 2007, the following were added: hepatitis A and B, H. influenza (HiB), seven-strain strep vaccine (Prevnar), Rotavirus, Chickenpox, Human Papilloma Virus (Gardasil) and influenza. That is at least 110 vaccine antigens, plus traces of more than 100 chemicals, injected into children by the time they enter middle school. It seems to me that instead of focusing on what is happening now – an epidemic of childhood cancers, bowel disorders, asthma, allergies and autism, the medical establishment is still focused on either diseases of the past or diseases not typically seen in children at all. Most of the diseases that these inoculations are protecting our children from were illnesses that ran rampant long ago and although these diseases are rare now, please don't give all the credit to vaccinations. I, like some other medical professionals, think it may actually have been the Industrial Revolution that caused the demise and decline of most of those diseases! With the advent of food refrigeration, safer food handling practices, clean water supplies, adequate heat in the winter, cooling in the summer, proper ventilation, proper year-round nutrition, less crowded living conditions, modern personal hygiene practices and sanitary conditions, indoor plumbing and proper sewage systems, people were less prone to acquire diseases. Vaccines have only been around for 50-60 years, yet these diseases were on the decline long before that. Other diseases, such as hepatitis, commonly affect only those people with high-risk sexual or drug addiction behaviors. So, why do our one day old babies (who are neither sexually active nor have any drug habits) need all this 'protection'?

Ask yourself this: What would happen to all the 'well baby visits' if you didn't have to comply with a vaccination schedule? If you weren't going to the doctor to get a prescription, would you still go? Medicine is a business like any other. The shoe salesman sells shoes and the doctor sells ...?

I urge you to please read, 'Vaccination Is Not Immunization' by Dr. Tim O'Shea, before you agree to any vaccines. This is an extremely important book which provides easy-to-understand, important information and data. Available at: thedoctorwithin.com

Doctors are trained to hold themselves in very high regard. They rarely disparage one another, even when their diagnoses are drastically at odds. Doctors are notorious for toeing the establishment line and anyone who dares to buck the current trend is often ostracized, has a hard time getting his findings published, finds it difficult to acquire research funding, is labeled 'a maverick' and pooh-poohed by his peers. Small wonder few question the status quo. *In The*

Structure of Scientific Revolution, it is noted that new ideas are first ignored, then ridiculed, then vehemently attacked, then finally accepted as obvious, and then claimed to be the establishment's own all along. I suspect that this will be the case when history judges our present vaccination schedule interfering with normal childhood development, physiology and immunology.

I would never presume to tell you what to do, but if I were a new parent I would not be lazy. I would make 'education before vaccination' my mantra and I would vigorously research vaccination concerns. I might ask the doctor to provide me with literature that describes: 1) an independent, standard double-blind, long-term study that proves that vaccines actually work; 2) the vaccine's package insert, disclosing of all the risks involved; and 3) a standard study showing the long-term safety of each vaccination. I would study this material _before_ allowing anyone entry into my child's body. I don't think that is too much to ask, considering that I would be giving someone permission to literally invade and inoculate my healthy, viable human baby with multiple toxic substances. (Hence the term 'toxoid.') I would postpone all vaccinations, at least until the age of two. I would bring a big, fat, red marker to the hospital, and write into the patient chart that "I do not give my permission for the Hepatitis vaccine to be given" at birth. If I did decide to permit some of the injections or nasal vaccination sprays, I would expect my pediatrician to limit the number of vaccinations given to my toddler and allow only one vaccine at a time. No trivalent, or combined injections. I would offer to come back to the office numerous times, in order to achieve any necessary vaccinations. I would choose which of the vaccinations are appropriate for my child. This may cost additional co-payments, but I'd be willing.

If I determined that I didn't want my child to be vaccinated, I would expect my pediatrician to respect my parental rights and decisions and provide the appropriate exemption form. Exemptions are permitted to government-mandated schedules. Mandated does not mean mandatory.

Please read Dr. Donald W. Miller Jr. and Dr. Sears articles for more on this subject.
lewrockwell.com/miller/miller15.html askdrsears.com/thevaccinebook/vaccine_faq.asp

I'm not suggesting that you distrust your doctor. I'm only suggesting that you become an informed parent/consumer before allowing anyone to do anything, or inject any foreign substance into your child's body. Once it's injected, there's no going back.

A physician from Strongsville, Ohio, Dr. Sherri Tenpenny states, "Doctors have an illusion that vaccines are "safe, protective and cause no harm." Pediatricians and other vaccinators are under-educated, uninformed and blindly follow the recommendations of the American Academy of Pediatrics, parroting the five-color glossy information (brochures) distributed by eager drug company salespersons."

The vaccine safety and informed consent debate is becoming more intense because more parents are reporting that their children are regressing into poor health after receiving many vaccines. Vaccines carry risks of seizures, brain inflammation and even death and often high-risk children are not screened out of the program.

For another perspective on vaccines, read Dr. Mercola's point of view: articles.mercola.com/sites/articles/archive/2011/11/03/right-vaccine-dosage-for-babies.aspx?e_cid=20111103_DNL_Art_2

Update: FDA, *Associated Press, Nov. 23, 2007*: Flu drugs affecting kids' behavior. Government health regulators recommended adding label precautions about neurological problems (including hallucinations and convulsions) seen in children who have taken flu drugs.

For more information please visit:
National Vaccine Information Center on the web at NVIC.org, VacTruth.com, nmaseminars.com, sayingnotovaccines.blogspot.com, cdc.gov/vaccines

* Flu vaccines are grown in egg protein (albumin.) If your child is allergic to eggs or chicken, DO NOT allow these immunizations to be given, even if they are said to be "safe."

An eloquent summation of everything I've tried to say:

We have more degrees but less sense, more knowledge, but less judgment, more experts, yet more problems, more medicine, but less wellness.   George Carlin

Getting a Shot

After all that I've said, if your child is going to get an injection, try distracting him/her by singing, tickling, counting, telling a joke, coloring, or focusing on a book, picture, TV, blowing soap bubbles or reciting the ABC's. Once the injection is delivered, give your child lots of positive attention, but don't harp on the shot. Do a fun, distracting activity afterward, like going to the park, getting an ice cream cone or going to a friend's house to play.

Always bring and apply an ice pack to the injection site immediately after the injection is given and continue to apply the cold compress as often as possible for the next 2 days. Neurosurgeon, Dr. Russell Blaylock also suggests that you increase the amount of Vit. D your child takes to at least 2000 IU. per day, for a few days before and after the injection to help reduce systemic, brain and autoimmune reactions to the toxic vaccination injections.

Source:http://articles.mercola.com/sites/articles/archive/2009/09/19/The-Truth-about-the-Flu-Shot.aspx

Call your doctor right away if your child gets welts or hives (which can indicate an allergic reaction), a fever of 101 degrees or higher, or convulsions.

Keep Records of X-rays

When you take a medication for pain or infection, you trust that it will do its intended job and then be eliminated from your system in a few days. But when you have an X-ray, no one tells you that the radiation that accumulates in your body will never be discharged or eliminated.

Granted, the radiation exposure is limited and it is generally safe. But we are now exposed to more X-rays than ever before, with the advent of airport screenings, dental checks and more and more diagnostic procedures and tests. Therefore, it is wise to write down and record every time your child has an X-ray, especially CT scans. The radiation and risk from one CT scan is low, but because a CT scan is actually a series of X-rays taken in very rapid succession, it carries a dose 50 to 100 times greater than a traditional X-ray. It has also come to light that some people may actually be getting cancer from too much exposure.

Update: CBS/AP, Nov/2007. Millions of Americans, especially children, are needlessly getting dangerous radiation from "super X-rays" that raise the risk of cancer and are increasingly used to diagnose medical problems, a new report warns. The report estimates the percentage of cancers caused by CT scans -- currently 0.4 percent -- will increase to as much as 2 percent in a few decades because the number of scans has increased so dramatically, reports CBS News medical correspondent Dr. Jon La Pook. "Our concern is there are so many CT scans being done right now that we should really be starting to think: Do we need to all of these CT scans?" says Dr. David Brenner of the Center for Radiological Research at Columbia University. Some experts say that estimate is overly alarming. But they agree with the need to curb these tests, particularly in children, who are more susceptible to radiation and more likely to develop cancer from it.

Medical Consent

Ask your doctor's office for a medical consent form. Fill it out completely and make several copies. Sign all the copies with a blue pen. Distribute the forms to your child's caregivers and grandparents, keep one in your child's medical file at home, one in the pediatrician's chart and one at your next-door neighbor's house. If your child should need medical attention, surgery etc. and you are on vacation, out of town on business, or involved in an accident yourself, all the necessary and appropriate 'consent for treatment' forms will be available in your absence.

Antibiotic Primer

OK, you're tired of the complaining, the crying and cranky behavior. You pack up the kids and go to the doctor's office. You wait 1 hr and 53 minutes in the waiting room, listening to other kids cry, scream, toss books and toys onto the floor - then you wait another 47 minutes in the exam room, watching the doctor skip back and forth, visiting every room but yours - you have a headache, you're tired, you need relief!

One of most common sources of childhood pain stems from ear infections. Prevalent causes of ear infections are: daycare outside of the home, parental smoking, and pacifier use. Your doctor knows that your child's ear infection, (technically acute otitis media) will spontaneously resolve 80% of the time with absolutely no intervention, or in 5 - 7 days with antibiotic therapy. (Even though the antibiotic may be prescribed for 7 - 10 days.) (Most doctors think that children younger than 2 years should always be treated.) The pediatrician recognizes your frustration, anxious expression, mournful plea for help as well as his/her own need to move on to the next patient. As the prescription pad emerges from the white-jacket pocket, you feel yourself begin to relax - relief is on the way! For the doc, it's just so much easier to write the order than send a patient home empty-handed and angry, because they 'came for nothing.' Antibiotics are over prescribed and because so many millions of antibiotics are consumed, the microbes we want to eradicate are mutating and becoming even more of a problem. Let me explain: Bacterial microbes are like us - some stronger, some weaker. As the weaker bugs are killed off, you begin to feel better. Waiting in the wings are the stronger back-up team players which have been kept in check by your normal, healthy flora. But as the antibiotics attack the healthy organisms too, the stronger bugs can take the stage and cause a rebound infection. Because bacteria are single-celled organisms with just a few genes, reproducing in just a few hours, it takes a very short time and only a couple of generations of bugs for them to reorganize, mutate and become totally resistant to our antibiotics. This is exactly how and why we are facing the problem of superbug and MRSA infections today. Bacteria have very sophisticated and complex DNA, which has adapted and survived millennia ... let's face it, those little organisms are beating us at our own game and I think the MD's are to blame.

Heads up, doc - get a grip.
You're the one who wrote that scrip'!

New evidence suggests that using antibiotics for much shorter periods of time may keep more of the healthy bacteria in your system, instead of unintentionally creating a selection that favors the development of antibiotic resistant strains.

The food industry also carries much of the blame, as they have been adding 28 million pounds of antibiotics each year to cattle, pork and poultry feed in an effort to keep the animals healthy so that they can reach your dinner table. Now drug-resistant bacteria are flourishing. So even if you are not actively taking these medications, if you eat animal products you are consuming them, whether you want to or not!

If your child really, really, really needs antibiotic therapy, then use it; that's what it's designed for. But don't encourage your doctor to write a scrip' just to soothe your frayed nerves. And if you do have occasion to use these drugs, remember that they don't make a beeline and attack only the harmful bacteria that are making you feel ill - they aren't that discerning; they go after every cute little bacteria in sight, knocking out even the most beneficial critters. So replenish the good bacterial supply by consuming a probiotic or serving live culture yogurt morning and evening, for the duration of the prescription and for the following week. But be advised that milk and dairy products block the absorption of tetracycline (and its derivatives) so make sure there is a 3 hour delay between medication and yogurt time. Also noteworthy: antibiotics do nothing to cure viruses (although doctors happily write 10 million useless prescriptions for viral infections a year), colds or the flu - it's like asking the doc to perform an appendectomy to cure a broken leg - apples and oranges - it won't work. Stop asking.

Related Update
In a recent retrospective study, it was noted that 65% of all children received some type of oral antibiotics (mostly broad spectrum) during their first year of life. Children who received antibiotics for non-respiratory infections were about twice as likely to have asthma by age 7, as children who hadn't used any antibiotics. According to F. Bruder Stapleton M.D., these results confirm those of previous studies that found an association between multiple doses of

antibiotics and development of childhood asthma and provide yet another reason to avoid unnecessary use of antibiotics, particularly broad-spectrum agents.

Related Update
Norway has completely eradicated MRSA. Completely. (Except for the cases that tourists bring back into the country.) How did they do it? They simply stopped using antibiotics! Completely. In the 1980's doctors began isolating MRSA carriers, prescribing herbal remedies, chicken soup, menthol balms and the like, and voila - the country's collective immune system woke up! In a few rare cases, when a life is on the line they treat the infection with simple, basic antibiotics. Simple as that! We can do it too of course, but then Big Pharma's stock would lose its value ... completely ... Not going to happen.

Measuring Medication

Never use kitchen spoons for medication dosing. It's so easy to innocently overdose medication if you rely on non standardized kitchen utensils, or mistake a teaspoon with a small soup spoon or tablespoon. Medication should be only poured using a measuring cap, a dosing syringe, a medicine dropper or medical dosing spoon.

Hack, Sniffle, Ha-choo

If your child has a cold or cough, stop all dairy products. They increase mucus secretions. Medicate with the oldest, safest antibiotic on the planet - homemade chicken soup. At bedtime elevate the head of the bed and/or prop the child up on extra pillows. Do not use over-the-counter medications. They have been found to be useless, if not dangerous. A safe and effective alternative, for children older than one year, is honey. Honey has been used for centuries to treat upper respiratory infection symptoms. Honey has both antioxidant and antimicrobial effects, and also soothes the back of the throat. (Source: Google Health News 12/07) Inhaling steam (in a steamy bathroom or via a humidifier) and squirting a few drops of a saltwater solution into the nose to flush out thick mucous should provide some relief, too. (Source: The Associated Press 2007)

Pushing Fluids

To get your child to drink more fluids, try serving the juice, tea, or soup from a small 'tea party' service. It's much more fun and it's not as intimidating as having to drink down a whole glass liquid.

Halting the Hiccups

Hiccups are caused by a harmless spasm of the diaphragm. It is an annoying disruption that can eventually become painful. Leave babies and toddlers alone as the condition will stop as spontaneously as it started.

For children and adults, try these home remedies;

- Touch the tip of your tongue to a teaspoon of sugar. Or...
- Drink some water from the edge of the glass while bending over at the waist. Or...
- Name 5 bald men you know. Or...
- Drink a cup of peppermint tea. Peppermint is an antispasmodic agent.
- Gently massage the soft spots just behind the bony prominences of the ears.

Pills Can Be A Pill To Swallow

If a child has trouble with, or is afraid of swallowing pills, have the child place the pill in his/her mouth, then have the child drink water, or any other liquid, out of a glass WITH A STRAW. It easily and quickly flushes the pill down the hatch. No muss. No fuss.

D. Vinegrad, Ottawa, Canada

Paper Cuts

Paper cuts hurt! For instant relief, coat the cut with a dab of lip-gloss which will smother the nerve endings and relieve the pain. If you are very careful you can mend a child's small cut with a tiny dab of Crazy Glue or New Skin. Make sure you wait several minutes and make sure it's completely dry before s/he resumes any activity.

Ouchless Bandaid Removal

Carefully blow warm air from a hairdryer over the bandaid for a few seconds and it will easily peel right off. (The blow dryer trick works to remove stickers, price tags and labels from packages too!)

Mosquito bites

Before reaching for the insect bite cream, try rubbing the affected area with the inside of a banana skin. Many people find it amazingly successful at reducing swelling and irritation.

Chew - Chew Chewing Gum

If the kids are in the habit of chewing gum make sure it's sweetened with Xylitol which has been shown to reduce cavities.

Not So Sweet Feet?

Warts - Cut a circle of duct tape slightly larger than the wart and apply to area. The immune reaction will attack the growth and dissolve it. Replace the plaster every 1-2 days.

Smelly feet? Sprinkle baking soda into smelly shoes to absorb smells. Foot odor is caused by bacteria buildup. Soak feet in a 'tea bath' or Alka-Seltzer bath for 15 minutes, twice a week.

How To Grow Fresh Air

You might be shocked to learn that benzene, formaldehyde and other similar toxic chemicals are being leached into the air as they evaporate from our carpets, pressed board cabinets, furniture, plastics and cleaning products. One easy and dependable way to freshen and clean the air we breathe is simply to grow a few indoor plants. Some excellent choices are bamboo palms, rubber plants, spider plants, English ivy, dracaena, dwarf date, Boston ferns, peace lilies, corn plants or schefflera. The National Aeronautics and Space Administration (NASA) also recommends mass cane, pot mums, gerbera daisies, warnecki, and ficus plants.

To Avoid Sneezing

Don't silly human glitches happen at the most inopportune times? To stop a sneeze in its tracks, try thinking of a pink elephant standing right in front of you.
To release a sneeze that seems stuck in your nose - look at a bright light.

Eye Drops

Warm the eye drops by rolling the container between your hands for a few minutes. It will be much easier to hit your target if there's no cold shock to the eyeball.

Insect Bites

Apply toothpaste to an insect bite to help relieve the itch, instead of using an alcohol-based product.

or

Apply a paste of baking soda and water to take the ouch out of bug bites, bee stings, sunburns, rashes, poison ivy, or pour some baking soda into the bathwater to relieve the itch of chicken pox and measles.

Avoid scratching, (which releases more itchy histamine into the area) and try slapping the spot instead.

Sun Burn Remedies

Milk: Apply a washcloth which has been soaked in cold milk.

Yogurt: Smear yogurt on your skin as soon as it turns pink to help cool the skin, reestablish pH balance and promote faster healing. It is best to use plain unsweetened full-fat yogurt that contains few additives. Let it sit on your skin until it warms up and then rinse it off with tepid water. Apply as often as needed. Better still, use a paste made of barley, turmeric and yogurt in equal proportions. Apply it over the affected areas for sunburn relief and healing.

Tea: Make a large pot of very strong tea, use a towel to soak up all the tea and then apply to the sunburn area. Alternately, use a large number of teabags and make a bathtub full of tea and soak in the bath when the temperature is tepid to barely warm. The tannins in tea help draw out the burn and heal the skin. You can also apply cold, used tea bags to sunburned eyelids to relieve pain and swelling.

Aloe Vera gel: Wonderful for minor scrapes and cuts and an all around wonderful substance for the skin. One superior good remedy for sunburn is to combine Aloe Vera, vitamin E oil, and cucumbers. Liquefy cucumbers in a blender and mix with Aloe Vera gel, and vitamin E oil.

Soothing Small Aches

Sports injuries, spills and falls can injure young muscles. Alternate ice packs (or bags of frozen peas or corn) with heat packs. To make a 'rice sock' fill a cotton sock with uncooked rice and microwave it for 1 – 2 minutes. Test it to make sure it's not too hot and wrap it around the sore knee, ankle etc.

RICE It!

For sprains, strains and tendonitis, treat injuries with the 'RICE" method. Rest, Ice, Compression and Elevation. Use an ace bandage to support the muscles and an ice pack or package of frozen peas to mold around the injury.

Regarding Medications

Point of information: the USA makes up only 5% of the world's population, yet we use 42% of the world's prescription medications. And still, we are faaaar down the list when comparing the health of this country to other industrial nations. Every $1 spent on advertising equals $4 of pharmaceutical sales. As a result, people in this country have been persuaded that we have a lot of medical problems! Over the past several decades we have watched relatively rare disorders become reclassified as diseases, for which there are suddenly a host of medications at the ready. Makes you think, which did come first, the chicken or the egg?

We are lucky to have meds available to us, but we should be more cautious about using them. I have seen people suffer many ill side effects from years of taking prescription drugs. People need to understand that there is always a price to be paid when taking powerful chemicals on a long-term basis. Weigh the pros and cons of taking these medications carefully, and encourage your doctor to reevaluate the need for these meds, instead of just reordering them continuously.

I was shocked to learn that there has recently been a 500% increase in the amount of antipsychotic drugs being prescribed to children in the U.S. Are our kids really that mentally ill? If so, we had better find out why!

As described above, doctors have so over-prescribed antibiotics, that certain bacteria are now resistant to the drug's curative properties. Makes me wonder what the next unintended consequence of over-prescription will be. The moral of the story is when it comes to medication, question the need, take as little as possible, understand the long-term side effects and stop it as soon as possible.

Addiction by Prescription

So often we go to the doctor complaining of a painful condition and we're rewarded for the visit with a prescription for a drug - a chemical painkiller. As a result we now have a new, socially acceptable, prescription drug addiction epidemic. We've created a society that avoids physical and psychological pain at almost any cost because if a doctor ordered it, it can't be a 'real' addiction, can it? Instead of using ice packs, heating pads, exercise, massage, pressure points and mind body remedies, we rush to the pharmacy for a quick fix and swallow pills without a second thought. I'm not advocating suffering but I am suggesting that we (and our children) shouldn't be so intimated by a little pain. To build muscle strength, we exercise. To build up pain tolerance don't medicate, meditate!

When the Flu Strikes

When children get sick or have the flu, make their bed (or crib) in several layers: put a waterproof pad (or large plastic garbage bag) on the bottom, cover with a sheet, then another waterproof pad, and another sheet on top. If they vomit, you need only take the top layer off, and they can fall back into bed in a flash. If they are older and you're afraid they might not make to the bathroom in time to vomit – put a plastic-lined garbage pail by the bed.

Mental Illness

If you broke down the human body into its elemental parts, you would find that we are nothing more than a few chemicals (albeit quite a magical brew) stirred into an electrical system. Sometimes we run smoothly, other times we short out, become unbalanced, hiss and backfire.

If we have a heart problem, we feel mildly annoyed at the inconvenience. We expect a trip to the body mechanic (the doctor) who will diagnosis the chemical or mechanical problem, offer an alternate chemical (a little potassium or digitalis, for example) or a mechanical roto-rooting, (angioplasty) to fix the ailing ticker. Have a backache? Headache? Cure it with the chemical acetaminophen. Tummy ache? Reach for the Pepto Bismol! (Fantastic stuff – no home should be without it.) No big deal.

If, on the other hand, a malfunction occurs in one's brain – it's a chemical imbalance like any other, so why do we feel so embarrassed, humiliated and/or angry? Silly, isn't it? Mental illness is just as prevalent as physical illness, yet people are still reluctant to discuss it openly. I recently had a discussion with a middle-aged woman about the disastrous effects of her sister's untreated bipolar disease. She was astounded that our experience with a family member was so similar to hers. She had never discussed her sister's eccentric, manic behavior with anyone before and like so many others, her family suffered in silence.

Talk to your children about mental illness. Mental illness tends to be familial, but it's not always. As I have already stated I am not a big advocate of prescription medication but our kids should understand from a young age that if there's ever a problem with their 'chemical mix or faulty wiring' there are some medications that can help. No one would ever hesitate to take insulin if they were diabetic and their body forgot to make this essential human juice, would they? If we plant the seeds of expectation and understanding early, perhaps we'll be better able to deal with serious mental health issues if the need arises later on.

Not sure where to get help? Contact the National Alliance on Mental Illness. (1-800 – 950-6264) on the web at: nami.org

Hospitals Are Necessary but Dangerous

If you or a loved one needs acute care for a medical emergency, never hesitate to call 911. If you need urgent care, proceed to your nearest Emergency Room. If you fear a broken bone, have severe pain, are bleeding profusely or you need surgery – the hospital is the place to go!

However, once you are there, please participate in the medical process by staying calm and becoming an advocate for your ill loved one. Unfortunately, many people have died as a result of medical errors. In fact, in a recent report, the Institute of Medicine stated that 100,000 patients are actually killed by medical errors each year. Yes, they are killed by their care, not by their disease! Additionally, The Institute for Health Care Improvement has calculated that 15 million 'incidents of harm' are inflicted on Americans annually. Never leave your loved one without an advocate. Arrange for someone to be there at all times. Literally 24/7. The job of an advocate is to watch, listen, question, speak up and oversee the patient's care.

Duties of the guardian angel:

- Make sure that <u>anyone and everyone</u> who is going to touch the patient or the patient's equipment has washed his/her hands with real soap and water. Don't be shy!
- Bring a supply of sanitary wipes (a bleach based sanitizer) to the hospital. Wipe down all surfaces, doorknobs, handrails, toilet handle, faucets, telephone receiver, TV remote, etc.
- Ask the nurses, technicians and doctors to clean their stethoscopes and equipment with one of your cleansing wipes before using anything on your loved one. Suggest they use similar precautions between every patient. Remind them that cell phones, writing pens, lab coats and men's ties, also serve as transports carrying lots of organisms from patient to patient!
- Do not allow the rubber band that was just strangling someone else's arm to be used again for drawing blood tests. Ask for a new, clean tourniquet to be used whenever blood specimens are going to be drawn.
- Make sure that the right medication is being given at the right time, to the right patient. Medication errors are the most common medical mistakes. Always ask what you're being given, what it does and if there are any side effects (there always will be). Then ask to see the label. It's your right, and if they can't or won't show it to you, please refuse to take it. Until all prescriptions are ordered electronically, we still struggle with doctor's illegible handwriting, leading to thousands of tragic pharmaceutical mistakes. Imagine – our fast food restaurants are more technologically advanced than our hospitals!
- Ask questions, get answers, and take the patient home as soon as possible. Nosocomial (hospital induced) infections are becoming increasingly common so skiddadle as soon as you can. Don't delay going home.

Your notes...

MONEY, MONEY, MONEY...

Money makes the world go around, but ...

Children learn by watching what you do, not what you say you are going to do. Parents work in order to earn the money that their family can spend. I think we should expect our kids to do the same. Seriously! When we mindlessly hand over an 'allow-ance' aren't we silently saying, "I ALLOW you to have this money – there are no strings attached." Instead of an 'allowance' perhaps our children should be given an 'EARN - IT- ance.' A small salary paid for the chores they complete. Their 'wages' should be age-appropriate of course. And the financial rewards should be tied to the kids' efforts: If a job is really well done, give that kid a bonus! If he does a lousy job, give him the equivalent of getting fired - don't pay him at all! Or, better yet, delegate the chore to another sibling and pay that child for it! That will certainly get your children's attention! To teach the kids how the real world works, deduct a small amount of 'family taxes' from their salaries and put the money into a central pot. (This money can later be used for a family outing or special purchase.) It is so important for a child to feel that s/he is really contributing to the family and the family finances. With his/her monetary contribution, however small, s/he will earn feelings of self worth that simply can't be measured in mere dollars and cents. Cleaning your room and making the bed every morning: $5. Learning the value of a dollar – priceless!

On Allowance

My children did not receive an allowance. When they wanted money for something, it was discussed and usually given. Then they learned that "Everyone Else's Mother" (Remember her---she's the one all us other Mothers wanted to lynch to the nearest tree) gave her kids an allowance for doing chores. "Everyone should receive an allowance for chores," the kids said.

So, we agreed on an amount to be paid every Friday night. The kids were ecstatic.

Friday night after dinner, I presented them with a bill for my chores. The bill was itemized and included the week's food, cleaning, transportation and laundry services, which just incidentally, totaled the exact amount of their weekly allowance. They realized that receiving an allowance wasn't all it was cracked up to be.

This was our compromise: Everyone has responsibilities that do not warrant compensation. But, if you take on a special task, you should be compensated. The children still received money when the need was there, and they began taking an interest in chores around the house being done by others and offering to help which was well worth the extra dollar of two.

Laura Cox, Hollywood FL

A Stretching Exercise

One night after dinner put a ten, twenty or fifty dollar bill, down on the table. With your supervision, let the kids figure out how to stretch that money. One week, focus on how to get the most 'food buying power' out of that dollar amount. Have them open the newspaper (or internet) to search for coupons and specials. One week let them budget and squeeze the most recreational fun out of the money. We learn much faster by doing and planning, than talking or watching.

On a related note: If you clip and use a coupon, you will only really save the money if you actually take the change out of your purse and put it away in a piggy bank. We don't really 'save' anything if we just spend it on something else, do we?

Happy Birthday Stock

Consider buying this unusual birthday gift: Buy shares of stock in a company that makes something your child is interested in, a sports outfit or an entertainment company. Explain how the market works and let him/her track his/her investment online or in the newspaper.

On Money Management

When my children reached the age of getting their first jobs, I was concerned about them having too much spending money and wanted to encourage them to save some of their hard earned cash. They weren't keen on the idea, so I presented them with this option: either put half of your paycheck into a savings account, or give me the money to pay household bills with.

Needless to say, they all chose to save their money rather than give it to me to spend. We had fun watching their savings grow and had a family celebration every time one became a "thousandaire". If any one of them had chosen the household bills option, I would have put their money in a savings account for them and given it to them for college or another legitimate need.

Judy Smith Williams, Arkansas

More On Money Matters

Most couples often fight about money. Stop the argument before it starts by having a well-balanced budget and sticking to it. Know what your household finances are all about. Even if your husband pays all the bills, know what your income and expenses are. Know what your holdings and debts are and look at your bank statements. Most financial experts agree that you should have your own savings account and/or money in your name. This is crucial for your own self-esteem and financial well - being. Divorce happens, and you shouldn't be left with nothing. Invest in a pre-paid college program for your children. If you work, put money aside every month without fail, for your retirement – it happens faster than you think. Experts say that you should save ten percent of your earnings, or $1,000. per month.

Now that you're a parent … Have a 'will' drawn up; we're all going to die sometime!

Take A 'Passion To Purchase' Vacation

We are so stuff driven! Are we unconsciously teaching our kids that 'we are what we have'? Do we feed our need for more and more 'things' to satisfy a learned material craving, which we've been schooled to believe is our "raison d'etre"? Let's be honest, we don't really buy what we need, we buy what we want. We've been brainwashed to think that our cars, homes and clothes represent who we are. Then we feel pressured to update and buy more, bigger and better. What are we doing? Let's stop this addiction, this 'passion to purchase.'

The best way to save money is simply not to spend it. Challenge yourself to stay away from all retail shops for just one week… all they want is your money. It's easier than you think. For one week, do not buy anything other than food. If this sounds too difficult and you're squirming at the thought - then I'm talking directly to you! Then, when you go back to any-shop-America before you buy anything, stop, think and ask yourself, "Do I really need this?" Most of the time you don't. Instead of spending, trade clothes, books, DVDs, CDs and toys with your friends.

Our Kids Want Too Much $tuff!

Are your eight year olds bemoaning the fact that they don't have an iPod, or iPad yet? Or an X Box, or whatever the fad-of-the-day is? Do your kids see a film and yearn for the day that they can 'own' a DVD copy? Can someone please explain to me why there's a need to watch the movie over and over again? Don't they get it the first time? If they loved it so much, why didn't they pay close attention and why don't they remember it now? Do all kids now require virtual 'game systems'? Not only are they expensive, but I understand that if you buy 'a system,' the games are just like potato chips - you can't have just have one! Before you commit to this pricey 'gotta have it' ask yourself if you are ready to feed the game addiction that comes with it. What happened to cheap ball-o-bats and hoola-hoops? Fashion trends always abound, but you don't have to allow the insanely overpriced sneakers, jeans or whatever the fashionistas decide you neeeeed to wear, to get the better of your kid's psyches. Another pricey trend - 10 year olds who demand their own cell phones! Why do little kids need cell phones? And as for spring or summer breaks, are you being coerced into taking an exotic trip? "It's just not fair. All my friends are going on trips!" OK, then plan a trip - go to the local library where the kids can still find excitement between the covers of a good book and live vicariously through the characters' exciting lives, just like we did in the olden days. Excessive spending has gotten completely out of control, even if you can afford it. All this buying is just not good for them, or us. It has the potential to turn kids into spendthrift adults or people who can never be satisfied unless they have all the stuff their friends and neighbors have. Let's protest all the consumerism directed at our children and help our kids see through all the slick merchandising. The kids might sulk but you will save, and you'll put some sanity back in our society too. It's just common cents!

Let's Do What Warren and The Donald Do!

What do Warren Buffet and Donald Trump have in common? They're both very, very wealthy. Although their children aren't running ragged in the streets, neither have they ridden on their father's tuxedoed coattails. In both cases, the children were provided excellent educational resources and then they went to work. They understand that their parent's 'money and stuff' isn't their money and stuff. These men made sure their children understood the value of a dollar, because a person's value is much more important than their money.

Don't rob your child of the luxury of being hungry.   Donny Deutsch

Avoiding Instant Junk

Whenever we attended a live show, such as ice-skating, the circus, a baseball game or a character theme show, we'd have a car discussion about the cost of the tickets and what to expect to see at the show. Because all kids want 'something' to hang onto, I came up with an idea to satisfy my kids' need for 'take home stuff.' My Mother always called souvenirs 'instant junk' because as soon as you leave the event these expensive items become meaningless, obsolete dust collectors. But I do understand that kids want something tangible to remember the experience, so I buy small inexpensive, theme-related trinkets beforehand, stash them in my purse and distribute them to my kids at the show. We're all happy.

On Cost Sharing *(When your child gets older.)*

We always found that if we agreed to split the cost (50/50) of any of the bigger items that were wanted, suddenly the item was not so coveted. And if they did want to spend 1/2 from their savings and allowance, it was something that got lots of use and wasn't put aside quickly.

Reba Heyman, Baltimore, MD

On Earning Money

My 15-year-old son was going on a school trip to Spain that would cost $2400. The school encouraged fundraising and since we do not have a money tree in our backyard (the gardener cut it down by mistake), I was determined to have him raise as much money as possible on his own. When the chocolate bars came home, I went with him to the first few neighbors to show him how easy it was to sell. He got so into it and was so determined to raise as much as possible to finance his trip. In the end he was the top fundraiser – with just a little push from Mom.

On the other hand, my 19-year-old son is pretty lazy. He is fairly low maintenance and he doesn't usually come to us with his hand out for money. However, I have refused to allow him to sleep his summer away. He really needed a push, and the only way that I could get him to find a job was to threaten to take his cell phone away. I left the classified ads open for him, with possible jobs circled, and wrote down phone numbers for him to call at local stores

who were looking for workers. Despite his protests, he landed a job at a jean store 5 minutes from our home. Now that he sees a regular paycheck coming in, he is thrilled. We're both happy – me because I don't have to see him lazing around the house and him because he is making money!
Arlene Stoffmaker, Montreal, Quebec

If you want children to keep their feet on the ground, put some
responsibility on their shoulders.

Women's $alaries

Beginning in the 1960's, the feminist movement made us aware that women really weren't being given our due. We women needed to step up and take our rightful place on equal footing with men, to effect necessary change in our society. The mantra became "Equality" in graduate schools, funding for women's college athletics, in the workplace, boardrooms and government. Slowly, we've been making progress. We've proven that we have the brains and the brawn - but where are the bucks? In 2011, the median weekly earnings for women in full-time management, professional, and related occupations was $941, compared to $1,269 for men. (Bureau of Labor Statistics, 2012) We need to demand pay equity.

It's 2007, but women are still only paid 77 cents for every dollar men are paid. Equal pay has been the law since 1963. However, for every $100 worth of work women do, they have $23 less to spend on groceries, housing, childcare and other expenses, than men have. Aren't we tired of seeing red? How many pennies do we have to pinch to make our 77 cents stretch as far as the dollar a man earns for doing the same or equivalent job? Why don't we have equal pay for men and women? Why don't our paychecks provide a livable wage for all of us, regardless of gender, race or type of work? (National Organization for Women, April 16, 2007 email alert)

Let's bring up our daughters, the next generation of 'womb-in' to expect and demand exactly what they deserve – real equality.

$orting Out $$$

When I was growing up money was a taboo subject - don't ask, don't tell. All we were told was that 'money doesn't grow on trees.' How to make money and how to make your money work for you was, and still is, a wonderment for most of us. Ninety-nine percent of us struggle with money and it's no wonder - educators make it a priority to teach history and spelling (though I'm not sure why) but the one thing that we all deal with every day, namely 'MONEY,' is never included in the school syllabus. We need to change that!

Once our kids leave the nest and get a job, an apartment and a few threads to wear at 'the job,' they need to understand what to do with their hard earned dollars. Most experts suggest that you advise your kids how to get started when they're getting started:

First of all, until we have a real, universal health care system (sound-off: like grown-up, mature countries who actually have an interest in looking after their citizens' needs!) the first investment must be health insurance. Most young people are healthy so you don't need a fancy plan. To find a suitable policy check out: ehealthinsurance.com

Next, learn to control your plastic or it will control you. Having a good credit rating is extremely important in our society so learning how to get and maintain a good credit history is vital. Start by using one card that offers the best rewards available and use it to pay for regular expenses, but be sure to pay it off completely every month. Keep another low-rate credit card to be used for emergencies only. One great trick is to keep the extra card in the freezer, imbedded in a can of frozen water so that it's difficult to access and not subject to frivolous use. Use cash for all other purchases and remember this rule: If you don't have the money in your wallet, don't buy anything! For financial networking and advice check out the web sites: youngmoney.com, wesabe.com, mint.com and geezeo.com

Always invest in yourself; contribute to your 401(k) as much as your employer will match and open a Roth IRA. If you want to learn about investing in stocks, look at: better-investing.org.

And finally, take a lesson from Warren Buffet, one of the wealthiest men on the planet. To hang onto your money - don't spend it! He certainly practices what he preaches - he drives an old car and lives in the same house he bought in the 1950s! He's not at all cheap, he just doesn't buy stuff he doesn't need. So brownbag your lunch; don't buy $3 cups of coffee; check out current movies, DVDs, CDs, best-selling books and monthly magazines which are all available for free at your local library; shop at thrift and discount stores for clothes and furniture; and join forces with your friends to buy food in bulk. 'A penny saved is a penny earned' still applies.

To find additional good advice and information on money matters, read *'The Laws of Money'* and *'Women and Money'* by Suze Orman.

Teen Time

Be The Mom

You have a job to do - you are the parent. Don't try to be your children's friend. They'll find lots of friends, but you'll be their only Mom.

Modeling - No Runway Required

Encourage your kids to model their behavior after a positive role model. Tell them, "Wanna be successful? Pick out a highly successful person, research how s/he achieved this level of success/wealth/position and imitate them." The only truly original people who ever lived on the planet were the proverbial couple, Adam and Eve. Everyone else has copied to some extent, so watch, listen and learn from those you admire.

Math with Meaning

The next time you're at a restaurant and the bill comes, pass it to your 3rd - 12th grade child. Have him/her check it and calculate the appropriate tip. Give him/her the cash, let him/her pay the bill and count the change. Kids don't always understand why they have to learn the things they do in school. This is a great opportunity to see that math is very much part of everyday life.

Fail to Succeed

Sarah Blakely, founder of Spanx, (women's foundation apparel) says that her father would motivate her by asking, "What did you fail at today?" He didn't ask this to ridicule or belittle her, but because he wanted her to understand that you can never succeed if you don't learn from your mistakes. Failing leads to success! It's only when you don't try, that you are really failing.

Teen Talk Translations

Is there anything worse than teen angst? Slamming bedroom doors, yelling, screaming, crying, hurling insults... Here's a short primer to help you decipher the drama...

"You're embarrassing me, Ma." "You're crazy." These announcements are usually made in front of friends. S/he just wants to leave the impression that s/he's in charge. Don't worry, they don't buy it. Just be cool, don't say a word and roll your eyes.

253

"Trust me, Mom." Sure... what they're really thinking is that what you don't know won't hurt them!

"Don't worry. Relax. I've got it covered." Means they really haven't done anything yet, they're scrambling to get 'it' done while trying to appear very cool and in control. Don't get involved let them handle their illusion of mastery.

"I hate you." "You're the worst mother in the world!" "You make me sick." She's angry and frustrated with herself, you and the world at large ... it's a lot to figure out... this too shall pass. Venomous words sting for the moment; just reflect on her past sweetness and future virtues.

"Whatever!" "You just don't understand!" Try to reflect her emotions by stating, "You seem angry, sad, frustrated, or frightened. What's bothering you?"

"I look so fat." "I'm ugly." "I hate my hair." She wants to fit in, look like the rest of the herd and be accepted. Didn't we all want to be 'different' carbon copies of the group at some point? Praise her attributes, both physical and emotional. Express admiration for her mind, creativity, humor and kindness.

"Leave me alone!" Take him at his word - we all need down time. Give him a hug and leave him be. Tell him you'll talk later - and when you do, don't pry. Let him spill what's on his mind without making any judgments or comments. Then ask him what you can do to help. This puts the ball back in his court and puts him in a position of accepting your help if he wants it.

Mood of the Day

Humor can really help. If your teen has left the park swings and is headed for the mood swings instead, hang up a circular "Mood of the Day Wheel." (Use two paper plates. Inscribe each 'mood' listed below, in each of 10 equal sections around the circumference of one plate. Cut a window equal to one section, on the top of the second plate. Lay that plate on top of the first. Attach the two together, using a pronged brad - button.) The chart can alert your family to your teen's emotional temperature. Here are the emotional variables:

Euphoric - Delirious - Excited - Cheerful - Somber -
Smoldering - Reactive - Poisonous - Explosive – Biohazard!

Do You Know Auntie Eem?

When I was a teen I met a wonderful woman named, 'Eem.' I'm sure you met her too. In fact I've never known anyone who hasn't met her and loved her! Everyone Else's Mom (Eem) is an intelligent, patient, wise woman who is always gracious, forgiving and kind. All kids make it their business to meet her. No wonder they love, honor and respect her. She stocks her pantry with every type of junk food imaginable, doesn't require you to eat your vegetables, and she cooks only the things you love. She willingly hands over the car keys without knowing where you're going or when you're returning. She allows phone calls at any time. She's totally OK with unchaperoned parties, even at her own house! She wouldn't blink an eyelash at the sight of your room or your piles of laundry. She's totally OK with whatever sloppy, inappropriate outfit you are wearing. She would never bug you regarding homework, term papers, assignments, exams or grades. She would never embarrass you and, best of all, she would never say "No!" So when your kids meet her, send her your best wishes and carry on carrying on.

I'm always surprised when I push my kids' buttons and they react ...
then I remember, I installed them!   Chris Smither

Zit Zapper

Use toothpaste! Put a dab on the blemish before bed and it will help dry it out.

Touchdown - and Out?

Girls who play soccer, and boys who play football or similar contact sports, incur the vast majority of teenage traumatic brain injuries. Of the 3 million concussions reported annually 150,000 affect high school athletes. MRI scans have shown that kids and teens are much more vulnerable to any kind of traumatic encephalopathy (brain trauma) than previously thought. This is certainly something to keep in mind when choosing which team sports teens participate in. Because although the damage caused may not show up decades, the consequence of today's tackle maybe tomorrow's early onset dementia, which will give a whole new meaning to joining the NFL, No-Fun-Living.

Her First Period

Remember getting your first period? Of course you do. You know where you were, who you were with, the exact date, what time of day it was – everything! Hopefully you knew why it was happening, what to expect and where your supplies were kept. Ask any woman you know and she will remember every minute detail of the event. Ask a man about his first experience shaving and you'll get an incredulous, blank stare... clueless! I guarantee it! Sadly, I had a friend who was totally freaked out because she thought she was dying and her insides were disintegrating. If you haven't already, at the first sign of your daughter's physical development discuss the natural course of events with her. Discourage negative commentary like 'expecting the curse' and focus on the beautiful journey of becoming a woman. Plan ahead and when the day comes, celebrate! Present her with a small gift to mark the occasion - perhaps a necklace, a charm or a pin featuring the moon or a ruby red stone, costume jewelry or otherwise. Life is certainly a miraculous journey and reaching special landmarks should be welcomed and cherished as sacred rites of passage.

Remember:

- It is not unusual for each breast to develop unilaterally, appear to be different sizes and feel tender. Don't worry - they'll even out, more or less.
- Young girls may have a (normal) vaginal discharge when they are developing, no need to worry about yeast infections or STDs.
- Expect your daughter to get her first period about 2 - 2 1/2 years after breast development, but some girls take longer.
- Make sure your daughter keeps a couple of pads in her purse (before she really needs them!) and that she knows how to use them.
- Cycles are always counted from the first day of one period to the first day of the next period. Normal cycles range from 21 - 45 days, but may take 5-6 years to become really regular. We are people, not machines!

Tomorrow Begins Today – Planning For Independence Day

Think of a Mother bird looking after her brood. She feeds them, warms them and protects her fledglings while they peer out of the nest. And then one day, she has one final task to accomplish - pushing them out to take leave of the nest. Her 'push' is really the greatest gift she has to offer her young. She may be thrilled with the expectation of seeing them soar, but the first time must begin with every Mother's fear - that her chicks might not be ready after all, and that they just might fall.

May I suggest that when your teen is a high school sophomore or junior, you sit down together and talk about the facts of life? (No, not 'those' facts, that's in another section.) Talk about life on the outside (of your home) and start to plan for your child's life in the REAL WORLD. Ask what your child aspires to do – does s/he want to go to vocational school or to college and then to graduate school? Does s/he plan to find a job right out of high school? Get a feel for what his/her plans are. Now choose a date – a real date, corresponding to his/her future plans and declare that day will henceforth be known as 'I.D.' or 'Independence Day.' Add a few months grace period following any graduation to allow for finding a job and an apartment. Print the date in large, bold font, frame it and hang it on his/her bedroom wall. Be clear and let your child know that from that date forward s/he will need to be responsible for him/herself – financially and personally. Kids need to know that there will be a 'cut off day' – we can't look after them forever. Create an expectation of self-sufficiency and let them know that they need to achieve 'personhood' by a date certain. To some this approach may sound like 'tough love,' but it's necessary because our kids expect us to 'be there for them' forever. Too often we hear of kids who take 5 or 6 years to graduate with a four-year college degree. And it's now commonplace for many to move back into the nest to avoid doing laundry, cooking or paying rent until 'they get on their feet.' But there's no incentive to stand on your own when you're lying on the folks' sofa, watching their flat screen and chowing down their food! As the saying goes, 'Ships are safe in harbor, but that's not what ships are for.'

Consider this: We set dates well ahead of time for inaugurations and retirements, graduation ceremonies and weddings, as a way to mentally, emotionally and financially plan for the change and the responsibility yet to come. In the same way, our kids need to know that 'Indy

Day' is coming! The impending 'I.D.' shouldn't be regarded as a threat or a signal that we won't support them to the best of our ability if they should ever need us, but rather as an endorsement of our confidence in their ability to take responsibility and look after themselves. When the date finally does materialize on the calendar, it should be a day of celebration – a real coming of age. We invited our kids into the world and into our lives, we fed them and taught them and nourished them with our love. Their job is to grow up and our job is to let them.

What's the matter with kids today?

Well... the kids are the same but the world is crazier. I think that our kids' 'acting out' is a reflection of the difficult, dysfunctional time we're living in. As proof of my hypothesis, I offer you a brief history lesson of adolescent lunacy:

The 1950s were an idyllic time, very innocent by today's standards. Boys and girls dressed in shirts, ties, skirts and ironed blouses! They had formal dates and chaperoned parties. In those days, 'risky behavior' meant swallowing live goldfish to show off. Oh those poor little fish! The next behavioral fad saw kids packing themselves into phone booths in order to see how many bodies they could squeeze into such a small space and secure some kind of quasi human sardine record. (I heard you thinking: A what? A phone booth, circa 1950-1990, was a 2 1/2 - foot square, glass-lined structure equipped with a local phonebook, a built-in seat and a pay phone. Initially it cost 10 cents to make a local call and you could talk as long as you wanted. Over time the fee increased and you could only talk for 3 minutes before more money was required. This freestanding structure was usually found on busy city streets, in shopping centers and/or at gas stations.) These sophomoric pranks were silly and harmless, notwithstanding the poor little fish.

The 60's were tumultuous – the country's emotions ramped up and so did 'the counterculture' generation. As the world swirled with angst over civil liberties issues and the very unpopular Viet Nam war, the kids' behavior escalated as well. Teens began to experiment en masse with sex and street drugs. Drugs are drugs – they aren't good for you no matter who offers them to you. Prescription drugs maybe legal, but your body doesn't know that. So even though numerous studies show that smoking marijuana, grass, pot and hashish are all less hazardous to one's health than the present day legal drugs of nicotine and alcohol, oxycontin and vicodin, they were and still are illegal. Using these soft drugs was a definite reflection of the times. Kids were rebelling. They were trying to escape the 'establishment' and find something to soothe their angry souls.

Fast forward to 2012. Once again we live in precarious times, with bad news flung at us wherever we turn. Picture our 16 year olds flipping on a TV, a PC, or scrolling through the news on their cell phones. First there's news about another unpopular war, conflicts and genocide, then they hear about school shootings and natural disasters. But you're only 16 and so far there's no military draft, so hey, what do these terrible things have to do with you? It's just some depressing news that's happening to someone else. Right now you're primarily interested in making friends. Girls. Boys. Hey, what's this on the PC - somebody's started a rumor about you - and the whole world is reading it??? Kids seem to be getting meaner, nastier and more vicious. And now that they have the power to show off their insults, one's tattered reputation can go 'viral' at the touch of a button. Cyberbullying. And you are totally powerless to stop it! Maybe you wanted to meet a pretty girl or handsome guy online, but everybody is online, so now everybody who's alive on the entire planet is your competition! Like for real! From a teen's perspective, that's pressure.

Yup, the world sure is cranked up and crazy right now. So, as I said before, the risk behavior is escalating right along with it. But we're not talking little goldfish anymore. Some teens are taking the blues to a whole new level, self-mutilating by cutting themselves, or displaying eating disorders such as anorexia and bulimia; other kids are dabbling with death ... sex, biting, drugs, self- asphyxia and suicide... read on...

Sex: The Beauty and The Beast

Of course, sex is only new if it's new to you. But with the sexual transmission of herpes, HIV and HPV, sex has never been deadlier. HIV, although now considered a chronic disease, is still no picnic. And it is estimated that 50% of the population is carrying HPV which, if left untreated might cause cervical cancer. Cancer is cancer, and nobody wants it but kids don't always 'get it.' They've been persuaded that a vaccine can shield them and if not – there'll be some medical quick fix. But it's not true. People die. So when you talk to your kids about the beauty of making love, be sure to tell them that if they don't protect themselves adequately, with everyone, every time – they may encounter more than love – they may face a deadly, infectious beast that they will have to battle forever.

If your teen is diagnosed with a sexually transmitted disease it's only right to inform 'the partner.' But how? An Internet STD Notification Service is now available in several states. It allows you send a private, specialized e-card to break the news. The site promises that you can send the card anonymously and no data about either the user or recipient is collected. Check out: www.inspot.org/gateway.aspx

Biting: Blood Suckers

Bizarre teen trends have been horrifying parents for generations, but health officials are warning that a vampire-inspired biting fad can be dangerous, not to mention disgusting. Thanks to a few best selling teen books and movies, kids are just in love with vampires these days. And now some wannabe teen couples have started biting each other hard enough to purposely break the skin and suck some of their sweetheart's blood... which may carry any number of pathogens, including hepatitis B and C and HIV. I'd advise teens to stick to old fashioned hickeys!

Drugs: Generation RX

Today, teenagers who want to get high are turning away from marijuana. They are turning to what's legal, close at hand and easy to acquire: prescription drugs. *"Upper-middle class individuals from good families, solid families, are becoming addicted to pharmaceutical drugs,"* said Sgt. Lisa McElhaney of the Broward County, FL. Sheriff's office. *"Lock up your medicines. These are dangerous, tempting substances to inquisitive children,"* she said. *"Don't leave them where they are accessible to kids."* But even if you don't store these drugs in your home, your child still might be enticed to try them, because increasingly kids are trading these drugs at school like we used to trade baseball cards and our kids traded 'Garbage Pail Kids' cards. Sadly, even kids in middle school are involved. And where are they getting these drugs? There are doctors who now specialize in selling prescriptions – they are legalized pushers, until they're caught.

The Choking Game

Another high-risk fad is playing 'the choking game.' Most of the time, kids play this (so called) 'game' using their hands to encircle someone's neck, thereby cutting off the air supply. The resulting 'self asphyxia' or self-strangulation causes hypoxia, a shortage of oxygen to the brain, which creates what the kids consider to be a 'high.' They report seeing colors and/or feeling a 'dimming' sensation. Of course the danger increases if the child 'plays' this deadly game alone, because no one will be there to revive him when this 'playing' becomes disastrous. Kids report using belts, bags, ties, ropes or even their own bare hands. Remarkably, kids will repeat this behavior even after blacking out. Police, medical and forensic experts estimate that 250 to 1,000 young people die in the United States each year from some variant of the choking game. Many are accidents but are reported as suicides. (Some signs to look for are: flushed face, bloodshot eyes, tiny red marks and bruises on the neck or face, and headaches.) For information check out: failuremag.com/arch_flop_choking_game.html, or kidsbesafeonline.com/index.html

Makes you want to bring back the wriggling sushi, doesn't it?

Look At Me! No, Really – Look at Me!

The latest in teen adventure? Anything outrageous enough to be youtube-worthy. Kids have recently been caught videoing themselves 'flash robbing' stores (which involves a band of teens sweeping through a store and shoplifting en masse,) or performing acts of vandalism just for the sake of (hopefully viral) peer voyeurism. Seems like kids will do anything as long as someone has a camera running. Because we live in a time of high tech, self-produced instant celebrity, our kids seem more desperate than ever to be noticed. What they forget is that the police also have access to youtube.

The Saddest Sad of All – Suicide

Most teens experience a period of dramatic moodiness. That's a quintessential right of adolescence. They start wondering about the whole life experience: What is the meaning of life? What is the purpose of life? Why are we here? What do I want to do with my life? What does everyone expect of me? Will I measure up? Often hormones escalate every emotion, and feelings become very intense. Remember?

Some kids experience some depression while struggling to find answers to life's big questions. Others get so caught up in their inner turmoil that they just can't see what we 'adults' already know – that this time of inner angst shall pass and the road ahead will, in time, become smoother. Talk to your kids about your own experiences. Let them know that we all feel bad, hung up, blue, sad, anxious and depressed from time to time in our lives. It's called 'being human.' Talk about all the different ways we can climb out of our despair and remind them that how we deal with life is a choice we make every day. Tell them that sometimes people lose their way, get lost in the dark forest and instead of calling out for help, they crawl into a cave and hide. If you want to see the light, you never find it by self-isolating. You need to get back on the trail and enjoy the journey even when you stumble and fall, skin your knees and experience some pain.

Sometimes teens might feel so spent, so hopeless, that they consider suicide. They see it as a quick fix for ending their pain or punishing someone else. It's scary to think about and I'm sure you'd rather not, but I'd rather be scared now than sorry later. If they're talking about thoughts of suicide, never leave them alone. Arrange for friends to come over, keep them busy where you can keep watchful eye on them. Some kids talk about suicide just to test you, others may be seriously contemplating and planning, but there's really no way tell to tell them apart. So keep them talking while you find the professional help you need. The most important thing to tell them is that 'suicide is a permanent solution to temporary problems and feelings.' Many, many others have weathered the same storms and they have found that if one makes the choice to wait for the sun – it will come out and shine.

ADD and ADHD

Science has recently determined that kids who are diagnosed with ADD are just wired differently. As a result they may be developmentally delayed, but will eventually outgrow their problems. Still, children who have ADD - ADHD present parents with even greater challenges than your run-of-the-mill, misguided teen. An excellent resource can be found at wrightslaw.com

Pete Wright's 'Four Rules for Raising Children' are: provide consistency and structure, establish clear standards and rules, have high expectations and teach your child to behave.

And before you allow your child to take prescription medications, try Mother Nature's remedy, commit to an hour of aerobic exercise, daily. Recent brain studies show that the same brain chemicals that are soothed by prescription meds, are also calmed by the natural endorphins released by vigorous exercise. It's fun, it's safe and it works!

Video Games May Help

Ian Glasscock, the managing director of the not-for-profit, Games for Life, has reported that new mind-controlled educational video games are proving to reduce ADHD symptoms, without any drugs! What? Watching video games could actually hold the key to helping children learn to concentrate? Yes ... riotous researchers are proposing that you seat your already-bouncing-off-the-walls-kid and let him play lots of video games! Yes, I know it sounds crazy. But read on...
Researchers had a group of children diagnosed with Attention- deficit/hyperactivity (ADHD) play educational video games three times a week for 12 weeks. The kids were fitted with brainwave-detecting helmets. Anytime their attention wandered the game would stop, which trained the kids to focus in order to keep playing. At the end of the study, the kids ADHD symptoms had measurably improved.

ADHD drug sales are big, big, BIG business. Sales have nearly quadrupled since 2000. That's more than $3.1 billion a year to treat (what some feel) is a questionable disorder. And make no mistake about it - these drugs are far from benign. They are stimulants whose neurological effects are very similar to cocaine. Potential side effects range from tics to psychosis and possible addiction. Any treatment that can yield benefits, and decrease symptoms without adding new ones (from adverse drug side effects) should really be given some serious attention. With nothing to lose, it's certainly worth trying it.

ADHD Bag

My son was diagnosed with ADHD, which often is marked by a low frustration level and a quick temper. To reduce his outbursts and temper tantrums, I created an 'angry book-bag.' It's a bag he keeps in the car and it goes everywhere with us. It contains a hand-held video game, extra batteries, paper and colored pencils, a yo-yo, a paddleball, a stress squeeze ball, a headphone cassette player with music CDs and books on cassette. It also has some items that change from week to week. I usually stock it with sugar-free gum and some other little goodies. The most important item in the bag is a 'journal with invisible ink pen.' The end of the ink pen has a black light on it, so he can see the secret thoughts he writes. Some of the items in 'the bag' help him release pent up energy without disrupting others, for example, the yo-yo and paddleball. Quiet activities such as the journal help him redirect his emotions when he begins to feel out of control. I have found a few minutes of 'alone time' keeps him calmer and as it allows him to refocus. He has learned to control his emotions rather than getting out of control and then getting in trouble, thereby teaching him that he can control himself, rather have someone else control him.

Billie Lister, Swannanoa, NC

Don't Run To The Rescue

T + I = SS   (Teen + Immaturity = Sticky Situations)

This is a common yet difficult law of human psychology. The solution to this age related problem is a negative theorem. The more you do nothing, the faster the problem will resolve itself.

How to do nothing:
Listen to what happened. Close your mouth. Breathe. Sit on your hands. Breathe again. Think to yourself: "What will s/he learn if I jump in and fix it? What will s/he learn if I let the situation do the teaching?" Stand aside. Be quiet. Breathe some more. Assume that your child will find a way to resolve the problem. Turn to the child and recite this incantation, "Wow. What a bummer. How are you going to handle that?" This allows him/her to resolve the situation and develop what we adults call 'wisdom.' With no other options, kids will learn to think first, be responsible for their actions and problem solve. They do the work and you get an 'A' ! Fabulous. Go to the head of the class!

All we need is to illuminate that which is already hidden within us.
The Rebbe of Kotsk

Another Inconvenient Truth: The World Has A Testosterone Problem

A personal sound-off …

The world is definitely heating up and it's not just from carbon emissions or estrogen surges. We all watch the news. Night after night we hear about terrible, depraved acts committed against innocent people. So I ask you, 'who' are the people committing all these horrendous crimes? 'Who' exactly are we talking about? Can we identify the people responsible? Is there a profile? Who has it in them to commit the crimes of: armed robbery, carjacking, school shootings, street crimes, arson, gang warfare, domestic violence, rape, kidnapping, burglary, acid mutilations, machete amputations, sexual abuse, pedophilia, child abduction, child pornography, child internet corruption, murder, suicide bombings, terrorism and genocide? Do you see a pattern? I do. Sadly, these crimes are committed overwhelmingly, by the genetically endowed XY carriers among us.

In terms of evolution, yes we have taken a few intellectual steps forward – we have lovely high-tech equipment to help us communicate easily and we have some very macho machinery to do our heavy lifting. But emotionally speaking a large number of humans who carry the XY chromosome are still living in the Stone Age! I think that individually men are great – collectively, they are making a mess. For the record, I absolutely LOVE my husband! And I like a lot of other men, too. I think that men have an equal and important role to play on our little twirling planet. But when you look at the state of the world all throughout history, you have to ask: what is up with all the misogyny, prejudice, racism, aggression, mindless conformity, insecurity, blind hatred, territorial jealousy and greed? Let's connect the dots and face a few facts. Men dominate the world scene and hormones dominate men. Diagnosis: We have a global testosterone problem.

Have you ever noticed that (generally speaking) people don't really change as they get older? They just become more of who they were as kids. If they were nice, they become nicer. If they were mean, they become meaner. And men are just larger versions of themselves as little boys. As I watch the news it seems to me that the world scene is just a magnified version of what goes on between little boys in any playground sandbox. "I'm bigger, I'm stronger. I can hurt you – you better be afraid!" "I want that! Gimme that! Now it's mine and you can't have it." "I'm playing here! You go somewhere else!" Am I right, Moms? The problem is that instead of quelling the immature male attempts to dominate, own and occupy, most societies continue to feed and massage the male ego.

Even today, many cultures still revere 'the male' and allow testosterone to rule. As a result, women are still widely regarded as possessions and are kept utterly powerless by male-dominated religions and governments, which are quite happy to maintain the self-serving status quo. When I see women shrouded in garments so that the men around them 'shouldn't be tempted' I'm astonished. News flash: arms, legs and faces are beneath those swaths of cloth! Honor killings and female genital mutilation are still very much the norm in much of the world. Who is fooling whom? No real god would ever condone this – this is submission thinly veiled as religion. These traditions keep women on the treadmill of emotional humiliation. Whole cultures continuously reinforce this immature mentality, and all to satisfy the boy-men who want and/or need more and more power.

262

Violence against women is not culture, it's not custom -- it's criminal.

Hillary Clinton

Even in more modern egalitarian world cultures, the older well-established organized religions refuse to loosen their ironclad grip, stubbornly clenching onto their male power.

I think that global hatred is only a symptom of an untreated disease. We have a spiraling, massive, worldwide male hormonal crisis. The male urge to dominate remains exactly the same as in the sandbox - control, possess and prevail. The only difference is that the adult expression of these immature urges, are channeled into religious zealotry/ fundamentalism/fervor (control), corporate greed or governmental expansionism (possession) or a desire to reign politically (prevail and rule.) Too many men all vying to be kings and as we now have so many killing machines, war and carnage abound. The world is full of way too many nuts! Sorry, the pun is intentional.

Here at home violence and domestic abuse are rampant, perpetrated by raging males who have a strong need to dominate. It's as if these males need a 'fix' so they control their women for self-gratification and pleasure. Women are easy targets because we still (however unconsciously) teach girls to be submissive. Fact; most of the women who are incarcerated in the US have committed reactionary crimes, usually in self-defense. 90% of the women in our prisons have been abused. Most were psychologically imprisoned by their men as well as being victims of poverty and circumstance. Many made the mistake of not realizing that they could have left their situation and found help. Most murdered the men who held them, in order to escape relentless physical and mental torture, rule and command of their possessive abusers.

Street crime and gangs are also disproportionately male, and what do they fight for? They vie for power, riches and turf. The world's militaries are of course primarily male, and they fight their wars to gain each other's power, natural resources or land. So, we see the same issues played out again and again, in the playground, in the home, on the street, in ancient stagnant cultures and in wars all over the globe. We can't seem to get out of the sandbox.

What can we do? I don't have the answers. When in doubt, I often turn to the Mother of us all – Mother Nature. She'll show us the way if we just stop, look and listen. Consider the animal world. Animals don't treat or train their young differently after a quick glance at their newborn kid's genitals! Regardless of gender all offspring learn to find food, shelter and to protect themselves. They either learn to survive on their own or cooperate within a group. What do we do? The exact opposite. We categorize, pigeonhole and teach different skill sets based solely on gender. Aren't we tired of the gender bias we keep feeding our kids' psyches? Do we really think there are pink brains and blue brains? No? Then why, oh why, do we keep buying gender specific toys? Fuzzy toys for girls, footballs for boys. Easy Bake® ovens and BB guns. Tutus and tomahawks. Without giving any conscious thought to what messages we're sending, we perpetuate societal roles with the mechanics of childhood – toys. We are teaching our kids how we expect them to behave with these toys!

Sporting activities are another area where we have allowed gender bias to creep into children's souls. We encourage our boys to be combative, roughhouse and attack as we pretend that 'sports' are healthy outlets for aggression. We cheer on professional sports teams and pay them a fortune to satisfy some voyeuristic fascination of dominance and blood lust: Pro football, wrestling and boxing are the modern-day equivalents of Roman barbarism. There are so many games of skill and strategy, and cooperative sports that we should be encouraging instead. Tennis, fencing, baseball and soccer are just a few that come to mind.

We've bought into mistaken societal norms, expecting and accepting different standards of behavior from our children too. We teach our girls to cry and our boys to suck it up. We expect our girls to verbalize and our boys to act out, often sulking and punching. If a female exhibits a powerful persona and is assertive, she is called aggressive. If a male does the same, he is proclaimed a great leader.

Enough already – it's just not working! We MUST find a way to transform old habits and cultural sexism. Are males and females different? Yes, of course, but we need to do a better job accentuating all our positive human attributes. We need to calm and douse the fires fueling the testosterone psyche. For the world to progress and become a kinder, gentler place, we need to establish some new rules. We must start at the very beginning, in each new Mother's arms, in every home, in every country. No more excuses. No more gender bias. No more massaging the male ego. No more acceptance of female submission. We need to insist on emotional maturity, gender equality and neutrality.

Is this a simplistic (male bashing) view of the so-called 'complicated' world I see playing out on my TV screen? I don't think so. On the whole, I don't see women promoting endless anger, building up weapons arsenals or starting wars. Although women in some cultures do suffer from the generational curse I outlined above, I concede that they certainly aren't blameless as they hand down legacies of hate. They tend the fires of centuries-old resentments and continue to teach tribal hostilities, just as they themselves were once taught. The key to change is, of course, education. We must make sure that every female on the planet is given the education she deserves. Because when you educate girls, you really do change the world! (We can see clear evidence of this when the men of misogynist cultures begin to see themselves losing their power and resort to burning girls' schools to the ground, or shooting brave girls like Malala Yousafzai.) We must insist that every single girl is taught to read so that the Internet can 'reach and teach' every heart and mind and advance our world community. The Internet (if not Oprah!) is our best hope – it can inform the planet and show all cultures that there is a better way. The Internet should be the world's great equalizer, brain library and idea pool. Can we work together to put a computer into the hands of every child on earth? How can we achieve and monitor this educational aspiration? Peer pressure! The eyes of the world should be watching every country and culture. Perhaps we can 'encourage' resistant societies by tying an equal opportunity educational requirement to acceptance into the UN, or aid packages, or economic incentives, or how about some old-fashioned public ridicule… whatever works. Because if nothing changes, nothing changes.

We Moms don't control the world (yet), but we do have the power to change the world, one child at a time. Mother Nature shows us that when tiny raindrops come together they effortlessly create a stream. When streams join together they form rivers. And just a few rivers from around the world can quickly fill an ocean. Moms of the world, let us each do our part to change the world, one child at a time.

If there is light in the soul
There will be beauty in the person.
If there is beauty in the person
There will be harmony in the house.
If there is harmony in the house
There will be order in the nation.
If there is order in the nation
There will be peace in the world.

Chinese Proverb

We can also start by stopping. Stop passing down stories of ancient tribal hatreds and centuries-old disputes. (See: Education/Teaching History.) Stop passing down violence and abusive language by holding still your own angry hand, and your own vicious tongue. Stop teaching old prejudices with your words and deeds. Stop allowing our children to go to war. Start teaching our boys there's a better way to resolve issues. Might is no way to fight. Fight with your intellect, words and ideas; not with fists, guns, bombs or war. Start buying only gender-neutral toys. Start teaching ALL our children to cook, to clean, to do the laundry, to speak up, to speak out, and to stand up. We need to start electing more women into politics all over the world. We need to demand women be given leadership roles in religious institutions – or we need to leave those institutions. We need our world to become more emotionally intelligent. We can start by teaching our sons to talk more, to express their emotions and to cry. Human tears are not an exclusive part of female anatomy and physiology. Tears are not gender sensitive; if more men had been taught to vent their frustrations, talking and spilling a few tears, perhaps they wouldn't need to release their fury by punching, beating and raping human targets. I'm tired of hearing that 'boys will be boys.' Real men cook, cry and wear pink. A character in the Broadway play 'My Fair Lady' once asked, "Why can't a woman be more like a man?" Perhaps the question is really, "Why can't a man be more like a woman?"

Is it raining yet?

When the power of love overcomes the love of power,
the world will know peace.

Definition of Insanity:
Repeating the same action, expecting a different result.

We'll only see peace when they love their children more
than they hate our children.   Golda Meir

We learn from experience that men never learn anything from experience.
George Bernard Shaw

Women Say No

Women say No to war
Women have borne the child
Out of our bodies comes
Each new life
We will not stand to see
Our sons and daughters be
Drawn to a flame, not in our name
Women say No, Women say No!

If we survive the wars
We are left holding on
Healing the wounded ones
Mourning the dead
Finding a place to sleep
Water and food to eat
Calming the fears, so many tears
Women say No!

Are you waiting? Grieving?
Shaken to your core?
Are you willing? Start now
Put an end to war.

Women say yes to love
We know the strength of peace
We have been practicing all our lives.

Voices of hope resound, all of the world around
Life is worth more and to the war
Women say No! Women say No!

Where Have All the Manners Gone?

Moms, can we please put the 'Man' back in manners? What's happened to us? We're a country of slobs! I'm not advocating going back to three-piece suits or long, corset dresses, but let's be honest - our men and boys need a makeover!

Heads Up:
Baseball caps and all other hats are OK at sporting events and outdoors, but they should be removed whenever you enter a home, at all meals, when attending the theater and at parties.

When dating:
Don't blow your horn to announce your arrival. Get out of your car and ring the doorbell when you pick up your date. Open the door for your date. Offer to pay the bill; if she wants to pay her half accept her contribution. After your date: Call her, even if you just want to remain friends instead of becoming more romantically involved. Don't kiss and tell! It's nobody's business and you'll appear to be both classy and respected if you keep your thoughts to yourself!

Table Manners:
Do - Pretend that the queen or some very, honored guest is sitting with you. Remove your hat. Put your napkin in your lap. Put your fork down and relax between bites... nobody's going to take your food away from you. Take small bites. Thank your host.

Don't - Tuck the napkin into your pants, shirt or shirt collar. Don't toss your tie over your shoulder. Don't stuff your mouth. Don't talk with your mouth full. Don't plow through your meal without adding to the conversation. Don't announce that you're stuffed. Don't pick your teeth or floss at the table.

The Real World

Open your teenager's eyes to the real world by taking him/her on a few field trips. Attend shareholders' meetings, town meetings, and county commission meetings. Sit in on courtroom trials. These forums are all open to the public. They offer more insight into the way our daily lives are impacted than any textbook can offer. 'Take your child to work day' offers the perfect opportunity to take your teens and explore.

Invite an Exchange Student Home

Hosting an exchange student is a terrific way to open the hearts and minds of your teenagers and those around the globe. Most exchange programs work out the logistics, matching host families with student adventurers for either a semester or a summer session. This is a real opportunity to impact global understanding. Most people cherish their experience and maintain lifelong friendships.

Divide your life into ten-minute units and sacrifice as few
    of them as possible in meaningless activity.   Ingvar Kamprad, IKEA Founder

Need A Teen-Friendly Ally?

Have your kids check out 'The Six Most Important Decisions You'll Ever Make.' It describes and discusses (in kid-friendly language) some tough subjects. On the web at 6decisions.com

On Trust and Teenagers (a work-in-progress)

All of us want to be certain that our teenagers are not involved in sex, drugs and god-knows-what-else. I'm not sure what works, but here's something that doesn't. If you're a control freak and want to know where your teen is and with whom and doing what at every hour of the day, and you start making rules about what they can and can't do, the likely result is that s/he will just learn to be very deceitful ("I'm going over to Mary's house to study for the algebra test.") The only thing that will work in the long run is if the child has learned for him/herself how to set appropriate limits, and I think that is what all of us parents have to try to encourage.

Catherine Joyce, New Haven, CT

When Kids Go Astray

Cry. You're not alone. I don't know anyone who hasn't at some point been terribly disappointed by his or her kid's behavior. And the first response, other than "I'd like to kill that little idiot!" is, "What did I do? Where did I do wrong? Did I forget to say something? DO something? Did I step on too many cracks? Did I forget to cross my fingers? Why did this happen?" It's our instinct to take ownership of our children's problems and search for 'a reason.' A reason might be comforting initially, but realistically it doesn't change a thing, so searching for one may not be a constructive use of your energy. Whether your child is ill, defiant, troubled, involved with drugs or alcohol or in trouble with the law, the heartache it provokes is excruciating. There are those who have studied families, patterns and parenting styles and come away wondering if 'parenting' makes any difference at all. They surmise that at least fifty percent of our behavior is genetically programmed. Twenty five percent may be determined by outside influences such as friendships, socio-economic status and geographic location, and that only twenty five percent of our makeup may be due to parental guidance. So take heart and remember that not every bud will bloom, nor does every recipe taste good. Please don't blame yourself. You are not in charge of the universe.

Sex Is Getting More Complicated!

Sexting

A recent survey done by Teenage Research Unlimited found that 22 percent of girls have sent nude or seminude images of themselves to boys on their cell phones, and not necessarily to their boyfriends, even though 75 percent of teens understand that this behavior may be risky, because one day that college you want to attend, or the prospective employer you want to impress, just may decide to Google your name and those pictures will still be there! And, in our present 'zero tolerance' era, the police may arrest both the sender and the receiver for transmitting pornography! Tell the kids to apply the 'Grandpa test' to anything they post online and ask themselves, "Would I be OK if my Grandpa saw this?"

Desire
We pleasure our children's senses daily with perfumes and aromas, good food, nice music, soft fabrics, beautiful vistas and paintings ... all the 'normal' five senses we usually talk about. And although they (like us) are bombarded with sexy pictures and sexual innuendo everywhere, we never tell them how to satisfy their natural sexual instincts. Little boys need no help of course; they figure it out all by themselves. But our daughters? Well, that's a different story. Sex therapist Dr. Laura Berman suggests that we should casually encourage our girls to explore and get to know their own bodies. Self-pleasuring is completely normal, natural and harmless. She brings up another interesting point to ponder; perhaps if teen girls are assured that's it okay to satisfy themselves, then maybe they wouldn't be in such a hurry to get involved with boys in order to quell their curiosity and normal sexual urges. They can 'feel good' safely, without risking STDs or pregnancy. In the spirit of attaining complete gender equality, let's encourage our teenage girls to own their sexuality. Now that's real 'Girl power!' Check out Dr. Laura's excellent advice on talking to kids about sex at: media.oprah.com/lberman/talking-to-kids-about-sex-handbook.pdf

When it comes to discussing oral sex, you'll probably feel more intimidated than talking about the mechanics of 'the act.' But oral sex is so commonplace in today's teen culture that you need to steel yourself and forge ahead. Our teens seem to have forgotten that desire is a two-way street, something that seems tragically lost on this particular generation of teenage girls who are so intent on pleasing the boys, that they don't give much thought to their own desire for pleasure. Ask your kids if they think that having oral sex is more or less intimate than intercourse? That should open the floodgates of discussion. Biology is mechanical. Tell them of the pleasures of real intimacy. You might want to plant the idea that if a girl rushes to 'service' a boy just so he will call her again, it really isn't much different than acting like a junior hooker. And while we're on the subject, have you heard about 'rainbow parties' where every girl wears a different color lipstick and every boy sees how many colors of lipstick he can collect on his penis by the end of the night? (I know you are cringing just the way I did.) I'm not sure if this is myth or reality but you might ask your teen about it and open a discussion. It could lead to a talk about the 'morning after' feelings of regret, shame and embarrassment the girls must feel, especially if the guy then acts cool towards them, or if people start talking about them. And the latest craze? Apparently some girls have started wearing 'jelly bracelets.' The different colors indicating which sexual acts the girl is willing to do. What will these kids dream up next?

If you talk about sex with your kids often, you'll get pretty good at these conversations. Try asking them if these things are going on in their school and how they feel about it, rather than delivering lectures. Keep talking even when they roll their eyes. It's tricky - and it means that you have to maintain your cool. You can't be judgmental or punitive.

If you think your teen is considering exploring their sexuality and going to the next level, you might want to strike up a conversation and toss around these questions... Why do you want to do 'it' now? Do you feel you need to have sex now just to please or keep your partner? Or because you're curious? Or because everyone else is? What do you expect to happen after your experience? How long have you been in this long-term relationship? How long do you expect to be together? What would happen if you broke up soon after? Will you regret doing this if you do break up? What are your partner's expectations of this relationship? How long does s/he think you'll be together? Do you know the correct way to apply condoms? (Answer: Always leave room at the tip of the condom.) Do you know that 30% of teen girls become pregnant by age 20? So, because condoms sometimes break, what secondary form of birth control are you going to use?

Discussing the pleasures of the flesh this way, may lead your teen to realize that it's a little more complicated than they thought. Encourage your kids to make the decision whether to have sex or not, before the moment of passion arrives. The more you talk the easier it will be - for both of you. And even though it isn't realistic, (did you tell your Mother 'everything'?) "You can tell me anything" should become your mantra. But don't worry, as Dr. Laura says, "Information does not equal permission."

Too much information? When it comes to sex there's really no such thing.

Show and Tell, Family Style

It wasn't long ago that network TV wouldn't allow a 'married TV couple' to be seen sitting on a bed together. Now, of course, you can watch soft porn in the middle of the day. What are we thinking? Sex is so much a part of life. We shouldn't hide it, nor should we flaunt it. I think it's healthy to have had the kids catch my husband and I display a little romance. We've 'accidentally on purpose' let them see us showing a little affection. They always saw us holding hands, smooching, dancing in the kitchen, hugging up and full-blown, all out kissing! Oh wow! Come on – they listen to explicit descriptions of pimps and ho's on their iPod's! Kids learn by watching, whatever they're watching, and I'd rather they imitate us – a real life couple in a healthy, stable, loving relationship, than try to imitate all the dysfunctional hook-ups portrayed in movies and music-video's on the tube and net.

SEX - 'THE TALK'

I told my children that when choosing a life partner to make sure that you are marrying your 'best friend.' Make sure your relationship is based on a love that is patient, not rude, not easily angered and not self-serving; a love built on trust and hope and the ability to carry you through life's storms, because no one is exempt from the seas of uncertainty. But when it came to discussing SEX, I let my husband handle it, in his own unique way...

He had 'the sex talk' with our kids before they hit their teens. After the basics were covered, he used one of his favorite songs, "Paradise By the Dashboard Light" from the album 'Bat Out of Hell' (1977) by Meatloaf, to help him explain the pitfalls of premature, unplanned sex between inexperienced, naive teenagers. It describes, in baseball analogy and terminology, a young couple who get carried away in the moment and the unintended consequences which follow...

boy: "Though it's cold and lonely in the deep dark night,
I can see paradise by the dashboard light."

girl: "Ain't no doubt about it- we were doubly blessed
cause we were barely seventeen and we were barely dressed."

But as they are about to slide into 'home plate' the young girl screams,

"Stop right there!... Do you love me? Do you need me? Will you never leave
me?
Will you make me so happy for the rest of my life?
Will you take me away and will you make me your wife?"

The boy in his exasperation and overwhelming lust agrees

"I couldn't take it any longer, I was crazed
And when that feeling came upon me
Like a tidal wave ...
I started swearing...
that I would love you to the end of time.

and years later he laments...

"I'll never break my promise or forget my vow
But God only knows what I can do right now -
I'm praying for the end of time, that's all I can do
So I can end my time with you!"

You can see the full version of "Paradise By the Dashboard Light" on Youtube.com

Michelle Leeds, Plantation, FL

Also worth mentioning: Sex hasn't changed in billions of years - it's only new to you. Most people are disappointed by their first experiences.

For all those men who say, "Why buy the cow when you can get the milk for free", here's an update for you. Now 80% of women are against marriage. Why? Because women realize it's not worth buying an entire pig, just to get a little sausage.

Andy Rooney

There's NEVER an Excuse for Abuse

Seems like 'the kids today' have no respect for themselves, or for each other. They have poorly developed emotional filters and no sense of relationship boundaries. Teen rage and date-rape are on the rise. Discuss the potential for abuse with your teen and be very clear that there's no room for second chances. Life isn't a baseball game: THREATEN TO STRIKE AND

YOU'RE GONE. STRIKE ONCE AND THE POLICE WILL ESCORT YOU OUT OF THE PARK. If there's ever an incident of emotional or physical abuse, there should be an automatic, 'no ifs, ands or buts' immediate severing of the relationship. As one TV psychologist states, "The best predictor of future behavior is present and past behavior." In other words, zebras don't change their stripes - people rarely change.

Here are some signs and symptoms to watch for: jealousy; controlling behavior; verbal abuse (comments regarding your weight or insulting put downs); threats to harm you, your family, or your pet; attempts to isolate you from your family or friends.

Don't be a victim; walk away. The 'Help Hotline' is: 1- 800 - 799 SAFE

Remind your teen that not every 'Mr. Right Now'
has what it takes to be 'Mr. Right' forever.   Narissa Nields

If I Had a Daughter
© Laurie Jennings Oudin 2009
Hear her great music at jenningsandkeller.com

If I had a daughter we'd sit by the river
Eat ice cream together and play skipping stones
We'd gallop through fields, the tall grass would tickle
We'd flop down in giggles on the welcoming ground

If I had a daughter I'd make sure to teach her
The limitless world is hers to explore
If I had a daughter no ceiling would stop her
She'd go the distance aware of her power

If I had a daughter I'd want her to know
Her body will never be a war zone
A body to serve her, propel her forward
Never constrained by fear or by shame

She'd make her own choices regardless of voices
Telling her she must conform to fit in
If I had a daughter she'd dress as it serves her
Never by rules of some magazine spin

On Piercings, Tattoos, Hair dye and Crazy Cuts

It's A Hair Thing

Let your kids do whatever they would like to their hair. Pink, red, black, blonde, orange, blue, faux hawk, short, long, whatever. But when they come to you the summer before their senior year of high school and announce they want dreadlocks, compromise and say "Sure! AFTER SENIOR PORTRAITS!"

Cindy Bowers, Asheville, NC

Tattoos are permanent, piercings may leave a scar, hair dye isn't forever and crazy cuts are only momentary madness. Your teen should know that the risks of getting a tattoo or body piercing are: contracting hepatitis or an infection, paralysis, numbness or loss of sensation to the area of the piercing and allergic reactions. You may cringe when your teenager adopts a fad haircut but I suggest you grin and bear it, and take lots of pictures so their future children and grandchildren can have a good laugh. Remind your teenager that today's hair color and style will show up on tomorrow's resume when they're ready to search for a serious job. Thanks to the Internet nothing will ever be forgotten! If that isn't enough of a deterrent, perhaps the following song lyrics will have more of an impact ...

Sometimes Mother Really Does Know Best
Printed with permission © Christine Lavin Music
ASCAP/administered by Bug Music
Check out her great music at: ChristineLavin.com

Daughter looked in mother's eyes and pleaded, "Please say yes!
You never criticize my friends, my hair, or how I dress
A tiny eyebrow piercing on me would look <u>sublime</u>!"
Her mother thought about this for a quite a long, long time

Then she said, "Hmmm, an eyebrow piercing . . .
That's a permanent reminder of a temporary fad
When you're old and gray my dear, you'll think back and be glad
That your mother had the foresight to turn down your request
Sometimes mother really does know best"

"Just a tiny tattoo, mother, dancing on my skin
All the other kids have one and I want to fit in
A delicate butterfly - right here on my wrist?"
Her mother thought about it, then she said this

"Hmmm, a tattoo . . . That's a permanent reminder of a temporary feeling
Think 'Angelina & Billy Bob' before you hit the ceiling
You think a tattoo on your teenage skin would make you look unique
But when you're older you'd look like a circus freak!"

The mother and the daughter barely spoke for the next year
Except for the occasional "huh!" and snotty sneer ("whatEVer")
It looked like there was nothing that could mend this sorry rift
'Til the daughter overheard the mother on the telephone, discuss getting a facelift!

"Hmmm. . . a facelift, Mother . . .
That's a permanent reminder of a temporary fear
Only the lucky ones grow older every year
And I don't think you, like, look <u>that bad</u> for someone of your age"
The mother sat there in a smoldering rage.

(This song can end two ways: It can have a beautiful, wholesome ending where everyone learns healthy lessons of self-acceptance and they live happy, productive lives. Or it can go to the dark side... pick your favorite!)

(Wholesome ending)
Mother and the daughter shook hands and took a vow
No facelift! No tattoo! No bloody punctured brow!
Instead the mother gave the money to 'Guide Dogs For The Blind.'
At the annual gala they met a blind father and son, and had the grandest time!

We're a permanent reminder of a temporary bad day
When we couldn't see our natural beauty and almost threw it all away
As we cuddle with our (blind) sweethearts now they, too, will attest,
"Yes! Sometimes Mother Really Does Know Best!"

(Be Careful What You Wish For Ending)
The mother said to daughter "OK, let's make a deal
Though your words stung me, at least now I know how you feel
If you let me get my facelift you can get that tattoo now
And yes, I'll even let you pierce your brow"

Both had their procedures done on the same day
If only they had known the heavy price they'd have to pay
The mother had her facelift done by Dr. Fronkenschteen
She came out looking like a combination monkey and drag queen.

And the daughter's tattoo went just fine but not that eyebrow ring...
It contracted an infection . . . too gross for me to sing
And both of them died disgusting painful, stinking deaths
But both had this to say with their dying breaths . . .

"We're a permanent reminder of our temporary insanity
We sacrificed our looks and our lives for our foolish vanity"
And at the reading of their wills they left this last bequest
A pillow upon which was embroidered:
"Sometimes Mother Really Does Know Best!"

On Peer Pressure

Life is so complicated for teens. Peer pressure is such a determining influence. Sometimes it's so hard to find the right words to get your intentions across... thankfully songwriters have a gift and they can deliver a message directly into a teen's heart. Maybe one day this lyric will help you teach a valuable lesson.

Courage

(Diane) © Bob Blue, Black Socks Press – printed with permission
Check out his great music at: bobblue.org

A small thing once happened at school
That brought up a question for me
And somehow it taught me to see
The price that I pay to be cool

Diane is this girl that I know
She's strange, like she doesn't belong
I don't mean to say that that's wrong
We don't like to be with her though

And so when we all made a plan
To have this big party at Sue's
Most kids at our school got the news
But no one invited Diane

The thing about Taft Junior High
Is secrets don't last very long
I acted like nothing was wrong
When I saw Diane start to cry

I know you may think that that's cruel
It doesn't make me very proud
I just went along with the crowd
It's sad – but you have to at school.

You can't pick the friends you prefer
You fit in as well as you can
I couldn't be friends with Diane
Cause then they might treat me like her

In one class at Taft Junior High
We studied what people have done
With gas chamber, bomber and gun
In Auschwitz, Japan and My Lai
Like robots obeying some rule
Atrocities done by the mob
Or innocents, doing their job
And what was it for-- was it cool?

The world was aware of this hell,
But how many cried out in shame?
What heroes and who was to blame?
A story that no one dared tell.

I promise to do what I can
To not let it happen again
To care for all women and men
I'll start by inviting Diane

Just Be You

Be who you are and say what you feel because those who mind don't matter
and those who matter don't mind.   Dr. Suess

Not everything that can be counted counts and
not everything that counts can be counted.   Albert Einstein

Never doubt that a small group of thoughtful, committed citizens can change the world.
Indeed it is the only thing that ever does.

Margaret Mead

A real friend is one who walks in when the rest of the world walks out.

It's New To You!

A sibling's 'hand me downs' are so yesterday - but other kids' clothes are so cool! At the end of the school year arrange a 'clothes swap' with some friends. 'Still cool' jeans, outgrown shoes, school uniforms, sweaters and jackets are so much better when they're 'worn in!'

When the temperature is sub zero (Celsius, below freezing F.) The Mother must insist that teen-age children at least TAKE their jacket with them when they go out, even when the child insists that it is really not that cold out and a T-shirt will do. Rule #147, paragraph 6, subsection A, states that the Mother must try to prevent hypothermia at all costs.

Andrea Grossman, Cranbrooke, B.C

Trust But Verify

Trust yourself. If you have a gut feeling that something isn't right, pay attention! Your inner voice is screaming "Warning! Warning!" Your teen may be smiling to your face and acting as if everything's normal, but if your instinct is flashing red warning signs and you suspect that something's up – it probably is. Mother's intuition is rarely, if ever, wrong. Don't worry about bruising their feelings – they'll get over it. Remember that these children are your responsibility, they live in your house and their expectations of privacy should be limited to the bathroom only! Feel free to look through their closets and drawers, behind books and blinds, under the bed and between the mattresses. If you find nothing, you'll both have nothing to feel bad about. If you do find something, your finding it will be the least of their problems - so don't worry about it.

I never hesitated to say, "I will always love you but I don't like you right now."

M. Cohen

276

Just Do It!

In our home, when there were tasks to be done, we expected the chores to be completed. No excuses. Whatever it takes. Just do it. "Just do it!" wasn't a Nike commercial – it was our motto!

Hazel Case, FL (90 yrs. young)

When Did High $chool become Big Bu$ine$$?

First, there might be a small charge to cover the rising cost of team sports equipment. Next comes the call to participate in chocolate bar sales, magazine sales, and Christmas tree sales. Soon after comes a plea for 'donations' to support the athletic and academic clubs. Of course you need to have a class T-shirt, be included in club pictures and Homecoming!

Junior year means expenditures for a suit or prom dress, limo rental and tickets for the prom, and accompanying girl-prep for prom night: hair, nails and makeup. I wish someone would explain the need for junior prom. Do the kids need a training session? But all of this has just been a prelude to the big one.

Senior year requires the purchase of school rings, senior pictures, yearbook, memory book, cap and gown, banquet night, grad' night, prom night dress/ tux rental, and again, prom night prep; hair, nails and makeup. And of course, there's the limo rental and tickets for the prom night event, which now rivals a grand, celebrity Oscar extravaganza. As for the academic side of high school – you'll probably want to invest in a SAT prep course and of course you have to pay for actual SAT test.

Whoa! How did this happen? What are we thinking? "Toto, I don't think we're in Kansas anymore..." We send our kids off to school for an education and the next thing we know, we neeeeed to buy all this stuff. Not that we're not getting our money's worth... sure they'll have days-long memories of the $300 gown she wore for a few hours. And the all-important 'senior class school ring' will last at least until a college friend makes a comment about how cute it is that 'you seem to be going steady with your high school chums.' Wow, it took three whole months before 'the $500 - $700 ring' got chucked into a memory box or underwear drawer. At least the yearbook will be of some value down the road, so you can look back, identify old buddies and catch a glimpse of those great old days when a junior prom dress cost only $300. And now that many yearbooks are replicated on CDs and DVDs, I wonder how many will get lost along the way? 'In the olden days' we didn't spend as much time or money feeding the high school memorabilia industry... we just did the things that created our cherished memories, free of charge. Can we find a way to get our kids back to Kansas?

On Self Reliance

High school seniors should brush up on self-reliance skills such as making and keeping their own dental, doctor and haircut appointments. It's helpful to use a daily planner, to think ahead and organize their time.

Beverly Low, Dean of First Year Students, Colgate University, NY

Rules of Life (attributed to Bill Gates)

Rule 1: Life is not fair -- get used to it.

Rule 2: The world won't care about your self-esteem.
The world will expect you to accomplish something BEFORE you feel good about yourself.

Rule 3: You will NOT make $60,000 a year right out of high school.
You won't be a vice-president before you earn it.

Rule 4: If you think your teacher is tough, wait till you get a boss.

Rule 5: Flipping burgers is not beneath your dignity.
Your Grandparents had a different word for burger flipping: they called it opportunity.

Rule 6: If you mess up, it's not your parents' fault, so don't whine about your mistakes, learn from them.

Rule 7: Before you were born, your parents weren't as boring as they are now. They got that way from paying your bills, cleaning your clothes and listening to you talk about how cool you thought you were. So before you save the rain forest from the parasites of your parents' generation, try delousing the closet in your own room.

Rule 8: Your school may have done away with winners and losers, but life HAS NOT. In some schools, they have abolished failing grades and they'll give you as MANY TIMES as you want to get the right answer. This doesn't bear the slightest resemblance to ANYTHING in real life.

Rule 9: Life is not divided into semesters. You don't get summers off and very few employers are interested in helping you FIND YOURSELF. Do that on your own time.

Rule 10: Television is NOT real life. In real life people actually have to leave the coffee shop and go to jobs.

Rule 11: Be nice to nerds. Chances are you'll end up working for one.

Internet Rules

May I suggest that you not allow computers in children's bedrooms, EVER. Keep the computer in the family room or kitchen where you can monitor its activity. Explain to your children that the PC is the equivalent of a TV or phone – that you can, and will, monitor what they are seeing and/or who they are talking to, at any time. I'm a big proponent of the Aussie philosophy, "no worries." Be up front and tell your kids that they should have no expectations of privacy. Remind your children that just as they would never give their name, telephone number, address or name of their school to a stranger on the street or in the mall, the same rules apply to the Internet, as they may be talking to a stranger there, too. Do not allow your children to enter chat rooms. Do not allow them to open any emails from unknown screen names, or pop up IM's – and teach them to block those that filter in. Explain that if they should happen to enter a forbidden space in error, they should tell you about it, without worrying about getting into trouble. Statistics listed on the website "Enough is Enough" (enough.org) mention that 12 percent of all websites are pornographic in nature which translates to 4.2 million pornographic websites, 420 million pornographic web pages, and 68 million daily pornographic search engine requests (or 25% of total search engine requests) (Internet Filter Review, 2006). Apparently 79% of unwanted exposures to pornography, occur in the home by children. (Online Victimization of Youth: Five Years Later, 2006.) Teach your child not to share passwords even with their 'best friends' or girl/boyfriends! (More on that later.) Install monitoring and filtering software. They are available for free at safefamilies.org and k9webprotection.com. Monitor your child's screen name(s) and web sites. Save and print out any evidence if your child ever experiences cyber-bullying. And use the computer to reinforce your family values; don't be afraid to limit its use and attach consequences for its misuse.

It's Not 'MySpace' It's Everyone's Space!
(or why Facebook should sometimes be Shut Your Face-book!)

A study, posted in Oct. 2007, examined publicly available 16 and 17-year-old MySpace web-profiles and the 'shared' information was truly astonishing! 47% of the websites contained risk behavior information: 21% described sexual activity; 25% described alcohol use; 9% described cigarette use; and 6% described drug use. 97.2% contained personally identifying information; 74% included an identifiable picture; 75% included subjects' first names or surnames; and 78% included subjects' hometowns.

Kids today face social pressures we could never have dreamed of. The new "If you love me, you'll do it," doesn't have anything to do with sex. It's all about...(can you believe it?) passwords. Apparently, the 'in thing' is for kids who are romantically involved to trade each other's passwords for e-mail, Facebook, ATM cards, etc. Let's see - how long would it take to text a disaster after a fight or breakup? An angry 'ex' could create a calamity within seconds. While you're talking to your teenagers about this, remind them that buried somewhere in the Facebook terms of service, it actually states that one can lose their Facebook account for sharing a password. Uh-oh...banished from the Facebook world? Now that would be a fate worse than death! Ah! Life was so much easier when your boyfriend was just pressuring you to get to third base!

The Internet is the modern-day equivalent of a masquerade ball. One teen killed herself after 'an online boyfriend' abruptly broke up with her. It turned out that the 'boyfriend' was actually the mother of one of her classmates who was trying to access information about her own daughter. The WWW seems magic, but it can also be tragic. Remind the kids that today's play (including 'sexting') might be tomorrow's 'nay,' because college admissions officers, potential employers or future boyfriends will all have access to whatever silliness they put online for display. The best IT rule I've heard of is 'The Grandpa Rule' - if they wouldn't feel comfortable showing grandpa whatever they are posting, it shouldn't be there. Remind your teens that scholarship companies (and/or committees) routinely check what candidates have posted, and scholarship money is often denied based on what they have posted on social media.

Clearly our kids don't understand what should be private about their personal lives. The time will come when our most treasured possession will be what we so nonchalantly give away – our privacy. Wise parents routinely check out MySpace.com, Facebook.com and Twitter.com to see what the kids are revealing about themselves.

Child Predators

How sad that we should have to worry about whom we can trust. We all know that 'pillars of the community' - priests, teachers, doctors and cub-scout leaders - have all been caught preying on children. Be vigilant and be cautious. Know where your children are and who they're with. Never allow your child to be alone with any adult or authority figure, no matter who they are! Most abused children become the victims of people they know and trust. If they walk home from school or the school bus drop-off point, have them always walk with a buddy or two. Predators plan their attacks carefully, and search for a victim who has a predicable path, a long walk home or who is alone.

If you work, set up a mandatory phone call upon your child's arrival home. Establish a secret code. Have one word that means everything is OK, and another word to let you know s/he needs help.

For more tips see: safeside.com and familywatchdog.us

John Walsh, from 'America's Most Wanted', developed this site. It is a valuable tool to help us keep our kids safe. When you visit the site you can enter your address and a map will pop up with your house as the small icon and other houses noted as colored dots surrounding your entire neighborhood. The colored dots indicate where registered sex offenders live. When you click on these dots, a picture of a person will appear with an address and a description of the crime s/he has committed.

On Dating

Be careful of your commentary. Never make fun of your child's boyfriend or girlfriend – they may end up being your son or daughter-in-law.

Lucie Lerner, Montreal, Canada

Tips For Dating

Who said dating was easy? No one who has ever tried it. Remind your kids: You'll fall in love and you'll fall out of love. You'll inadvertently hurt someone and you'll probably be hurt by someone. And it's all part of learning about the process we call love. Here are some things to keep in mind:

First Impressions Last
You only have one chance to make a good first impression. People are judgmental – that's just a fact of life. So, take a second and look presentable no matter where you're going. Fix your hair and wear clean clothes. You are who you think you are, present yourself confidently.

Know yourself - Be yourself
Don't let others make you into someone you're not. Just be you. If you're not, how can you expect others to be comfortable around you? When you just relax and act naturally, you'll find someone who really complements you.

What Do You Really Want From Love?
Everybody's got a list of ideal "must-haves." Those are the things that you absolutely, positively, MUST SEE in someone just to give that person a chance. Don't look for movie star looks - they are few and far between. Look for someone who makes you laugh and with whom you're comfortable.

Recognize Your Imperfections - To Thine Own Self Be True
Look, no one wants to admit they have any flaws, but there's a very good chance you do. Acknowledge your imperfections and learn to work with them. Recognize that you're only human and accept that others will have their faults, too.

After A Break-Up, Take Time To Get Over It
Maybe you think you're ready to date, but maybe you're not quite done mourning your last relationship. If that's true, take the time to get over the relationship. Otherwise, you're just wasting your own and your date's time. When you're ready to start dating again be honest with your 1st date and tell him/her that you're starting over, but don't talk about your 'ex.' Your past history is yours, and no one wants to hear about it for very long.

Don't Keep Repeating Past Mistakes
Dating is an opportunity to get to know what we definitely want or don't want in a partner. But, unfortunately, we generally forget what we've learned once the next relationship comes along. If you see the same problems arising in a new relationship, stand back and re-evaluate. As much as it feels right, it probably isn't if the problems are the same as what broke up a previous relationship. People are creatures of habit and some people keep slipping back into their comfort zone - even if it's negative or destructive.

Girls – don't listen to a word of what boys say,
just pay attention to what they DO.

Randy Pausch

On Winners vs. Losers

The winner is always part of the answer
The loser is always part of the problem.
The winner always has a program
The loser always has an excuse.
The winner says, "Let me do it for you"
The loser says. "That's not my job."
The winner sees an answer for every problem
The loser sees a problem for every answer.
The winner says, "It may be difficult, but it's possible"
The loser says, "It may be possible, but it's too difficult."
A winner listens
A loser waits until it's his turn to talk.
When a winner makes a mistake, he says, "I was wrong."
When a loser makes a mistake, he says, "It wasn't my fault. "
A winner says, "I'm good, but not as good as I could be."
A loser says, "I'm not as bad as a lot of other people."
A winner feels responsible for more than his job.
A loser says, "I only work here. "

Submitted by Marilyn Green, Hollywood, FL

How to Handle a "Pro" Procrastinator

Is your kid the 'pro' in procrastinator? One of my daughters certainly was. This is one trait she didn't inherit. My husband is always early, the first to arrive wherever he needs to be. I tend to arrive 'on time,' start projects on the day I'm given one, and have it completed in plenty of time. But our daughter - she did things 'her way!' Whatever the school project, there she was burning the midnight oil, working furiously in a race against the clock. Drove me crazy! We used to kid her that she should be a newspaper journalist because she thrived working under the gun with a deadline looming. It took some time but I learned to let go - she owned that frenzied countdown to the finish. One day I put up this sign above her desk and went to bed...

If it weren't for the last minute, I wouldn't get anything done!

Tomorrow is the busiest day of the week.   Spanish proverb

Arguing with a teenager is like wrestling with a pig in the mud. You both get dirty but, the problem is, they like it!

Listen honey, nobody knows how to raise teenagers – you just live through it and one day they're people!

When you cannot stand to have your child around you, it is probably the time when they need you the most.
Andrea Grossman, Cranbrooke, B.C.

The Keys Please...

Vroom, Vroom – Just A Shortcut To A Tomb?

Please Moms, I implore you to forbid your kids to ever ride on a motorcycle. I've had both a good friend and my nephew die in horrific accidents while driving cycles. They were both wearing helmets. No matter how careful you are or how great you may think your reflexes are, you are no match for any car, truck, or poor highway road conditions that you might encounter. When I hear people tell me about the open road, their wonderful traveling experiences, and the feeling of freedom they feel; I imagine the tens of thousands of people on organ transplant recipient lists who are patiently waiting to feel those very same things - just as soon as the donor-cyclists are finished having their turn. In my opinion, 'vroom, vroom' means you'll die too soon.

Driving Lessons

Did you know that originally teens were given a license to drive a tractor, only on the family farm in order to help bring in crops? Most of our kids don't help with anything even remotely similar to hauling hay, so why do we cling to the same age criteria as the bygone agricultural era? Tradition! Let's face it - sixteen year olds are not mature enough to drive. One needs to focus on the tasks of steering a motor vehicle at a reasonable speed, keeping track of what's happening ahead, beside and behind you, watching and planning for any eventuality a few car lengths ahead, knowing your route, using directional blinkers appropriately, changing lanes with room and time to spare, responding to traffic lights, pedestrians and cyclists and negotiating several different methods of parking in a variety of settings... all this from the same teen who can't direct his dirty clothing into the hamper, in a bedroom he's being occupying for most of his life! Now add friends in the back seat, the music blasting, the escalating conversation, the distractions on the road, the occasional "it was only one!" beer, and you have a disaster waiting to happen. Auto accidents are the #1 cause of teenage death in this country. My advice: Postpone, delay and deny! The world and your children will be safer if they both wait a few years. No one ever died from erring on the side of caution. That said, here's some advice I've gleaned from the experts ...

Steering Kids To Safety

If you're getting ready to hand over the car keys, this fact should keep you up at night: The number-one killer of American teenagers is car accidents. Teen drivers not only have the highest collision rate of any age group, but teens who have driven for one year or less have the worst crash rates by far. According to the AAA Foundation for Traffic Safety, when teens cause accidents, pedestrians, passengers and occupants of other cars account for two out of every three fatalities! You can never absolutely positively crash-proof a new driver, but the following 10 steps will help reduce the risks:

1) Is your teen mature enough? Take a good honest look and assess your teen's readiness to get behind the wheel. Measuring maturity can be tricky, but academic performance is a good yardstick. Does your teen get good grades, complete assignments on time, and generally

take responsibility for schoolwork, without your nagging? If not, you might want to reconsider and delay handing over the car keys.

2) How's your driving? Here's a troubling truth: Bad drivers beget bad drivers. Ouch! The AAA Foundation for Traffic Safety found that a teens' driving behavior is a reflection of their parents' driving behavior. The correlation is the same regardless of parents' educational level or socioeconomic status. Like it or not, you are a behind-the-wheel role model for your teen long before s/he reaches driving age. Did your child sit in the back seat and watch you ignore speed limits, yak on the cell phone, cut off other cars or 'flip the bird' to other drivers? Then why be shocked if your kid does the same?

3) Practice makes progress. First, hire a professional instructor to take your child out on the road. Make sure they drive in all conditions (snow, rain, heavy traffic and on the highway.) Then, after s/he's mastered the fundamentals with a real pro, hold your breath, grit your teeth and let him/her practice taking the wheel. Schedule regular road sessions to practice the skills and techniques s/he's learned from the hired pro, such as parallel parking, making three-point turns, merging into traffic and getting off an exit ramp. Try to correct mistakes calmly and provide praise when your teen does well. Kids should learn how and when to check under the hood too. They should practice checking the tire pressure, the brake fluid, transmission fluid, oil, window-washer fluid and radiator antifreeze levels. And absolutely, positively have a dress rehearsal so they learn to change a tire before they need to do it on the side of a busy highway.

4) Say no to peer passengers and night driving. Statistics overwhelmingly identify the two biggest risk factors for teens as driving at night and having other teens as passengers. The more passengers, the higher the risk - that's a fact. Most states now have 'graduated driver licensing laws' that phase in night driving and the number of passengers allowed. These restrictions really do reduce new-driver crash rates. But you can enforce your own laws, too: Set strict curfews and allow them to drive only in a specific geographical area for the first few months.

5) It's not where your hands are – it's where your head is! Limit distractions. Cell phones, CDs, iPods, fast food, mascara - the list of potentially dangerous behind-the-wheel distractions goes on and on. Insist that your teen never eat, use a phone, fish around for CDs, text or scroll through their iPod playlists while driving. Studies have shown that talking on a cell phone while driving decreases our mental and visual acuity causing 'inattention blindness.' People are 4 times more likely to have an accident while cell – talking, which is the same rate as driving while legally drunk! And texting doubles that rate to 8 times more likely to get in an accident! As Oprah suggests, make your car a NO PHONE ZONE. Don't tempt fate, that call or text can certainly wait!

6) Have your teen get in the habit of buckling up and locking the doors. Girls should get in the habit of putting their purses on the floor behind them.

7) Draw up two written contracts. One contract will be the terms and conditions allowing your teen to drive your vehicles. Once you all agree on the terms, conditions and restrictions of driving privileges (and the consequences of violating them) write everything down on paper and have all parties sign the document just to make everything crystal clear. Next, take out a medical 'living will' and discuss what heroic end-of-life procedures your child would want, and which vital organs s/he wishes to donate should s/he be involved in a terrible accident. Bingo! This should wake 'em up and get your child's attention! And this one conversation, coupled with a

signature on the bottom line, may very well insure that irresponsible driving, drag racing and speeding will never become 'issues' in your home. Furthermore, you will have opened a very important discussion because after watching the Terry Shiavo case play out on television, we all learned that end-of-life issues should be decided and documented clearly, by each individual. There's nothing like a written, signed contract to make people become more aware of their commitments. (You can find actual living - will documents tailored for each state at: http://www.caringinfo.org/i4a/pages/index.cfm?pageid=3289) Of course, your teen must agree to always wear a seat belt, observe speed limits, say no to alcohol and drugs, and obey all laws. Your agreement should also spell out all the responsibilities of driving, such as vehicle maintenance and driving expenses such as gas and insurance.

8) Set some rules and stick to the consequences of breaking them. Traffic violations earn (police) tickets, and violations of your rules should bring consequences too. Depending on the offense, penalties might include fewer driving hours or the loss of driving privileges all together for a time. Good behavior should earn some perks too. Experts emphasize that rewarding good behavior reinforces the learning process.

9) Kitchen Table Talk. According to an AAA Foundation study, better parent-teen communication leads to better driving. Gather around the kitchen table every few weeks and talk about your teen's driving performance. If s/he has been violation-free for 90 days, then maybe it's time to let your teen have the car for an extra hour on the weekends.

10) High-tech help. Several companies offer Event Data Recorders (EDR or black boxes.) These devices keep track of maximum speed, acceleration rates, instances of hard braking and other parameters that indicate aggressive driving. Some EDRs even sound alarms when the vehicle exceeds certain pre-set limits. They cost around $200 plus installation. Many teens might balk at what they consider electronic eavesdropping. But you aren't spying when you install this device, you're just making them accountable for their behavior. Never install an EDR secretly. You want your teen to think twice about speeding, knowing that the EDR will catch the incident even if the police don't. Once installed, you just download EDR readouts and review them together. If you use the EDR to monitor your own driving behavior, you can compare the results with your teens. This way, everyone will view it as a family safety tool, not just a way to spy on kids.

11) Have your teen drive the safest car. Often the hand-me-down teen-mobile may not be the wisest choice, because the least experienced driver should really use the safest car. When it comes to collisions, size really does matter and large sedans make up in crash worthiness what they lack in cool. The newest cars offer the latest safety technology: side airbags, anti-lock brakes and stability control. Never give a teen driver a small, high-powered sports car, convertible (which have higher injury rates), or an SUV (which tend to roll over). And in order to feel true ownership and the subsequent responsibility, kids should have a financial stake in 'their own car.' The car should always be registered in their name because if they are in an accident, you can't be held liable.

In the end, if all of your efforts fail and your teen is involved in a crash, you'll know that you've done your best to maximize his/her protection.

Regarding Drinking and Driving

We all know how important it is to reinforce, reiterate and 'drive home' the message about the responsibilities of driving and the dangers of alcohol consumption, and how deadly and disastrous it is to mix them together. Sometimes a poem or a song can reach a teenager's heart in a way that conversation alone can't.

I Didn't Mean It, Don't Get It

Printed with permission; ©Mindy Lou Simmons
Find her great music at: mindysimmons.com

He's a very handsome boy, a strapping twenty-two.
He's got jet-black hair, long lashes and eyes so blue.
He's the life of the party. He makes everybody smile.
He even makes you laugh, and you haven't been there for a while.
But he drives drunk... and you lost your mother that way.
It doesn't matter how he's feeling now, it doesn't matter what he says.
Cause there's no comfort in the cold 'I'm Sorry Morning Blues'
"I didn't mean it" doesn't help when someone's grieving for their mother
Or sister... or father... or brother.

She's a beautiful woman, a shining thirty-four.
She's worked like a dog to get what she's got, struggled to open every door.
And her kids they look up to her. They want to be just like their Mom.
She might be the one you've been looking for,
But she's a ticking time bomb.
Cause she drives drunk and you lost your brother that way...
There's no comfort in the cold 'I'm Sorry Morning Blues'
"I didn't mean it" doesn't help when someone's grieving for their mother
Or sister... or father... or brother.

He's only 19 years old ... his young wife great with child.
She wakes him up in the middle of the night with a craving so wild.
And he smiles as he's driving, thinking about the child she's going to bear.
And he just can't wait to get back home... but he never gets there.
You've got a lot of money, so you can buy your way out of this mess.
But you've just destroyed a new family, and you can't escape the press.
When will you learn that the loss of life isn't worth that fifth martini?
You just turned a simple trip to the grocery store into such a tragedy,
Cause you drive drunk. Now she's lost her lover to you.
It doesn't matter how you're feeling now, it doesn't matter what you do.
There's no comfort in the cold 'I'm Sorry Morning Blues.'
"I didn't mean it" doesn't help
When someone's grieving their mother, sister, father, brother...
Or their daughter, son, friend, or lover.

Tweens, Teens and Twenteen-agers ... who knew?

Have you heard the expression 'sometimes things get worse before they get better'? This is a truism and I have noticed that it applies to 'human becomings' as well. Girl 'tweens on the brink of physical maturity have one foot in a sneaker and the other foot precariously balanced on a 5 inch spike heel. They're moody, a little irrational and sometimes silly, but we can handle that. All teens are prone to fits of rage, moodiness and dumb adolescent mistakes. This is a given. But I need to warn you the worst is yet to come, because if teenagers are dumb, twen-teens are dumber.

Somewhere between the ages of twenty and twenty-five, I call this unnamed stage 'the twenteens,' your angel child will enter a peculiar stage of life whereupon billions and billions of brain cells will suddenly, but thankfully temporarily, switch off. They simply freeze and remain static. Your child will simply wake up one morning and although all outward appearances remain the same, the inner workings of his/her mind will have totally ceased to function. S/he will walk around the house like a familiar stranger. It's as if some alien has snatched your tempestuous teen's demeanor and replaced it with a zombie-like, semi-comatose spirit. Your 'darling' may lack even the limited cognitive awareness you have come to expect. Be warned, symptoms include, but may not be limited to, spending money s/he doesn't have, losing all interest in the college courses s/he just spent years aspiring to gain access to, lying or cheating in school, doing things totally out of character, sneaking around and doing things behind your back, delaying life, denying responsibility, experimenting with drugs, drinking way too much beer/booze and being totally obsessed with exploring the opposite or same sex... or simply lying around accomplishing absolutely nothing. S/he may drop out, flunk out or 'take some time to find her/himself.' In short, s/he'll have entered into the dumbest phase of life – a time I call the 'Twenteens Coma,' so named because these kids are totally oblivious to real life as we know it. They give no thought to consequences of their actions or inactions. And they just float through life while you are pulling your hair out, wondering where your real kid went.

"YOU don't understand!" "It's MY life!" and "Leave me ALONE." "I'LL decide!" are the hallmark phrases, a sure sign that you've entered this trying twilight zone. Often this state of (un)consciousness is accompanied by an 'it's all about me' state of mind. Seemingly the planet takes its cue from your progeny and simply won't rotate unless it has an impact on her/his life. Have I struck a chord here? Do you recognize these symptoms?

Take heart... one day s/he'll awake from this brain freeze, revert to her/his old personality and be totally amazed at how much *you've* learned in the past few years!

Update: The teenage brain, Laurence Steinberg says, is like a car with a good accelerator but a weak brake. With powerful impulses under poor control, the likely result is a crash. The most recent research on the adolescent brain indicates that the juvenile brain is still maturing in the teen years and reasoning and judgment are developing well into the early to mid 20's." "As any parent knows," wrote Justice Anthony Kennedy for the 5-4 majority, youths are more likely to show "a lack of maturity and an underdeveloped sense of responsibility" than adults. "These qualities often result in impetuous and ill-considered actions and decisions." (Source; CNN.com/health 12/07) Oh no, a new defense strategy... the twenteen coma.

The Trouble With Tough Love

It is the ultimate parental nightmare: Your affectionate child is transformed, seemingly overnight, into an out-of-control, drug-addicted, hostile teenager. Many parents blame themselves. "Where did we go wrong?" they ask. Many anguished parents put their faith in strict residential rehab programs. At first glance, these programs, which are commonly based on a philosophy of "tough love," seem to offer a safe respite from the streets. However there is little data to support these institutions' claims of success. Nonetheless, a billion-dollar industry now promotes such tough-love treatment. Sadly, tough love often looks as if it works: For one thing, longitudinal studies find that most kids, even amongst the most troubled, eventually grow out of bad behavior, so the magic of time can be mistaken for the magic of treatment. Second, the experience of being emotionally terrorized can produce compliance that looks like real change, at least initially. But the bigger picture suggests that tough love tends to backfire. In late 2004, the National Institutes of Health released a "state of the science" consensus statement, concluding that "get tough" treatments "do not work and there is some evidence that they may make the problem worse."

The most effective help for troubled teens, oddly enough, is family therapy, done with the child at home. This has been shown to help even some of the roughest kids in the juvenile justice system. A lot of the time, teens are acting out because of family factors like divorce or new stepparents or moves -- but if you focus on the problem as one that "we are fighting together" rather than one in which the teen is "the problem," it is a lot easier to get him/her engaged. Have an independent psychiatrist (who is unaffiliated with any residential program) evaluate your child for signs of depression or mental illness. Then, the most important criteria for insuring that the therapy will work, is finding someone whom the teen likes (or at least, doesn't hate): the better the connection, the more likely the success. Some family therapy techniques that have proven results include cognitive behavioral family therapy and multidimensional family therapy. But if things don't improve overnight, don't give up!

Maia Szalavitz, New York, NY

The End of the Beginning

Emptying the Nest

It's time. He's getting ready to head out the door for good, and I can hear you thinking … "All I really want for him is to hear and feel my love, to take everything I've taught him (or tried to teach him) to heart and to be happy. I want him to be happy, to be healthy, to go out into the world and enjoy his life. I want him to take pride in himself and in his work; and do whatever he's going to do with a smile on his lips and a little flourish in his style." (Because anyone can be mediocre at a job, but only a special few will sparkle no matter what the job is. This is the most telling sign of inner happiness because when you're really happy on the inside your light will shine on everything you do.) Our children's leaving home is like fine chocolate, bitter sweet. We weathered the scraped knees, the dented car, the screaming matches and occasional slamming of bedroom doors; we savored the giggles and soft cheeks and cuddles. Now we have to face the most challenging part of Mothering – that gentle (or firm) 'push' out of the nest. It's such a difficult transition for some Moms that it might be helpful to remember that we, all of us, are both dependent and independent our entire lives. As infants we are dependent on others to nurture us, yet we must breathe, metabolize and acclimate to the world on our own. And all through life it's much the same. So, fear not: even when your last baby is heading out the door, s/he will always need you.

We spend so much time preparing our children for their independence but we so often forget to prepare ourselves! One day we wake up and it's time to let them go but we are the ones who aren't ready. When our oldest daughter was preparing to leave for college, I thought that I was perfectly OK with it. As we prepared for her departure, my bitchy mood seemed to escalate in sync with the stack of clothes piled up along the walls. She was ready. Obviously I wasn't. When our youngest was heading out the door, I was prepared, reconciled and a little more mature. The first night we became 'empty nesters' my husband and I lit candles, had a romantic dinner and celebrated the new chapter we were embarking on. We had come full circle. It was just us - alone at last, with the computers, the phones, all the hot water, all the cupboard space, and the TV clicker all to ourselves.

For everything there is a season, turn, turn, turn.

On Letting Go

Some say there's strength in hanging on. But I think there's strength in letting go.
I held on to my cats, my houses, my kids and husbands way too long!
Anne Marie Tague, Asheville, NC

Things every child should know by the time they leave home or go to college :

How to swim, tread water and throw a lifeline to someone else.

How to defend him/herself without a gun, using karate or some form of self-defense.

How to sew on a button. How to sew a hem. How to shorten pant cuffs.

How to do the laundry. How to use bleach. How to iron a shirt and fold a shirt.

How to prepare a full meal – from scratch.

How to wrap a gift.

How and when to write a thank-you note.

How to use good table manners. Knowing which utensils to use for what, at a formal dinner.

How to answer the phone and transfer the call without screaming into the receiver.

How to take a complete phone message: record the time, person calling, return phone number or message and then read it back to the caller to verify the info.

How to hold open the door for others when entering or exiting stores and buildings.

How to clean the bathroom, use a plunger, vacuum and dust.

How to sort out and throw away unnecessary papers and clutter.

How to write a condolence note. What to say to a person who is in mourning.

How to pay bills, balance a checkbook and keep a reserve in one's bank account.

How to budget and save.

How financial investment works. How a mortgage works. How insurance works. How and why we pay taxes.

How debit and credit cards work. What debt and credit means. How to get and keep a good credit rating. What APR means.

How our government works, or doesn't work.

How world religions differ, or how they are the same.

If your kids know all this by the time they leave your home,
you've made it - consider yourself a Master Mom!

Let My Children Go?

I know. Letting go is hard to do. We're so involved in our children's lives. We've been so 'there' for them. How do you wave goodbye? How do you let go? Whether you drop them off at a college dorm or help them settle into their first apartment, here are some tactics to cut the ties that bind you:

<u>Can You (not) Hear Me Now?</u> Resist the urge to call and check on them. Easier said than done. But really, once a week should suffice. (Read that again. Once a week!) Remember, the object is for your daughter/son to be responsible and make it on her/his own. S/he should not feel the need to report to you or seek your approval. Agree to a scheduled time to talk, like a weekend date. No long-distance hyper-parenting allowed. Be confident in your child's independence and don't worry about him/her until s/he misses the regularly scheduled call.

<u>This Bud's For You!</u> Suggest that your child and a friend develop a buddy system to keep tabs on each other when either of them is going out jogging, or on a date, or away for the weekend, etc. Stress that it's important to always let someone know where you are and when you expect to be back. This is called 'being a responsible adult.'

<u>I'm On My Own - Now What?</u> It's scary being on your own. Sometimes you need a little encouragement or professional advice but you'd rather not admit it. Provide your child with phone numbers for the school's professional counseling center, a tutoring service or the peer/residence advisor, but leave it to your child to make the call.

Gen X Is Becoming Gen XXL

Note: Talk to your college-bound or 'leaving the nest' kids to be wary of the 'freshman 15' (pounds, that is.) These kids are morphing into "Generation XXL." Pizza, beer, all-you-can-eat cafeterias and exam binging at 2 a.m. are just too easy to pass up. A Rutgers study found that consuming an extra 112 calories a day amounted to a weight gain of 7 pounds in just 2 semesters. (Note: just one 12-ounce beer contains 150 calories.) Encourage them to walk, get involved in a sport and hit the gym. For more info see: dineoncampus.com

Easy Credit – Easy Debt

Credit companies have targeted 'young adults' (usually on college campuses) to aggressively market their credit lines. What they don't tell the kids is just how easy it is to run up big monthly balances and get stuck with sky-high interest rates. (Gosh, that fine print was tiny!) These young 'customers,' who rarely have a steady income, easily fall behind on payments and get stuck paying the debt for years. For example did you know that paying the minimal monthly payment, on a $1000 credit card balance, will actually take 16 years to pay off? Tell the kids to beware of all the 'offers' they may receive.

College Loan Caution

Point of information: If a student incurs sixty thousand dollars of college loan debt, it will actually cost half a million dollars to pay it off over 30 years!

Cults Seek Intelligent Kids

Every year thousands of kids are inducted into destructive religious cults. New recruits are usually sought on college campuses, where kids are apt to feel a little lonely and isolated from time to time, and hungry for friendly camaraderie. The come-on is often subtle - "Hey, we're having a group over for dinner at our place tonight, why don't you come? We'll even pick you up." Before the kids know it, they're in a van, heading out to an obscure location. They may be served a meal and then they're brought into 'a meeting' which may involve music, rituals, singing, dancing, clapping, a lot of smiling, instant friendships and no resting ... it doesn't take long to feel embraced and 'a part' of this new family, and too exhausted to decline their strong invitation to stay over. In just days, the impressionable, idealistic kids are convinced, brain washed and manipulated to stay and work for the leader of a 'cool' new quasi-religion.

Most cults recruit young, intelligent, lonely individuals who are seeking answers, direction or community. It doesn't take long to surrender to your 'new family' and adopt the 'group think.' A cult is typically defined as a religious sect whose members are controlled by a manipulative organization or individual. Most have a strong charismatic leader who professes 'to know' the way. Cults fall under the radar as modern-day religious movements and are therefore exempt from government surveillance, and very difficult to shut down. How can you prosecute a religion, after all? They hold their followers tightly in their grip, using sophisticated mind control techniques. They convince the new devotees that their 'new family' cares much more about them than their parents ever did and that they should leave their old families behind. Cults often use deceptive techniques to acquire their devotees and require absolute loyalty from their followers. Their aim is to gather more and more into the fold and then exploit them to work and raise money.

Parents may only begin to detect a problem when they either hear their child's speech patterns change, or they sense personality changes as their child starts becoming more secretive and uncooperative. Tragically, the government will not intercede and many families have had very trying ordeals in order to rescue their child from a destructive cult.

Before your kids leave your home, make it a point to have a serious discussion regarding cults, gangs and secret clubs. Warn them of the dangers. Reiterate that if anyone says they have 'the answers' or that they can show them 'the way, the truth' or that 'the group' is going to be their new family - RUN! RUN VERY, VERY FAST! Please find more information at: howcultswork.com

College Is Not For Everyone

Not everyone is going to go to college. That's fine. There are so many other opportunities for kids to choose. Encourage your teen to consider all the career colleges and vocational schools. They offer training in everything from diamond cutting to real estate, health care to baseball umpiring. Point out that there's no need to fret about an absent 'college degree' because in today's world we are finding that some of the most valuable (vocational) careers are recession proof. Help your kids figure out what they feel passionate about and then find a way to build a career around it. Once they have learned a trade and start down that path, remind them not to be afraid to go wherever life leads them... even if it's in the opposite direction! Sometimes the road less traveled is much more interesting than anything you could have envisioned for yourself.

Life happens while you are making plans.

On Choices and Destiny

I believe that the path we choose in life could be a lot more productive and less painful if we paid more attention to the "signs" along the way. They tell us when we need to make a correction. If a college student fails the first couple of semesters, college may not the right choice at this time. Perhaps he is just not 'college material' or he lacks the drive and motivation necessary to achieve passing grades. In any case, it is counterproductive to push a rock uphill and damaging to the psyche to pursue something that is not working. Parents naturally choose the gold standard for their child, which usually means they have college in mind. But not everyone need go in this direction. Keep an open mind, be encouraging, loving, supportive, and firm. Do not allow your child, or yourself, to indulge in self-pity or wallow in disappointment. Get busy. Push your child forward. Small decisive steps and successes will soon lead to larger ones and serve to illuminate a productive new pathway.
Robin Vasquez, Pembroke Pines, FL

The future is yours as you chose it.

Sometimes the path you're on is not as important as the direction you're heading.
Kevin Smith

On Sending Them Out Into the World

When my college student son was preparing for a job interview, he balked at having to dress up. "It's a casual office," he argued. "Why should I show up in a suit and tie?" I simply told him, "You have to make the team before you get to wear the uniform."

If you're going to an interview, do some homework first. Call the potential office and ask to speak to an associate. Ask what the customary office attire is. If you want the job, show up looking as if you already are a team player. If you're not sure, wear a conservative, wrinkle-free, dark suit and appropriate shoes. Minimize your jewelry and tone down accessories and your makeup.

Sometimes They Take You At Your Word

When our children were younger I always told them that they were 'children of privilege' in that they had been born into a family that was able to provide them with many opportunities. I explained that with all they had been given they had an obligation to use their gifts not just for themselves but also to improve the lot of others. I still believe that. Now here's the tough part. Our daughter recently graduated from university magna cum laude and was class valedictorian. She had been mentored well by all her professors and her academic path lay open before her. When she announced that she was reconsidering academia and was instead contemplating going overseas to do development work, my heart fell. Why? Didn't I teach her about her responsibility to others? Shouldn't I be proud? Well, the answer to both is, of course, yes. So why did I have such a negative reaction? I think the answer lies in the fiercely protective instinct that every mother has for her children. From my perspective as a mature and probably somewhat jaded adult, I could see the dangers, difficulties, and potential disillusionment that might lie ahead, and I was afraid. In my heart I just wanted to keep her safe, nearby and happy. (Preferably married to a wealthy, gracious, and handsome man, if the truth be told!) The hardest part for me now is learning to honor and respect what my daughter may bring to the world and having the courage to support her in her choices. So, to the young mothers who may read this I would say stay open to the gifts that your child brings to you and the world. Accept that his/her path in life may not be what you anticipated. And finally, remember that love really can change the world.

Debby Taylor, Winnipeg, Canada

Finding A Mate

In the December 2009 issue of Glamour Magazine, Katie Couric asked first lady Michelle Obama, how she would counsel young women on dating and finding a mate. She answered, "...cute only lasts so long, and then it's, who are you as a person? That's the advice I would give to women: Don't look at the bankbook or the title. Look at the heart. Look at the soul. Look at how the guy treats his mother and what he says about women. How he acts with children he doesn't know. And, more important, how does he treat you? When you're dating a man, you should always feel good. You should never feel less than. You should never doubt yourself. You shouldn't be in a relationship with somebody who doesn't make you feel completely happy and make you feel whole. And if you're in *that* relationship and you're dating, then my advice is, don't get married. Get out of it. And find another person who brings you complete and utter joy with who you are at the moment."

I would add, don't settle for someone who doesn't make you laugh. If you don't share lots of personal little 'in jokes,' if s/he doesn't crack you up and keep you giggling, then s/he's not the right one for you. Life is tough enough - find someone who can soften the edges.

Is This Really Love, Lust or Fascination?

If you see your child stumbling in love, write this out and tuck it in his/her pocket...

How do you know?

You meet someone and suddenly your heart is a flutter. Your body cries out with demanding desire. You feel an aching need, a hunger to be intimate. There is an urgency screaming to be fulfilled, an attraction that demands your immediate attention. This is not love at first sight - this is just LUST nagging at your loins.

You're enthralled, captivated and fascinated by this person. But during the time you spend together a few things begin to bother you; flaws of character, subtle doubts, and some unanswered questions that leave you with an uneasy feeling. You're nervous about their sincerity and check voicemail, email or FB for clues. Still, you're charmed by this frivolous romance - this is INFATUATION tugging at your mind.

You talk at length, you joke and share secrets. You work together, play together, build a foundation of friendship first, and then explore a deep understanding of each other's soul. You share experiences, go for walks, meet each other's family and friends. You see if, and how your two worlds can mesh. Feelings and shared history come together as trust. You are comfortable, calm and secure together. Yes, there's laughing, excitement and fun. Yes, there's longing and lust and sex. Then, suddenly all of these things come together and you realize that best friends make the best lovers. This is real LOVE - informing your heart.

I'm not falling at all - I am rising in love!   David Roth

What? My Baby's Getting Married?

Teach by example and when the time is upon you, remind your children that a good marriage is always a work in progress. It doesn't just happen, life is not a movie or a sitcom - it takes work.

Popping THE Question

Presumably, the answer is a foregone conclusion, so girls and boys, when you're ready to pop THE question, make sure you give some serious thought to HOW you do it. If everything goes according to plan this will only happen once in your lifetime, so think about it. Where, when and how you ask will be part of your 'life story' forever. Plan to make it special, but not necessarily youtube worthy. Don't include any parents... this should be a grown-up, personal and private moment. So, no matter which one of you is doing the asking, make it unforgettable! Shocked? I know lots of girls who popped 'the question' - I was one of them. (My husband says it was the best idea I ever had!)

Bad – a - Bling

When considering buying a diamond engagement ring, it has been customary to look for the 4 C's: Carat, Color, Cut and Clarity... now consider 2 more C's – the Cost and your Conscience. We've all bought into the diamond industry's mythology that these rocks are sacred, rare and 'very special.' But the truth is that they are plentiful and quite ordinary. 'Conflict diamonds' have funded devastating civil wars in Africa, ending millions of lives. Conflict diamonds, also known as 'blood diamonds,' are associated with human rights abuses, environmental damage and terrorism, and all because we want to decorate our digits. Now that science and technology are able to replicate Mother Nature's bling at a fraction of the cost (and with no possibility that a human being will ever be harmed in the process), I wonder why anyone would choose to buy or wear anything else. Manufactured diamonds are produced in laboratory conditions. Carbon is compressed under pressure, just as it is in the earth. The resulting rocks are just as hard, just as brilliant and beautiful, and they are virtually identical to mined diamonds. Even jewelers can't tell the difference! Some might say 'they aren't real' but I ask you, is a hydroponic tomato any less real than one grown with its roots in the soil? Is the voice you hear coming from your iPod any less real than the voice you heard at the concert? Is a baby conceived in vitro any less real than a baby made in the conventional manner? My daughter once told me that everyone wants 'bigger D's' – girls want bigger diamonds and boys want bigger dicks! I laughed realizing that she was right and now at least one of them can get what they want! And no one but your bank account and your clear conscience will ever know the difference.

I would also advise the young man make a pre-visit to the jeweler, to discuss how much he feels comfortable spending on a ring so that only those in his price range will be presented to his girlfriend when they come in together. An engagement ring may be a gift, but because she will be wearing it, she should choose it. Not all surprises turn out to be pleasant ones.

You can also choose to 'go-green' by buying a pre-owned diamond at an estate sale, jewelry or antique shop or at a jewelry pawnshop.

Mothers and Mother-in-laws: You may be well meaning, but you'll be setting the stage for a much better in-law relationship if you do not get involved with this purchase.

The Wedding is Just A Party

Although it's obvious to us parents, too often couples forget that the wedding is only a party ... it's the relationship that's the real big deal. Wedding parties have escalated into very showy extravaganzas and have become a multibillion-dollar industry. Is it really necessary to spend soooo much money for just a few hours of celebrating? Perhaps a smaller party and some money put away for the future might be a wiser investment. There's a television series, which chronicles the wedding industry and time after time, you see 'the father of bride' look quite bewildered at the costs, as they dutifully repeat the mantra, "It's her day – she should be a princess"! OK, he's on national TV, what's he going to say? But I beg to differ. A lavish wedding does not a happy couple make. Actually, the fun and stress of planning a wedding may bring into sharp focus the way a couple really works together, complements each other or illustrates how well or poorly they handle problems together. Often it is a harbinger of things to come. If a couple is at odds just looking at invitations and arguing about wedding plans, perhaps they should take some time and reassess their decision to spend the rest of their lives together.

The Best Gift Ever

Anyone can go out and buy an engagement or wedding gift for their new son or daughter–in–law, but only you can give him or her, this unique gift. Go through your photo albums and assemble a tableau of pictures from your child's birth to the present. Be sure to include some baby faces, kid shots, funny faces and bad hair days. Try to make it represent the full spectrum of life before they found each other. This is as close to giving him/her the gift of 'time in a bottle,' filling in the period before they found their beloved. Have the photos copied and assemble them with a few other treasures, (poems or artwork that you have saved) in a book. There are online services that specialize in producing professional compilation books as well.

Time-Tested Advice

Don't marry for all the wrong reasons: Don't marry to save someone or change someone – it never works. Don't marry for money or status – both can evaporate in an instant. Don't marry to escape your present or to heal the past – those are 'single' tasks. Don't marry because 'it's time,' 'it's the thing to do,' or 'everyone else is doing it.' Don't marry because you feel you have to. Opposites may attract, but then they often attack. Look for someone who has similar interests and values. We all learn from watching our parents' relationship, so if you want to see the lessons (good and bad) s/he has learned, spend some time watching your intended's parents' relationship traits. Be engaged at least six months before you get married. If you come from different religious backgrounds, study the other's religion, because often our outlooks and value systems are rooted in long held beliefs. Before you get married, discuss and decide which religious affiliation will be used to bring up your children.

Marriage is a committed, equal partnership; Two whole personalities coming together to complement, not to compete, or to complete one another. Both of you have to share. Both of you have to listen, though sometimes you have to pretend that you're deaf. Both of you need to learn how to talk it out and how to bite your tongue. Both of you will have to learn the art of compromise.

Assess your love's faults and ask yourself, "Can I live with the things that bother me?" Because all the good, funny, generous aspects of his/her personality may be there - but so will all the faults: the temper, the lustful eye, the gambling habit, the drinking binges. If you can't live with 'em, maybe you're better off without 'em. If you have troublesome issues, remember that these will not change because a little gold ring encircles your finger. If he's not for you - don't be shy to say good-bye. You cannot change anyone but yourself, ever. Step into your evolving life as a couple understanding and expecting that your relationship will continue to change. Nothing ever stays the same, change is the only constant.

Expect each other to change,
but don't expect to change each other.

Learn to dance together. Learn how to fight constructively
together. Learn how to laugh together.

True love is neither physical, nor romantic.
True love is an acceptance of all that is, has been, will be and will not be.

When you have a disagreement, try this: listen first. Practice 'active listening.' Listen until the other person is finished speaking and explaining his/her point of view. Repeat what you just heard, as you rephrase it in your own words. Then explain what you think while the other person listens. Don't interrupt. Don't bring up the past. Don't raise your voice. Discuss the issue, not the person.

Sometimes you just have to agree to disagree. During those times ask yourself: "Would I rather be happy or right?"

Laugh. If you don't play and laugh together, your relationship is doomed.

Dancing is both a real and metaphorical lesson for love's union. Sometimes you'll step on each other's feet and sometimes you'll be perfectly in sync. You may like to dance to different rhythms. Or you may want to sit and watch your beloved take the floor.

First Step

Chris and Meredith Thompson (c) 2004, printed with permission
Listen to their great music at: cmthompson.com

Come and take my hand and draw me ever closer, for this is our moment, our moment to share.
Nothing is as sweet as the time we have together, time to remember how lucky we are.
Remember that the first step should be on the right foot. Count up to eight before we begin
Learn to turn away and when to step apart. Remember how we come together again.
You lose your place. You lose track of time, but I will be there to remind you
Your hand in mine, my hand on your shoulder, we keep track of time together.
I can still remember our first steps together. You reached out your hand and we stepped alone.
Here we are today after so many steps together, surrounded by people who make our lives whole.

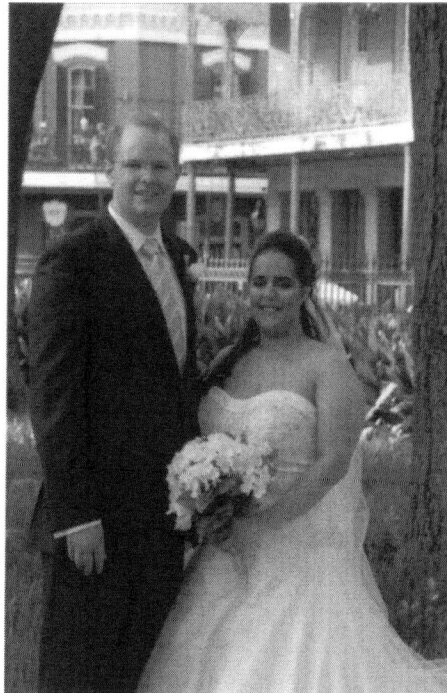

Real love is finding that he replaced the kitchen garbage bag.
Elaine Boozler

Life is too short for drama and petty things, so kiss slowly, laugh insanely, love truly and forgive quickly.

Keep your eyes wide open before marriage, half shut afterwards.   Ben Franklin

Will We Ever Stop WORRYING About Them?

Is there a magic cutoff period when offspring become accountable for their own actions? Is there a wonderful moment when parents can become detached spectators in the lives of their children and shrug, "It's their life," and feel nothing?

When I was in my **twenties**, I stood in a hospital corridor waiting for doctors to put a few stitches in my son's head. I asked, "When do you stop worrying?" The nurse said, "When they get out of the accident stage." My Mother just smiled faintly and said nothing.

When I was in my **thirties**, I sat on a little chair in a classroom and heard how one of my children talked incessantly, disrupted the class, and was headed for a career making license plates. As if to read my mind, a teacher said, "Don't worry, they all go through this stage and then you can sit back, relax and enjoy them" My Mother just smiled faintly and said nothing.

When I was in my **forties**, I spent a lifetime waiting for the phone to ring, the cars to come home, the front door to open. A friend said, "They're trying to find themselves. Don't worry, in a few years, you can stop worrying. They'll be adults." My Mother just smiled faintly and said nothing.

By the time I was **fifty,** I was sick and tired of being vulnerable. I was still worrying over my children, but there was a new wrinkle. There was nothing I could do about it. My Mother just smiled faintly and said nothing. I continued to anguish over their failures, be tormented by their frustrations and absorbed in their disappointments.

My friends said that when my kids got married I could stop worrying and lead my own life. I wanted to believe that, but I was haunted by my Mother's warm smile and her occasional, "You look pale. Are you all right? Call me the minute you get home. Are you depressed about something?" Can it be that parents are sentenced to a lifetime of worry? Is concern for one another handed down like a torch - to blaze the trail of human frailties and the fears of the unknown? Is concern a curse or is it a virtue that elevates us to the highest form of life?

One of my children became quite irritable recently, saying to me, "Where were you? I've been calling for 3 days, and no one answered I was worried." I smiled a warm smile. The torch has been passed.

Author unknown

Just A MOM?

A woman, renewing her driver's license at the county clerk's office was asked by the recorder to state her occupation. She hesitated, uncertain how to classify herself. "What I mean is," explained the recorder, "do you have a job or are you just a...?" "Of course I have a job!" snapped the woman. "I'm a MOM." "We don't list 'Mom' as an occupation, 'housewife' should cover it," said the recorder emphatically.

I forgot all about her story until one day I found myself in the same situation, this time at our own Town Hall. The clerk was obviously a career woman, poised, efficient and possessed of the high sounding title of "Town Registrar."

"What is your occupation?" she probed. What made me say it? I do not know. The words simply popped out. "I'm a Research Associate in the field of Child Development and Human Relations." The clerk paused, ballpoint pen frozen in midair and looked up as though she had not heard right. I repeated the title slowly, emphasizing the most significant words. Then I stared with wonder as my pronouncement was written, in bold, black ink on the official questionnaire. "Might I ask," said the clerk with new interest, "just what you do in your field?"

Coolly, without any trace of fluster in my voice, I heard myself reply, "I have a continuing program of research, (What mother doesn't?) in the laboratory and in the field. Normally I would have said indoors and out. I'm working for my masters, (first the Lord and then the whole family,) and already have four credits (- all daughters.) Of course, the job is one of the most demanding in the humanities (any mother care to disagree?) And I often work 14 hours a day (24 is more like it.) But the job is more challenging than most run-of-the-mill careers and the rewards are more of a satisfaction rather than just money." There was an increasing note of respect in the clerk's voice as she completed the form, stood up and personally ushered me to the door.

As I drove into our driveway, buoyed up by my glamorous new career, I was greeted by my lab assistants -- ages 13, 7, and 3. Upstairs I could hear our new experimental model, (a 6-month-old baby) in the child development program, testing out a new vocal patter. I felt I had scored a beat on bureaucracy!

And I had gone on the official record as someone distinguished and indispensable to mankind!

Awww Mother's Day

Every day should be Mothers Day - no cards or gift wrapping required. But once a year the florists, chocolateers, and commercial card makers encourage a fuss:

Some kids will buy you $5 cards, when you'd much rather they sit down and write you a poem. Some will buy smelly lotions, potions and perfumes...for you to ha-choo! Maybe they will buy you some clothing that will hang in your closet until it lands in the give-away pile. Or, maybe you'll get lucky and score some dark chocolate.

We Moms don't want any of this stuff – except for the chocolate of course. What we really want is for our children to just pay attention to us. Not just on Mother's Day but every day. If only they'd listen to what we teach them and then, give it all back to us, we'd be thrilled: To watch our children live happy, productive, responsible lives. That precious gift would be worth all the money in the world – and it would never cost a dime.

Sometimes I look at my children, and I say to myself "Lillian, you should have remained a virgin."
Lillian Carter (mother of President Jimmy Carter)

Wisdom

If not for the photographs, I might have a hard time believing they ever existed. The pensive infant with the swipe of dark bangs and the black button eyes of a Raggedy Andy doll. The placid baby with the yellow ringlets and the high piping voice. The sturdy toddler with the lower lip that curled into an apostrophe above her chin.
ALL MY BABIES are gone now. I say this not in sorrow but in disbelief. I take great satisfaction in what I have today: three almost-adults, two taller than I am, one closing in fast. Three people who read the same books I do and have learned not to be afraid of disagreeing with me in their opinion of them, who sometimes tell vulgar jokes that make me laugh until I choke and cry, who need razor blades and shower gel and privacy, who want to keep their doors closed more than I like. Who, miraculously, go to the bathroom, zip up their jackets and move food from plate to mouth all by themselves. Like the trick soap I bought for the bathroom with a rubber ducky at its center, the baby is buried deep within each, barely discernible except through the unreliable haze of the past. Everything in all the books I once pored over is finished for me now. Penelope Leach, T. Berry Brazelton, Dr. Spock. The ones on sibling rivalry and sleeping through the night and early-childhood education, all grown obsolete. Along with 'Goodnight Moon' and 'Where the Wild Things Are,' they are battered, spotted, well used. But I suspect that if you flipped the pages dust would rise like memories. What those books taught me, finally, and what the women on the playground taught me, and the well-meaning relations -- what they taught me, was that they couldn't really teach me very much at all. Raising children is presented at first as a

true-false test, then becomes multiple choice, until finally, far along, you realize that it is an endless essay. No one knows anything. One child responds well to positive reinforcement, another can be managed only with a stern voice and a timeout. One child is toilet trained at 3, his sibling at 2. When my first child was born, parents were told to put baby to bed on his belly so that he would not choke on his own spit-up. By the time my last arrived, babies were put down on their backs because of research on sudden infant death syndrome. To a new parent this ever-shifting certainty is terrifying, and then soothing.

Eventually you must learn to trust yourself. Eventually the research will follow. I remember 15 years ago poring over one of Dr. Brazelton's wonderful books on child development, in which he describes three different sorts of infants: average, quiet, and active. I was looking for a sub-quiet codicil for an 18-month-old who did not walk. Was there something wrong with his fat little legs? Was there something wrong with his tiny little mind? Was he developmentally delayed, physically challenged? Was I insane? Last year he went to China. Next year he goes to college. He can talk just fine. He can walk, too.

Every part of raising children is humbling, too. Believe me, mistakes were made. They have all been enshrined in the, "Remember-When-Mom-Did Hall of Fame." The outbursts, the temper tantrums, the bad language, mine, not theirs. The times the baby fell off the bed. The times I arrived late for preschool pickup. The nightmare sleepover. The horrible summer camp. The day when the youngest came barreling out of the classroom with a 98 on her geography test, and I responded, What did you get wrong? (She insisted I include that.) The time I ordered food at the McDonald's drive-through speaker and then drove away without picking it up from the window. (They all insisted I include that.) I did not allow them to watch 'The Simpsons' for the first two seasons. What was I thinking?

But the biggest mistake I made is the one that most of us make while doing this. I did not live in the moment enough. This is particularly clear now that the moment is gone, captured only in photographs.

There is one picture of the three of them, sitting in the grass on a quilt in the shadow of the swing set on a summer day, ages 6, 4 and 1. And I wish I could remember what we ate, and what we talked about, and how they sounded, and how they looked when they slept that night. I wish I had not been in such a hurry to get on to the next thing: dinner, bath, book, bed. I wish I had treasured the doing a little more and the getting it done a little less.

Even today I'm not sure what worked and what didn't, what was me and what was simply life. When they were very small, I suppose I thought someday they would become who they were because of what I'd done.

Now I suspect they simply grew into their true selves because they demanded in a thousand ways that I back off and let them be.

The books said to be relaxed and I was often tense, matter-of-fact and I was sometimes over the top. And look how it all turned out. I wound up with the three people I like best in the world, who have done more than anyone to excavate my essential humanity.

That's what the books never told me. I was bound and determined to learn from the experts. It just took me a while to figure out who the experts were....

Anna Quindlen

A child can always teach an adult three things: to be happy for no reason, to always be busy with something, and to know how to demand with all his might that which he desires.

Paulo Coelho, The Fifth Mountain

In The Land of 10,000 Mothers
© Cosy Sheridan
Hear her great music at: cosysheridan.com

In the land of 10,000 mothers every song is a lullaby
Nobody marches to war no one stands in the airport and cries
Nobody dies on the highway with too many words left unsaid
In the land of 10,000 mothers we all sleep safe in our beds
In the land of 10,000 mothers - milk and honey flow without end

Nobody goes away wanting. You are welcome wherever you've been.
You are welcome to lay your head down
And get a kiss for every wound
In the land of 10,000 mothers you will get better soon.

You are welcome no matter what chases you
Whatever road you chose through the wood
In the land of 10,000 mothers somebody loves you
And knows you are good.

In the final analysis it is not what you do for your children but what you have taught them to do for themselves that will make them successful human beings.

Ann Landers

When you teach your child, you teach your child's child.

304

In the end, the best thing you can do for your child is:

Let your child figure out who she wants to be.

Help her get there.

Then stand back and let her be herself.

Made in the USA
San Bernardino, CA
19 July 2013